BY LYNNE OLSON

*The Sisterhood of Ravensbrück: How an Intrepid
Band of Frenchwomen Resisted the Nazis in Hitler's
All-Female Concentration Camp*

*Empress of the Nile: The Daredevil Archaeologist Who
Saved Egypt's Ancient Temples from Destruction*

*Madame Fourcade's Secret War: The Daring Young Woman
Who Led France's Largest Spy Network Against Hitler*

*Last Hope Island: Britain, Occupied Europe, and the
Brotherhood That Helped Turn the Tide of War*

*Those Angry Days: Roosevelt, Lindbergh, and America's
Fight over World War II, 1939–1941*

*Citizens of London: The Americans Who Stood with
Britain in Its Darkest, Finest Hour*

*Troublesome Young Men: The Rebels Who Brought
Churchill to Power and Helped Save England*

*A Question of Honor: The Kosciuszko Squadron; Forgotten
Heroes of World War II* (with Stanley Cloud)

*Freedom's Daughters: The Unsung Heroines of the
Civil Rights Movement from 1830 to 1970*

*The Murrow Boys: Pioneers on the Front Lines of
Broadcast Journalism* (with Stanley Cloud)

THE SISTERHOOD
OF RAVENSBRÜCK

The
SISTERHOOD
of
RAVENSBRÜCK

How an Intrepid Band
of Frenchwomen Resisted
the Nazis in
Hitler's All-Female
Concentration Camp

Lynne Olson

RANDOM HOUSE

NEW YORK

Published in the United States by Random House, an imprint and division of Penguin Random House LLC, 1745 Broadway, New York, NY 10019.

RANDOM HOUSE and the HOUSE colophon are registered trademarks of Penguin Random House LLC.

Photo credits appear on pages 345–46.

LIBRARY OF CONGRESS CATALOGING-IN-PUBLICATION DATA
NAMES: Olson, Lynne, author
TITLE: The sisterhood of Ravensbrück / Lynne Olson.
DESCRIPTION: First edition. | New York, NY: Random House, [2025] | Includes bibliographical references and index
IDENTIFIERS: LCCN 2024048861 (print) | LCCN 2024048862 (ebook) | ISBN 9780593732304 hardcover | ISBN 9780593732311 ebook
SUBJECTS: LCSH: Ravensbrück (Concentration camp)—Biography | Women Nazi concentration camp inmates—Germany—Biography | Women Nazi concentration camp inmates—France—Biography | World War, 1939–1945—Underground movements—France | World War, 1939–1945—Deportations from France | Postel-Vinay, Anise | Tillion, Germaine | Gaulle-Anthonioz, Geneviève de | Pery d'Alincourt, Jacqueline, 1919– | Association nationale des anciennes déportées et internées de la résistance—History | LCGFT: Biographies
CLASSIFICATION: LCC D805.5.R38 O47 2025 (print) | LCC D805.5.R38 (ebook) | DDC 940.53/1853154—dc23/eng/20241118
LC record available at https://lccn.loc.gov/2024048861
LC ebook record available at https://lccn.loc.gov/2024048862

Printed in the United States of America on acid-free paper

randomhousebooks.com
penguinrandomhouse.com

2 4 6 8 9 7 5 3 1

FIRST EDITION

Book design by Barbara M. Bachman

TITLE PAGE IMAGES: *Top:* Ravensbruck, *U.S. Holocaust Memorial Museum archives*
Bottom: Creative Commons—Attribution: Centre des archives diplomatiques de La Courneuve

The authorized representative in the EU for product safety and compliance is Penguin Random House Ireland, Morrison Chambers, 32 Nassau Street, Dublin D02 YH68, Ireland, https://eucontact.penguin.ie.

For Stan and Carly

At the end of my journey, I realize how fragile and malleable man is.
Nothing can be taken for granted. Our duty of vigilance must be absolute.
Evil can return at any time, it smolders everywhere.
And we must act while there is still time to prevent the worst.

—GERMAINE TILLION

The only response to absolute evil is fraternity.

—ANDRÉ MALRAUX

Contents

....

Author's Note

....

LIKE OTHER NAZI CONCENTRATION CAMPS IN GERMANY, Ravensbrück, the only camp designed specifically for women, was built in the middle of nowhere—a sandy, boggy tract of land, deep in a dense forest, about fifty miles north of Berlin. Its secluded location was hardly an accident: SS head Heinrich Himmler, who was in charge of the camps, was adamant that they be concealed as much as possible from public view.

An estimated 130,000 women from Nazi-occupied Europe, many of them members of their countries' resistance movements, were sent to Ravensbrück during World War II. As many as forty thousand died there—of starvation, disease, torture, shooting, lethal injections, medical experiments, and, beginning in December 1944, in a newly installed gas chamber.

While word of the horrors of Dachau, Buchenwald, and other male-only camps filtered out to the West during the war, virtually nothing was known at the time about Ravensbrück and its atrocities. Even after the war, its story remained largely untold. Liberated by Soviet forces, Ravensbrück was located in the Soviet zone of postwar Germany, which remained off-limits to Westerners. Unlike at Buchenwald and Dachau, which had been freed by American troops, with

American journalists as witnesses, at Ravensbrück no photos or film footage existed of the piles of dead bodies and skeleton-like survivors.

"History forgot Ravensbrück," the British historian Sarah Helm observed in her magisterial 2015 history of the camp. "Today [it] is hidden from view; the horrific crimes enacted there and the courage of the victims are largely unknown."

So, too, is another vital fact. Even in the midst of the most extreme savagery, a sizable number of Ravensbrück's inmates refused to behave like victims; instead they joined forces to continue their passionate fight against the Nazis. Foremost among them was a tight-knit group of *résistantes* from France, whose resilience, audacity, and esprit de corps were unparalleled. *The Sisterhood of Ravensbrück* is their story.

In writing it, I was aided not only by the recollections of the Frenchwomen themselves but also by a series of stunning pen-and-ink drawings by one of the *résistantes,* which are prominently featured throughout the book. In these primitive, searing images, Violette Lecoq, who worked as a nurse in the camp, depicted the hellish reality of Ravensbrück, putting the lie to official photographs staged by the SS and released to the International Red Cross, which showed inmates working peaceably in clean, orderly surroundings.

Knowing that she risked a brutal beating or even death if her drawings were found, Lecoq hid away in her barracks night after night, illustrating the barbarism she'd witnessed with pens and paper stolen from the camp's offices. Like her compatriots, Lecoq was determined to bring to justice those who'd committed these heinous crimes. In doing so, she and the others were honoring the shouted command of a French comrade as she was trucked off to Ravensbrück's gas chamber: "Tell it to the world!"

THE SISTERHOOD
OF RAVENSBRÜCK

Prologue

As a child, Aline Corraze de Ziegler loved spending time with her widowed grandmother. Tall, slender, and graceful, Jacqueline Péry d'Alincourt was an inveterate traveler, but when she was in Paris, her base was an elegant five-room apartment in the 17th arrondissement. It was filled with many lovely things—paintings, furnishings, objets d'art from all over the world, and a magnificent grand piano. But what Aline loved most was her grandmother's enormous collection of books—shelved in bookcases in every room and piled high on bedside tables, atop and under desks, and on each side of the living room sofa.

"For a child, it was like a wonderland," Aline recalled. "There were lots of places to hide because of the books. When I went there, it was like entering a treasure chest." Jacqueline Péry d'Alincourt considered books "living things," her granddaughter observed. "They were her companions."

As a young girl, Aline was equally taken with Jacqueline's human companions—a circle of women whom her grandmother considered her closest friends and who regularly came to her apartment for afternoon tea. "They looked like perfectly ordinary old women, gray-haired and appearing somewhat fragile," Aline said. "But their looks did not match who they were. They were not ordinary at all."

Over tea and cookies, the women often talked about world affairs, about the need to combat such injustices as racism and antisemitism. Sometimes, though, their conversation would take a startling turn. The decades would fall away, and they became young women in Nazi-occupied Paris during World War II, no longer answering to their given names—Jacqueline, Germaine, Geneviève, Anise—but to aliases like Violaine, Danielle, Kouri.

Back then, one of them was helping to organize Paris's first resistance network. Another was spying on German military positions. Still another—Aline's grandmother—was sending coded messages to London and bicycling around Paris carrying radio sets and secret reports, all the while dodging the Gestapo. Sitting there, Aline realized, were "true Resistance heroes, doing the amazing things we read about in books and see in films and on TV. These old ladies, drinking their tea, had been brave and intrepid warriors."

In fact, the women had been *résistantes* twice over, defying not only the Germans but also their own deeply conservative, patriarchal society, in which women were largely confined to the roles of wives and mothers and still did not have the right to vote. Indeed, under the authoritarian Vichy government of Marshal Philippe Pétain, wartime France had become, in various ways, eerily akin to the society portrayed decades later in Margaret Atwood's dystopian novel *The Handmaid's Tale*.

None of these constraints, however, had stopped Jacqueline Péry d'Alincourt and her guests. "We committed ourselves to fight for the freedom of a country that refused to give us basic human freedoms," one of them would write. "But it was still our country, and we were prepared to die for it."

Chapter 1

"Something Must Be Done"

Germaine
Tillion

W HEN WORLD WAR II ERUPTED IN SEPTEMBER 1939, IT DIDN'T
mean much to Germaine Tillion, who at that moment was living in a
cave on the side of a cliff overlooking the Sahara. For the previous five
years, the young French anthropologist, following in the tradition of
her American counterpart Margaret Mead, had been studying semi-
nomadic Berber tribes in the Atlas Mountains in northeast Algeria.

One of only a handful of female anthropologists in France, the petite, dark-haired Tillion was a protégée of Marcel Mauss, who, like
Franz Boas, Mead's mentor, was regarded as one of the world's pre-
eminent authorities in cultural and social anthropology. Also like Boas,
Mauss encouraged his students to travel across the globe, searching out

remote, primitive places and collecting information about their inhabitants' behavior, society, and culture.

Mauss and Boas were alike in another important way: They emphasized the similarities among peoples rather than their differences. While both accepted the idea that humanity was divided into different races, they rejected the idea that some races were superior to others. To his students, Mauss repeatedly stated his fundamental principle: "There is no such thing as an uncivilized people."

Fascinated by anthropology's broad sweep, Germaine Tillion, from the beginning of her career, was "impatient to decipher the riddles of the world," according to her biographer Jean Lacouture. At first glance, such grand ambitions seemed far-fetched for anyone, let alone a young woman who'd been brought up in a small village tucked away in the Auvergne, a rural province in south central France. Today the Auvergne is considered "peasant France," filled with farms and little villages, famous for its cheese and charcuterie. Its landscape and history, though, belie the mundane nature of its everyday life.

The Auvergne is part of the Massif Central, a spectacularly beautiful mountainous region noted for its volcanic peaks, yawning canyons, deep green valleys, and rocky, windswept plateaus. It got its name from the Arverni, a warlike tribe best known for its fierce resistance to the conquest of ancient Gaul by Julius Caesar and his Roman legions, five decades before the birth of Christ. Almost two thousand years later, the region would again become a stronghold of French resistance, this time against the Nazis.

But when Germaine Tillion was growing up in the early years of the twentieth century, life in the village of Allègre was undramatic, slow-moving, and mired in tradition. Her parents had been born into prosperous, well-connected families from the area, many of whose members had been lawyers and public officials for generations. Men on her mother's side had served as the hereditary mayors of their ancestral town since the reign of Louis XVI.

But Tillion's father, Lucien, who was a magistrate, and his lively, outgoing wife, Émilie, an art historian, had always set their sights beyond Allègre. Cultured and well read, the couple wrote several vol-

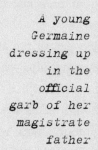

A young
Germaine
dressing up
in the
official
garb of her
magistrate
father

umes of *Les Guides Bleus*, the venerable travel book series issued by the French publisher Hachette, focusing on the history and cultural heritage of France and other European countries. In the early 1920s, they and their two daughters—Germaine and her younger sister, Françoise—moved to Saint-Maur-des-Fossés, a leafy, affluent suburb of Paris.

In 1925, when Germaine was eighteen, Lucien Tillion died suddenly of pneumonia. His wife continued working on the *Guides Bleus*, writing four more volumes with Marcel Monmarché, the creator of the series. Known for her erudition and sparkling sense of humor, Émilie also delivered lectures, wrote articles for art publications, and became a leading figure in a circle of intellectually and culturally minded women in Paris.

From the time her daughters were little, Émilie encouraged them to go to college and pursue careers of their own—a rare attitude in patriarchal France. Françoise studied at the Institut d'Études Politiques de Paris, one of the country's most prestigious, selective institutions of higher education, where women were still very much in the minority. Germaine, for her part, took her time deciding which path she should follow. In her quest to "decipher the riddles of the world," she studied psychology for a while, then archaeology, before discovering Marcel Mauss and anthropology. In 1933, after three years of coursework at the Sorbonne, the Collège de France, and other schools, she was awarded her first fieldwork mission.

Germaine, now twenty-six, had hoped to get as far away from France as possible—Tibet or Tierra del Fuego, perhaps—but instead was assigned to the North African country of Algeria, which the French had colonized a century earlier. Yet even though Algeria was only a few hours from Paris by plane, the desolate, mountainous territory of Aurès was as wild and remote as any place she could have wished for. Lacking trade and roads, it was populated by fierce Berber tribes whose members, according to French colonial officials, were thieves and murderers with low intelligence who'd never had any contact with Europeans, much less a young European woman. The idea of Germaine's trying to insert herself into this virile, violent Muslim society, they declared, was sheer madness. She paid no attention to their warnings. In fact, she later said, their racist comments only added to "my initial sympathy for the population in question."

She settled in the most inaccessible spot she could find—on the side of a mountain with a stunning panoramic view of the Sahara. The closest town with the rudiments of civilization—a doctor, a store, a school—was a fourteen-hour horseback ride away. Once she'd pitched her tent and set up camp in a cave, she began to learn the dialect of the first tribe she'd decided to investigate—a grouping of about sixty families in the Chaouia tribe, who eked out a living in a terrain as dry and rocky as the surface of the moon.

Germaine was extremely careful in the way she approached this insular society. She began by inviting the old men of the tribe to her cave, where over cups of coffee and with the help of an interpreter she invited them to tell stories of their people—their history, rituals, and religious beliefs—and in turn told them about her own. The elders, whom she called *les grands vieux*, entered into the dialogue with gusto, spinning "tales of travel, of ghosts, of battle." Devout Muslims, "they were very sorry at the thought that I, whom they considered a good person, was doomed to hell as a Christian," she later said. "But I pointed out that their beliefs were not that different from those expressed in the Old and New Testaments."

Having won the trust of *les grands vieux,* Germaine turned her attention to the rest of the tribe, leaving her cave at dawn and traveling by horseback to their encampment, where she got to know the younger men, as well as the women and children. "If nature had given me a Cyclops eye in the middle of my forehead or a dog's muzzle, I would have astonished them less than with my jodhpurs, camping gear, and endless scribbling," she later told an interviewer. "Once recovered from their amazement, however, they realized I was harmless."

Germaine Tillion with Chaouia tribal members in Algeria

Germaine's respectful, restrained approach impressed the tribe members, as did her attempts to make herself useful, helping out when someone was sick or writing letters to government authorities on their behalf. Before long, they were opening up to her, happy to teach her everything she wanted to know about their community.

Over the six years Germaine Tillion spent with the Chaouia, she was "accepted wholeheartedly" and "received everywhere like someone from the family," she said. "I had no problem being a woman in this extremely manly society. Even though the men had more or less locked up their wives, keeping them on the sidelines, they saw me as a person of authority. In cultures like these, when a woman by chance does have authority, it sometimes gives her more influence than a man."

Germaine felt equally at home with the tribes; indeed, their members' behavior, traditions, and customs reminded her of those of the peasants in the Auvergne. The Berbers, she declared, were neither "narrow-minded nor thieves, and no more fierce" than their contemporaries in rural, out-of-the-way places in France.

During her stint in Algeria, Germaine took several long breaks in Paris, spending time with her mother, to whom she was very close, and consulting with Marcel Mauss and her other mentors. When she was on her mountaintop, though, she led a solitary, isolated existence, with no radio or newspapers to keep her abreast of what was going on in the rest of the world.

In the spring of 1940, she finally completed her mission, having filled a multitude of notebooks and written reams of field reports about the Chaouia's family structure, as well as their economic, cultural, and social organization. In Paris, she would begin writing her doctoral thesis and present her findings to Mauss and other prominent members of France's anthropology circles.

On May 21, Germaine began her trek back to civilization, stopping to spend the night at Arris, the closest town to her encampment. There, over a makeshift radio, she heard stunning news: The Nazis had invaded France and were on the verge of occupying the country. Only eleven days before, the Germans had launched a blitzkrieg of Western Europe, slashing through the Netherlands and Belgium, then breaching France's borders. Struggling to hear the announcer's voice through the crackle of static, Germaine learned that the French front had been smashed and that the defending French and British troops were in full retreat.

Even as thousands of people streamed out of France, Germaine continued her journey home; at every stop, she was greeted with increasingly dire news. In Algiers, as she tried to find a berth on a ship, she heard a broadcast by French president Paul Reynaud declaring that only a miracle could now save the country. Germaine, completely overwhelmed, broke down in tears. Surely, she thought, the French military would be able to rally its forces to produce that miracle.

But when she finally arrived in Paris on June 9, she learned otherwise. The capital was a ghost town, the vast majority of its panicked residents having fled the Nazi onslaught that was momentarily expected; five days later, German troops would march in and occupy the city. Collecting her mother and grandmother in Saint-Maur, Tillion headed out of town, too, convinced that the French government would continue the struggle from Brittany or North Africa.*

On June 17, the three women were passing through a village in southwest France when the new French president, Marshal Philippe Pétain, went on the radio to announce that he had asked Hitler for an armistice. Invited into a house to listen to Pétain's broadcast, Germaine was so sickened by it that she ran out to the street and vomited. "The shock, the disgust was brutal," she later said. "To ask for an armistice was to open one's door to the enemy, to submit to an enemy completely. That was completely unacceptable."

It takes one second for the course of a life to change forever, Germaine later observed; for her, it came on that hot June afternoon. She bitterly reproached herself for her previous indifference to France's political affairs and suddenly realized "how essential my country's dignity and independence were to me." Blind with rage toward Pétain, whom she labeled a traitor, she decided that "something must be done immediately." A few days later, she drove back to Paris to take up the fight.

---

* Françoise had married a French colonial official and was then living in Indochina.

———

WITHIN DAYS OF RETURNING to the capital, Germaine Tillion had begun challenging the Nazis at a time when virtually no one else in the country was doing so. The suddenness and magnitude of the collapse of the French army and government had traumatized the vast majority of her compatriots, producing a wide range of emotions—shame, shock, anger, and despair, as well as, for many, a sense of relief that the fighting had come to an end for France.

In those very early days, a sense of hopelessness and helplessness prevailed. How could anyone possibly stand up to these seemingly all-powerful conquerors? For most of the French, the main goal was obvious: to keep one's head down and focus on survival. "Something has been broken in this country," Jean Guéhenno, a noted French writer and literary critic, observed at the time. "The people don't think or feel anymore. Two weeks of chaos have turned them into a herd."

Like Germaine, however, a tiny minority of French citizens thought differently. Germaine's mantra, "something must be done," was theirs as well—four words that appear repeatedly in their memoirs and other writings. With no clear notion of what that "something" was, they began cautiously sounding out others who they thought might share their rage and determination.

Germaine's first sounding board was a retired French army colonel named Paul Hauet, whose name had been given to her by an acquaintance. An artillery officer who had served for many years in the Sudan, the seventy-four-year-old Hauet came from a long line of army officers; his grandfather had accompanied Napoleon on his ill-fated invasion of Russia. Hauet was tall and ramrod-straight, with an impressive white mustache and "a boiling fury" over what he considered the treachery of Marshal Pétain.

Germaine and Hauet joined forces, transforming an organization he had formed to aid former soldiers into a fledgling escape network for French troops taken prisoner by the Nazis in the battle for France. They then recruited seventy-year-old Charles de la Rochère, another retired French army colonel and a close friend of Hauet, who, along with several associates, had begun collecting information on German troop movements and other military intelligence.

Germaine's mother, Émilie—who, according to her daughter, "was as fiercely committed to resisting the Germans as I was"—was another member of the group. Having accompanied her daughter and mother back to Paris, Émilie offered the use of her house as a "mailbox," where secret messages could be dropped off and picked up, as well as a hiding place for escaped Allied troops and Jews.

Years later, Germaine Tillion, who adopted the code name Kouri, would refer to her embryo resistance unit as a nucleus, seeking to join other nuclei to create an explosion. Within weeks, she and her two elderly partners found new allies at the Musée de l'Homme (Museum of Man), France's premier anthropology museum and research center. Housed in a massive curved Art Deco building on the Right Bank and overlooking a marble plaza with spectacular views of the Seine and the Eiffel Tower, the museum, under the leadership of its director, Paul Rivet, had served in the 1930s as a hotbed of opposition to Nazi racist theories promoting the innate superiority of Aryan peoples. At a time when anthropologists in Germany and elsewhere, including antisemitic elements in French academic circles, embraced the notion of an Aryan super race, Rivet co-founded an antiracist journal, *Races et Racisme*. He also organized a group called the Vigilance Committee of Anti-Fascist Intellectuals, which included several members of his staff.

When German troops marched into Paris in mid-June 1940, the Museum of Man subtly signaled its opposition to the Nazis with what one writer called "a defiant gesture and sly call to arms." The only museum in the capital to remain open, it prominently displayed on its massive front doors a French translation of "If," Rudyard Kipling's poem celebrating courage and independence, which read in part, "If you can keep your head when all about you are losing theirs . . . you'll be a Man, my son!"

The following month, Paul Rivet cast aside any semblance of subtlety, making public an impassioned open letter he'd written to Pétain. In it, he warned the collaborationist French president that "the country is not with you. . . . History must not associate your name with such a disastrous work." Pétain's Vichy government fired Rivet almost immediately, and he soon fled the country, but not before planting the seeds of what would become the first major resistance network in occupied France, with the Museum of Man as its base. Its initial organizer was Yvonne Oddon, the museum's head librarian.

A diminutive woman like her friend Germaine Tillion, the thirty-seven-year-old Yvonne was—again, like Germaine—"a big brain, with a big, brave heart," according to a colleague of both women. With most of the museum's male employees in the French army at the time of the occupation, Yvonne Oddon and Paul Rivet had jointly decided to keep the museum open, making clear their refusal to capitulate to the enemy. To guard against pillaging by Paris's invaders, Yvonne slept on a camp bed in the library stacks.

An influential figure in French library circles, she had grown up in Gap, a market town in the foothills of the Alps in southeast France. She came from a staunchly Protestant family whose ancestors had suffered several bouts of official persecution over the centuries in this predominantly Catholic country, making her particularly determined to rebel against current-day injustices.

In the early 1920s, Yvonne had studied at the American Library School in Paris, founded by U.S. librarians to train their French counterparts in modern methods and to promote the then revolutionary idea in France of opening libraries to the public. After her studies there, she traveled to the United States to take graduate classes at the University of Michigan, followed by a year of work at the Library of Congress. When she returned to France, she became one of its leading specialists in modern library science, turning the Museum of Man's library into a showcase research center for scholars as well as providing access to the general public.

Days after the Germans marched into the city, Yvonne began sending books and clothing to French prisoners of war. With the help of one of her library staffers, she then set up a rudimentary escape line for prisoners. The staff member's apartment near the museum served as the nerve center for the line: Escaped prisoners were secreted there until they could be smuggled across the demarcation line into France's unoccupied zone.

In the late summer of 1940, Germaine Tillion, who had had close ties with the museum since her student days, contacted Yvonne with the idea of joining forces. She'd been in classes with several of the anthropologists currently working there and had spent countless hours doing research and writing papers in its library, in the process forging a strong friendship with Yvonne.

Also joining the Museum of Man group in its early days was another prominent female scholar: Agnès Humbert, a forty-three-year-old art historian and divorced mother of two grown sons. An expert on the French painter Jacques-Louis David, Agnès was a curator at the National Museum of Popular Arts and Culture, located in the same complex as the Museum of Man.

Like Germaine and Yvonne, the fiery, irreverent Agnès had a razor-sharp intelligence and a wicked sense of humor, which she often aimed at herself. She also shared their fierce sense of outrage about France's capitulation to Germany, as well as their determination to take immediate action. "I will go mad, literally, if I don't do something!" she exploded when she learned of Pétain's quest for an armistice.

This newborn network was distinctive not only because it was the first significant resistance group in Paris but also because of the overarching importance of women in its creation and operation. Yvonne Oddon, Germaine Tillion, and Agnès Humbert were far from the only women who played key roles in the upper reaches of the network— a stark contrast to later, male-dominated resistance organizations in which women were relegated to supporting roles.

Years after the war, Germaine pinpointed a major reason for that fact: "At the time of the great French collapse in June 1940, there were very few men left in Paris. There were a million prisoners of war, and the men who weren't prisoners were mobilized, dead, or in hiding. Women had to respond immediately to the situation, and they took control of it. . . . In essence, women kick-started the resistance."

Others on Yvonne Oddon's contact list were two women staffers at the U.S. embassy in Paris, who were among her many friends in the capital's American community. Even though the United States was still officially neutral in 1940, William Bullitt, its ambassador to France, was unabashedly anti-Nazi and turned a blind eye to the efforts of embassy staffers to aid French acquaintances in their resistance efforts. Yvonne's embassy contacts passed on to her U.S. newspapers and other vital sources of information about what was going on outside France. Even more important, they used the embassy's diplomatic mailbag to smuggle confidential documents out of the country for the network. When Germaine's group had military information it wanted to share with the United States and Britain, Charles de la Rochère would visit the Museum of Man library, ostensibly for research, then casually drop by Yvonne's office to hand over reports meant for the mailbag.

In the early fall of 1940, two anthropologists from the Museum of Man who had fought in the short-lived war for France returned to Paris. One of them, Anatole Lewitsky, had been demobilized from the French army; the other, Boris Vildé, had escaped from German captivity. Lewitsky, who was Yvonne Oddon's lover and the head of the museum's European-Asiatic department, and Vildé, an expert on Arctic cultures, immediately joined the nascent network and, together with Yvonne, drew up its plan for action. From then on, the charismatic Vildé would serve as chief of the group, with Lewitsky and Yvonne acting as his deputies.

An unlikely collection of rebels, the original members of the Museum of Man group were mostly scholars—anthropologists, archaeologists, art historians, museum curators and directors, linguists, writers, and librarians. With no experience in politics or insurgency, they set out to encourage their countrymen not only to reject collaboration with the enemy but to actively defy them. As Germaine put it, "What we wanted to do in 1940 was to somehow wake up France, force it to become aware that we were not at Pétain's service and that he did not represent us."

Years later, she emphasized how primitive the group's early effort was. "Don't forget, the resistance was just beginning," she said. "We were deprived of everything. We did not have any radio transmitters.

We had not yet formed real networks. We were improvising all the time. We tried to be careful, but we couldn't hide. We were almost forced not to hide, because somehow we had to advertise the resistance."

Although thoroughly ill-equipped to take on the German military and Gestapo, this ragtag band plunged ahead. "It was," one British historian remarked, "as though the upper echelons of the British Museum had turned to new careers as urban guerrillas and saboteurs." In the first weeks of the occupation, network members recruited friends and colleagues, made new contacts, and brought other small, fledgling resistance groups into the museum's orbit. Within a few months, the organization had "transformed itself into a veritable spider's web covering the whole of France," noted the French historian Tatiana Benfoughal.

Among its earliest efforts was the creation of flyers, leaflets, and posters that denounced the Nazis and their French collaborators, as well as the printing of news from BBC broadcasts and extracts from speeches by U.S. president Franklin Roosevelt and British prime minister Winston Churchill, including Churchill's famed "We will fight on the beaches" address. Staffers used a mimeograph machine in the museum's basement to run off copies while German soldiers playing tourist tramped through its galleries overhead. The posters and flyers were then plastered on walls, stuffed into mailboxes, and deposited on park benches and store counters.

The network also engineered the escape of captured French and British troops from temporary prisoner of war encampments set up by the Germans throughout France. The more than a million Allied soldiers rounded up during May and June 1940 were scheduled to be shipped to Germany to do slave labor. Before that happened, network members helped hundreds of them slip out of the camps, providing them with civilian clothes and false papers and smuggling British soldiers into the unoccupied French zone and starting them on their way back to freedom.

But the group's most significant achievement in those early days was to publish the earliest underground newspaper in France's occupied zone. Called *Rèsistance,* it gave a name to the mass movement that would follow, equating "resistance" with a rejection of the occupation and a resolution to work against it. First published on December 15, 1940, the newspaper was initially distributed mainly in Paris and then throughout the country. An editorial from the first issue proclaimed: "Resistance! That's the cry that goes up from your hearts, in your distress at the disaster that has befallen our nation. Your immediate task is to get organized like us so that you can resume the struggle."

Under Vildé's leadership, the network would soon shift into higher gear, allying itself with even more groups, opening escape routes over the Pyrenees into Spain and collecting and transmitting military intelligence to London, including information on German military installations and airfields. In early 1941, it would provide British authorities with drawings of the German submarine pens and huge dry dock at the Atlantic port of Saint-Nazaire—information that would result in arguably the greatest Allied commando raid of the war: a March 1942 assault on the Saint-Nazaire dock that would put it out of action for the rest of the conflict.

THROUGHOUT THE BRIEF EXISTENCE of the Museum of Man network, its members considered themselves a team of equals. There were none of the rivalries, feuds, or power struggles that plagued many if not most of the resistance organizations that followed them. Members of the network who survived the war described a deeply collegial atmosphere, in which they and their comrades felt themselves part of the same family, united by their love of country and outrage against the Germans.

That solidarity was accompanied by a sense of joy in one another's company. Although "joy" seems, at first glance, an inappropriate word to use when referring to those dark and dangerous times, several prominent members of the network noted the lighthearted, cheerful atmosphere that pervaded their work. In his memoirs, one of them—Jean Cassou, the director of Paris's Museum of Modern Art—recalled, "For me, there is one word for this time in my life: happiness."

"Although [the network's members] were serious people," the journalist and historian David Schoenbrun wrote, "they looked upon what they were doing as a lark, a gay adventure for cultured men and women who had always led a cloistered life." Echoing that view, Cassou noted: "We did not slink about in cloaks and daggers, looking grim. We laughed a lot and felt younger than we had in years."

Even when their world began to fall apart, their laughter and hope continued. As total novices in clandestine activity, the Museum of Man agents were organizing on the fly, making things up as they went along, with little idea of how to operate in this dark new netherworld. The dangers they faced were heightened by the network's explosive growth. Put simply, it was trying to do too many things—publish a newspaper and other propaganda material, run escape lines, and collect military intelligence—all while failing to pay close attention to security. Some of its agents were involved in all these actions, which, as they soon would find out, was a prescription for disaster.

"I think that if our network had survived, we would certainly have separated the activities of escape and intelligence," Germaine Tillion said after the war. "But that was something we couldn't do in the beginning, when we were starting from scratch. We simply didn't have the resources or the experience."

Six months after the network was launched, the arrests began. Its leaders were betrayed by one of its own members, Albert Gaveau, who served as a top lieutenant to Boris Vildé but was in fact a double agent working for the Gestapo. In the first of several Gestapo roundups, Vildé, Lewitsky, and Oddon were captured. Soon to follow them to prison were Humbert and more than a dozen others. Several more key members, including Jean Cassou, managed to escape to the unoccupied zone.

For almost a year, those under arrest were kept in prisons and jails in and around Paris while the Germans investigated their resistance activities. On January 8, 1942, eighteen network members—twelve men and six women—were put on trial by a German military court at Fresnes prison near Paris. At its end, ten were sentenced to death by firing squad—seven men, including Boris Vildé and Anatole Lewitsky, and three women, among them Yvonne Oddon. (The judge, however, would commute the women's sentences to deportation to German concentration camps.) Agnès Humbert and five others were sentenced to five years in German prisons. The three remaining defendants were found not guilty.

In the late afternoon of February 23, the seven condemned men were loaded into a bus and driven to Mont Valérien, a snow-covered hill overlooking the Bois de Boulogne and the main execution site for members of the French Resistance. As they walked to the clearing where the firing squad awaited, the men were asked if they wanted blindfolds. They all said no. As they faced their executioners, they began singing "La Marseillaise," haltingly at first, then louder and louder. They didn't stop until the shots rang out. The German prosecutor at their trial, who witnessed the executions, later declared, "They all died as heroes."

GERMAINE TILLION AND HER small cell within the network escaped detection because it had few day-to-day dealings with Vildé. Distraught at the news of the arrests of her friends, Germaine became obsessed with the idea of engineering their escape from Fresnes prison, a massive gray fortress-like structure near Paris that served as the Gestapo's main holding facility for captured French resisters. When she brought up the idea to Paul Hauet, however, the elderly colonel told her they didn't have the resources—human, material, or financial—to stage a successful escape. Germaine then sought out leading Catholic prelates in Paris, urging them to intercede with Third Reich officials to commute the death sentences. All those she approached refused to do so.

Germaine's failure to save her friends' lives left her with "an unbearable pain and impotent anger." For a time she thought about hunting Albert Gaveau down herself and neutralizing him, she told the British historian James Knowlson decades later. What exactly did she mean by the verb *neutraliser?* he asked. She calmly answered, "I had a revolver at the time." Raising her hand, she pointed her index finger at her head: "Pfut!"

"Since then," Knowlson wrote, "I can never hear this verb, either in

English or in French, without thinking of that tiny, bespectacled, ninety-year-old lady, sitting in her armchair in the sitting-room of her country house in Brittany, calmly announcing her intention to blow out someone's brains and regretting that she had not been able to do so."

As the only high-level leader of the group still at large, Germaine gave up her ideas of revenge and devoted all her energies to resurrecting the network and overseeing its work. "I was the head of the *réseau* and also its godmother for more than a year," she later said. Although she and the other surviving members no longer were able to publish their newspaper, they continued to hide and smuggle out Jews and fugitive Allied troops as well as to collect military intelligence.

One of Germaine's first priorities was to find a new way of transmitting that information to London. In late 1940, the American embassy had moved from Paris to Vichy, making the network's previous method of transmission—sending material via the embassy's mailbag—no longer possible. In her search for such a link, Germaine forged relationships with other networks, including one called Gloria SMH, which also specialized in intelligence gathering and was backed by the Special Operations Executive (SOE), one of Britain's two top intelligence services. Attracted by Gloria's resources, which included substantial funds and the ability to transmit by radio to London, Germaine entered into an informal alliance with its leaders. Two years later, she would join forces with one of Gloria's feistiest agents, a nineteen-year-old university student named Anise Girard.

Chapter 2

"Hold On!"

Anise
Girard

I N JUNE 1940, WHEN ANISE GIRARD ANNOUNCED TO HER MOTHER
that she planned to escape to Britain to join the fight against the Nazis,
Germaine Girard hardly batted an eye. After pointing out the obvious
dangers of such a plan, she told her eighteen-year-old daughter she
could go if she found someone to accompany her.

"Freedom was one of my mother's great principles," Anise observed years later. "So was independence. It was important to her that
her children grow up in that kind of atmosphere." As a teenager herself, Germaine Girard had put into practice what she would later preach

to her children. Hungry for knowledge, she periodically took the train to Paris from her home in Le Havre to attend lectures by renowned French intellectuals like the philosopher Henri Bergson and the sociologist Émile Durkheim.

After marrying a doctor, moving to Paris, and giving birth to five children in short order, Germaine made their education her life's work. Rejecting the rigid French educational system, in which the teacher has absolute authority and rote learning is the norm, Germaine home-schooled Anise and her siblings until they went to high school.

She followed the child-centered approach of the famed Italian educator Maria Montessori, giving her children the freedom to learn through their own experiences and at their own pace. "We worked in the morning from nine to noon, but not in the afternoon at all, and we never had homework," Anise recalled. "We played a lot, learned a lot, and visited every place that was interesting in Paris."

She described her mother as "a tall, blond, attractive woman with a fiery temperament and an exceptionally keen intelligence," which was an apt verbal portrait of herself as well. From her earliest days, the blond, blue-eyed Anise was high-spirited, impulsive, and outspoken— traits that her teachers tried to curb when she finished her primary education and attended the Lycée Moliere, an elite public high school for girls in Paris. The lycée's exacting academic regimen was, to put it mildly, not to her taste: "I didn't enjoy myself at all there. I didn't fit in." Years later, she would tell an interviewer, "I was rebellious, insolent, restless, and I had discipline problems. When I later went to prison, it reminded me a lot of high school."

She did well enough, however, to graduate and win admission to the Sorbonne, where she decided to study German. Even though her parents, both of whom had grown up in French provinces adjacent to Germany, were strongly anti-German and hated the Nazis, they insisted that their children learn German as a second language. Anise's goal was to become a teacher and then the director of a lycée. "I thought our high schools had appalling methods of education," she said, "and I wanted to run one that put its faith in young people and gave them freedom."

When German troops occupied France in the summer of 1940, her only thought was how to fight back. She decided to join the small group of young Frenchmen who had fled to Britain to join forces with General Charles de Gaulle, the only official in the French government to leave his homeland and continue the struggle against Hitler. It was a pipe dream, and Anise's mother knew it, but she allowed her daughter to pursue the idea as long as she found a friend to make the effort with her. Her failure to persuade any of her friends to do so, Anise later said, "was the first big disappointment of my life."

Although she eventually accepted the fact she would never see actual combat, Anise, like Germaine Tillion and a mushrooming number of her compatriots throughout the country, was determined to "do something." But she had no idea where to go or whom to contact. Perhaps not surprisingly, it was her mother who provided the key.

For months, Germaine Girard, who had taken in a number of Jewish refugees from Nazi Germany at various times, had been discreetly putting out feelers to friends and acquaintances, seeking leads to Resistance groups that Anise might join. She finally was put in touch with Suzanne Roussel, a philosophy professor at the Lycée Henri IV, one of Paris's most prestigious high schools for boys. Roussel agreed to meet with Anise. A few days later, she was accepted as an agent for a newborn intelligence network working with the British. Its name was Gloria.

STUNNED BY THE NAZIS' lightning-fast conquest of most of Western Europe, British officials were desperate for information about German military activities in the countries now under German control. Their main focus, though, was France. As the occupied nation closest to Britain, France was Hitler's springboard—the country from which the Luftwaffe would bomb British cities and the German navy would dispatch submarines to sink British merchant shipping. As a result, information about the movements and disposition of German troops, ships, submarines, barges, and aircraft there was of vital importance.

Dozens of intelligence networks sprang up in France to meet that need. Gloria was one of the earliest, named after the alias of the young woman who was its head. She was Jeanine Picabia, the daughter of two of the leading figures in Paris's exuberant avant-garde art scene during the first two decades of the twentieth century.

Jeanine's father, Francis Picabia, was a flamboyant Cuban French artist who is widely credited with producing—in 1909—one of the first abstract paintings in the history of Western art. Her mother, Gabrièle Buffet-Picabia, was also very much ahead of her time, studying for five years at conservatories in Paris and Berlin with the aim of becoming a composer of modern music. "We wanted to free ourselves from all the traditional techniques, from all the old syntaxes and grammars, to explore what we called pure music," Gabrièle later wrote.

In 1909, Gabrièle gave up her promising career to marry the fiery, seductive Picabia, who had already made a name for himself as an impressionist painter but wanted to break out of that mold. He saw Gabrièle as the muse he needed to do that. "She seemed so rebellious and sure of herself that Francis perceived her as a feminine double, on all levels," according to her great-granddaughters, the writers Anne and Claire Berest, who wrote a 2017 biography about her. "Conversations with her galvanized and inspired him. He wanted her to always be there, watching him paint, giving her opinion on each brushstroke he made."

From the beginning of the couple's relationship, she pressured him to break away from the traditional and become more radical in his art, just as she had earlier hoped to do with her music. She applied the same pressure to some of their artist friends, particularly the painter and sculptor Marcel Duchamp, with whom she formed a close if complicated relationship.

In early 1913, less than four years after the Picabias' marriage, Francis Picabia and Marcel Duchamp took center stage at an incendiary art exhibition in New York City that caused an international sensation and marked the dawn of modernism in the United States. Known as the Armory Show, the exhibition featured avant-garde art from all over America and Europe, but the most controversial paintings came from France. Duchamp's Cubist-inspired *Nude Descending a Staircase,* de-

picting a deconstructed human figure in abstract brown panels seemingly in motion, was considered especially provocative. According to
the art historian Valerie Paley, the Armory Show, in its questioning of
classical traditions, emerged as a significant countercultural moment
that created a revolution in American art.

After returning to Paris, the Picabias and Duchamp established
themselves at the center of a glittering social circle whose other members included some of the biggest names in the city's frenetic modern-
ist scene—the poet Guillaume Apollinaire, the sculptors Constantin
Brancusi and Alexander Calder, the photographer Man Ray, and the
writers Samuel Beckett and James Joyce, among others.

Some, prominently including Francis Picabia, thumbed their noses
at convention in the way they lived as well as their art, indulging in
considerable partying, drinking, drug taking, and, in the case of Picabia, womanizing. While Gabrièle was not as heedless as her husband,
she was unable—or unwilling—to rein him in. "Francis took all her
attention, all her energy," wrote Anne and Claire Berest. "He drained
her of her strength. There was almost nothing left for her." And certainly nothing left for their four children, who were handed over to
nannies and governesses and virtually ignored by their parents.

As a child, Jeanine, who was the second youngest, had no interest in
Francis and Gabrièle's free-living, free-thinking ways, but she did take
after her mother in at least one important aspect: an early determination to lead her own life and follow her dreams without interference
from others. In her late teens, Jeanine left home, went to nursing
school, and began earning her own living.

When World War II broke out, Jeanine joined the Red Cross. After
France capitulated to the Germans in June 1940, she became part of a
Red Cross group that traveled throughout Brittany, Normandy, and
other areas near the coast of western France to tend to the medical and
other needs of French soldiers held in German internment camps there.
As she did so, she took careful notes about the considerable German
troop and supply movements she witnessed.

When she was demobilized in December 1940, Jeanine took off
for the south of France to visit her father, whom she hadn't seen since

the beginning of the war and who, long divorced from her mother, was living in Cannes. On her way, she stopped on impulse at the U.S. consulate in Marseille and showed American officials the considerable information she had collected about the German military presence on and near the Atlantic coast.

After examining her notes, the Americans urged her to remain in Cannes while they decided what to do with the material. Several days later, a man identifying himself as a British intelligence officer came to her father's house. He asked Jeanine to return to Paris and head a group, to be financed and overseen by a new top-secret British government agency, which would recruit agents throughout France to gather intelligence of the kind she had already assembled. The agency, known as the Special Operations Executive (SOE), had been set up in the summer of 1940 to foment sabotage, subversion, and other resistance activities in occupied Europe.

Jeanine Picabia's code name would be Gloria, and her network would be christened Gloria SMH (an inversion of HMS, which stands for His Majesty's Service). SOE also assigned her a partner—an intelligence operative named Jacques Legrand, a chemical engineer in civilian life who'd fought in the battle for France and had been taken prisoner, then escaped en route to a German prisoner of war camp. The pair's Paris-based network, which eventually numbered more than two hundred agents, gathered information throughout the occupied zone, but its specialty was intelligence collected from ports, shipyards, and submarine bases on the Atlantic and English Channel coasts, particularly in Normandy and Brittany.

Although casting a wide net in their recruitment of agents, Picabia and Legrand each had a favored group from which to draw. Legrand focused on high school and university students and professors, among them Suzanne Roussel, who in turn tapped Anise Girard. Intriguingly, Picabia, who had long distanced herself from her parents' hedonistic milieu, enlisted the help of several members of their former entourage.

One was Mary Reynolds, a wealthy socialite from Minnesota who was the longtime lover of Marcel Duchamp and whose house on rue Hallé in Montparnasse became a favorite rendezvous point and hiding place for network members. It was secluded and surrounded by a high wall, allowing operatives to enter and leave without being seen. On more than one occasion, Reynolds, whose code name was Gentle Mary, uprooted shrubs in her garden to bury tin boxes containing important reports and supplies, including an official German seal for identity papers, stolen by Jeanine Picabia and retrieved whenever an agent needed forged ID documents.

Samuel Beckett was also on Gloria's roster. Born and educated in Dublin, the novelist and playwright, who would win the Nobel Prize decades later, first traveled to France at the age of twenty-two and spent most of the rest of his life there. He had known Jeanine Picabia since her childhood, and she recruited him for a key role: analyzing and translating into English the intelligence reports that now flooded into Gloria's headquarters. "They would bring all this information to me on various bits and scraps of paper—everything that concerned the occupying forces—and I would rank them in order of urgency, translate them, and type them up," he said. He would then take the documents to the network's photographer, André Lazaro-Hadji (known as Jimmy the Greek), who would photograph them and reduce them to the size of a postage stamp, to be hidden in matchboxes, cigarette packs, and other small containers. These in turn would be transported by couriers from Paris to France's unoccupied zone, where they would be sent on to Britain.

Crossing the demarcation line between the Nazi-occupied north of the country and the so-called free zone was always a highly dangerous mission. German soldiers minutely scrutinized each traveler's *ausweis,* a German-issued identity card allowing French citizens to pass back and forth between zones, and often subjected those carrying them to a thorough body search.

One of Gloria's veteran couriers, however, never seemed to mind the perils involved in the crossings; in fact, she seemed to welcome them. Gabrièle Buffet-Picabia, the onetime muse of France's leading modern artists and Jeanine's mother, was arguably her daughter's most unconventional recruit. Gabrièle, who had been divorced from Francis Picabia since 1930, had once bemoaned the fact that she didn't have enough adventure in her life; now she had all she could handle, which pleased her immensely.

Known as Madame Pic, she usually began her missions early in the morning, catching a train from the Gare de Lyon to Lyon or other destinations in the south, carrying a shopping bag filled with food and other goods that concealed the contraband she would soon hand over to comrades in the free zone. If challenged by German police or soldiers, as she occasionally was, she adopted the façade of a gentle, kindly grandmother, explaining in fluent German that she was on her way to visit her cherished grandchildren in the countryside. This "sweet little old lady" persona reportedly never failed her.

DURING THE YEAR ANISE GIRARD spent as a Gloria agent, she never met Madame Pic or Jeanine Picabia. The only operative she saw on a regular basis was the melancholy-looking Irishman to whom she delivered her intelligence reports at his Montparnasse apartment. She would not learn the famed writer's true identity until decades after the war.

When she joined the network, Anise, who was assigned the code name Danielle, was given no formal training in intelligence gathering; all she received was a leaflet displaying the insignia of the various German armies, with a description of their ranks and weapons. Her first assignment was to find out the type of gun mounted on German tanks at Fort Vincennes, a military fortress on the eastern edge of Paris that had been turned into a Wehrmacht base. "It was a task for which I was wholly unfitted," she recalled. "I could hardly tell a corporal from a general, let alone distinguish between different types of cannon."

Nonetheless, she rode her bicycle to Vincennes and, keeping a wary eye out for German guards, spotted a couple of tanks in the woods outside the base. "My descriptions of the guns with which the tanks were equipped were anything but exact," she said. "Something told me that this was not the way to tackle the business of resisting the Germans."

Her next mission was more successful. Asked to pinpoint the location of German barrage balloons in Paris, she joined forces with another Sorbonne student to cycle around the city and note the types of balloons being used, where they were moored, and their Luftwaffe serial numbers. Helped by her brothers, she entered the information on a large map of Paris, which was then photographed and sent to London.

Like Anise, most members of Gloria SMH—and, for that matter, of other early French Resistance groups—were rank amateurs. They had joined this clandestine world with little idea of what was required for success or even simple survival. Few of the networks, for example, followed the lead of French Communist resistance groups, which were organized into cells of a few members, with cells having minimal contact with one another. Members of the cells had to abide by strict rules, including not sleeping in the same place for more than two or three nights in a row and not gathering in public places like bars and restaurants.

Such strict secrecy was not something that most of the French were good at. As one French historian wrote, his compatriots "had a hard time taking security measures seriously because they interfered with their social habits and natural garrulousness." Another Frenchman noted, "We have no experience of clandestine life. We do not know how to be silent or how to hide."

Further increasing the risk of German detection for Gloria were the close ties between it and other resistance groups, like the reconstituted Museum of Man network, led by Germaine Tillion. Germaine now relied on Picabia's organization to transmit to London the intelligence gathered by her network's members.

In March 1942, that radio link was abruptly severed when Pierre de Vomécourt, a wealthy young French aristocrat who acted as SOE's liaison with Gloria and other networks, was arrested by the Gestapo, along with two associates. From then on, neither Gloria nor the Museum of Man group was able to pass on its information to British officials.

Vomécourt was one of SOE's most valuable agents in occupied France, and the British agency pressed Jeanine Picabia and Jacques Legrand to devise a plan to help him escape from Fresnes prison, where he was being interrogated. As they both knew, the chances of success were slim to none. But then Germaine Tillion paid a visit to Legrand, and suddenly there seemed to be a glimmer of hope.

As Picabia and Legrand were debating what to do, a man in clerical garb showed up unannounced at the front door of the spacious house that Germaine shared with her mother in Saint-Maur-des-Fossés. Short and dark-haired, with a receding hairline and steel-blue eyes, he introduced himself as the Reverend Robert Alesch, the assistant pastor of a neighboring Catholic parish.

Alesch told Germaine he was a native of Luxembourg, had studied theology in the German town of Freiburg, and had moved to France two years after his ordination in 1933. He said he had heard about her Resistance work from a young mutual acquaintance and wanted to know if there was anything he could do to help.

Understandably wary, Germaine said she didn't know what he was talking about. After sending him away, she asked several people about him, including Pierre Maurice Dessignes, the university student who had referred Alesch to her. Two years before, the nineteen-year-old Dessignes had organized a small resistance group of young people in Saint-Maur and La Varenne, a neighboring Paris suburb, to hide escaped Allied soldiers and air crews and smuggle them across the demarcation line into the unoccupied zone. The group began working with Tillion's cell, and then, following its example, joined the Museum of Man network.

Dessignes corroborated Alesch's story. He told Germaine that the priest had become well known for his fiery sermons opposing the Nazi occupation and the Vichy government's collaboration with Germany. He also had established close ties with members of Dessignes's group and encouraged them and other young members of his parish to do all they could to resist the Germans. Indeed, he had become so outspoken about the German menace that some of his parishioners feared for his safety. A few days before, Alesch had asked to meet Dessignes's boss in the Resistance, and Dessignes gave him Germaine's address.

Reassured, Germaine was more receptive to the priest when he paid another call several days later. The priest told her he had met someone who might be useful to her group—a German noncommissioned offi-

Robert Alesch,
the priest who
offered to help
Germaine Tillion in
her Resistance
activities

cer who had fallen in love with and become engaged to a young French-woman in Alesch's parish. According to Alesch, the German, who was a high-ranking guard at Fresnes, had informed him he was about to be transferred to fight on the Russian front and was desperate to escape to the unoccupied zone with his fiancée. He asked Alesch if he could help him.

When Germaine relayed Alesch's story to Jacques Legrand, he saw the possibility of an exchange: the guard arranging for the escape of Pierre de Vomécourt in return for Gloria's help in smuggling him and his fiancée out of Paris. Legrand conducted his own investigation of Alesch, which, because time was of the essence, was somewhat cursory. Still, everything that Alesch had said seemed to check out.

Legrand told Germaine to go ahead. After consulting the guard, Alesch informed her the German was willing to orchestrate Vomécourt's escape but needed a considerable amount of money to do so. SOE agreed to his demand, and Alesch signed a contract at Germaine's home, in the presence of Émilie Tillion, who had been there for all his visits. In early August, 400,000 francs were handed over to Alesch to set the operation in motion.

On August 13, 1942, Germaine met Alesch at the Gare de Lyon to go over final plans with the priest before he boarded a train for a meeting in the south with several people he identified as co-conspirators in the operation. After their discussion, she accompanied him to his gate. As he headed down the platform toward his train, Germaine felt a hand on her shoulder. Turning around, she saw three men in civilian clothes. One of them demanded her papers, then ordered her in German-accented French: "Come with us." Surrounding her, they hustled her to a black Citroën waiting outside and drove to Gestapo headquarters on rue des Saussaies.

Germaine would not find out until later that Robert Alesch, who was indeed a Catholic priest, had been working for the Gestapo since 1941. He had offered his services to the Germans in Paris in exchange for 12,000 francs a month, along with bonuses for every Resistance member he betrayed. His fierce anti-German sermons were meant to win the sympathy of his parishioners and to persuade the young people in his congregation to defy the Nazis. Once they did, he reported them to the Gestapo.

Known as Agent Axel, Alesch spent his considerable earnings on a luxurious apartment in Paris's 16th arrondissement, living there with two mistresses and artwork he'd bought from the Nazis, who had stolen it from Jewish art collectors. The only time he spent at his church was to celebrate mass every morning.

As a result of Alesch's treachery, Gloria SMH was decimated, as was Germaine Tillion's network. Her arrest was followed two days later by those of Suzanne Roussel, Jacques Legrand, and dozens of others. Anise Girard, who had just returned to Paris after spending much of the summer in Le Havre, was aware of none of this.

Anise had had two missions in Le Havre, a bustling port city on the English Channel coast of Normandy. She worked as a counselor at a summer camp while at the same time gathering intelligence for Gloria. Britain's Royal Air Force had staged several recent bombing raids on the German naval base and other military targets in Le Havre, and Gloria, responding to an SOE request, wanted Anise to document the extent of the damage. In her off hours from the camp, she traveled around the city and its outskirts, taking careful notes about the destruction she observed. She had the "incredible joy" of witnessing firsthand the bombing of an ammunition train at the Le Havre railway station, watching as deafening explosions ripped the air and flames leaped high into the sky.

When she came back to Paris, she carried in her backpack a large map of Le Havre on which she'd marked the bomb sites she'd seen, as well as detailed notes about the sites and the extent of damage to each. She'd been told to call Jacques Legrand when she returned, but she had never met the co-head of Gloria and was shy about approaching this "massively important, mysterious man." Instead, she decided to drop off the map and notes at Suzanne Roussel's apartment.

Outside Roussel's apartment house, Anise noticed a parked red convertible. She thought it odd, since the Germans had banned all but a few thousand French-owned vehicles from the capital. But the convertible's windshield displayed a sticker allowing the car's use, and Anise remembered that her father, a doctor, had a similar sticker. So, shaking off her uneasiness, she climbed the five flights of stairs to Roussel's apartment and rang the bell.

A handsome young man in shirtsleeves opened the door, and, looking past him into the apartment, Anise saw upended chairs and tables and books and papers littering the floor. Turning around, she dashed for the stairs, but the man caught her halfway down the first flight. He and two Gestapo confederates marched her down and into the convertible. As it crossed the Pont de la Concorde, Anise pulled the map from her backpack and tried to throw it into the Seine, but one of the men snatched it away and pushed her back into the seat.

She was taken to La Santé prison, a sprawling jail in the 14th arrondissement, east of Montparnasse. At its entrance, she had to surrender all her personal effects and sign a waiver acknowledging she had done so. To her horror, she saw that the signature preceding hers was that of her sixty-two-year-old father. Convinced he had been arrested because of her, Anise was consumed with guilt, a burden she carried for the rest of the war. Not until its end did she find out that Dr. Louis Girard, a prominent ear, nose, and throat specialist, had also been a Gloria agent. He had allowed his office in Passy, an elegant neighborhood in the 16th arrondissement, to be used as a mailbox, where the network's intelligence reports could be dropped off and picked up. Neither he nor his daughter knew about the other's resistance activities.

Yet even though the Gestapo dragnet had swept up the Girards and most of Gloria's other agents, several key members managed to get away. Samuel Beckett and his wife were hidden by Mary Reynolds for a few days before fleeing across the demarcation line and hiding out in a village in the south of France for the duration of the war. Reynolds herself later escaped across the Pyrenees to Spain, as did Jeanine Picabia, who fled in December 1942 with the assistance of the Brandy Line, an escape network set up by de Gaulle's Free French forces. In London, Jeanine joined the Free French women's service.

Jeanine's intrepid mother, meanwhile, remained in Paris, continuing to hide stranded Allied airmen and troops in her apartment. In early 1943, the head of the Brandy Line recruited Madame Pic to help organize an extension of his group into southern France. After being named the Brandy Line's second-in-command, she traveled throughout the south for the next several months, recruiting couriers and setting up safe houses. With the Gestapo hot on her trail in late 1943, she finally acknowledged it was time for her to leave. An experienced mountain climber, she had no trouble making her way across the Pyrenees, and in early 1944 she was reunited with her daughter in London.

Although both Gloria SMH and the Museum of Man network were smashed relatively early in the war, they still managed to make important contributions to the burgeoning Resistance in France. The Museum of Man group in particular served as an inspiration—a ray of light—to would-be resisters, showing them that it was indeed possible to oppose the Nazis in action as well as in spirit. It was its members' readiness to fight and die that lit a fire in others, noted the *New York Times* correspondent Alan Riding, who wrote a book about cultural life in Paris during the war. "At a time when most of the French were coming to terms with the occupation," Riding observed, "they were almost alone in acting on their belief in the idea of resistance." According to the French historian Julien Blanc, the Museum of Man group "fed and watered the Resistance to come."

———

ON ANISE GIRARD'S FIRST NIGHT at La Santé, a German soldier entered her cell to tell her she was to be executed at four-thirty the following morning. While seized by a "visceral, terrible fear," she was not surprised. She knew that the penalty for military espionage was death.

Throughout the night, she waited in a daze for the inevitable, as the loud chime of an unseen clock sounded every quarter of an hour. At three o'clock, she knelt at the side of the cot in her cell and began to pray. The chimes continued—3:30; 3:45; 4:00; 4:15; 4:30. Still no sign of her executioners.

At seven, she braced herself as a key turned in the lock. A female guard came in, bearing a cup of coffee. "Either my death warrant had been countermanded, or I had been the victim of a standard procedure for demoralizing new prisoners," she later wrote. But escaping death failed to ease Anise's deep depression and sadness over being confined indefinitely to this tiny, filthy cell, its walls scarred with the signatures of previous inmates. "The loneliness was unbearable. I came from a house with five children, and suddenly all that was gone. The first few days I hated myself. Why had I gotten involved? Why had I inflicted this on my family?"

On her first night at La Santé, Germaine Tillion, too, was threatened with death. A German guard entered her cell and informed her she would be killed the next morning. "I believed him," she later said. "And I entered into an intense state of thought. I began to think about life, about the philosophy of life. And I shrugged my shoulders."

The guard was incredulous. "You're shrugging your shoulders?" he shouted. At that moment, Germaine roused herself from her meditation: "I told him, 'Oh, excuse me, sir, I had forgotten you.' This staggered him so much that he began to gasp for air. Then he began yelling again and left.

"The fact that I had forgotten him—that sent him into a rage. It was instinctive on my part, but it was also a way of dominating. In effect, I was saying to him: 'I look at you, I judge you, I weigh you, and you are . . . what are you? You are a minuscule flea that I study under the microscope.'"

Her sense of detachment, however, proved fleeting. "The two months I spent [at La Santé] were one of the two most difficult periods in my life," she observed. "I was like a corpse. For weeks, I was frozen with horror and anguish." She added, "Entering this new world of captivity—being walled up alive—results in a complete dislocation of a human being, no matter how strong they are."

For more than a week, Germaine couldn't sleep or eat. Denied contact with members of her family or anyone else from the outside world, she was barred from receiving mail, packages, and reading and writing materials. To "keep in touch with time and prove that I still existed," she used the metal spoon she'd been issued to scratch notes on her cell's plaster walls: "Aug. 18, I eat a little"; "August 22, I kill a hundred bedbugs"; "September 2, I sleep a little for the first time."

In October 1942, Germaine, along with Anise and several dozen other inmates, was transferred to Fresnes prison. While conditions there were grim, they still were far better than at La Santé. The cells were larger and cleaner, and many of them had windows, which, even though barred, allowed inmates at least to see out. Although members of prisoners' families were not allowed to visit, they could drop off packages and walk around the prison's perimeter, shouting out messages to their loved ones.

Best of all, in the eyes of the newcomers, were the various ingenious ways of communicating with fellow prisoners that were available to almost everybody there, including those, like Germaine and Anise, who were still in solitary confinement. When she arrived, Anise immediately broke a pane of glass in her cell's window so she could shout to inmates above and below her, who had done the same. Prisoners also used vents and water pipes to exchange messages and information with others, either by voice or in Morse code. Germaine's main method of communication was her cell's heating vent, directly below the ceiling. Standing on a chair, she could reach the vent and talk to the woman in the cell above her and those in the cells of the three floors directly below her.

Four months after arriving at Fresnes, she finally was allowed to receive parcels of food and clothing from friends. A fellow Resistance member had taken charge of Germaine's laundry, washing it and sending it back in a small linen bag. Germaine discovered that the bag had a double lining, which concealed a piece of silk with a sheet of paper sewn to it. Typed on it was a synopsis of the latest bulletins from the BBC's French-language news program, which was broadcast every night throughout the country. Through her heating duct, Germaine read the bulletins to her neighbors. The inmate in the cell directly below her—a young Czech girl whose code name was Jeannette—repeated the information to Anise Girard, who in turn spread the news with her "very loud voice," shouting it out through the window and through her own ducts and vents.

Without ever seeing one another's faces or knowing one another's real names, the women resisters at Fresnes gradually coalesced into a community. Those who received packages of food, like Germaine, sent some of their booty through the pipes and vents to those who did not, like Jeannette. They shared with each other stories about themselves and their families, their fear and terror about what was to come, and their hopes and dreams for life after the war—that is, if they survived. When inmates were taken out to be executed, which happened not infrequently, their fellow prisoners sang "La Marseillaise" at the top of their voices. When their guards shouted at them to be quiet, they sang all the louder, even when it resulted, as it often did, in a beating.

For many prisoners, that burgeoning solidarity reignited the flame of resistance. Although they could no longer defy the enemy outside the prison's walls, they would find ways to do so within. "Hold on!" became their mantra. "*Courage!* We will defeat them."

ANISE GIRARD'S DEFIANCE IN prison also took the form of devising various schemes to escape. During her time at La Santé, she established contact with a young male resister in the cell above hers who had managed to acquire a piece of wire and make a device that he claimed would pick the cells' locks. But before he could put his scheme into action to free himself and her, she was transferred to Fresnes.

There she came up with the idea of overwhelming the elderly fe-male guard who brought her food by hitting her on the head with the wooden handle of her hairbrush. She then planned to stuff a piece of cloth in the guard's mouth, take her keys and uniform, lock the door, and slip out of the prison.

Early one morning, Anise lured the guard into her cell by claiming she had seen bedbugs in her mattress and asking the woman to check for herself. As the guard leaned over the mattress, Anise closed the cell door behind her, then hit her with the brush. The blow failed to stun the woman, however, and she began to scream. Anise pushed her down on the cot and tried to stuff the gag in her mouth. As the two women wrestled on the mattress, the cell door was flung open, and the German commandant of Fresnes and two subordinates, having heard the screams as they walked past, burst in.

The commandant demanded to know what was going on. Thinking fast, Anise, who spoke fluent German, said she had attacked the guard because the woman had beaten her several times when both were at La Santé, which, as she later admitted, was "an outrageous lie." The guard insisted that wasn't true, that she had never hit Girard or, for that mat-ter, ever worked at La Santé. But the commandant told her to be quiet, preferring to believe the pretty French blonde with her perfect Ger-man. Instead of receiving the severe punishment she expected, Anise got off with a nearly literal slap on the wrist—she was handcuffed for three days—as well as a temporary removal of her mattress and noth-ing to eat for the same period of time.

In the days to come, the commandant made it abundantly clear that he had developed a soft spot for Anise. His adjutant visited her during her brief punishment period, removing her handcuffs for a few minutes to allow her to wash and to eat the soup that other guards surreptitiously brought her. Before the incident, she had not been allowed to receive parcels from her family; afterward, she began to get packages from her mother containing food, clothing, and books. On several occasions, the commandant visited her cell to chat with her. During one of his visits, Girard predicted that Germany would lose the war. "This seemed to amuse him," she later said. "He was courting me a little, I think."

———

FOR GERMAINE TILLION, TOO, life in prison showed considerable improvement. Several months after she arrived, she finally was given access to her field reports and notes from her six years of research in Algeria. She was ecstatic. "In this abyss of absence," she later said, "I felt as if I had been given opium. A complete universe—the most exciting work in the world—was given back to me." With all her material at hand, she returned to work on her doctoral dissertation. "I read line by line what I had already written, interspersing notes not yet inventoried. I had the reassuring feeling that I could stay twenty years in prison without exhausting what I had before me." By the autumn of 1943, she had completed several hundred pages.

At the same time, however, she received disturbing news about her mother. Until early 1943, she had been given no information about Émilie Tillion's fate. Then, during a visit by the prison's chaplain, she learned that Émilie, too, had been betrayed by Robert Alesch and arrested on August 13, 1942, just a few hours after her daughter. Like Germaine, she was now an inmate at Fresnes.

Distraught at the news, Germaine caught a glimpse of Émilie several weeks later when she peered out her open cell door and spied her in the doorway of a cell one floor below, on the other side of the prison block. "For a brief moment, we looked at each other," Germaine recalled. "The pain was unbelievable. It broke my heart."

Thanks to the chaplain, they were able to exchange letters over the next few months. In one, dated July 4, 1943, Émilie urged her daughter to stay fierce and strong. "It's the only way to hold on," she wrote. "Otherwise, we'll dissolve."

A month later, Germaine was told that Émilie was no longer at Fresnes. Desperately hoping that her mother had been released, Germaine found out not long afterward that she had been transferred to another prison. Then, in late October, Germaine was informed that she herself was about to be deported to Germany.

Chapter 3

"We Are Here to Be Killed"

ON THE MORNING OF OCTOBER 21, 1943, GERMAINE TILLION found herself, along with twenty or so other female prisoners from Fresnes, on a platform at the Gare du Nord railway station. Her luggage consisted of a suitcase and a huge jute sack stuffed with her dissertation manuscript and the notes and reports from her research in Algeria.

Neither she nor her fellow inmates knew where they were headed that day, although they'd heard rumors that their destination was a labor camp somewhere in Germany. After being closeted in a jail cell for more than a year, Germaine hoped she would get a chance to work outdoors. Perhaps, she thought, she might even find time to finish her dissertation.

As she struggled down the platform with her suitcase and sack, she was spotted by Anise Girard, who was getting ready to board the train. Anise had spent the last three months at Fort Romainville, a former military fortress outside Paris used by the Germans as a transit center for Ravensbrück and other concentration camps.

At the moment, Anise was furious with herself. Earlier that morning, on the bus that would take her and several other women to the Gare du Nord, she had reviewed her latest escape plan—to melt into the crowds of travelers at the station and slip away. The guard who had accompanied the women from Fort Romainville was a regular German soldier, not an SS man. He had been kind to Anise, and she thought there was a good chance he would allow her to flee. But one concern made her hesitate: If she succeeded, she feared the Nazis might arrest one or more of her younger brothers in retribution. In the end, Anise decided not to try. "I don't know if it was because of this worry or because of general lack of courage, but I didn't leave," she recalled. "I was ashamed—it was quite hard to bear."

The sight of the petite, dark-haired Germaine on the platform, wrestling with an overstuffed sack almost as big as she was, roused Anise from her funk. "I thought it must be Germaine Tillion, the famous Kouri," she said. "I knew her by her name and voice, had heard all about her, but had never seen her." As Germaine came closer, Anise called out, "Hello, Kouri! I'm Danielle." Germaine smiled, and the two boarded the train together.

During their journey, the women formed an intense bond that would last the rest of their lives. "She made me talk about myself, gave me courage, and helped me swallow the cowardice I had felt in abandoning my plan of escape," Anise said. Germaine also did her best to hearten the other women in the compartment, spinning lighthearted stories about her time with the Berber tribes in Algeria. She pointed out that they were traveling in a regular passenger train, surely a good omen for the future. Perhaps life at their final destination, whatever it was, would be better than what they imagined or feared.

After a week of zigzagging across Germany, the train began slowing down at dusk on Sunday, October 31. Outside, the terrain was heavily wooded and marshy. A small lake lay in the distance, its shore bristling with gorse bushes and scrub pines and surrounded by dunes of white sand. It was a desolate, brooding landscape, made ghostly by wisps of fog clinging to the trees.

A nervous silence fell over the train. Then, as it pulled to a stop, all hell broke loose. Even before the doors opened, a cacophony of noise—screams and shouts, the barking of dogs, the cracking of whips—ripped the air. "*Raus! Raus!*" ("Out! Out!") SS guards yelled, yanking women and their luggage from the cars. Several tumbled to the ground, and those who stooped to help them were kicked, attacked by dogs, or lashed with whips. The stream of invective continued: "Line up by fives, you dirty bitches! Hands at your sides, lazy cows!"

Struggling with their luggage, the women were herded down a dusty road lined with pine trees. After half an hour or so, they approached a high gray wall, topped by electrified barbed wire. As a gate slowly opened, they saw before them an enormous square. Behind it were rows of narrow bottle-green tarred-roof barracks, separated by a wide main road and alleys of black coal gravel. Facing the women were female SS guards in hooded black capes, gripping the leashes of lunging, howling dogs. German soldiers pointed machine guns at them.

Ravensbrück

But those weren't the images that burned themselves into the minds of Germaine, Anise, and their compatriots. It was the sight of emaciated, wraithlike figures, dressed in shapeless rags, who were creeping around the square, some staggering under the weight of vats of soup, others pushing immense wagons overflowing with garbage. According to one of the new arrivals, it was like something from a horror movie: "I barely noticed their skeletal forms or their shaven heads. What shocked me to the core was the sight of their dead, vacant stares. They were living zombies."

As Germaine viewed the ghastly scene before her, she "felt what animals probably feel when they arrive at the slaughterhouse—that death is in this place." Turning to Anise, she whispered, "We are here to be killed."

But first they would be stripped of everything they'd brought to Ravensbrück—their possessions, their dignity, and finally their very identity. Marched into a building, they were ordered to surrender everything they'd brought with them—a wide array of items that included wedding bands and other jewelry, clothing, watches, books, photos, letters, food, toothpaste, and soap. Germaine watched as her jute bag was thrown into a corner of the room. She would never see it or its precious contents again.

Caught up in the chaos of the moment, she had no time to process the loss. She and the other women were ordered to take off all their clothes, then were thrust into a room where several had their heads shaved. There was no rhyme or reason to the selection process; both Germaine and Anise left with their hair intact. But no one escaped the next humiliation: submitting to rectal and vaginal probes to make sure no one had hidden anything inside her body cavities.

Numb with shock and mortification, the women, still naked, were next herded into a shower room. Following the shower, which consisted of a trickle of lukewarm water, they were issued threadbare, stained uniforms—striped cotton dresses and caps, along with rough wooden clogs. The underclothes were also hand-me-downs. The underpants Anise received came down to her knees and had black fringe on the sides. She concluded that the garment once had been a Jewish prayer shawl.

On the dresses' left sleeve was a red triangle, indicating the women's status as political prisoners. On top of the triangle, a numeral was written in black ink—24,588 for Germaine and 24,589 for Anise—denoting the number of women who'd been imprisoned at Ravensbrück before them. From then on, that's all they were to their jailers—just a string of ciphers.

FOR THE NEXT THREE WEEKS, the Frenchwomen were confined to a quarantine barracks, as a precaution to make sure none had an infec-

1. — Welcome...

Sketch by Violette Lecoq of the arrival of a
convoy of French résistantes, including herself,
Germaine Tillion, and Anise Girard, at Ravensbrück
in October 1943. Note how fashionably dressed many
of the women are. Like many of the captions for
Lecoq's drawings, this one—"Welcome"—is meant to
be savagely ironic.

Sketch of the
same convoy
of women two
hours later

2. — Deux heures après...

tious disease. Germaine and Anise shared a top wooden bunk so
narrow—less than two and a half feet wide—that they had to sleep on
their sides, packed like sardines in a can. It was cold and damp in the
barracks, and just six days after her arrival, Germaine, who had been in
robust health all her life, fell deathly ill. Notwithstanding all its quarantine efforts, Ravensbrück was a giant petri dish of disease, and no
one escaped unscathed. After coming down with a high fever, Germaine became almost comatose, barely able to move or speak.

The Czech inmate in charge of the barracks, known as a blockova, knew something about Germaine and Anise that they themselves were not yet aware of. Before arriving at Ravensbrück, they'd been classified by German authorities as *Nacht und Nebel* (Night and Fog) political prisoners, who eventually were to be put to death in secret, with no record of what had happened to them. The blockova, who'd been a member of the Czech resistance, alerted a compatriot of hers, a doctor who worked in the camp infirmary, about the presence of Germaine, and her illness. The daughter of a prominent Czech musician and philosopher, Dr. Zdenka Nedvedova had been a pediatrician in Prague before her involvement in anti-Nazi activities. Arrested in 1940, she was sent to Auschwitz with her husband, who died of tuberculosis there. In 1943, she was transferred to Ravensbrück.

After arranging for Germaine to be brought to the infirmary, Nedvedova diagnosed her illness as diphtheria. She injected her with an antitoxin and installed her in the diphtheria ward, which German officials and guards, terrified of acquiring a contagious disease, never entered. Also in the ward was a Czech inmate recovering from the disease, whom Nedvedova put in charge of watching over the newcomer. "Thanks to this small group of courageous women," Germaine later wrote, her life was saved.

It was in the ward that Germaine Tillion, having just lost six years of her research from Algeria, embarked on a new study—an in-depth anthropological investigation of Ravensbrück. Her fieldwork began with an informal tutorial in the infirmary by Nedvedova and her fellow Czechs, both medical personnel and patients, about the concentration camp system in general and Ravensbrück in particular. A number of the Czechs, like the Poles and other early political prisoners at the camp, spoke German and had been put to work by the Nazis in administrative and medical positions. They described to Germaine what they had seen and heard during their time at the camp: the brutal forced labor, the beatings and whippings, the executions by shooting and injection.

Several of the Czechs, mostly Communists, had initially been imprisoned at Auschwitz in Poland, where they had witnessed the beginning of the Holocaust. They told Germaine about the mass gassing there of millions of Jews from all over Europe. She also learned about so-called black transports—trucks shuttling women from Ravens-brück to the Auschwitz gas chambers.

Germaine, who began secretly writing down the information she received, using a pen and paper smuggled to her by her new Czech friends, was also given a short history of Ravensbrück. When it opened in May 1939, three months before the war began, almost all its pris-oners, numbering some two thousand, were German. About a third had been convicted of criminal offenses, while most of the rest were Romany and women arrested for anti-Nazi activities, among them members of religious sects, like Jehovah's Witnesses.

In the war's early months, resistance members from the first coun-tries occupied by Germany—Austria, Czechoslovakia, and Poland—began flooding in. As the number of prisoners expanded, so did the camp bureaucracy. Needing more workers to handle the influx, Ravensbrück officials assigned German-speaking inmates, some of them former resis-tance members, to jobs throughout the camp. At the time of Germaine's arrival, they were in charge of the barracks; staffed the kitchen; served in the infirmary as doctors, nurses, and technicians; and worked in the camp offices as typists, secretaries, bookkeepers, and filing clerks.

In early 1942, as thousands more political prisoners poured into the camp from German-occupied countries in western Europe, Hitler's as-sault on Russia, launched in the summer of 1941, was floundering. The German army was in desperate need of more munitions and other ma-tériel, and concentration camp officials provided the workers to supply them. Over the course of the war, tens of thousands of women from Ravensbrück were deployed as slave laborers to make uniforms, arma-ments, and other military equipment. While many prisoners were dis-patched to factories scattered throughout Germany, thousands more worked at subcamps in and around Ravensbrück, including a Siemens factory that made electrical parts for Germany's V-1 and V-2 terror weapons.

From her new Czech friends, Germaine learned the difference be-tween so-called extermination camps like Auschwitz and forced labor camps like Ravensbrück. The sole and immediate purpose of extermination camps was to kill. Even though the term "forced labor" sounds less extreme, the aim of the other camps was also to kill, although much more slowly. Nazi officials schemed to make as much money as possible from the prisoners' labor before they died.

As she dug deeper into the history of Ravensbrück, Germaine learned that it was operated by a limited company, whose main shareholder was SS head Heinrich Himmler, the creator and administrator of all German concentration camps. Himmler, who owned the lease of the land, about fifty miles north of Berlin, on which the Ravensbrück camp was built, made enormous profits from its slave labor trade.

To keep those profits high, Himmler mandated a constant churn of workers—fresh new prisoners brought in to replace women exhausted by twelve-hour workdays and weakened by disease, beatings, and lack of food. "To maintain the prosperity of [Himmler's] business, it was considered necessary to periodically destroy the human equipment that was no longer useful—at first, a quarter or a fifth of the population each year," Germaine later wrote. As long as prisoners were fit for work, they were to be kept alive. As soon as their productivity dropped off, they were eliminated. Adding to the pressure to reduce the camp's population was the mushrooming influx of new inmates.

In early 1942, the black transports to extermination centers began. There were about ten transports that year, each delivering roughly 160 women—some sixteen hundred victims in all—to a gassing center in a sanitarium in the town of Bernberg, south of Berlin. Most of the women were sick or elderly or both, but there was also a scattering of inmates convicted of common crimes, along with prostitutes and others considered "asocial," Jehovah's Witnesses, and Jews.

Always a small minority of Ravensbrück's population, Jews there were not singled out for extermination until the Nazis officially launched the Final Solution in January 1942. By the end of that year, virtually all Ravensbrück's Jewish inmates had perished at Auschwitz. Several thousand more prisoners had died at Ravensbrück from a variety of causes—disease, lack of food, extreme punishments, and execution by shooting and injection.

Yet despite all the efforts to cull the population in 1942, more than

eighteen thousand women were in Ravensbrück when Germaine's convoy arrived there the following year. In each barracks, more than seven
hundred women were jammed into a space meant to hold three hundred,
and the already abysmal food rations were further reduced, amounting
to a bowl of watery rutabaga soup and a piece of bread a day.

Once Germaine had recovered from her bout with diphtheria and
returned to the barracks, she kept adding to her list of informants and
acquiring more intelligence about the workings of the camp, which she
surreptitiously jotted down in copious notes that she secreted in various hiding places. For her, this was familiar work. "My experience in
Algeria had already taught me how to live in an environment that was
completely foreign to me and figure out how that society was put together," she wrote.

By doing so, she was essentially resisting—searching for the truth
of that monstrous place and determined to understand and reveal it at
some point in the future. By rejecting the status of submissive victim,
she had turned the tables on the camp's system of domination, becoming an investigator, a hunter rather than the prey.

Germaine's study also allowed her to remove herself emotionally
from Ravensbrück's horror, to give her the professional distance she
needed to control her own fear and to help others do the same. "It was
a way of diminishing the power of the enemy: 'I look at you, I judge
you, I weigh you.'" For the next year and a half, she devoted herself to
uncovering the camp's secrets and sharing her knowledge of its terrible
logic with fellow prisoners.

Germaine was assiduous in building a network of informants, particularly among the Czech, German, and Polish prisoners who worked
as secretaries and other staffers in the camp's administrative offices. She
was given considerable help in this effort by Anise Girard, who, with
her fluent German and ebullient personality, won the trust and friendship of many of those well-placed sources, turning them into accomplices and collaborators. They passed on to her not only lists of arrivals,
departures, and the number of deaths and illnesses, but also news, gos-
sip, and warnings about the German staff at Ravensbrück, as well as
intelligence about the war itself. Much of the war news came from Ger-

man newspapers, including a journal for SS members, that inmate office workers smuggled out to Anise, which she in turn translated for her fellow prisoners. "We called Anise 'the Great Danielle,' " recalled one of her compatriots. "She was one of the leaders there."

EARLIER, WHILE GERMAINE WAS still in the diphtheria ward finding out about the camp's workings, Anise was informed about one of the most heinous crimes committed there—a crime that the Germans were so determined to keep secret at the end of the war that they plotted to kill everyone involved.

She was told the story one morning in November 1943 when she herself was in the infirmary, suffering from abscesses all over her body. A Polish inmate about Anise's age approached her bed. Introducing herself as Nina Iwanska, the young woman, who spoke excellent French, told her she'd come to talk to Anise on behalf of more than seventy of her compatriots, all of them members of the Polish resistance, who had been used as guinea pigs in medical experiments that ended up killing several of them and crippling the others for life.

"You are a Frenchwoman, so you're going to live," Nina said. "I'm a Pole, and I'm going to die." She explained to Anise that she and the other Poles who'd been experimented on were all under a blanket sentence of death. Then she held out a small bottle. "This medicine will help you survive. My father sent it to me through the underground. He heard about the infections in my operated legs and he thought this would help them heal. It's of no use to me if I am going to die, but I want you to have it so that you can live and tell the world our story. You must make people aware of what they did to us."

The genesis of the experiments could be traced to the assassination of Reinhard Heydrich, Heinrich Himmler's murderous deputy, who'd been head of the Gestapo and the main architect of the Final Solution. In September 1941, Hitler had appointed Heydrich as the Nazi governor of Czechoslovakia. Nine months later, his automobile was ambushed in downtown Prague by two Czech resistance fighters, one of whom hurled a small bomb at the car, sending it several feet into the air and showering shrapnel everywhere. Heydrich, whose spleen was pierced by shrapnel fragments, was rushed to a hospital, where German doctors fought to save his life.

When a bacterial infection set in, Hitler ordered Dr. Karl Gebhardt, a boyhood friend of Himmler's whose clinic treated top Nazi dignitaries, to travel to Prague and take over Heydrich's care. Once he'd arrived, Gebhardt rejected the idea of using new sulfa drugs to try to stop the infection, declaring they were ineffective. Heydrich died of sepsis a few days later, and Gebhardt came under severe criticism from other physicians in Hitler's entourage, one of whom accused him of malpractice.

Knowing he was in deep trouble with the Führer, who had raged that "losing Heydrich is the equivalent of losing twenty battalions," Gebhardt sought Himmler's advice about how to redeem himself. The SS chief suggested that his friend conduct experiments to prove that sulfa drugs were worthless in the treatment of infections. As subjects for his experiments, Himmler offered him the use of young, healthy Polish inmates from Ravensbrück.

As brutal as the Germans were in their retribution against members of the resistance in France and other Western European countries, they were even more savage in their treatment of the Poles, whom they regarded as *untermenschen* (subhuman). Hitler was determined to wipe Poland off the map and absorb its territory into Germany.

The Poles, however, had other ideas. Their nationwide resistance operation, called the Home Army, was the largest, most sophisticated, and best organized in all of Europe. When the Germans shut down Polish government institutions such as courts and the national legislature, the Poles re-created them as part of a remarkable underground society. They did the same with schools and cultural institutions, also banned by the Germans. All Poles were expected to defy the Germans in every possible way, from noncooperation to outright sabotage. Girls and women were an integral part of that effort.

Many of the Polish inmates at Ravensbrück, including nineteen-year-old Nina Iwanska, came from Lublin, a university town southeast of Warsaw that was known as a hot spot of the country's resistance. On the morning of July 22, 1942, several dozen young women from Lublin, most in their teens and early twenties, were ordered to the camp's main square for a special roll call. They were told to lift their skirts while German doctors stooped to inspect their legs. Four days later, seven of them were summoned to the infirmary, where they were ordered to undress and don hospital gowns. They were given no explanation of what was about to happen.

After being given a general anesthetic, they were taken to operating rooms. There, Gebhardt and other Nazi doctors sliced open their legs, then inserted tetanus and gangrene bacteria into the incisions, along with dirt, pieces of glass, and wood splinters, to insure an even more rapid spread of infection.

When the young women regained consciousness, they were in excruciating pain. Most developed high fevers, drifting in and out of consciousness. Pus seeped from their bandages, and when the bandages were changed, the women, screaming and crying, looked in shock at what was left of their legs, now grotesquely swollen, with incisions so deep that some could see their leg bones. They were divided into two control groups: some were given sulfa drugs, the others no drugs at all. Gebhardt did his best to ensure that his opposition to the use of sulfa would be vindicated. The women in the sulfa-treated group received little or no nursing care, while those in the untreated group received more attention.

In August, nine more young Poles, among them Nina Iwanska and her sister Krystyna, were ordered to report to the infirmary. After her surgery, Nina woke up with a raging fever and agonizing pain, both of which lasted for weeks. When the plaster cast on her right leg was removed, she saw that her calf muscle was barely still connected to her fibula, which was plainly visible. Pus was oozing from the wound, and within a few minutes, the new dressing placed on it "was soaked with odorous black and red slime."

In a later letter to Anise Girard, Nina noted, "Of all those who underwent the operation then, I was the most affected. I don't know whether my depressed morale explains this, nor can I tell whether the greatest suffering was physical or psychological. . . . Nothing seemed clear. Did God exist or did he not? Why did this happen to me? Should I kill myself or should I not?"

Unable to walk, Nina was still in the infirmary several weeks later when a new group of Polish women, six this time, were brought in for surgery. Late that night, they were all delirious, with high fevers, and in excruciating pain. No one was there to give them medical attention, not even a glass of water.

Getting out of bed to tend to them, Nina hopped on one leg as she brought them water and put cold compresses on their foreheads. Then she began tentatively putting weight on her injured leg, shuffling with one foot, then the other. By dawn, she was only slightly limping. "I suddenly felt a great calm," she told Anise. "The girls' fever had dropped. The day was breaking. Physically I was very tired, but morally I was strong. I felt only joy that I had kept my faith, that I had passed the test, that never again would I ask why did this have to happen to us, and not to others. Why to me?"

From then on, Nina wrote in a postwar report, she could walk, "but I would feel the consequences of the bacteria spreading throughout my leg long afterward. Every two weeks or so, my fellow prisoners would have to carry me to the hospital, my fever shooting up to more than 40 degrees [104 degrees Fahrenheit]. Those periods of high fever became more and more frequent."

As grievous as her injury was, Nina was more fortunate than a number of her compatriots. She underwent only one operation; several were forced to undergo multiple surgeries. With some women, Gebhardt decided to intensify the seriousness of their infections by increasing the amount of bacteria introduced into their bloodstream. Five of them, injected with what turned out to be fatal amounts of gangrene and tetanus bacilli, died in agony within days of their surgery.

Instead of halting the experiments, Gebhardt and the team of doctors assisting him broadened their scope. In addition to continuing the infection trials, the doctors broke and removed the leg bones of other women for grafting experiments, some of the bones shattered with a hammer. They removed muscles and tendons from the legs of still others to see if they would grow back. For more than a year, seventy-four women, almost all of them Polish, were subjected to this horrifying array of experiments.

Eventually, most recovered enough to leave the infirmary, but their legs had been mutilated beyond repair. Many of the incisions were never properly sewn up, and they oozed blood and pus for weeks. The huge wound of a fourteen-year-old girl, from her ankle to her knee, was held together with staples. The pain was still extreme for many of the women, and most could not walk without crutches. Some would never walk again.

Word of the atrocities had spread with lightning speed throughout the camp, and inmates responded with an outpouring of sympathy and help for the young Poles, who were called *kaminchen,* the German word for rabbits, by their fellow prisoners. Their countrywomen formed a committee to take care of them. Each rabbit was assigned a Polish "mother" to look after her needs, which involved scrounging for more food, blankets, and warm clothing.

While appreciative of the help, the rabbits refused to be confined to the role of passive victims. The first to rebel were Nina Iwanska, her sister Krystyna, and two other Lublin resisters, Krystyna Czyz and Wanda Wojtasik. In January 1943, as they struggled to recover from their maiming, the four began to discuss how to get word to the Polish resistance about what the German doctors had done to them.

Sixteen-year-old Krystyna Czyz, who was called Krysia, came up with the answer. She and the other three had all been scouts, and one of the things they'd learned from that experience was how to write in invisible ink, using lemon juice and other acidic liquids to do so. At Ravensbrück, their only communication with the outside world was one letter a month, which, after being heavily censored, was sent to their parents. Their next letters, Krysia said, should contain a message in invisible ink in the margins and between the lines.

When they discussed which liquid to use, Nina Iwanska suggested urine. Krysia seconded the idea. Her mother, who was a major in Poland's Home Army, had once told Krysia how Polish spies had used urine for secret messages during World War I. If they could tip her off that they were using it, she would know how to make the writing appear by running a hot iron over the paper.

As children, Krysia and her younger brother had been fans of a Polish author of adventure stories, whose hero often sent coded information in letters. In her next letter home, she referred to that author and how much she had enjoyed his stories. Her brother immediately understood what she was trying to say. When the four rabbits received indirect word from Krysia's mother that their message had been received, they sent more secret information, including reports of a new round of surgeries in November 1942, during which the doctors, who were identified by the girls, performed surgery on a number of rabbits whose legs had already been mutilated.

Krysia's mother passed the girls' accounts to her Home Army superior in Lublin, who sent them to the Home Army headquarters in Warsaw. It in turn forwarded them to the Polish government in exile in London, which called on the Vatican and International Red Cross in Geneva to make public protests against this savagery. Both declined to intervene.

With no one from the outside coming to their rescue, the rabbits decided they must take on the job themselves. In March 1943, word came that a new round of surgeries was in the offing; five rabbits who'd already been operated on were recalled to the infirmary. They refused to go. When another list was sent, no one responded.

On March 14, the dozens of women who'd been maimed staged an extraordinary protest march to the main office of the camp. Some were using crutches, others leaned on walking sticks. Those who couldn't walk were carried by their compatriots. "It was a breathtaking sight," recalled a camp inmate, one of hundreds who had gathered to watch.

The women stood outside the office for several hours. No one came out to talk to them, but at the same time, there was no attempt to stop the march or interfere with the gathering. When the rabbits returned to their barracks, no retribution followed for that quiet show of rebellion.

In the summer of 1943, there was one last assault on the rabbits. Several were taken, kicking and screaming, and were operated on once again. Warned of a potential explosion of anger on the part of the camp's population, officials apparently became worried about setting off a mutiny. There had been no surgeries since then.

Of the seventy-four women operated on, sixty-three were still alive and were being closely guarded by fellow Poles. But they still feared that they would not be allowed to leave the camp alive, that the Germans would execute them before the war ended to get rid of the main witnesses to their crimes.

After Anise Girard heard Nina Iwanska's story, she accepted the medicine offered by Nina, and her abscesses did in fact heal. In return, she promised that if she and Germaine Tillion survived, they would tell the world about the crimes committed against Nina and the other rabbits. Over the next several months, the two Frenchwomen collected more evidence of the surgeries, including undeveloped photos of the butchered legs of several victims, taken by a camera one of the Poles had stolen from the luggage of an incoming inmate. Germaine added the film and reports to the growing cache of information she had hidden throughout the camp.

Shortly before the war ended, Ravensbrück authorities did indeed embark on a campaign to murder Nina and the remaining rabbits. They weren't expecting the extraordinary camp uprising that followed, led by Anise and dozens of other inmates fiercely determined to save the lives of their Polish comrades.

Chapter 4

"Keeper of the Flame"

Geneviève
de Gaulle

ON A BITTERLY COLD DAY IN EARLY FEBRUARY 1944, GERMAINE
Tillion slipped out of her barracks and headed for a quarantine block
containing a just-arrived convoy of women from France. It was the
third transport of French *résistantes* since the beginning of the war and
by far the largest, totaling almost a thousand women. Germaine had
received word the day before that her mother, Émilie, was among
them.

The news of her mother's presence at Ravensbrück had been passed
along in whispers from one inmate to another as they stood motionless

during the daily early-morning roll call. When it reached Germaine, she was devastated. She had hoped that Émilie would escape being sent to the camp. Although still vigorous and lively, Émilie was sixty-nine years old, which, as Germaine knew, meant her chances for survival were slim. "I was almost paralyzed with grief when I heard she'd arrived," she recalled. "I never really recovered."

Now she was on her way to see her mother. In doing so, Germaine, as was her habit, was defying one of the camp's myriad regulations—in this case, the rule forbidding prisoners to leave their barracks without permission. "Unlike most of us, Germaine seemed totally without fear," Anise Girard said. That, however, was not true in this case: While intrepid when it came to herself, she was filled with anxiety where her mother was concerned.

Standing in front of a window outside the quarantine block, Germaine shouted to the women inside, asking if Émilie Tillion was there. Her mother pushed her way to the window, opened it, and yelled back, *"Oui!"* Then she delivered a brief report on the women's journey: *"Voyage exultant! Cologne, Düsseldorf, Elberfeld en ruine. La fin de la guerre est proche."* ("Fabulous journey! Cologne, Düsseldorf, Elberfeld in ruins. The end of the war is near.")*

Émilie's acerbic wit was clearly still intact, as was her sunny, ebullient personality. "She didn't seem to feel any sadness or fear about being there," Germaine said. "Indeed, she seemed joyful—happy to see me and happy to be with the others. Everyone loved her."

Just as Émilie tried to ease her daughter's fears, Germaine did the same when she talked to the other women in her mother's convoy. Most of them were in their thirties or younger, with a good many still in their teens and early twenties—"well-behaved little girls who had come straight from the convent," in Germaine's words. Convent-educated Geneviève de Gaulle, the twenty-two-year-old niece of General Charles de Gaulle, was one of them.

---

* By early 1944, an intensive Allied bombing campaign of Germany had wreaked great damage on many of its cities and towns.

When Geneviève and the others arrived at Ravensbrück, they had stared at the guards, dogs, and skeletal prisoners—"looking like figures in a painting from the Middle Ages"—in stunned disbelief. "We had been dropped into an unknown land," Geneviève remembered, "a universe that was not only terrifying but absurd, contrary to everything we knew."

Through the open window that frigid February morning, Germaine gave her and the others a brief description of the functioning of the camp, seemingly absurd in many ways but actually following a certain logic. "Nothing is more terrifying than a complete mystery," Germaine said later. "By explaining these mysteries, I was conscious of giving a degree of moral strength to my comrades. . . . If you can understand a mechanism that crushes you, if you can mentally dismantle its springs and consider in all its details an apparently hopeless situation, that can become a powerful source of composure, serenity, and fortitude."

She advised the newcomers that the single most important thing in their lives now was to form tight bonds with one another. Without that, none of them would survive. They must also do their best to stand up to the Germans. Still in shock from her first view of the camp, Geneviève de Gaulle was "amazed and filled with admiration" by Germaine's analysis. "The first thing she did was give us knowledge," she said. "That was a lifesaver for me. When you understand, you can fight back."

IN TRUTH, GENEVIÈVE DE GAULLE had been fighting back against the Germans for as long as her famous uncle, who, on the day after Pétain asked Hitler for an armistice, urged his compatriots via the BBC to defy the French government and rebel against the Nazis. As he was calling for resistance from his new base in London, Geneviève was on the ground in France putting his appeal into action. She initially delivered intelligence reports, money, and false identity and ration cards to Resistance contacts, then wrote for the country's largest underground newspaper. As a Resistance propagandist she played a major role in persuading her countrymen to accept de Gaulle as the sole leader of undefeated France.

Unlike her outspoken, prickly uncle, who had viewed himself as a man of destiny since childhood, the small, dark-haired Geneviève was soft-spoken and reserved, trying her best to avoid attention. Late in her life, she would be called a hero, a description she strenuously resisted. "I don't like the word 'heroism,'" she told a journalist. "And I don't think that we should seek to have a great life or grand destiny. I think we should simply seek to do what is right." A friend of hers once observed, "She would say, 'Yes, I am a de Gaulle and it opens doors for me,' but when those doors opened, she used that as a way of helping others."

In doing so, she was following a family tradition. Devoutly Catholic, the de Gaulles prided themselves on their uncompromising patriotism and respect for human rights and freedoms; the motto on the family's coat of arms—TO DIE IS TO SERVE—reflected their commitment to these goals. During World War I, Charles de Gaulle and his three brothers all took up arms against the Germans, and all were seriously wounded.

After the war, Geneviève's father, Xavier, the eldest brother, served as a military engineer in the Saar, a demilitarized region of Germany placed under French control. When Geneviève was four, her twenty-seven-year-old mother, Germaine, died in childbirth, leaving her husband with three small children. After her death, Xavier, inconsolable with grief, placed a portrait of his wife on her chair in the dining room and kept it there for years afterward.

As the eldest child, Geneviève devoted herself to easing his pain. When she was ten, he remarried without telling his children beforehand, which threw her into an emotional tailspin. "I was very unhappy about it," she acknowledged. "Suddenly this little girl who thought she was essential to her father was replaced." But instead of making a public show of her devastation, she adopted a polite, cool, smiling demeanor that served as an implicit rejection of her stepmother. According to her brother, Roger, their father's remarriage prompted the first instance of Geneviève's "quiet resistance."

Having lost her status as her father's favorite, Geneviève took solace in her close relationship with her vivacious, witty sister, Jacqueline, who was fourteen months younger. Despite their very different personalities—Geneviève was far more reticent and bookish—the two girls were inseparable, sharing a room and often dressing alike. They thought of themselves, Geneviève later said, "almost as twins." Then in October 1938, sixteen-year-old Jacqueline developed a high fever after eating salmon tainted with salmonella. She died several days later, on Geneviève's eighteenth birthday.

Geneviève was shattered. The emotional wounds from losing her mother and sister early in her life never completely healed. Yet she found the fortitude to surmount her pain and turn it into action, demonstrating what the French psychiatrist Boris Cyrulnik has called "psychological resilience." As Cyrulnik put it, "The agony is there, painful and incessant, but instead of triggering a groan, it provokes a challenge."

It was Charles de Gaulle who helped her cope. With Geneviève, he was a much different person than with most people he encountered, including Winston Churchill and Franklin Roosevelt. To them he came across as haughty, arrogant, and temperamental, acting like a king in exile rather than a lowly former official without a country. Even his own staff sometimes found it impossible to get along with him.

But with Geneviève he was tender, warm, and affectionate. She could confide in him in a way that was impossible to do with her father, whom she deeply loved but who had always put his emotional needs before hers. Charles, by contrast, gave her the support and guidance for which she hungered. She adored him, one family member said, and he cherished her, in large part because he saw a bit of himself in her. Like him, she was stubborn, strong-willed, serious, fascinated by history, and passionate in her love of her country and her antipathy toward the Nazis.

At the age of thirteen, she had read *Mein Kampf*, Adolf Hitler's outline of his political philosophy. She was appalled by its hatred and bigotry, but above all, by its explicit blueprint for German aggression against much of the rest of Europe. When she discussed it with Charles, he told her of his fear that the ill-prepared French army would never be able to stop the onslaught he saw coming.

WHEN GERMANY INVADED FRANCE in May 1940, both her uncle and her father headed back to war. Charles de Gaulle led an armored division in an unsuccessful counterattack against German troops, while Xavier, who had returned to the army as a reserve officer, was taken prisoner by the Germans and sent to a POW camp in the German city of Nuremberg.

After learning of Pétain's capitulation to the Germans, Geneviève, a student at the University of Rennes, had the same reaction as her uncle. "I felt as if I'd been burned by a hot iron," she said. "To lie down so abjectly in front of the enemy was unbearable." In early 1941, she moved to Paris to study history at the Sorbonne and try to find a way to resist.

Her accomplice in Paris was Madeleine de Gaulle, the lively, non-conformist young wife of the youngest de Gaulle brother, Pierre. Madeleine, whom one acquaintance described as behaving "like an escaped colt," had been involved with the Resistance since shortly after the armistice. When Geneviève moved in with her, Pierre, and their four children, Madeleine pressed her into service, too.

They both served as couriers for the Museum of Man network, and, on their own, they replicated and distributed photographs of Charles de Gaulle, whose BBC broadcasts had begun making waves in the country's newly formed resistance movements. Among a growing number of their members, he had become the symbol of a France that wanted to fight back, but they knew virtually nothing about him, not even what he looked like. Madeleine and Geneviève were determined to rectify that situation.

In the early spring of 1941, French police inspectors raided and searched Madeleine's apartment. While Madeleine kept the men occupied in the sitting room, Geneviève threw stacks of photos of de Gaulle into the woodstove in the kitchen. A week later, the Gestapo conducted another search of the apartment, again finding nothing. This time, they took Madeleine de Gaulle away for interrogation. Released after a few hours, she later learned that her arrest was part of the first roundup of Museum of Man leaders. Although she was suspected of belonging to the network, there was no evidence linking her to it.

For a while, Madeleine cut back on her Resistance activities, and Geneviève moved out of the apartment to avoid further compromising her aunt and uncle. In 1942, she was recruited by a new Resistance group as a courier, ferrying clandestine messages and reports across the Pyrenees to contacts in neutral Spain. After twice making the trip, she visited her father in the Haute-Savoie, a mountainous, heavily forested region in southeast France, near the Swiss and Italian borders. After being released from German custody in 1941, Xavier de Gaulle had taken refuge there with his wife, although he reported to his daughter that he was being kept under surveillance by French gendarmes.

During the two months with her father, Geneviève spent considerable time at a camp training young resistance fighters for future guerrilla activities against German forces, including ambushing convoys and derailing troop trains. The only woman among several dozen men, she helped produce false identity papers and carried out a number of intelligence and courier missions.

While at the camp, she had a fleeting romance with one of the group's leaders—twenty-two-year-old Hubert Viannay, whose affluent, conservative Catholic family lived nearby. Their relationship ended when she returned to Paris that fall, but not before Hubert introduced her to his twenty-five-year-old brother, Philippe, the co-founder of a large Paris-based resistance movement called Défense de la France. Its members were mostly students from the Sorbonne, and its primary activity was publishing an underground newspaper that bore the same name. In the months to come, Défense de la France would emerge as a major force in the French Resistance, and Geneviève de Gaulle would play a key role in its operation.

When she joined the organization, Geneviève went underground, assuming a false last name, severing ties with her family, and moving into a one-room apartment on rue Cardinet in the 17th arrondissement. The tiny space had minimal furnishings and just enough books and clothes to indicate that a student lived there.

A FORMER SEMINARIAN WHO won a Croix de Guerre as a sharpshooter in the failed 1940 fight for France, Philippe Viannay had enrolled in the Sorbonne as a philosophy student after France's capitulation. Tall and handsome, sporting an unruly shock of dark hair, he was a whirlwind of energy and ideas.

Yet he failed to impress a fellow Sorbonne student who was an acquaintance of his—Hélène Mordkovitch, whose mother, a revolutionary in czarist Russia, had been imprisoned and then exiled to Paris. Mordkovitch, who combined her studies with writing and distributing leaflets urging Parisians to defy the Germans, considered Viannay a spoiled rich dilettante. When he talked vaguely about doing something to fight the occupiers, she snapped, "You're always talking about patriotism, but what are you doing that's concrete? Why haven't you left for England?" He responded, "This is where we have to fight. It's much more difficult, but we have to stay." Then he looked her in the eye and asked, "How about starting an underground newspaper?"

Publishing a newspaper aimed at counteracting German propaganda and providing the French public with accurate information about what was happening in the war and their country was the first step taken by many embryo resistance groups. The newspapers themselves were tangible proof that the French were beginning to fight back. Producing and distributing them also involved considerable risk and ended up serving as the seedbed and training ground for more overt and dangerous kinds of rebellion.

Hélène Mordkovitch soon realized that Viannay's proposal was hardly a spur-of-the-moment notion. He had gotten the idea from Marcel Lebon, a family friend and the owner of a gas and electric company in Paris. After the armistice, Viannay had turned to Lebon for advice about how to resist the Nazis. Lebon advised him to start an underground journal, pledging financial and technical support. Changing her mind about Viannay's seriousness, Hélène Mordkovitch became a partner in the venture—and later Viannay's wife. Also joining the effort was Robert Salmon, another Sorbonne student who had won a Croix de Guerre during the fighting in France.

In the spring of 1941, with Lebon's help, Viannay and his two partners purchased a rotary press, christened it Simone, and set up the machine in an abandoned building near the Sorbonne. Rather than hiring outside printers, Viannay and Mordkovitch, for security reasons, did most of the work themselves, learning as they went along. The first issue of *Défense de la France* was published in April 1941, with a print run of three thousand copies.

Learning in July that the Gestapo was nosing around the neighborhood, Viannay and Mordkovitch moved the press to the home of one of Viannay's relatives, who a couple of weeks later developed a case of nerves about its being there. This time, it was taken to the home of Viannay's father, on the west side of Paris, until Mordkovitch got hold of a set of keys to a cellar at the Sorbonne, where it was hidden next. In all, Simone was moved seven times in its first year of operation.

On publication days, dozens of Défense de la France members gathered at whatever location the press was currently being stored. After the latest issue, usually two to four pages, was printed, they stuffed copies into their backpacks or satchels and took them away for distribution. Some were sent by mail, but the majority were handed out in public places such as churches and subway stations.

The paper's circulation skyrocketed when, shortly after its first few editions, a student group called Volunteers for Freedom, made up of several hundred teenagers from elite high schools in Paris, took on the main responsibility of distributing it. By the time Geneviève de Gaulle joined Défense de la France in 1943, the paper's circulation had grown to three hundred thousand.

Geneviève soon discovered that Viannay was, to put it mildly, not a fan of her uncle and his call for rebellion against the Vichy government. Although he rejected Vichy's collaboration with Hitler, Viannay had not lost all faith in Marshal Pétain. Like many of his countrymen, he remained convinced that the old hero of World War I was playing a double game and in the end would safeguard France's interests and join with the Allies to drive out the Germans. As for de Gaulle, Viannay was strongly opposed to his cooperation with the British and his reliance on them for help, believing that France must get out of its predicament on its own, without enlisting allies. Many in his group, including Robert Salmon and Hélène Mordkovitch, were strongly anti-Pétain and considered Viannay's views to be wrongheaded. But even though she disagreed with Viannay, Mordkovitch never dreamed of challenging him directly, nor did she consider writing anything expressing her doubts.

Until then, women members of Défense de la France had not taken part in its journalistic operations. According to Mordkovitch, it was not because of misogyny on the part of Viannay or other male members, but because she and the other women never considered pursuing such a role. She felt equal to the men, she explained, but didn't think about asserting herself: "Back then, women still had the mentality of letting men take center stage."

Decades after the war, an American author researching a book about women in the French Resistance interviewed Mordkovitch and two other key female members of the group. She asked the three to tell her about the articles they had written for the journal. "We looked at each other and burst out laughing," Mordkovitch recalled. "We told her that we didn't write anything and that it had never occurred to us. It's hard to believe now, and it proves how backward we were in terms of our education and thinking."

Geneviève de Gaulle felt differently: She was determined to do everything she could to persuade her colleagues at Défense de la France, not to mention the rest of her countrymen, to support her uncle. What better way than to publish information about him in the highest-circulation underground paper in France? "Even in the Resistance, people didn't know who de Gaulle was and what he wanted," she later said. "My comrades never really understood that he embodied France. They said 'But it's the English who are conducting the fight.' I thought at the time—and it was not out of sympathy for my good uncle—that a resistance united behind him was absolutely necessary."

As Philippe Viannay remembered it, Geneviève repeatedly pressed her case with him "with great skill and conviction." Although he initially rejected her arguments, she refused to give up, handing him copies of what she considered de Gaulle's most important speeches and other writings and insisting he read them. Albeit reluctantly, he did so.

In June 1943, she finally persuaded him to let her write a biographical article about de Gaulle for the paper—an act that made her the first and only woman to publish a piece in *Défense de la France*. Signed with the pen name Gallia, the Latin word for France and an allusion to Geneviève's last name, it ran on the front page. In the story, Geneviève recounted de Gaulle's stellar if controversial military career, which she said was marked above all by his "independence of spirit." A man of courage and honor who would never capitulate to cowardice or evil, he had escaped to London to continue the fight, she wrote. "He knows that France demands more of him than merely dying for his country. It is the hardest sort of combat that he must undertake, while carrying on his shoulders the faith of an entire people. . . . Charles de Gaulle left France, but it was so he could lead it into combat and victory."

Two weeks later, she produced another piece under the Gallia pseudonym, this one entitled "De Gaulle and French Independence." Explaining to readers the reasons for the alliance between her uncle's Free French movement and the British government, she decried as "nonsense" the claims that de Gaulle was ceding control of postwar France to Britain. "All he wants, all he ever wanted, is to ensure France's total independence," she declared. His cooperation with the British, she added, was simply a strategic tactic to achieve that end.

Geneviève's nonstop lobbying finally paid off. By the end of the summer of 1943, *Défense de la France* and Philippe Viannay had become staunch de Gaulle supporters. "It was Geneviève de Gaulle who completely converted us to Gaullism," said Jacqueline Pardon, a leading member of the group. "That change of policy provided an inflection point to the paper and organization that we did not have before."

Geneviève's cause was also helped by the fact that her uncle's Free French movement finally had acquired the clout to pressure recalcitrant underground groups to fall in line. Earlier in 1943, most of the key Resistance movements and networks in the country had joined together to acknowledge de Gaulle as their leader. In return, they began receiving considerable financial and logistical support from the Free French—aid that was actually supplied by the British. If Viannay and Défense de la France wanted to participate in such largesse, Geneviève made clear, they would have to follow suit.

Until then, Défense de la France had been financed by donations from Marcel Lebon. Now it was receiving hundreds of thousands of francs a month from the Paris staff of Jean Moulin, de Gaulle's official representative to the Resistance. Jacqueline d'Alincourt, a member of Moulin's staff and an acquaintance of Geneviève's, traveled by bicycle to Geneviève's tiny apartment to hand over the money.

Thanks to the infusion of aid from London, the group was able to buy several more presses, which led to another big jump in *Défense de la France*'s circulation and to public support for de Gaulle. The paper followed up Geneviève's initial articles with several major pieces about de Gaulle, occasionally devoting an entire issue to what its editors considered a particularly important speech. Expanding its other activities as well, the movement emerged in the war's final two years as one of the most important Resistance organizations in the country. It became the Resistance's key source for false identity papers, as well as a major player in collecting military intelligence and conducting sabotage missions against German forces.

Geneviève de Gaulle, meanwhile, took on more responsibilities within the newspaper and the movement in general. Named a member of the organization's steering committee, she also became the paper's managing editor, assigning, selecting, and editing articles for publication and overseeing its distribution. Its most valued readers were people like priests, lawyers, and doctors, who interacted with large numbers of people and were regarded as important influences on public opinion. "We had the physicians' directory, so every doctor got a copy," she recalled. "We delivered it to anyone who dealt with the public because we had to change people's minds and convince them that they could and should resist."

Groups of students were dispatched across Paris and other cities to buy small quantities of stamps and envelopes. Other teams addressed and stuffed envelopes with the current issue before fanning out to mail them from different locations. Still others circulated on city streets throughout France to hand out the paper, keeping an eye out for German soldiers and French policemen.

On July 14, 1943—Bastille Day—the leaders of Défense de la France decided to stage a dramatic demonstration of the movement's fast-growing reach and influence. Hundreds of members blanketed Paris to distribute copies of the paper's latest edition. A chief target was the city's subway system. After boarding a Métro train, members waited until just before it reached its next stop, then ran at full speed through the cars, handing out papers to every passenger, including Germans in uniform. When the trains stopped, they jumped off and melted into the exiting crowds.

Taking part in the free-for-all, Geneviève offered the paper at one point to a German soldier, who reddened with anger as he scanned the front-page headlines that included a quotation from her uncle exhorting FRANCE, UNITE WITH US. The soldier put his hand on his revolver but hesitated to take it out of his holster, knowing full well that the Frenchmen jamming the car despised him. He "couldn't kill me in front of other passengers, not in those tense times," she said later. She hurriedly left the train at the next stop.

Earlier that day, she had joined her comrades in handing out the paper at church entrances. At one church, she offered copies to parishioners going in and out while a male associate observed the scene from the other side of the street, watching for the approach of German or French police. Although a few parishioners crumpled up the paper and threw it away, many more folded it up and hid it in their pockets or read it openly, nodding to her in support.

On July 20, Geneviève left work a little early to attend evening mass at Notre Dame Cathedral. On the way, she stopped at a bookstore on the Left Bank, used as a Défense mailbox, to drop off some forged identity documents. Nobody was in the bookstore, which she found odd. After hiding her briefcase containing the documents behind a shelf in a back room, she moved quickly toward the front door. As she was about to step outside, a bespectacled man suddenly appeared. He asked what she was looking for. A Bible, she said, edging away from him.

The man said the owner would be back in a few minutes and invited her to wait. An alarm went off in Geneviève's mind: the owner, she knew, was on vacation. As she bolted toward the door, she was grabbed by the man, whose name was Pierre Bonney, and two of his confederates, who were waiting outside. A former Paris policeman who'd been fired for corruption, Bonney was the co-leader of the infamous Bonney-Lafont gang, a group of French criminals and rogue ex-cops who were paid handsomely by the Gestapo to arrest, torture, and turn over suspected members of the Resistance.

When asked for her identity papers, Geneviève produced a document identifying her as Geneviève Garnier. While Bonney examined it, one of the other men approached him with her briefcase. Inside were the false identity documents and an article for the paper she'd been working on. Brandishing the papers, Bonney barked, "Do you maintain that these documents are real?"

"Actually, no," she said. Bonney demanded, "What is your real identity?" "Geneviève de Gaulle," she answered. Years later, she said she had decided that if she was arrested, she would give her real name: "I wanted them to know there were members of the de Gaulle family who were opposing them in France, too."

Prodded by a machine gun pressing into her back, Geneviève was marched to a car outside and taken to the gang's headquarters for interrogation. When she refused to reveal any information but her real name, one of her interrogators pummeled her several times with his fist, then threw her violently to the ground and slapped her hard on her ear, which caused several days of deafness.

Geneviève had often wondered whether she'd be able to withstand physical violence if and when she was arrested. In her encounters with the Bonney-Lafont gang and later with the Gestapo, she found the answer was yes. While she was never tortured, she later said, she was subjected to a series of beatings. She found that the blows only served to increase her defiance: She would not give her persecutors the satisfaction of intimidating her.

After getting nowhere with Geneviève, Pierre Bonney turned her over to Gestapo officials on rue des Saussaies. When they, too, learned nothing from her, she was sent to Fresnes. Throughout her various interrogations, little attention was paid to her last name. Among his countrymen, Charles de Gaulle might have been increasingly regarded as the future savior of France, but he was not currently on French soil leading the Resistance and hence was of little interest to them, at least for the moment.

Through the jury-rigged prisoner communication system at Fresnes, Geneviève soon learned the circumstances behind her July arrest and those of dozens of her colleagues. As was true of most mass Resistance roundups, they were triggered by a double agent, in this case a young medical student named Serge Marongin, who helped distribute the newspaper. Marongin had learned a great deal about the journal's distribution process and the people who were involved in it. But he knew little, if anything, about the paper's editorial operations or those in charge of the movement and its other activities. The list of some one hundred names he had given to the Gestapo was largely confined to those who handed out the newspaper. Viannay, Mordkovitch, and most of the other high-level members of Défense de la France evaded arrest and rebuilt the distribution system. By the end of the war, the newspaper had a circulation of 450,000.

ONE DAY, SHORTLY AFTER Geneviève was sent to Fresnes, she was returning to her cell after taking a shower when she heard a familiar voice cry out from a cell two doors down from hers: "Where is Geneviève de Gaulle?" The voice was that of Marie-Agnès Cailliau de Gaulle, Geneviève's aunt and Charles's only sister. Before guards could stop her, Geneviève ran to her aunt's cell and reached through the bars in the window to hug her. Guards separated the two women before leading Geneviève away and chaining her to the wall as punishment.

Although virtually all of Charles de Gaulle's immediate family was involved in some way with the Resistance, the de Gaulle women were at the forefront. Marie-Agnès had been working against the Germans since 1940; two months before Geneviève's arrival at Fresnes, she'd been sent there for her own Resistance activities.

Geneviève took great solace in having her feisty aunt close by. When guards weren't around, the two engaged in brief conversations. Every morning, the women in adjoining cells would call out to one another: "Bonjour, everyone! Good day! Good luck!" Each of them would be mentioned by name: "Bonjour, Marie-Agnès!" "Bonjour, Simone!" "Bonjour, Claire!" "Bonjour, Geneviève!"

Geneviève reveled in that sense of community, but she had relatively little time to take part in it. In mid-January 1944, she and dozens of other *résistantes* were transferred from Fresnes to a transit camp near the town of Compiègne, about fifty miles north of Paris. More than nine hundred women resisters, belonging to movements and networks throughout France, were assembled at the camp, having been dispatched there from jails and prisons all over the country. Housed in rudimentary barracks rather than cells, they were free to roam around the camp and speak to whomever they wanted. "I was amazed to discover the range of diversity of my fellow prisoners: young and old, from very different backgrounds and geographic locations," Geneviève recalled. "Some belonged to intelligence units, others had hidden Allied aviators who were shot down over France, still others had given refuge to those clandestinely sent by the Free French from London to France." They ranged from doctors, teachers, artists, and lawyers to housewives, florists, civil servants, and seamstresses. Among them was the owner of the Paris bookstore where Geneviève had been arrested.

Every morning, the Germans called the roll of prisoners in the camp's main square. "As each name was shouted out, a woman stepped forward," Geneviève said. "There were very young girls and grandmothers, pregnant women, robust rural workers, and elegant city girls.

Despite the tragedy of the hour, we looked at each other with joy and pride. It was an extraordinary image of the strength of the Resistance— and also of France."

When her own name was called, the throng erupted in cheers and applause, which the German guards tried in vain to suppress. That explosion of feeling, Geneviève said, revealed the deepening influence of Charles de Gaulle in France. In addition to commanding the French Resistance, de Gaulle was now regarded by millions of ordinary French men and women as the leader of their country. His Free French forces totaled more than four hundred thousand, many of whom had fought in North Africa and Italy. He also headed the French Committee of National Liberation, an Algeria-based organization that served as the main governing body of North Africa and other liberated French colonies.

"To my comrades," Geneviève said, "I was sort of a de Gaulle in miniature."

THE WOMEN'S EXHILARATION AT being together ended abruptly on the morning of January 31, 1944, when they were taken to the nearest railway station and loaded aboard a train. It was not a regular passenger train like the one in which Germaine Tillion and Anise Girard had ridden in comfort three months earlier, but an unheated freight train comprising ten foul-smelling cattle cars. More than eighty women were jammed into each car, making it impossible to stretch out or even sit down. An oil can served as a toilet for all of them. The trip lasted three days and four nights, during which there was no food and little water.

When the train came to a halt outside Ravensbrück, it was the middle of the night. Its exhausted passengers were met with the same terrifying chaos as the thousands of women who had preceded them: the screaming guards and lunging dogs, the blows of truncheons if one stumbled or didn't move quickly enough. In a long column, the women, chilled to the bone by an icy wind, trudged down the snow-covered road to the camp. Once there, they experienced the same shock and humiliation felt by their predecessors over being stripped naked, losing everything they owned, having their heads shaved, and surrendering their names for a string of numbers.

They were still struggling to come to grips with the insanity they'd experienced when Germaine Tillion showed up to help them try to make some sense of it. Looking back decades later, Geneviève de Gaulle observed, "Germaine provided the key to understanding that demented universe. When you understand something, you can struggle against it. When you can't grasp any logic to it, you're doomed. Germaine taught us how to read our enemy."

For the younger French prisoners, the thirty-seven-year-old Germaine became what German inmates called a *lagermutter* ("camp mother"), an older, experienced leader to whom they looked for advice, encouragement, inspiration, and protection. Just as she had on the train to Ravensbrück, she tried to take their minds off the hellishness of the place by telling jokes or spinning stories of her varied travels as an anthropologist.

Geneviève de Gaulle recalled one icy predawn morning at the camp, when she, Germaine, and several other inmates were assigned to fetch cans of hot water from the camp kitchen. As they stood there, shivering in subzero temperatures, waiting for the kitchen to open, Germaine told them in intricate detail about going hummingbird hunting once during a trip to a rainforest. "Hummingbirds are very, very fragile," she told her listeners. "Of course, you don't use guns to hunt them. You just have to say, 'Hou, Hou,' and immediately they fall straight to the ground. Then you pick them up very delicately and feed them honey and flower petals." Germaine was a masterful storyteller, and as she spun these gossamer-light tales for her entranced listeners, they were taken, in the words of Geneviève, "to another world. It made all the difference."

Yet even as Germaine became a major figure in the lives of many of these newcomers, their arrival also served as a seminal event for her, Anise Girard, and the couple of thousand other Frenchwomen already at Ravensbrück. Until then, French resisters had made up only a tiny minority—less than five percent—of the camp's population. The best jobs within Ravensbrück had been claimed by Polish, German, and Czech inmates, a good number of whom regarded the French with disdain, particularly for their government's capitulation to—and collaboration with—Germany. That contempt was encouraged by camp officials, who worked hard to foment dissension among the various nationalities under their control.

The relatively few Frenchwomen in the camp had been scattered among the thirty-two barracks and had almost nothing in common, including language, with the other inhabitants. Only in a couple of barracks, including the block containing Germaine, Anise, and the other *Nacht und Nebel* prisoners, were they a notable presence. With no community to support them, the Frenchwomen were at a distinct disadvantage in the daily struggle for their physical and mental survival.

The inmates who coped best were those who, like Germaine and Anise, had formed a sort of surrogate family. They might be residents of the same town, members of the same resistance organization, or women who had met during their earlier stays in prison or on the train to Ravensbrück. Many if not most of the 956 newcomers had already formed such bonds, and with the addition of such a large group, the French *résistantes* felt a greater sense of solidarity and national consciousness.

Geneviève de Gaulle, as it turned out, would play a key role in bringing her countrywomen together. As a symbol and stand-in for her uncle, "she very quickly became the privileged comrade of all the Frenchwomen in the camp, crossing all political boundaries," Germaine remembered. Geneviève slipped from one barracks to another, covertly meeting with small groups of compatriots to talk about Charles de Gaulle and his campaign to free France. Decades later, Anise Girard still had vivid memories of the first time she saw his niece in action: "She was standing on a stool in the washroom of our block, a small, very thin figure who'd already acquired the gray complexion of an inmate. But in her presentation, she was so assured, so clear, so at ease. *Mon Dieu!* How important this woman was to all of us!"

When one Frenchwoman spotted Geneviève in her barracks, she exclaimed: "Here's Geneviève de Gaulle! Here's our little flag!" About that remark, Geneviève later said with a smile, "The little flag was more like a dirty rag. But what she said made me very happy. The fact that a de Gaulle was there gave them a bit of courage."

Jacqueline d'Alincourt, an acquaintance of Geneviève's from Paris who would arrive at Ravensbrück two months later, called her "our inspiration. She was the keeper of the flame." The close friendship that swiftly formed between the two young women would help keep both of them alive throughout the hellish months to come.

Chapter 5
....

The Seventh Circle
of Hell

Jacqueline
d'Alincourt

For the rest of their lives, Jacqueline d'Alincourt and Geneviève de Gaulle would struggle to find the right words to define the intensity and significance of their relationship. Interviewed for a documentary more than fifty years after the war, Geneviève remarked, "I don't think our friendship can be described. I always say that she's my sister." Jacqueline, for her part, thought their bond "was even stronger than blood ties." She added, "It was essential [at Ravensbrück] to have someone as close as we were to each other. It changed everything."

Twenty-one years old when they first met, they were both from well-connected, devoutly Catholic families that valued culture, intellect, and love of country. Each had suffered personal tragedies at a young age, with Geneviève losing her mother and sister, and Jacqueline her father and newlywed husband. Quiet and reserved, the two young women sometimes seemed delicate and fragile to others—a profoundly misleading impression that camouflaged their strong-as-steel inner toughness. Whatever the reasons for their bond, they became inseparable.

BORN TO ARISTOCRATIC PARENTS, Jacqueline de La Rochebrochard and her six siblings were brought up on her family's country estate in northwestern France. Her father, Henri de La Rochebrochard, was a descendant of King Louis IX, considered one of France's most distinguished monarchs and certainly its holiest: He was canonized as a saint in 1297. The family of Jacqueline's mother, Countess Nicole de Ligniville, was known for its long line of strong women, the most notable being Anne-Catherine de Ligniville, the doyenne of arguably the most influential literary and intellectual salon in eighteenth-century Paris. Among those who frequented it were Voltaire, the philosopher Denis Diderot, a young Napoleon Bonaparte, and two U.S. ministers to France, Thomas Jefferson and Benjamin Franklin. By all accounts, the witty, brilliant Anne-Catherine bedazzled her male guests, including Franklin, who, having fallen under her spell, asked her to marry him. She turned him down.

Almost two centuries later, her descendant Nicole was called on to show her mettle in a different way. When her husband died in 1931 from the aftereffect of wounds suffered in World War I, she was left with the family estate, almost no money, and seven children to raise. Taking charge with a firm hand, she closely supervised her children's intellectual development, with emphasis on literature, music, poetry, philosophy, and history. She encouraged them to be active in sports and games, and, making clear they would have to support themselves as adults, encouraged them to prepare for what she termed honorable professions. "We grew up very close to our mother," recalled Jacqueline, the eldest. "To us, she was the model of courage."

After several years of instruction by governesses, Jacqueline attended a convent school in Poitiers, a town in northwest France near her family's estate. She was preparing for a career as a preschool teacher when, at the age of eighteen, she met Joseph d'Alincourt, an artillery cadet in the French army and the scion of a prominent aristocratic family in eastern France. Smitten by the beautiful young countess, d'Alincourt proposed soon afterward; their wedding was scheduled for early September 1939.

Two weeks before the event, d'Alincourt, now an army lieutenant, suddenly appeared at Jacqueline's home. With war expected any day, he had just been ordered to report immediately to a base in eastern France. Deciding to get married at once, the couple awakened the mayor of the closest village, who married them that night in the village hall. Early the next morning, Jacqueline's parish priest celebrated a wedding mass. "We weren't expecting anyone," Jacqueline recalled. "When we entered the church, we were stunned to find it full of people from all the neighboring villages." An hour later, Joseph kissed his bride goodbye and was off to war.

Throughout the seven months of the so-called phony war, Jacqueline stayed with Joseph's parents in northeast France, and the two were able to spend a few days together during his occasional short leaves. When German troops marched into eastern France in May 1940, his antiaircraft battery was sent to the front lines, where it was swiftly overwhelmed and its members taken prisoner.

A few days later, Jacqueline traveled to the transit camp near the German border where her husband was being held. Standing in front of the camp's gates, she shouted out Joseph's name and heard "d'Alincourt! d'Alincourt!" echoed by his fellow prisoners inside. A couple of minutes later, he appeared at the gate, and, pushing past two rifle-toting German sentries, she reached out for him through the bars. They barely had time to clasp hands before the sentries separated them. The next day, her husband and his comrades were sent to a POW camp in Nuremberg, the same one where Geneviève de Gaulle's father was being held.

Jacqueline returned to her family in Poitiers to await Joseph's release, which everyone assured her would occur within months. In the meantime, she and her three younger sisters embarked on a campaign to defy the Germans occupying Poitiers. Several times a week, early in the morning, they crept into the downtown area to tear down the anti-semitic and anti-British posters plastered on walls and shop windows and doors. In their place, the girls put up homemade flyers and posters appealing to the residents of the town not to lose hope and to resist the Germans in every way possible.

At the end of March 1941, nine months after Joseph d'Alincourt and his men had disappeared inside Germany, Jacqueline received a letter informing her he had died of meningitis at the camp. At the age of twenty-one, she'd become a widow, having spent a total of less than a week with the husband she adored. Devastated by his loss, she vowed to avenge him by committing herself to the Nazis' destruction.

IN 1942, JACQUELINE D'ALINCOURT moved to Paris to teach pre-school and first grade at a convent school in the fashionable 7th arrondissement. Soon after she arrived, she saw a small Jewish boy on the Métro wearing a yellow star of David—"marked like cattle," she said. "The sight of him upset me so much that I thought I would rather die than live in a system where you could do such a thing. It was really at that moment I told myself I was ready to lose my life if necessary."

At about the same time, she met another young war widow who invited her to share a spacious apartment she was renting on nearby rue de Grenelle. There was a third tenant—Claire Chevrillon, a teacher of English literature and the daughter of André Chevrillon, a member of France's literary elite. A prominent critic and the author of more than twenty books, Chevrillon was noted as an interpreter of English literature and culture, having introduced Shelley, Ruskin, Galsworthy, and Kipling to French readers.

Having followed in her father's footsteps as an expert in English literature, Claire, unbeknownst to her roommates, was also freelancing as an agent for a Free French network. When Jacqueline indicated her interest in joining the Resistance, Claire introduced her to a jaunty, energetic young Frenchman who identified himself as Robert Gauthier, a salesman of meat-slicing machines. In fact, he was Jean Ayral, a Free French officer who had parachuted into France on a secret mission from London. He belonged to Charles de Gaulle's fledgling intelligence and sabotage service, known as the BCRA (Bureau Central de Renseignements).

Initially, de Gaulle and the Free French had paid almost no attention to Resistance efforts inside France. In his first BBC broadcast from London, de Gaulle had focused on recruiting Frenchmen outside the country—those who had escaped from France or were living in North Africa and other French possessions. "We knew that men of good will, dispersed here and there in France, were ready to engage in violent action against the Germans," André Dewavrin, de Gaulle's intelligence chief, later wrote. "But we had absolutely no idea how to get in contact with them, and as a consequence, how to organize them."

In the spring of 1942, the Free French sought to correct that situation by creating the BCRA. Its agents were charged with parachuting into France to recruit compatriots for intelligence and sabotage work and to prepare them to take part in an Allied invasion of France. Among its first operatives was nineteen-year-old Jean Ayral, a college student from Le Havre, who, two days after Pétain's capitulation to Germany, had fled to Britain to join de Gaulle's forces.

After intensive training by SOE experts, Ayral was sent back to France to set up an air operation between the two countries. His duties included overseeing parachute drops of agents, weapons, and supplies, as well as the landing of small RAF aircraft to ferry BCRA operatives, Resistance fighters, and other important individuals and matériel between France and Britain.

Soon after Ayral arrived in Paris, he recruited Claire Chevrillon to code his messages to BCRA headquarters, which then were sent by radio to London. At Claire's suggestion, he enlisted Jacqueline to work with her in what became a twenty-four-hour-a-day operation. Jacqueline was overjoyed. In effect, she said later, she and Claire, together with the radio operators, "served as the umbilical cord between the Resistance and London, transmitting messages citing its most pressing needs with respect to weapons, ammunition and money and giving the coordinates of the latest landing and parachute drop sites."

It was grueling, highly dangerous work, especially for the operators, whose transmissions were vulnerable to detection by the Germans. At the Gestapo headquarters in Paris, clerks worked around the clock to keep track of radio frequencies in the area. When they found signals they considered suspicious, they alerted agents cruising the city in unmarked vans containing sophisticated direction-finding equipment. The vans would then close in on the target.

In March 1943, the Gestapo did arrest Ayral's radio operator, but not because they detected his transmitter. He was betrayed by a double agent, who a month later did the same to Ayral himself. Taken to a nearby hotel for questioning, Ayral, after overpowering and killing a Gestapo guard, escaped and took refuge with another BCRA operative, who hid him for a couple of months. He was eventually spirited out of Paris, picked up by an RAF plane at a landing field in the countryside, and whisked back to London.

AT THE TIME OF Ayral's arrest, he had been working under the direction of Jean Moulin, who operated out of Lyon and Paris as de Gaulle's official representative to the various French Resistance movements and networks. A short, stocky, boyishly handsome former civil servant, Moulin was the top Free French official in the country. Today he is regarded as the greatest figure in France's wartime resistance.

When the war broke out, the forty-one-year-old Moulin had been serving as prefect (or governor) of the department of Eure-et-Loire, a region of northwest France. Unlike his fellow administrators, most of whom collaborated with the Germans, Moulin refused to accept Nazi rule. Just days after the occupation began, he was arrested by the Gestapo and tortured after refusing to follow their orders.

For the rest of Moulin's relatively short life, he worked to make the

French Resistance a force to be reckoned with. For much of the next year, he made clandestine trips around the country, contacting and collecting information about the various Resistance groups, most of which worked independently and had little sense of discipline or direction. He put his findings into a report and, after smuggling himself out of France, presented the report to Charles de Gaulle.

Impressed by Moulin and his work, de Gaulle sent him back to France as his liaison to the Resistance: His mission was to unite the organizations into a single entity under de Gaulle's direction. In return, they would get money and arms supplied by the British. It was an extremely difficult challenge, considering the deep divisions and rivalries, both political and personal, that bedeviled the disparate groups. Nonetheless, by the end of 1942, Moulin had succeeded in extracting pledges of support for de Gaulle from most Resistance organizations, including the Communists, who complied only when Moulin threatened to deprive them of all subsidies.

The culmination of a long and arduous fight, Moulin's triumph coincided with a pivotal moment in the growth of the Resistance. As long as Germany had seemed unbeatable, the idea of rebellion on the part of more than a few thousand French citizens had seemed quixotic in the extreme. In late 1942, that myth of invincibility finally began to crumble, thanks to Britain's first battlefield victory at El Alamein in November, followed a few days later by the Allied invasion of North Africa.

Adding to the cascade of events was the German takeover of Vichy-controlled France on November 11, 1942, just three days after the attack on North Africa. The whole of France was now under enemy domination, with the severe repression in the north spreading to the comparatively more relaxed south. The takeover also thrust Vichy's open collaboration with Germany into sharper focus. In the view of an increasing number of the French, Pétain and his officials had become nothing less than Hitler's henchmen.

But the biggest impetus for the Resistance's sudden growth spurt was the Reich's decision in 1942 to draft hundreds of thousands of young French citizens to work as forced labor in its factories and fields. The Service du Travail Obligatoire (or STO, as it was commonly called) was in effect a national draft for slave labor—imposed and administered by the French government itself.

For many, enduring the occupation was now no longer an option. Worker strikes and protests multiplied. More important, tens of thousands of men left their homes and went underground. The lightly populated, heavily wooded French countryside, along with mountainous regions in the east and south of the country, became favorite hiding places. In those out-of-the-way places, members of newly formed quasi-guerrilla groups, called *maquis,* lived off the land and began to plot sabotage and subversion. From that point, the Resistance began to count as a real force in France.

Under Moulin's auspices, a National Council of the Resistance was formed, consisting of representatives from eight Resistance groups, five political parties, and two trades unions. The council's acceptance of de Gaulle's direction gave him legitimacy with the other Allies at a time when he needed it most. Its first act was to recognize de Gaulle as chairman of a provisional government that would replace the Vichy government and prevent France from coming under an Allied military administration after its liberation.

BEFORE JEAN AYRAL WAS airlifted back to London, he met in secret with Daniel Cordier, Moulin's right-hand man and a fellow BCRA agent who had parachuted into France with Ayral the year before. The twenty-two-year-old Cordier was in command of Moulin's headquarters in Paris, which in effect was now the nerve center of France's resistance efforts. During their meeting, Ayral urged Cordier to hire the "two amazing girls" who had been his coders—Jacqueline d'Alincourt and Claire Chevrillon. Cordier agreed.

Notwithstanding his youth, the intense, hard-charging Cordier deeply impressed both women. Sixty years later, Jacqueline would describe him as "the epitome of intellectual independence, passion, and total commitment. Working with him was like being in a religious order, subjecting oneself to a very strict discipline and giving everything to the cause."

Daniel
Cordier,
1942

In his student days, Cordier, who came from a wealthy, conservative family in Bordeaux, was known for the stridency of his extreme right-wing, antisemitic opinions. But Germany's occupation of France and Vichy's collaboration with Hitler forced him to reconsider his views. Originally sent to France as a radio operator, he was chosen by Moulin as his chief of staff, and for the next eleven months was his closest collaborator.

Cordier, whose code name was Alain, hero-worshipped the charismatic man he knew only as Rex. Moulin was a committed leftist, and thanks to his influence, Cordier became one, too. In the words of the British historian Julian Jackson, Moulin served as "both Cordier's educator and a surrogate father figure." Yet he remained a man of mystery to his young admirer, who had no idea until after the liberation of France of his prewar background.

Cordier's own headquarters team was tiny, numbering only about a dozen people, most of whom, like Jacqueline, were in their twenties. "We could easily have used two or three times the number of people to carry out the work we had to do," he later wrote. "We slept little, we were everywhere at the same time, and everyone did everything."

That was certainly true of twenty-three-year-old Jacqueline d'Alincourt. Adopting the code name Violaine, after a character in a play by Paul Claudel, one of her favorite writers, she was constantly on the move. Among her multiple duties was to search for possible mailboxes—places like stores, restaurants, cafés, and offices, where intelligence reports and other messages collected from all over France could be left by couriers. Her greatest success was to persuade a friend who handled public relations for a well-known clothing designer to allow the fashion house to be used in that role. "Thanks to the many comings and goings at her workplace," Jacqueline observed, "our young couriers went unnoticed. No one was able to imagine Resistance activity in the heart of that great house frequented by, among others, German officials and their wives."

Her main task, however, was to supply lodging and other necessities of life for the fast-growing number of individuals needing temporary hiding places in Paris, from BCRA agents and high-level Free French officials parachuted in from London to Resistance group leaders and even Allied pilots evading capture by the Germans. "They couldn't go to a hotel, so I was constantly looking for places that were safe," she said. "We had to make sure they had everything—false identity documents, rationing coupons, even the right clothing and toilet articles."

From morning to night, she raced around the city, traveling by bicycle or Métro from one rendezvous to another. In a letter to her sister, Claire Chevrillon marveled at Jacqueline's "wonderful energy. She has some kind of taut inner life spring that keeps her going forever. She never seems to tire—and she looks about fifteen years old, with her beautiful, open, radiant face."

Jacqueline's seeming resilience, however, was at odds with her true feelings. "It was necessary for me to smile serenely and mask emotions that should never be shown," even to her closest friends, she wrote. In her view, iron self-control was essential at all times: "One could never give in to an impulse or share a confidence, never talk about one's pain, for fear it would trouble the other person."

Beneath that smiling façade was a turbulent swirl of feelings—

exhaustion, unrelenting tension, and above all a steadily mounting fear. Jacqueline was well aware that legions of people in the city, both German and French, were plotting the destruction of Jean Moulin's operation. By 1943, the Paris operations of the Gestapo and the *Sicherheitsdienst* (SD), the SS's counterintelligence unit, had grown exponentially. Both agencies had established multiple substations there, with armed guards, hundreds of French informers at every level of society, and fleets of black cars ready to sweep up their quarry at any hour of the day or night. "If there had been any bridle upon the terror before 1943, it was swept away now," one Resistance leader declared at the time.

As Jacqueline later put it, "Danger stalked us everywhere. Wherever we went, we knew there might be Gestapo informers, watching in the streets, the squares, the cafés, for secret meetings and taking note of the participants." Even when she was in her apartment, she couldn't entirely relax: "Every time the doorbell rang, you asked yourself whether it was a friend or enemy, and then you calmly opened the door just the same."

Yet in spite of her fatigue and fear, she took great satisfaction and pride in what she was doing; for the first time since Joseph's death, she later said, she had found true meaning in life. There were even occasional moments of joy, usually during the rare times she socialized with other members of Cordier's team, with whom she had formed close ties. She had a beautiful voice and, at these gatherings, was often called upon to sing.

According to Claire Chevrillon, who was not entirely approving, Jacqueline apparently had also found time for romance. About her, Claire cryptically noted to her sister, "There have been sentimental entanglements, as you can well imagine. She is so sweet, and the men in her life are so despotic!"

WHILE CORDIER AND HIS overworked staff risked their lives to support the new partnership between Resistance organizations and de Gaulle's Free French, many of the groups' leading figures continued the infighting, rivalries, and backbiting in which they'd engaged before the alliance. "Instead of thinking about winning the war, the leaders and many Resistance fighters are only concerned with politics," Cordier fumed in his journal. "The sole thing that interests them is preparing for their own political future after the war and protecting their independence." Throughout the spring of 1943, Cordier and Moulin spent almost as much time combating maneuvers to sabotage Moulin and the alliance as they did overseeing actual Resistance efforts.

In the end, however, they were victorious, at least for the moment. On May 27, the National Council of Resistance finally held its inaugural meeting in Paris and announced to the world that it had united behind de Gaulle and confirmed him as the leader of France.

Three weeks later, Jean Moulin was captured by the Gestapo, along with six Resistance leaders with whom he was meeting at a safe house in a Lyon suburb. For two weeks after his arrest, he was subjected to various forms of extreme torture by Klaus Barbie, the local Gestapo chief. After each torture session, Barbie, who was known as the Butcher of Lyon, ordered that the battered, unconscious Moulin be displayed to other imprisoned members of the Resistance as an object lesson. According to the Germans, he died while being transported by train to Germany.

Moulin's arrest and death hit Cordier and his team like a hammer blow. But even as they struggled with their shock and grief, they never paused in their work. Claude Serreulles, a former top aide to de Gaulle in London, took Moulin's place as head of the council, and Cordier remained as chief of staff.

The catastrophe in Lyon reinforced Jacqueline's conviction that she herself was living on borrowed time. Certain that she would be arrested soon, she was determined to visit her family before that occurred. In the late spring of 1943, she returned for a few days to her family's estate, where her mother, siblings, and maternal grandfather had all gathered: "I looked at them constantly, carving their features into my memory, reliving childhood experiences." When it was time to leave, her family walked with her across the fields to a little railway station at the estate's edge.

As she boarded the train, her twelve-year-old sister, Monique, climbed aboard for a moment, too, and, with a laugh, insisted on a second kiss. On the platform behind Monique, Jacqueline's usually controlled mother burst into tears. When the train began to move, Jacqueline took a seat and closed her eyes "with the radiant image of my little sister in my mind. I would keep that face before me regardless of what was to come. I would find solace in remembering her."

FROM THE MOMENT JACQUELINE returned to her duties, she was in nonstop motion. The number of people she had to house had turned into a flood, and she was having trouble finding enough rooms and apartments to hide them. Part of the problem lay in the requirements these boltholes had to have, such as two separate entrances, ideally located on different streets.

Previously, she had relied on friends and acquaintances to suggest such places, but those recommendations had run dry. Now, with the approval of Cordier, she began working through a real estate agency—a method that carried a great deal of risk. The agency required an authentic identification card, so she rented the apartments—more than twenty in all—in her own name.

As worrisome as it was, she was buoyed by the fact that she soon would be relieved of the grinding pressure of that task. Cordier had given her new duties, and she was getting ready to turn over her housing assignment to another operative. Just before she did so, she rented one last apartment—for a Free French colonel who had just arrived in Paris as military liaison to the National Council.

In late September, the colonel moved into the apartment, whose landlady, it turned out, was a Gestapo informant. Shortly after the new occupant arrived, she searched his belongings and found in the lining of a collar a handwritten note that left no doubt about his role and rank in the underground. In the early morning of September 24, when the Gestapo came to arrest him, he swallowed a cyanide pill and died two hours later. Although he had eluded their grasp, the Germans didn't leave empty-handed. The landlady gave them the name of the person who had rented the apartment—Countess Jacqueline d'Alincourt.

———

THE NIGHT BEFORE, JACQUELINE had not returned to her apartment until well after midnight, without a moment's rest since early that morning. September 24 promised to be an equally frenetic day, again with appointments from morning till night. She hoped to get a few hours' sleep before setting out again.

Just before dawn, she was awakened by a loud knock. Her heart racing, she put on a robe and opened the front door. Standing there was a courier sent by Cordier, who wanted her to meet him as soon as possible at the Métro station near his apartment in Montparnasse. After getting dressed, she cycled to the station, where Cordier was waiting for her.

He was concerned about the security of a radio transmitter that had been delivered to Jacqueline the day before, emphasizing she had to find a safe hiding place for it immediately. For the time being, she had put it in a tiny studio apartment she had rented on the ground floor of her building as a temporary storage place for the false IDs, ration books, clothing, and other items she needed in her job.

Assuring Cordier she would do so, she stopped at a café to call her apartment and ask Claire to move the radio to a more secure location. But the café owner was unable to get a phone line, and Jacqueline decided to go back to the apartment and do it herself. Throwing her bike down in the building's foyer, she raced up to the fourth floor, shouting "Claire! Claire!" as she entered the apartment. Hearing no answer, she ran toward her room just as four Gestapo agents appeared and surrounded her. When she tried to break away, her hands were cuffed behind her back, and their interrogation began.

When she refused to respond, they searched the room but found nothing. Dragging her downstairs, they asked the concierge if Madame la Comtesse d'Alincourt had access to any other apartments in the building. If the regular concierge, who supported Jacqueline's and Claire's Resistance activities, had been on duty, she would have said no. But she was on vacation, and her substitute, unaware of the situation, told the Germans that Jacqueline had indeed rented another apartment and led them to it.

After breaking down the door, they found the radio, as well as a host of other incriminating items, including a suitcase full of banknotes and rental receipts for other apartments. As she was hustled out, Jacqueline knew that the Gestapo would post men in both apartments to trap any of her comrades who, unaware of what had happened, might come to see her. Desperate to alert Cordier and the others to her arrest, she tried, unsuccessfully, to stage an accident by throwing herself at the driver of the black Citroën that sped her to the Gestapo headquarters on rue des Saussaies.

For five days and nights, she underwent a series of interrogations, always standing up, her arms handcuffed behind her, with nothing to eat but a couple of bread crusts a day. During occasional brief breaks, lasting an hour or so, she was thrown into a windowless cell, her arms still handcuffed behind her back, which made it difficult for her to lie down or sleep. Several teams of interrogators took turns during this twenty-four-hour-a-day marathon. Each had its own method. One repeatedly banged Jacqueline's head against the wall; another beat her with his fists; another burned her with lighted cigarettes.

When none of that worked, they told her that all her colleagues had been caught and would be tortured if she did not reveal information about the whereabouts of Serreulles, Cordier, and other Free French officials and Resistance leaders. She remained silent. They then informed her she would be shot, to which she repeated her mantra: "I will not speak." Years later, she would tell an interviewer that her worst fear was that she would break down and give the Gestapo the information they wanted. Throughout her time in prison, she kept one thought paramount in her mind: "I will not speak."

At their wit's end, her Gestapo interrogators inflicted what Jacqueline called "the cruelest punishment of all": the threat to arrest and torture her mother and send her brothers and sisters to concentration camps. One group of interrogators said her mother had already been sent to Fresnes and would stay there until Jacqueline told them what they wanted to know.

"I was always taught, in my family, that honor is worth more than life," she replied. "If I talk, I would betray that belief. If you arrest and torture my loved ones, you are monsters. But I will not give in because of that." One of her interrogators shouted, "When your mother is here, in front of you, you will talk!" She shook her head: "No, if I talked, my mother would spit on me."

On her fifth night at rue des Saussaies, Jacqueline's persecutors finally gave up. They removed her handcuffs and sent her to Fresnes. Inside the van taking her and several other prisoners there, she recognized one of her comrades from Cordier's staff, but her face was so bruised and bloodied that he had no idea who she was until she identified herself.

It took her several weeks to recover from the beatings and other physical abuse. Late one afternoon, she was lying on her straw mattress when she heard a familiar voice coming from her air duct. The voice directed her to roll up her mattress and place her chair on top. "Then climb on the chair and try to reach the air duct," it said. "We are going to send you something."

She was so weak that it took her several tries to accomplish what she called "this acrobatic exercise. I fell down over and over. Finally, I reached the height of the opening and put my arm in it." She pulled out a small package containing a sugar cube, a tissue-thin piece of paper, the stub of a pencil, and a scrawled message, identifying the sender as another of Cordier's staff members, who was imprisoned with a colleague in a cell two floors above. He wrote that the two had managed to establish communication with the outside world. "We will send you something every day at this time," the message went on. "If you want to send news to the outside, write on the tissue. You can send it to us tomorrow."

When she wrote back, Jacqueline asked to be sent a sewing thread of a certain color if her mother had been arrested and a thread of another color if she had not. She made the same request, specifying threads of various colors, to let her know the status of her siblings and of Claude Serreulles and Daniel Cordier. A few days later, she received the answers in another package. All the threads were the right color: Everyone she'd asked about was still free. In a masterpiece of understatement, Jacqueline noted, "I felt a great weight of anguish fall away."

———

ON APRIL 18, 1944, after six months in solitary confinement at Fresnes, Jacqueline d'Alincourt was deported to Ravensbrück, along with some five hundred other Frenchwomen. If anything, the conditions at their destination had become even more inhumane since Geneviève de Gaulle had arrived there in February. The number assigned to Geneviève had been 27,372, while Jacqueline's was 35,243. In just two months, eight thousand additional women had inundated the already vastly overcrowded camp.

The quarantine block to which the newcomers were sent was so jammed there was no place to lie down. "We couldn't even sit on the floor," Jacqueline remembered. In those tightly packed quarters, disease spread rapidly, and several women died before the convoy members were allowed to leave. A woman Jacqueline knew developed a toothache, which within days had become infected and evolved into blood poisoning. She received no medical treatment and died under the table set aside for the blockova's meals—the only place Jacqueline and the others caring for her could find where she could lie down.

The horror Jacqueline experienced in her first few weeks at Ravensbrück made her reunion with Geneviève de Gaulle that much more joyous. The two had first met in Poitiers in 1940 after the German occupation of France. They reconnected in Paris almost three years later, when Jacqueline, working at Moulin's headquarters, regularly delivered substantial sums of money to Geneviève for use by Défense de la France.

Along with Germaine Tillion, Anise Girard, and other French veterans of Ravensbrück, Geneviève was now in the habit of making immediate contact with French *résistantes* who had just arrived at the camp, communicating through the windows of their quarantine barracks and giving them tips on how to survive. Learning that Jacqueline was in the latest transport, Geneviève arranged for her to be assigned to her block, where for the next six months they shared the same narrow straw mattress. Conditions in the block were appalling. There were no panes in the windows, and there were only three toilets and

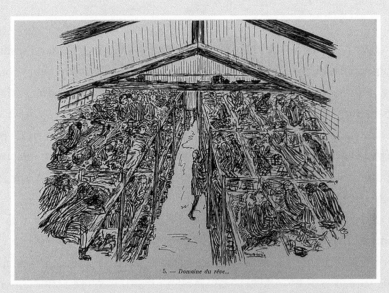

5. — *Domaine du rêve...*

"Domain of dreams": Violette Lecoq's sardonic caption for her sketch showing the appalling sleeping conditions in Ravensbrück's vastly overcrowded barracks.

two working water faucets for the more than six hundred women living there. Bedbugs, lice, and rats were rampant.

Few of the block's inhabitants had been members of their countries' resistance movements; many, if not most, were convicted criminals. Perhaps not surprisingly, the barracks was rife with violence and thievery. Inmates housed there slept with their most valued items—shoes, bowl, cup, spoon—under their mattress; if they failed to do so, these essential goods would be gone in the morning. "If someone steals from you what is most precious of all, your piece of bread for the day, you can easily feel defeated," Geneviève observed. "And if you can't get beyond that, you're doomed."

She and Jacqueline helped each other cope with that and the other brutalities, large and small, that they experienced in their daily struggle to stay alive. During the interminable predawn roll calls, which began at four o'clock, they stood side by side, frozen in rigid attention, know-

ing that the slightest move could result in the lash of a whip, a staggering slap, or the lunge of a dog. The most feared of the female guards
was their young blond chief, Dorothea Binz, who took particular delight in whipping and beating inmates until they were half dead. One
inmate recalled how Binz clubbed a woman "until she saw blood pouring out of her nose and mouth. She also used the heels of her boots to
kick women on the ground." When Binz appeared, "you literally felt a
wind of terror pass by," Germaine Tillion observed. "One felt touched
by the breath of evil."

9. — *La loi du plus fort...*

"The law of the strongest": The blond SS
guard depicted by Violette Lecoq is thought
to be Dorothea Binz.

No matter what the weather was—rain, snow, or bone-chilling
cold—the thousands of inmates were forced to stand motionless for up
to four hours during the morning roll calls, with nothing to cover them
but their skimpy prison dresses. The area around Ravensbrück, just a
few miles south of the Baltic Sea and known as "little Siberia," was buf-
feted by gale-force winds and winter temperatures that plunged to
minus ten degrees and below. "The pain of the cold was so intense that
the women who were not sick prayed that those who were—who also

had to be dragged out for roll call—would die before the nightmare began," Jacqueline d'Alincourt's biographer, François Berriot, wrote.

"It was really like Dante's seventh circle of hell," Jacqueline said. "Death was around us all the time. We learned to read its signs—we could see very well when one of our comrades had given up and could no longer live." When one friend died just before a morning roll call, Jacqueline and others had to take her body out and prop it up between them until the roll call was over.

A second roll call took place immediately after the first one ended. This muster was the daily "slave market," as Jacqueline called it, during which women who did not have a permanent job inside or outside the camp were assigned to backbreaking physical labor lasting twelve hours a day. Jacqueline's assignments included unloading coal and slabs of granite from railroad cars, putting them in wagons, and dragging them up a hill. On other days, she was harnessed to an enormous cast-iron roller, along with several other women, who, like oxen, pulled it behind them to flatten newly built roads.

Geneviève, meanwhile, was set to work draining marshes and creating roadbeds. Any sign of fatigue on her part resulted in a barrage of blows from club-wielding German guards; no prisoner was safe from their casual, incessant cruelty, which often resulted in death. At Ravensbrück, as Germaine Tillion noted, "One could be killed at any time, by anyone, in any manner." One day, a fellow worker of Geneviève's, judged by a guard to be working too slowly, was knocked to the ground. The guard took a spade and sliced open the woman's neck, killing her instantly.

Another dreaded workplace was the camp's huge sewing shop, with its long conveyor belt and lines of women sitting at sewing machines alongside it making uniforms for the SS and clothing for inmates of Ravensbrück and other concentration camps. Women who made mistakes or fell asleep at their machines during their eleven-hour shifts were routinely assaulted by the workshop foreman, an Austrian SS man named Gustav Binder. He hurled scissors at them, smashed their faces down onto their machines, battered them with a club, and kicked

An official German photograph, staged by the
SS, showing Ravensbrück inmates quietly
carrying out their duties in a camp workshop.
In reality, such work was more often than not
chaotic, brutal, and life-threatening.

them with his metal-shod jackboots. More than a few died immediately
after his assaults; others later succumbed to their injuries.

Equally horrific was another clothing workshop to which Jacqueline and Geneviève were assigned in mid-1944. The inmates there took
apart the bloodied uniforms of German soldiers killed on the eastern
front to salvage buttons and pieces of cloth for reuse. Although the
work was far less physically strenuous than Jacqueline's and Geneviève's outdoor labor, it proved to be every bit as exhausting and dangerous. "The SS overseer yelled at us, struck us mercilessly, and killed
some of the women by beating them to death," Jacqueline remembered. Geneviève, whose health had dramatically worsened after
months of abuse, was a frequent target. The corneas of her eyes were
ulcerated, impairing her vision, and oozing sores on her back and arms
often leaked onto the material she was unstitching, all of which brought
on a repeated fusillade of blows.

Jacqueline did everything she could to aid her friend, scrounging ointment to put on her sores, bathing her eyes, giving her some of her own ever-shrinking food rations, and trying to buoy her spirits by singing to her and reciting poetry. Nevertheless, she and Geneviève's other friends increasingly feared for her life.

Chapter 6
....

"The Maquis of Ravensbrück"

THE GENEROSITY SHOWN TO GENEVIÈVE DE GAULLE BY HER friends was a hallmark of many French prisoners: a commitment to sharing and community that had begun at Fresnes and other jails and flourished at Ravensbrück. "I have never experienced such strong demonstrations of solidarity and sharing as among my fellow inmates," recalled one Frenchwoman.

Anise Girard declared, "We absolutely needed to care for one another. Alone, you were finished." Years after the war, she recalled how Germaine Tillion insisted on giving her most of her own daily bread ration: " 'Take it,' she'd tell me. 'You're young, you'll survive, marry, have ten children!' She kept me going, raising my spirits."

Geneviève—who once remarked, "I experienced the worst at Ravensbrück, but I also experienced the best"—extended to others the generosity that Jacqueline and her compatriots had shown to her. When on occasion she acquired a special treat, like a lemon or a piece of sugar, she would divide it into tiny pieces to share with her friends. Women assigned to various outdoor work details did the same, smuggling pieces of wood and charcoal to provide heat for themselves and others in their barracks, pilfering potatoes and other vegetables to share with their bunkmates, bringing back a flower as a birthday present for a friend.

16. — *Amitié...*

"Friendship"

Jacqueline, for her part, spent part of her shifts at the uniform work-shop making mittens for her comrades. Keeping an eye out for the murderous SS overseer, she surreptitiously cut fabric and leather from the uniform jackets and sewed at least one pair of mittens a night. "I would slip them to my friends, who would have warm hands during the next roll call," she said. "It was my way of taunting our captors, to prove that we were not defeated."

Women assigned to other clothing workshops fashioned slippers, hoods, and even coats. Émilie Tillion, who worked as a knitter, surrep-titiously made extra pairs of stockings for her companions. A woman of "radiant spiritual beauty," in the words of a compatriot, Émilie was sought out by younger inmates for comfort and guidance in dealing with the horrors of Ravensbrück. "Madame Tillion radiated tender-ness and joy," one of them recalled. "She had a marvelous sense of peace, light, and warmth of heart." Even the daily savagery of the camp failed to extinguish Émilie's spirit of optimism: In a letter to a young friend of hers at the camp, she wrote that Ravensbrück, for all its bestiality, had widened their horizons, which would provide "all sorts of ideas and unsuspected possibilities" in their lives once they were free.

The Frenchwomen's sense of community also prompted the development of an astonishing array of unofficial cultural activities they offered to one another. Although camp rules strictly forbade meetings and other gatherings of inmates, Ravensbrück's exploding prison population meant that strict surveillance at all times was no longer possible. As a result, Frenchwomen who were experts in various fields began delivering a series of impromptu lectures and performances in their barracks.

Years later, Lidia Beccaria Rolfi, a young member of the Italian resistance, recalled with awe the wide variety of events staged by the French in her block: "lessons in history, literature, geography; travelogues; even lectures on how to raise rabbits and tame lions." In their respective barracks, Émilie Tillion discussed various aspects of French art and archaeology, her daughter delivered discourses on the history of mankind, and Geneviève de Gaulle talked about her uncle.

Singing was also forbidden, but the Frenchwomen engaged in that, too. "Often, it was only a single murmur, sometimes a three-person choir," said Jacqueline, who was a ringleader in that effort. "We sang old songs from the seventeenth century, folk songs, current popular songs, even prayers." When the siren shrieked at 3:30 A.M. to rouse inmates for the morning roll call, Jacqueline serenaded Geneviève and others sleeping around them with a silvery rendition of a Renaissance song: "Awake, O Sleeping Hearts, the Lord Is Calling You."

For the Frenchwomen, reciting poetry was yet another favorite way to raise their spirits. As they stood at attention during the early-morning roll calls, one group of women whiled away the time by reconstructing the poetry of Paul-Marie Verlaine, each woman whispering a favorite stanza of one of his poems.

Jacqueline, a poetry maven since early childhood, took the sharing of poems one step further. She transcribed her favorites by such poets as Verlaine, Paul Claudel, and Charles Péguy, and asked friends to contribute the poems they loved most. The paper, ink, and pen she used for this venture had been stolen for her by a young Austrian friend who worked in the camp's offices. Jacqueline then bound the pages, covered with minuscule writing, into a series of tiny volumes, christening her publishing effort the Éditions de la Croix de Lorraine.* The books were circulated among other French inmates, several of whom contributed their own offerings to the new publishing venture, including collections of word games, popular sayings, and recipes. As Jacqueline noted after the war, "These books were our escape from the ghastly reality of Ravensbrück, our oasis in the desert."

WHILE THE FRENCHWOMEN regarded these endeavors as one way of standing up to the Germans, many of them were also involved in far more direct and dangerous acts of resistance against their captors. A former Polish prisoner remembered how appalled she and other Poles had been at the way the French thumbed their noses at their jailers: "Coming from a nation that had not known captivity, they often— very audaciously though unwisely—opposed the authorities' orders." At the same time, she acknowledged that their defiance had been carried out "with a great deal of bravura."

For many of the French, rebellion took the form of doing everything possible to avoid working in munitions factories, military supply workshops, or any other setting that contributed to the German war effort. Having succeeded twice in eluding an assignment to the Siemens factory attached to Ravensbrück, Jacqueline was informed that another group would soon be sent and that she was on the list. She began researching possible diseases that would disqualify her from such work, one of which was scabies, a skin rash caused by mites burrowing into the skin. To give herself the appearance of scabies, she scratched her arms and legs with a needle, then rubbed the scratches with dirt to infect them. Her faux scabies turned out to be "entirely believable," she said, and once again she was rejected.

---

* The Cross of Lorraine, a two-barred cross, was adopted by Charles de Gaulle as the symbol of his Free French movement.

Stealing supplies during work details, from coal to lumber to food, was another form of defiance, albeit a highly risky one. At the end of the day, each worker was searched, and if any items were found in their possession, the punishment was often extreme. But French prisoners became highly adept at secreting stolen goods in the folds of their over-sized prison uniforms. "Once again, we rolled them!" one French-woman exulted at the end of a particularly productive work detail involving the delivery of charcoal briquettes to the living quarters of SS guards. "When we got back to the block, we pulled from under our dresses eight briquettes." For that night, at least, there would be warmth from the stove that heated her and her fellow workers' section of the barracks.

On at least one occasion, the payoff from an inmate's thievery turned out to be life-saving. Dr. Paulette Don Zimmet, a pediatrician from the Haute Savoie, was the leader of a work detail that unloaded railway cars filled with clothing, jewelry, and other treasures that the Germans had looted from Poland and other occupied countries. In one shipment, she discovered a large case of medicines taken from a Polish hospital. With the help of other inmates, she hid them in stoneware pots, which she then buried in nearby sand dunes. Each evening for the next week or two, she and her comrades smuggled the drugs back to the camp in small amounts. They were secreted in hiding places throughout their barracks, and Don Zimmet used them over the next several months to save the lives of sick and dying fellow prisoners.

Although Paulette Don Zimmet remained with this work detail for much of the time she was at the camp, it was not considered a perma-nent assignment. Like Jacqueline, Geneviève, and many of the other Frenchwomen at Ravensbrück, she was classified as *Verfügbar* ("avail-able"), in spite of being a physician. The term denoted unskilled labor-ers, whose assignments usually involved the backbreaking physical work of maintaining the camp.

According to Germaine Tillion, *Verfügbaren* were regarded as "gal-ley slaves," occupying the lowest rung on Ravensbrück's hierarchical ladder. Most prisoners at the camp, one historian noted, "would do nearly anything to get out of this category and into a regular job." But many of the Frenchwomen actively sought the classification, taking pride in their refusal to perform any work for the Germans' benefit. Within that cluster of rebels was an even more radical group, whose members did their utmost to avoid any work at all. Germaine Tillion was in its vanguard.

WHEN GERMAINE FIRST ARRIVED at Ravensbrück, she was physically unable to work for several months because her bout of diphtheria had left her with a partially paralyzed leg. But even after she recovered, she was adamantly opposed to serving the Reich in any way. For her, the camp was like her country: In both places, the Germans depended on collaboration by those they controlled. Having resisted such obeisance in France, she did the same at Ravensbrück.

Thanks in part to her many inmate friends and sources within the camp's administrative network, Germaine managed to evade work assignments for eighteen of the twenty months she spent at Ravensbrück. "The status of *Verfügbar,* which was my constant goal, required a repertoire of ruses, subterfuges, and conspiracies large enough to power an Oriental kingdom," she wrote. She was in hiding most days, using that time to continue her investigation of the camp, which included keeping a record of the names of all SS administrators, doctors, guards, and other staff members that she coded and disguised as recipes.

Another radical—Yvette Gouineau, a former high school teacher from Versailles—called herself and the other French *Verfügbaren* "the maquis of Ravensbrück." Gouineau, who used the code name Bleuette, argued that standing up to the Germans in the camp was as vital as fighting them on the battlefield. "We had to resist their efforts to debase us," she said. "It was a matter of simple human dignity."

As the camp grew more crowded and chaotic, an increasing number of Frenchwomen joined Germaine and Yvette in defying their captors' orders to work. "It was," said one of the evaders, "a life full of adventure. . . . The game consisted of inventing a thousand ingenious and very risky strategies for this purpose. We French were particularly good at it." Another referred to herself and her French compatriots as

"the queens of irregularity, of indiscipline, of sabotage by omission."
Still another noted that she and other members of the French sisterhood had a "very Gallic taste for chaos, obsessed as we were with freedom and equality. We were not the lifeless downtrodden."

At the same time, they were well aware of the extreme risks they
were taking, with potentially deadly consequences. If they were found
out, the penalties included severe beatings and the withholding of
food, either of which might well result in death. They also risked being
selected for immediate extermination, as part of the increasingly
frequent black transports from Ravensbrück to Auschwitz and other
death camps.

To avoid being caught, the *Verfügbaren* depended on the complicity
of other prisoners. According to Germaine, she and her fellow evaders
never had to worry that their compatriots would inform on them.
While prisoners from other countries might do so, she said, no French
inmates, not even those sent to Ravensbrück for criminal offenses, ever
turned them in.

That fierce sense of loyalty to one another prompted a young French
inmate, who was known as Denise Jacquier, to reveal to a few of her
comrades the fact that she was Jewish. She did so because she feared
that if she died at Ravensbrück, there would be no trace of her, since
she was registered under a false name. Approaching Anise Girard one
day, she said, "You know, my name is not Jacquier. It's Jacob . . ."

For a moment, Anise couldn't speak. She was terrified by Denise's
admission, she later acknowledged, because if camp officials ever discovered she was Jewish, she would be on the next black transport to
Auschwitz. But Denise's trust in Anise and the rest of her countrywomen was well placed: They kept her secret until the end.

....

Chapter 7

"To Laugh Is to Resist"

THE UNOFFICIAL HEADQUARTERS FOR FRENCH RESISTANCE AT
Ravensbrück could be found tucked away at the back of the camp, in a
barracks whose inmates were all slated to be executed. Yet even though
its occupants' future seemed impossibly bleak, Block 32 was a haven of
stability, camaraderie, and even high spirits in the midst of Ravensbrück's hellishness.

The dozens of Frenchwomen confined there were *Nacht und Nebel*
political prisoners, who, under Hitler's orders, were to be put to death in
secret, with no record of what happened to them. N/N prisoners were
not allowed out of the camp and therefore could not be sent to munitions factories; by definition, almost all of them were *Verfügbaren*—
and intensely proud of it.

The women of Block 32, who included Germaine Tillion and Anise
Girard, prided themselves on their steadfast support of one another
and their defiance of the efforts of camp officials to crush them. According to Germaine, it was the only block at Ravensbrück where theft
was a rarity, where the sick and weak were routinely given extra por-
tions of food, where residents worked hard at keeping it clean and
vermin-free, and where anyone in trouble with the camp administration could find accomplices to help her.

"We all helped one another, paying special attention to the oldest and youngest among us," Germaine said. "On national and religious holidays we held little parties. We had banished from our minds all thoughts of our forthcoming execution."

Every night, after the blast of a siren demanding silence throughout the camp, a voice in the French section of the block loudly announced, "Listen, ladies! Here is today's news communiqué." At that point, Anise Girard relayed war news she had picked up from German newspapers purloined and given to her by inmates working in the camp's offices. Before going to sleep, the Frenchwomen engaged in another nightly ritual—a call-and-response that originated at Fresnes prison. One of them would shout "France . . ." and the others would shout back ". . . will live!"

The Frenchwomen of Block 32 were known, too, for their robust, often caustic sense of humor, a trait they shared with many of their compatriots at Ravensbrück. A Danish resister said the French joked about everything, adding, "They were like a breath of free France." But there were more than a few non-French inmates who strenuously objected to their habit of making fun of the daily horrors they faced, including death. That was especially true of Polish prisoners, who, in the words of Geneviève de Gaulle, "had a tendency to talk about things in a tragic way."

Once, when several French inmates were given small pieces of soap, they were told by Polish prisoners that the soap had been made from the fat of bodies burned in the camp's crematorium.* The next day, as one of the Frenchwomen was using her bit of soap in the washroom, she said jokingly to her comrades, "And with whom are we washing today?" To the horror of the Poles, "that made us laugh a lot," Geneviève remembered almost fifty years later. "And when I tell this story to people who were not at Ravensbrück, they find it horrible. And it *is* horrible. But it was our way of coping with death."

No one was more addicted to jokes than Germaine Tillion, who

---

* During the war, the allegation that the Nazis manufactured soap from the fat of their victims was widely believed, but according to Holocaust scholars, there is no evidence that they actually did so.

had, in the words of the historian Julien Blanc, "an extraordinary propensity to laugh at everything, including herself." Emulating her mother, Émilie, who was also noted for her keen sense of humor, Germaine, even before the war, "took pleasure in composing little witty texts that were often inspired by everyday reality, distorting the facts and pointing out the ridiculousness of a situation," Blanc observed.

Earlier, as a young anthropologist, Germaine had learned the importance of humor in the structuring of human societies, particularly as a tool of subversion in resisting oppression. Jokes, slogans, anecdotes, caricatures, graffiti, and humorous songs and drawings aimed at ridiculing oppressive regimes had long been popular weapons of political protest. At Ravensbrück, she was "one of a small group who knew how to ridicule with a quip the monsters who persecuted us," one French prisoner said. "Made grotesque, they became less formidable, and by laughing, we recovered a little freedom." In the words of another Frenchwoman, "We laughed to prove to ourselves that we were still alive, that we were still able to react. To laugh is to resist."

BY MIDSUMMER 1944, HOWEVER, there was no longer much laughter at Ravensbrück. Its inmates' hopes of leaving the camp alive, which had surged with the news of the Allied invasion of France in June, had dwindled since then. For more than a month, Allied forces had been bogged down in Normandy's hedgerow country, with no sign they would break out soon. Liberation was still a far-distant dream, and many prisoners feared that for them, it would never become a reality.

The camp was filled to overflowing, and disease was everywhere. Several of the blocks had been turned into sick bays, and the hundreds of prisoners confined to them were weakening by the day. Despair had taken firm hold, and there seemed to be no way to ease its grip. All this was extremely worrisome to Germaine, who told Anise Girard that "we must find a way to laugh at our lamentable state. It is our only lifeline."

What could be done to change the situation? She thought about that question during one of her rare work stints—as part of a labor detail, composed entirely of N/N prisoners from Block 32, that unloaded and sorted goods pillaged by the Germans from occupied Europe. Overseen by Dr. Paulette Don Zimmet, the detail was made up mostly of Frenchwomen, along with a few Dutch and Belgian women. "Our work was sometimes very hard, we were occasionally beaten, and every evening, we were searched by the SS, but we trusted and took care of each other," Don Zimmet later wrote. "We turned our work column into an oasis of safety and fraternity."

As she retrieved clothing and other goods from railway cars, Germaine finally came up with a solution. She would try to do the impossible—write a musical operetta/revue, filled with wit and fun, about the miserable life of a *Verfügbar*. Its aim was not escapist; it would not deny the awful reality she and the other women faced, but rather poke fun at it. "I felt," she later said, "that high spirits and humor were a more invigorating intellectual climate than moaning. We wanted to laugh and joke, and we believed that we had the right to do so." Anise remembered Germaine telling her at the time, "Let's not pity ourselves! Let's write! Let's sing!"

For ten days, with the blessing of Don Zimmet and her other co-workers, Germaine hid in a large wooden packing crate in a warehouse next to the railway line while she worked on her creation, which she entitled "Le Verfügbar aux Enfers" ("The Verfügbar in Hell"). One of her Czech friends, who worked as a secretary in the camp's office, supplied her with paper and a pen.

The revue consisted of a series of satirical sketches interspersed with songs and dances. Germaine wrote the dialogue for the sketches and lyrics for the songs, which were a pastiche of music from a mind-boggling array of genres, from operas and operettas to cabaret and folk songs to military marches and catchy jingles from radio commercials of the 1930s. The varied repertoire of "Le Verfügbar aux Enfers" was made up of tunes Germaine obviously knew well, but they also were familiar to many if not most of her compatriots at Ravensbrück.

By all accounts, her familiarity with and knowledge of music were extraordinary. Both her parents came from musically inclined families. Lucien Tillion had inherited a collection of priceless antique violins and violas that had been in his family for more than a century. "I fell asleep every night to the sound of music," Germaine said. "My father was particularly passionate about it, from Beethoven to comic songs. He thought nothing of taking the train to Paris for a night to attend a performance or concert."

Spurred on by her parents, she frequented concert and opera halls from an early age—Wagner, Debussy, and Prokofiev were some of her favorite composers—but she also was fond of performances at cabarets and music halls. The French composer Christophe Maudot, who sixty years later would help stage in Paris the first production of *Le Verfügbar aux Enfers,* marveled at what he called Germaine's "deep awareness of the musical canon," which he considered striking, even for an educated woman whose parents had been amateur musicians.

GERMAINE'S OPERETTA/REVUE BEGINS WITH a solitary figure onstage, a character called the Naturalist, who launches into a lecture about a strange new species of animal life that he has just discovered. He has named it *Verfügbar.*

An enigmatic figure, somewhat like the master of ceremonies in the musical *Cabaret,* the Naturalist presides over the show, explaining to the audience the genesis, development, and present life of this bizarre creature he has come across. In passing on his observations, he makes clear he does not understand, nor does he particularly want to understand, the *Verfügbar*'s behavior.

As the Naturalist continues, a female Greek chorus made up of the creatures he's describing drifts onto the stage and gathers around him. Creeping closer, its members begin to interrupt him, calling into question his description of them and explaining to him the reality of their existence. When, for example, he mentions his befuddlement over why *Verfügbaren* assigned to outdoor work details are quiet most of the time but immediately start talking when noisy food carts pass by, they tell him it's the only time they can't be heard by their SS overseers.

As the *Verfügbaren* increasingly interrupt him, the Naturalist tries to quiet their outbursts and retake control. He fails miserably. By the end of the second act, he's been relegated to the background while the chorus is now at center stage, with its veteran members—"the old rats"—instructing the newer arrivals in the realities of camp life, passing on the various tricks of survival they've learned.

The first two acts of *Le Verfügbar aux Enfers* are filled with the irony and black humor so characteristic of Germaine and the other French prisoners. In one sketch, a young woman about to be deported sings about how she's being sent to a rest camp, "a model camp with all the comforts—water, gas, electricity . . ." She's interrupted by other members of the chorus, who point out, "especially gas."

In another, the *Verfügbaren* talk about the pitiful state of their bodies: their skeletal thinness, the sores and pustules covering their bodies, their swollen legs and flat feet. Then one of them adds, "There is another slump that we cannot, alas, completely pass over in silence." While the rest of the chorus hums a funeral march, she continues, "It's our breasts, which are no longer saints but fallen martyrs."

Yet while the revue is filled with this kind of deadpan humor, there are also a number of sketches and songs expressing lighthearted but poignant longing for what the women left behind in France. High on the list of those treasured memories is food.

Barely kept alive on an ever-shrinking diet of black bread speckled with sawdust and mold and a thin yellowish rutabaga soup, French inmates were obsessed by food. They talked about it incessantly, discussing favorite dishes, exchanging recipes, and recalling memorable dinner parties, with the main focus on the menus. One French inmate had a recurring dream of "a large piece of pink bacon, translucent, steaming, quivering on a dish of pink beans." The dish was so real in her dream, she said, she even managed to smell it.

Every morning, during the march to their work detail, Paulette Don Zimmet and her comrades would discuss the menu they would serve their husbands that night if they were home. "There was always a profusion of exotic meats, reminiscent of a menu from the court of the Sun King," Don Zimmet said. "I remember providing several recipes for pâtés and wild game. I also remember a certain recipe for a Grand Marnier soufflé which I thought very impressive."

Another song in Germaine's revue is *"Nous avons fait un beau voyage"* ("We've had a wonderful trip"), in which two *Verfügbaren* wax rhapsodic about their fantasy gastronomic pilgrimage throughout France to sample the specialties of each region:

> *Nous avons fait un beau voyage!* We've had a wonderful trip!
> *Nous arrêtant à tous les pas,* Stopping every step of the way,
> *Buvant du cidre à chaqu'village,* Drinking cider in every
>   village,
> *Cueillant dans les clos des lilas.* Picking lilacs in the
>   vineyards.
>
> *Nous avons dégusté* We've eaten
> *Du beurre et du pâté,* Butter and pâté,
> *D'la crème en Normandie* Cream in Normandy
> *Et du fromage en Brie.* And cheese in Brie.
> *À Riec, savourons* In Riec, let's savor
> *Coquilles et belons.* Scallops and oysters.
>
> *À Vire, de l'andouille,* In Vire, pork sausage,
> *À Nice, la ratatouille,* In Nice, ratatouille,
> *À Aix, le calisson,* In Aix, an almond fruit candy,
> *À Lyon, le saucisson.* In Lyon, hard spiced sausage.
> *Madeleines à Commercy.* Madeleines in Commercy.
> *Bergamotes à Nancy . . .* Bergamot oranges in Nancy . . .

By reminding her compatriots of the delights and comforts of their homeland, Tillion's aim was to bolster their spirits and keep alive their hope of returning to that world. In another scene, the Naturalist tells his audience that the *Verfügbaren* have only three techniques for survival: their quick movements, cunning, and ability to infiltrate other groups. Oh, no, says the chorus, they have another. Breaking into song, one of its members explains that she keeps in her heart a star of hope that shines every night and gives her the strength to bear all the miseries to which she's been subjected. When the Naturalist sneers that a being as wretched as she cannot possibly be hopeful about anything, she replies tartly that it's none of his business what she hopes for.

"The beauty of *Le Verfügbar aux Enfers* is that it allows us both to acknowledge the evil of [the camp], yet also marvel at how its victims could endure, challenge, and sometimes overcome it, with grace, humor and determination," the American historian Christine Holden observed. Above all, she added, the revue highlights "the power of the human spirit to rise above the horrific situations that confronted them."

As she was writing the show, Tillion reached out to her French companions, asking them to collaborate with her. Every evening, after they'd returned from their work detail, they would wait impatiently for her to read them the scenes she'd come up with that day, acting out the dialogue and humming and singing the musical interludes. She then would invite them to contribute dialogue and lyrics of their own or even suggest new scenes. More often than not, she would incorporate their suggestions.

Over those ten days, Tillion and her comrades lost themselves in the laughter and fun of the venture, allowing them to forget for a moment the bestiality of their everyday life. They particularly enjoyed singing the songs they'd come up with on their way to and from their labor detail. Singing while heading to work was de rigueur for prisoners in German concentration camps, but the tunes generally were traditional German songs. The Frenchwomen sang traditional tunes, too, but the lyrics were scathing anti-German screeds. "We marched in step singing verses in which we ridiculed our German guards," Tillion said. "They were delighted with them, but, of course, none of them understood a word of what we were saying." It was basically a collective joke—another way of triumphing over them, of making fun of the monster.

Tillion and her friends never staged an actual performance of *Le Verfügbar aux Enfers* at Ravensbrück; that would have been far too dangerous. But they did make several copies of the text and circulated them clandestinely among other French inmates in the camp, creating a minor sensation.

Twenty-year-old Béatrix Gontaut-Biron, a scion of one of France's oldest aristocratic families, recalled being approached one day by Paulette Don Zimmet, who asked her if she knew a fellow prisoner named Kouri. When Béatrix replied no, Don Zimmet passed her a copy of the revue, warning her "not to mess up and get caught with it." Béatrix was transfixed by what she read. "It summed up our lives perfectly," she said. "It was a masterpiece."

Chapter 8

"We Won't Make Your Bombs!"

On AUGUST 15, 1944, MORE THAN TWO THOUSAND MEMBERS OF the French Resistance—some fifteen hundred men and nearly six hundred women—were rousted from their cells in prisons and camps around Paris and herded aboard a flotilla of requisitioned city buses. Where were they headed? With Paris on the verge of liberation, it was difficult to believe that the Germans were actually going to waste their remaining resources on a last-minute deportation of their remaining French captives.

After breaking out of Normandy just days before, Allied troops were now only forty miles from the French capital; the noise of their advancing artillery was getting louder by the day. Meanwhile, French railway workers had walked off the job, and most of the capital's train stations had been badly damaged or destroyed. The French railway system was nearing a complete breakdown. Did the Germans really think they could get their last prisoners across the border?

Not even the German commandant of Fort Romainville believed they could—or would—succeed. Earlier that day, he'd told Virginia d'Albert-Lake, an American woman who'd worked for a Belgian-French escape network, that she was much more likely to be freed by her countrymen than deported to Germany. And yet here she was, crossing the Place de la Concorde in a vastly overcrowded, stiflingly hot bus, part of a long convoy on its way to God knows where. From a bus window, she observed German troops streaming out of the city, accompanied by trucks and cars jammed with clothing, food, wine, and other looted goods.

As it turned out, Hitler had indeed ordered the deportation of all imprisoned French resisters, no matter how difficult or time-consuming the effort might be. Once again, the Führer's rage at the effrontery of the French who had defied him took precedence over everything else. They would be sent to work in German weapons factories as part of a last-ditch campaign by Berlin to try to ward off defeat.

The buses finally pulled up at the Gare de Pantin in the far northeastern suburbs of Paris, one of the few remaining railway stations still in operation. After lining up on the station's *quai aux bestiaux* (animal platform), the resisters were given water by Red Cross workers, who assured them, "You'll never make it to Germany. It's impossible. You'll be liberated before then."

The men were loaded onto the waiting cattle cars first, then the women—seventy to eighty in each car. There was no room to sit, let alone lie down. During one of the hottest August days on record in Paris, the padlocked, unventilated cars remained at the station for over five hours, with no more water made available for its occupants, much less air.

Still, with every passing minute, hope grew that, because of the railway strike, no one would be found to operate the train. Minutes before midnight, however, German railway workers arrived, and the train pulled out of the station. Just prior to its departure, the bodies of six women who had succumbed to the heat and asphyxia were removed and dumped alongside the tracks.

AMONG THE WOMEN ON board was one of France's most important wartime spies. An interpreter for a syndicate of French businessmen in Paris, twenty-four-year-old Jeannie Rousseau was a member of Alliance, the largest and most influential Allied intelligence network in France. Begun in Vichy in the fall of 1940, it numbered about three thousand agents and was run by Marie-Madeleine Fourcade, the only woman to head a major French Resistance organization during the war.

Rousseau had used her pert good looks and disarmingly guileless manner to ferret out top-secret information about Germany's V-1 and V-2 terror weapons. The material she passed on to the Allies, she was told later, was one of the greatest intelligence coups of the war. Indeed, Rousseau had become so important to the Allied scientific intelligence effort that British officials decided to bring her to London for an extensive debriefing. She was to be picked up by a Royal Navy boat off the coast of Brittany, but the operation went awry and she was captured in April 1944.

Jeannie
Rousseau

At her side in the stifling cattle car was Countess Germaine de Renty, who, along with her husband, Robert, had been arrested in July. Fixtures of Paris society, the forty-nine-year-old count was a well-to-do businessman, the owner of an agrochemical company, while his forty-four-year-old wife was as well known for her charity work in Paris's poorest neighborhoods as for her grace and elegance. But, like Jeannie Rousseau, the de Rentys had led another wartime life: They, too, were members of Fourcade's network.

Although Jeannie and Germaine had never met before, they became extraordinarily close over the next six days—a deep friendship that lasted for the rest of their lives. In the last year of the war, "Germaine meant everything to me," Jeannie wrote more than fifty years later.

Also aboard the train were twenty-year-old Jacqueline Marié, the daughter of a career French army officer, and her mother, Marceline. The Marié family had been fiercely anti-German even before the war began; within a few months of the occupation, Jacqueline, who was still in high school, had joined the Resistance, together with her mother, father, and elder brother. She had worked initially for the Défense de la France movement, then joined her brother in gathering military intelligence for a Free French spy network. On February 3, 1944, Jacqueline and her parents were arrested by the Gestapo. After enduring several days of torture, she and her mother were sent to Fresnes, where they remained until they were transported to the train.

While Resistance members in most previous convoys to Germany endured appalling treatment, the conditions were particularly atrocious for this last transport. The train made excruciatingly slow progress, taking almost two days to cover sixty miles. Its frequent stops and detours were due to saboteurs' destruction of long stretches of track, as well as the train's having to give way to German troop transports also heading east.

On the morning of the second day, the train suddenly stopped in the middle of a tunnel. It was pitch black, and the heat was overwhelming. Smoke began seeping into the sealed cars, and their panicked occupants struggled to breathe. Shouts and screams ripped the air. Three and a half hours later, the train backed out, and its doors were opened. A bridge just beyond the tunnel had been destroyed, and the prisoners were ordered to get out and march five miles in the searing heat to another station and another train. Anyone who tried to escape would be shot, they were told, along with ten hostages from each car.

"Dante could not have imagined a worse scene," Jacqueline Marié later observed. "In a matter of days we'd been turned into wandering zombies. When we left Paris, we were still female prisoners. Now we were animals going to the slaughterhouse."

As they trudged down country roads, some captives still had faith that fellow resisters would appear in time to save them. Among the hopefuls was Virginia d'Albert-Lake, one of two Americans in the convoy. A teacher from Florida, Virginia had met and married Philippe d'Albert, a French businessman, shortly before the war. The two became agents in the Comet escape line, providing shelter in their Paris apartment and their country house in Brittany for more than sixty American and British airmen shot down over France and Belgium. Virginia, who was thirty-eight, was arrested June 12, 1944; her husband managed to get away.

As the days and miles mounted, "we realized that if we were to be saved, something would have to happen quickly," Virginia wrote. "But nothing did, and before we knew it, we were reading German signs. All hope had vanished."

The train stopped when it reached Weimar, a city in central Germany, and the wagons containing the male prisoners were separated from those carrying the women. Calling out the names of women whose husbands were also in the convoy, SS guards told them they would be allowed to say goodbye before the two trains went their separate ways. Germaine de Renty, who hadn't seen her husband, Robert, since their arrest, was one of dozens of women who scrambled off and ran down the block-long platform. When they finally reached its end, there was no one there: The train carrying the men had already left, bound for Buchenwald. The SS guards were doubled over in laughter, exulting in the success of their extraordinarily cruel trick.

The women prisoners finally reached Ravensbrück on August 21, 1944. On the day they'd left the French capital, the Allies had launched Operation Dragoon, their invasion of southern France. Three days after the convoy's arrival at Ravensbrück, American and French troops liberated Paris.

AS THEY ENTERED THE CAMP, the 594 French newcomers were still reeling from their journey. But to their compatriots at Ravensbrück, they looked as if they had come directly from avenue Montaigne, the center of Paris's haute couture. Some "wore ridiculously fashionable dresses they'd concocted somehow," a camp veteran remarked. One even sported an Hermès scarf. "It was as if a little of our former life had slipped illegally into the camp—a breath of France."

But that suggestion of normality quickly vanished. Like the seven thousand or so Frenchwomen who had come before them, the new arrivals were stunned by their surroundings, which continued to grow more vile than those that had greeted their predecessors. With thousands more women from all over Europe pouring into Ravensbrück each week, there was no order anywhere in the camp. Its administration and infrastructure were collapsing, disease was rampant, the mortuary was full to overflowing, and bodies were stacked up in the barracks' washrooms. Food and water were at a premium, and lice, rats, fleas, and bedbugs were endemic.

When the women arrived, there was no place to put them. Late that night, they were herded into a narrow alleyway at the back of the camp and pushed up against a line of open latrines. They would not learn until later that the alley served as Ravensbrück's execution ground, where hundreds of inmates over the last four years had been taken out and shot.

The next morning, the women were finally jammed into a quarantine block, filled with six-tier wooden bedsteads rising to the ceiling, which already housed some six hundred other inmates from various countries. To squeeze one's way through the thicket of bunks to find an empty space proved virtually impossible. Each straw mattress—little more than two feet wide and infested with bedbugs—had to accommodate at least three women. Every square inch of space was occupied.

The well-being of the newcomers was a matter of grave concern for veterans like Germaine Tillion and Anise Girard. Paradoxically, the later in the war that inmates arrived at the camp, the smaller were their chances of survival. "Ravensbrück was by this time divided into two worlds," one Polish prisoner recalled. "There were those who had been a long time in the camp and had had time to better themselves, and those who arrived now and struggled pathetically to keep their heads above water." Physical stamina had never been as essential as it was in the camp's final months.

Jacqueline Marié fell ill from dysentery almost immediately. Her mother, frantic to save her daughter's life, was overjoyed when they and most other members of the August 15 convoy, including Jeannie Rousseau, Germaine de Renty, and Virginia d'Albert-Lake, were assigned to a transport sent to a factory in Torgau, about two hundred miles south of Ravensbrück. Neither Marceline Marié nor anyone else chosen for the convoy knew what the factory produced, but at that point, she didn't care. She'd do anything to get her daughter and herself out of the squalor and death of Ravensbrück.

Two and a half weeks after their arrival at the camp, the Frenchwomen departed for Torgau. Compared with what they'd just experienced, it initially seemed like paradise. "We were actually treated like human beings," Virginia remembered. Instead of a thin gruel and the black sawdust bread of Ravensbrück, their first meal consisted of sausage, sauerkraut, and loaves of just-baked pumpernickel. The dormitories were large, spacious, and well ventilated, and each worker was given her own bunk, complete with a clean, bug-free straw mattress and wool blanket. The German guards were strict but not brutal or wantonly cruel like those at Ravensbrück.

But as the Frenchwomen soon discovered, there was a significant price to be paid for these comforts. The Torgau factory was a munitions plant owned by the Heinkel aircraft company—one of thirty-three arms factories throughout Germany whose workers came from Ravensbrück, now a crucial supplier of labor in Germany's desperate effort to ward off defeat. The women's job, they were told, would be to make bomb shell casings and fill them with explosives.

Many if not most of the women responded with dismay, then anger. Having resisted the Germans in France, they were not about to work for the Nazi war effort in Germany. Leading the charge was Jeannie Rousseau, who, during the journey to Ravensbrück, had made a pact with Germaine de Renty to refuse to perform any labor for the German war machine. If ordered to do so, she said, they must recruit other women to organize a protest.

"At the time, we did not think twice about our fearlessness, our audacity, our madness," wrote Jacqueline Marié, who, having recovered from her illness, was one of Rousseau's most vocal supporters. "We did not think of the possible consequences of this refusal or the fact that the German commander there had the power of life and death over us. The invasion of France by the Allies had given us hope. We knew that an act of rebellion was impossible in Ravensbrück. But in Torgau?"

Yet while Jacqueline and most of the others in the French contingent, especially its younger members, applauded Rousseau's stand, a group of older women counseled caution. "You are mad, little ones!" one of them declared. "You're forgetting that we're prisoners, in their hands. You'll receive nothing in return but retaliation, which will be extreme. You are young and ardent, but you need to think carefully about this." Her warning of reprisals was rejected by those who were its targets: No matter the cost to themselves, they would never make ammunition that would be used to kill their countrymen.

The morning after their arrival, the women were ordered to line up outside their barracks for an inspection by the commander of the camp. Before the SS officer could speak, Jeannie Rousseau stepped out of line and approached him. In fluent German, she told him that she and her compatriots were political prisoners, not ordinary criminals. As such, they should be considered combatants under the protection of the Geneva Convention, which prohibited all war work for captured prisoners of war.

"We have brothers, fathers, husbands who are fighting," Jeannie declared. "We cannot work on weapons that will be used to kill them. We refuse this job, and we know it is our right." She added, "We are not afraid of hard work. We will go and pick your potatoes, but we won't make your bombs!" The bemused commander asked Rousseau what she and the others were expecting when they were assigned to Torgau. Didn't they know it was a weapons factory? No, she replied. They had no idea what its purpose was.

Shaking his head, the officer said he would consult Berlin about how to handle the situation. In the meantime, the women would be required to work. Those willing to work temporarily in the factory would go there. The rest would be assigned to kitchen and other labor duties. But before he sent them back to their barracks, he delivered a chilling warning: In all likelihood, the recalcitrants would be returned to Ravens-brück.

As Virginia d'Albert-Lake remembered it, Jeannie Rousseau "had put a match to a fuse of dynamite," and the resulting explosion shattered the camaraderie of what had been up to then a close-knit group. Nobody wanted to return to Ravensbrück. Two lists were drawn up: those willing to work in the factory and those who refused and would face the consequences.

Initially, Virginia signed up to resist, but another woman convinced her that that was lunacy and she took her name off. "The war is nearly over," the woman told her. "The few munitions we might make will never be used." Others said they would surely die if they had to go back to Ravensbrück. "We all suffered that day," Virginia recalled. "We were torn between courage and fear, idealism and realism, pride and shame. . . . Women were lecturing and arguing, fighting and weeping. It was all madness."

At one point, Jeannie Rousseau got up on a chair and addressed her compatriots. "We have gone through so many difficult years," she said. "Now, after all that work, we can actually stand up to the Germans, tell them to their face that we can and will defy them. This is our chance. Let's not stop now!"

Describing the scene to a historian more than fifty years later, Jeannie explained why she felt she had to take charge: "I was convinced somebody had to do something. Somebody had to stand up. I decided to do it."

"Why?" the historian asked her.

"Because I was there." She paused a moment, then added, "And because I was very young."

AFTER JEANNIE'S CALL TO arms, the majority of the group, including Virginia, decided she was right. The others—some one hundred women—went to the factory, where they made shell casings, then dipped them in vats of acid to clean them. In sharp contrast to that dirty, exhausting, and dangerous job, those who resisted were sent to work in the kitchen and fields. Their ringleader, however, was severely punished. After being thrown into a dungeon cell in the camp's prison block, Jeannie Rousseau was taken out every morning for three weeks, sprayed with ice-cold water, then beaten.

As Torgau's commander had predicted, the *résistantes* were sent back to Ravensbrück, while those who had accepted factory work were dispatched to another plant near Weimar. When Jacqueline Marié went through the readmission process at Ravensbrück, she was assigned the number 75,537; her earlier number had been 57,978. These numbers were breathtaking: Since Jacqueline had left the camp just a month before, almost eighteen thousand more women had been added to its roster.

Jammed once again into a filthy barracks, the women from Torgau spent the next few days waiting to find out what was going to happen to them. Whatever it was, they knew it would be bad. For Jeannie Rousseau, the verdict was death. Authorities in Berlin had ordered Ravensbrück officials to execute her.

Amazingly, however, bureaucratic bungling saved her life. "They were going to kill me," she said, but the administrators of the camp couldn't find papers for a Jeannie Rousseau. When she was originally arrested by the Gestapo, she was identified as Madeleine Chauffour, her code name. But when Jeannie arrived at Ravensbrück and then at Torgau, she gave her real name to authorities, none of whom made the connection between her and the official dossier, sent separately to the camps, of the dangerous Allied spy Madeleine Chauffour. Having no idea who she really was or what she had done to warrant being sent to Ravensbrück, the Germans, who assiduously followed bureaucratic regulations, decided to let her live, at least for the moment. But they could, and did, make her life a living hell.

In the end, the Torgau rebels were separated into two groups. The first, which included Jacqueline and Marceline Marié, was banished to a factory at Abteroda, a subcamp of Buchenwald. When they arrived, they slept on a concrete floor without mattresses or blankets, were beaten by SS guards, and received barely enough food to survive. Dozens fell ill from typhoid, dysentery, and other diseases, and several died.

The plant, which was underground, made parts for V-1 and V-2 rockets—the terror weapons that Jeannie Rousseau had told the Allies so much about. If the Frenchwomen wanted to stay alive, they knew they would have to submit to German demands and actually do the work. But did that mean they would be complicit in aiding the German war effort? "Absolutely not!" Jacqueline Marié retorted. "We played at being incompetent morons, unfit for factory work, incapable of learning to operate the machines and causing constant breakdowns."

She and her mother, for example, became expert bunglers in their job of checking the quality of certain small parts, separating the good from the defective. "It often happened that we made mistakes, mixing up the good with the bad. The Germans would yell at us, saying we Frenchwomen were useless workers and harmful to the Third Reich. These insults, of course, delighted us."

The other band of Torgau rebels, which included Jeannie Rousseau, Germaine de Renty, and Virginia d'Albert-Lake, was never given the opportunity nor had the satisfaction of outwitting the Germans. They were sent to Königsberg, a punishment camp in East Prussia, about fifty miles east of Ravensbrück. Of the 250 Frenchwomen forced to go there, only ten percent survived.

The ostensible purpose of Königsberg, whose inmates also included Poles and Russians, was to build a military airfield. But with the war approaching its end, it was clear to the workers that the airfield would never be finished in time to be of actual use to the Luftwaffe. Indeed, they suspected, the Germans didn't care whether the work was completed: The camp's real purpose was to destroy those sent there. "It was hard labor of the worst kind, and the prisoners were clearly expected to work until their last breath and die," the British historian Sarah Helm observed.

Winter came early that year to east Prussia. Plagued by blinding snow and subfreezing temperatures, the Frenchwomen cut down trees and dug out their massive stumps, hauled rocks and gravel, and laid sod for the airfield and steel rails for a future railroad track. Lacking coats or any other warm clothing, some stuffed handfuls of straw from their mattresses down the fronts of their flimsy dresses to provide some protection from the icy blasts of wind.

Their only meal of the day—a thin soup and a piece of bread—came in the evening. The soup was doled out from a large vat by the camp's head guard, a fat, sadistic woman whom the prisoners called La Vachère (the Cowherd). Not infrequently, she would kick the vat over and watch with relish as the famished prisoners licked the soup up from the snow. Many women rummaged through the camp's garbage dump for rotten vegetables, potato peelings, or anything else that could be considered remotely edible. One by one, they fell ill from dysentery, tuberculosis, typhoid, and a plethora of other diseases. Every week, dozens died, some of them collapsing in the snow as they worked.

Jeannie Rousseau's health, too, was deteriorating by the day. The only thing keeping her alive was the care given her by Germaine de Renty, the elegant, seemingly delicate socialite from Paris who turned out to be one of the strongest women, both physically and mentally, in the camp. From the day she arrived at Ravensbrück, Germaine was determined to return to her four children, particularly to her youngest daughter, fourteen-year-old Claude. She made clear to Jeannie Rousseau that she would do everything in her power to survive. "This frail woman was indomitable," Jeannie recalled. "She let nothing stand in her way."

Germaine insisted that Jeannie follow her lead. She gave the younger woman much of her own pitiful food ration and scavenged bits of fabric to keep her warm. She nursed her, comforted her, and urged her to keep going. But even as she struggled to do so, Jeannie knew that neither she nor Germaine could last much longer. They had to find a way to escape.

Each day, she knew, trucks left Königsberg with the bodies of dead and dying inmates, which she assumed were being taken back to Ravensbrück to be disposed of. The thought of returning to the camp was horrific, but it was the only possible option, she told Germaine, who agreed.

Several days later, the two women climbed into the back of one of the trucks as it was about to leave. When the truck reached Ravensbrück, it stopped for a few minutes just inside the gate, and Jeannie and Germaine slipped out before it went on to dump its cargo at the infirmary. Their problem now was how to survive inside the camp, since without registration numbers, they had no place to go for either food or shelter. They fled to one barracks housing several other Frenchwomen, who agreed to hide them for one night. The following day, they were taken in by Polish friends in another block, spending nearly a week there until an informer reported their presence to the SS.

They were then thrown into the most fearsome place in the camp— the punishment cell block—where prisoners were tortured and sometimes killed. Had they come back to Ravensbrück only to meet their end in the Bunker?

Chapter 9

"The Dawn of Hope"

GENEVIÈVE DE GAULLE WOULD ALWAYS THINK OF HER LIFE at Ravensbrück as the height of absurdity. Never was that more true than in the last three months of 1944.

In the early summer of that year, Jacqueline d'Alincourt and Geneviève's other friends had feared she would soon die. Repeatedly beaten by Herr Syllinka, the sadist who oversaw the workshop in which she'd been laboring, she was emaciated, half blind, and close to collapse. It was then that Anise Girard persuaded Milena Seborova, a Czech friend who was the foreman of another workshop, to put in a word for Geneviève with the SS man in charge of Seborova's detail.

The man, one Herr Schmidt, was an anomaly among the Germans at Ravensbrück. A staunch Catholic who had been drafted against his will into the SS, Schmidt still possessed remnants of a conscience. On several previous occasions, he had allowed Seborova to transfer ill prisoners to his workshop, which dismantled fur coats and jackets taken from Holocaust victims at Auschwitz and other extermination camps for use as linings in SS officers' winter greatcoats. Undoubtedly his willingness to do as Seborova asked was influenced by her reminder that the war was not going well for Germany and that showing compassion to inmates would certainly help his cause with the Allies in case of a German defeat. Whatever the reason, he agreed to take Geneviève in.

So exhausted that she could barely move, Geneviève spent her first few days on the new job sleeping under a pile of rabbit skins. With the support of her fellow workers, she slowly began to regain her strength even as she struggled with the horror of having to unstitch garments which all "had a story, a first name," as her biographer, Frédérique Neau-Dufour, put it. "Each item of clothing was the shadow of a departed being."

In the late afternoon of October 3, 1944, Geneviève had just returned to her barracks when a female guard came to the door and called out her name. The woman told her that Fritz Suhren, the camp's commandant, wanted to see her. She escorted Geneviève across the camp's parade ground, through its main gate, and into another world, filled with trees, shrubs, attractive cottages, and an impressive stone building that housed Ravensbrück's administrative offices.

When Geneviève was ushered into Suhren's office, he was sitting on the edge of his desk, waiting for her. Aware that she was nothing but a cipher to him, she lowered her head and identified herself in German as "prisoner 27,372." He responded by asking, "How are you feeling?"

The ludicrousness of that question prompted her to raise her head and stare at the thirty-six-year-old commandant. He had pale red hair, blue eyes, and a round, boyish face, and he cut a dapper figure in his crisply tailored SS uniform. Suhren was "the kind of assassin who wore cufflinks," another French inmate noted. "He smelled like soap and wore ironed shirts. He was a consummate functionary who organized systematic exterminations in his camp but who didn't do the job himself."

The answer to Suhren's query was blindingly obvious. She was cadaverous, with a body covered with open sores and eyes that were red and swollen. She answered, "Very poorly, thank you," then couldn't resist adding a little dig, ". . . as you can see."

"Yes, I can see," he said. "You don't look at all well. What is your work detail?" She was still officially assigned to Syllinka's detail, and

Fritz
Suhren

when she told Suhren that, she saw him wince. When he asked which barracks she was in, her reply—Block 31—produced another cringe.

"Starting immediately, you'll be assigned to work in a desk job in the infirmary," he said briskly, "and you'll be transferred to Block 2. I think you'll find it less arduous." No, Geneviève protested, she couldn't possibly move. She'd already lost one sister, and she couldn't abide the thought of being separated from Jacqueline d'Alincourt, who'd become like another sister to her.

But Suhren refused to listen; he had given her an order, and she must obey. He asked if there was anything she needed or wanted. Some new underwear, perhaps? A warm jacket or sweater? No, she replied, but she'd appreciate it if he would help the other Frenchwomen: "As you well know, we are among the most ill-treated in the camp. The others' situation would be much improved if they were all quartered in the same barracks. They're also in dire need of medicines and warm clothing to get through the winter."

Suhren abruptly stood up, making clear that their discussion was over. "That's none of your business," he barked, then added, "If you personally are in need of anything else, let me know."

As Geneviève was escorted back to Block 31, she wondered why "this all-powerful master" was suddenly so interested in "a poor, humble person, namely myself. Until then, no one had shown the slightest interest in me. If I had not yet succumbed to the beatings or the lack of food or hygiene, or died of exhaustion, it was by pure chance."

She concluded that someone very high in the Nazi hierarchy had decided to make her welfare a priority. She was right. That "someone" was none other than Heinrich Himmler.

WHEN GERMANY STILL OCCUPIED France, there was no reason for Himmler or anyone else in Berlin to take special notice of the niece of General Charles de Gaulle. But by October 1944, most of France had been liberated, de Gaulle was the country's provisional president, and Geneviève was now regarded as a possible bargaining chip.

At that point, Himmler knew the war was lost. Allied troops were sweeping across France, heading for Germany. The Russians were doing the same from the east. With the Third Reich's days clearly numbered, it was time, Himmler decided, to open secret talks with the Allies about the possibility of a separate peace. In searching for ways to build bridges with the West, Himmler and his masseur, Felix Kersten, who became his middleman, decided to use European prisoners held in German concentration camps as pawns. A prime candidate was Geneviève de Gaulle.

As it happened, neither the top Allied leaders nor the International Red Cross, based in Geneva, had shown much interest in the fate of those held in Nazi camps, whether they were Jewish victims of the Holocaust or members of resistance movements. For the most part, the British and American governments chose to remain silent about the atrocities being committed in the camps.

But while those imprisoned in Germany were of little concern to U.S. and British officials, the same was not true in France, which had lost thousands of its citizens to the Nazi maw. Among the many Frenchmen appealing to the Red Cross for information about their loved ones was Xavier de Gaulle, Geneviève's father, who fled to Switzerland in 1943 after being warned of his imminent arrest by the Gestapo and who was now the French consul in Geneva.

Meanwhile, neutral Sweden, which had been criticized by some in the Allied camp for its pro-German policy early in the war, was intent on burnishing its tarnished image. One way to do so was to offer to act as a back channel in negotiations to rescue Scandinavian, French, and other Western European prisoners from the camps.

By the early autumn of 1944, Swedish officials had received reports of German preparations to liquidate the camps and kill all their prisoners, which spurred the Swedes to speed up the idea of a rescue operation. The central figure in the plan was Count Folke Bernadotte, a nephew of King Gustav of Sweden and the vice president of the Swedish Red Cross.

In October 1944, Felix Kersten, who lived part time in Sweden, informed Bernadotte that he believed Himmler might consider freeing some prisoners to show good will toward the Allies. That same month, Himmler wrote to Charles de Gaulle offering to free Geneviève in exchange for a German prisoner held in France. While waiting for an answer, he ordered Suhren to improve her treatment in the event of her release.

Knowing nothing about these behind-the-scenes machinations, Geneviève returned to Block 31 to say an emotionally wrenching goodbye to Jacqueline d'Alincourt and move her things to Block 2, a barracks for prisoners such as secretaries, bookkeepers, and technicians who worked directly with SS personnel. The only other Frenchwoman living there was the hairdresser for SS women guards.

Because of their proximity to the Germans, the women in Block 2 were under strict instructions to keep themselves and their surroundings impeccably clean and free of fleas and lice. To ensure such neatness, these privileged inmates lived "like the queen of England," as Germaine Tillion put it—each with a clean straw mattress all to herself, a pillow, and two new blue-and-white patchwork blankets. The clothing Geneviève was issued was immaculate, too: a crisp new blue-

and-gray-striped prison dress and jacket and wooden clogs. "Clearly I was no longer a part of the camp subproletariat, the lowest of the low, the ragged and tattered, those who were beaten at the drop of a hat," she wrote. Her outfit served as a badge of her new status, allowing her to move freely about the camp, which none of her old comrades was able to do.

Geneviève's new job—as a clerk in the infirmary office, updating prisoners' records—was as comfortable as her living conditions. After only two days there, she fainted during the early morning roll call, but instead of receiving a beating, which would have been her fate just days before, she was sent to the infirmary as a patient. There, her sores were disinfected and treated with ointment; she was dosed with vitamin pills and allowed to stay in bed for several days.

On October 25, three weeks after she'd been summoned to Suhren's office, Geneviève returned to Block 31 to celebrate her twenty-fourth birthday with Jacqueline and several other friends. They had made her a cake from bread crumbs they'd saved from their meager rations, mixed with a kind of molasses that was used as jam in the camp kitchen. For candles, they substituted twenty-four twigs, and for further decoration added brilliantly colored leaves collected by those in outdoor work details. Moved to tears, Geneviève pretended to blow the faux candles out. For the rest of her life, she remembered that evening as "a true moment of happiness."

Three nights later, as she slept in her bunk in Block 2, she was jolted awake by the beam of a flashlight shining in her face. Opening her eyes, she saw two dark figures, SS men, who curtly ordered her to get down from her bunk and put on her clothes. She was helped by the barracks' Polish blockova, who gathered up Geneviève's few belongings, including her tin spoon and bowl. With tears in her eyes, she hugged Geneviève tightly before the SS guards took her away.

And just like that, it was over. She'd gone down the rabbit hole again, snatched from the best place for prisoners at Ravensbrück and taken to the worst—the Bunker. Officially known as the *strafblock* (punishment barracks), it was a narrow two-story building, with eighty tiny cells overlooking a central atrium. It was Ravensbrück's nexus of terror—the spot where the most severe punishments were meted out and where prisoners were taken just prior to their execution.

Geneviève was panicked, her mind racing, as the guards hustled her into the building and down the steps to the dungeon. Why was she there? What was happening to her? The men unlocked a cell, shoved her into it, and shut the door behind them. She was enveloped in total blackness.

Her arm outstretched, feeling her way, she bumped into a bare wooden platform, clearly meant to be the bed but with no mattress or blanket. As her eyes became accustomed to the lack of light, she made out the shapes of a stool chained to the wall and a toilet, with a water spigot above it. There was a window near the ceiling, but it had been boarded up.

For three days she huddled there, shut up in the dark with no food or visitors. Her only guide to the time of day came from the wail of sirens. When she heard the first siren, she knew it was 3:30 A.M., time for the camp's prisoners to rise for the early morning roll call. The daily nightmare was beginning—women scuffling in the overcrowded barracks for a cup of what was loosely described as coffee and jostling one another to get access to the disgusting latrines, all of them preparing for another day of exhaustion, pain, and terror.

Entombed in her cell, Geneviève was spared the pushing and shoving, the agony of the roll call, the guards' cruelty, and the crushing fatigue of the work. But at what cost? She was convinced she was going to die in the Bunker, whether from starvation or in the alleyway where the executions took place just steps away.

What's worse, she would die alone. "No one will be there to help or comfort me, to hold my hand as I so often have held others during their final moments," she thought. "The last faces I shall see will be filled with hate and contempt. . . . My friends have no idea what has become of me, and here I have to confront my fate, whatever it may be, without their tenderness and compassion. Will they ever know how I died?"

Throughout the day, she heard a variety of sounds: the distant barking of dogs and harsh shouts of SS guards, the thud of boots in the corridor outside her cell, the click of keys opening other cell doors, no doubt those of guards bringing food to their occupants. But there was no food for her, which she found understandable: "Obviously, if they're planning to kill me in the near future, what's the point of feeding me?"

Geneviève's thoughts turned to Jacqueline d'Alincourt and her determination to raise her friends' spirits with reminders of life's beauty— noting the occasional pearly loveliness of a dawn sky high above the ugliness of Ravensbrück, reciting a favorite poem, or her bell-like singing of "Awake, O Sleeping Hearts, the Lord Is Calling You." Prompted by that last memory, Geneviève softly sang the hymn to herself and tried to pray but couldn't bring herself to do so. For the first time in her life, "God was strangely absent for me. I can't say I doubted his existence, but he wasn't there in the Bunker."

Although she tried hard not to despair, she was on the brink of losing that struggle after three days of living in a literal black hole that was fast erasing everything about her—hope, identity, self-respect, sanity, even life. Weakened by hunger, she felt herself succumbing to a dreamlike lethargy.

And then once again her world shifted. On the morning of Geneviève's fourth day in the Bunker, she was awakened by the loud click of her cell door being unlocked. When she looked up, a female SS guard was standing in the doorway, staring at her in astonishment. "Who are you?" she demanded. "What are you doing here? How long have you been here?"

Responding in German, Geneviève explained what had happened. The woman spun around and left. An hour or so later, she returned, informing Geneviève that a mistake had been made. No one knew why she had been put in a darkened cell. There was no order to punish her, and she should not have received the treatment she had. The board covering the window would be removed shortly, and she would be given food as soon as possible. From then on, Geneviève received a meal of soup and bread once a day, but her stomach, having been denied nourishment for so long, rebelled, and she found it hard to keep anything down.

She was never told the reasons for the topsy-turviness of her treatment. She didn't know of Himmler's initial offer to exchange her for a German prisoner in France, nor was she informed that her uncle had never responded to it, which apparently was the reason for the premature end of her privileged status. But Himmler hadn't entirely given up on the possible use of Geneviève as a future bargaining chip: He ordered that she be kept indefinitely in the *strafblock*. There has never been an explanation for the way she was initially treated there.

When the board was removed from the window, Geneviève could finally inspect her cell, which was about five feet wide and ten feet long. Although cold and damp, it was clean, albeit with a bevy of cockroaches to keep her company. They had kept out of her way until she started receiving her daily bread ration; at that point, they decided to make her acquaintance. For the next few weeks, they were her only companions.

For the first time since her capture by the Gestapo, Geneviève was denied the opportunity to communicate with her fellow *rèsistantes*. She never saw or heard from other inmates in the *strafblock*, nor was she allowed to have any contact with her friends in the camp and had no idea whether they were still alive. The only faces she saw were those of the guards who opened her cell door for the early morning roll call, during which she had to stand at attention, and an elderly prisoner who brought her food. The woman, whose name was Anna, was a member of the Jehovah's Witnesses, a religious group persecuted by the Third Reich for its strong opposition to Hitler and the Nazis.

After weeks in her cell, with no one to talk to and nothing to do, Geneviève was on the knife edge of a breakdown. One day, when she discovered a piece of meat floating in her rutabaga soup—an immense treat—she burst into tears. She did the same a day or so later, when a guard took her for a short walk in a tiny internal courtyard, and she saw the sky for the first time since she'd been shut up in the Bunker. Just as she was ordered to go inside, snowflakes began to fall. Back in her dank, dark cell, she couldn't hold back the tears. "I was," she said, "thoroughly astonished by my lack of self-control."

At that point, Geneviève decided to pull herself together. She was still alive, after all, and perhaps, just perhaps, she might actually survive until the end of the war. To regain her strength, she began to exercise and to eat all her food rations, repulsive though they were. To occupy her mind, she tended to her cockroaches, feeding them bread crumbs and organizing races for them to compete in. The fastest was the biggest cockroach, which she named Victor; the runner-up was called Félix. They received the most crumbs, although she kept back a few for the also-rans.

One Sunday afternoon in mid-December 1944, Geneviève's spirits received a further boost when Anna slipped into her cell. The SS guards were having a party, she whispered, and she was taking advantage of their carousing to bring Geneviève sewing supplies to fix her torn stockings. She produced a bit of wool yarn, a needle, and scissors. Later, she replenished the supply of yarn, enabling Geneviève to mend all her clothes. In return, Geneviève made a handkerchief for Anna, embroidering on it the woman's Ravensbrück identification number. She planned to give it to her as a Christmas present—the only thing she had to look forward to on what she was sure would be the saddest holiday of her life.

As it turned out, Christmas Eve 1944 was far worse than she expected, filled during the afternoon with shrieks and moans from prisoners who were being beaten in a special punishment room a few doors down from Geneviève's cell. The cries of pain seemed to go on for hours. That night, when silence again reigned, Geneviève heard a female voice singing "Silent Night" in German. Her own voice trembling, she sang "O Holy Night" and "It Came Upon a Midnight Clear" to herself. That night she dreamed of Jacqueline d'Alincourt.

On Christmas morning, when Anna brought her coffee, Geneviève slipped the embroidered handkerchief into her hand and, in German, wished her a merry Christmas. There was no reaction from Anna—no smile, no Christmas greeting. Stunned by her lack of response, Geneviève couldn't imagine a more miserable day.

Sunk in depression the following morning, it took her a moment to look up when Anna entered her cell. The blank look from the night before was gone; in its place was a big smile. With a flourish, Anna presented her with a box. "Your friends sent it to you for Christmas," she said. "I couldn't bring it yesterday, because we were being very closely watched. Now the SS are still asleep after staying up all night drinking." She pointed to the box. "Take everything out. I'll come and get it later."

Geneviève opened the box. Inside was a cornucopia of riches. There was a small fir branch, a piece of paper with the lyrics of a French Christmas carol, four star-shaped cookies, a red apple, a tiny bit of pork fat, and two pieces of sugar. Then she took out the most wonderful present of all—an exquisite little doll dressed like an eighteenth-century aristocrat, her hair in a powdered white pompadour, clothed in a white lace fichu and a pink satin skirt complete with petticoats. Embroidered on the skirt were the initials J and A, for Jacqueline d'Alincourt.

Jacqueline had labored for weeks over this gift. Shattered by Geneviève's sudden disappearance two months earlier, she had known nothing about what had happened to her. She had had no idea whether Geneviève was still alive, although she had heard rumors she was being kept in the Bunker. If that were true, Jacqueline was determined to create an elegant, whimsical Christmas present that would transport Geneviève, at least for a few moments, out of the ugliness and savagery of the world around her. To do so, she asked for help from Paulette Don Zimmet and her work detail, which was responsible for unloading railway cars filled with clothing, jewelry, and other valuables. Jacqueline asked Don Zimmet's crew if they could bring her small amounts of certain fabrics, like cotton, satin, silk, and lace. They managed to find everything she had requested, and from those remnants, she fashioned a doll that looked like the porcelain dolls sold in the most expensive toy shops in Paris.

Geneviève was overwhelmed by the gift, which she later referred to as "a very, very precious treasure." For the rest of her life, she cherished that doll, keeping it in a place of honor wherever she was living. She saw it and the rest of the presents as a sign from Jacqueline and her other friends that their sisterhood held firm and she was not alone. "Even in my dungeon cell," she wrote, "they managed to touch me, to join me." At the bottom of the box, she discovered yet another present—a neatly folded brown wool shawl. She wrapped it around her shoulders "just as if I were enfolding myself in their warm and gentle friendship." It was the first time in the two months she'd been in the Bunker that she wasn't cold.

Until then, Geneviève's nights there had mostly been dreamless. That night, however, she dreamed she was nine or ten years old and was walking with her sister, brother, and youngest uncle, Pierre, through a field of white daisies. It was the height of summer, and the sun shone brightly. Pierre, who was her godfather, wove a wreath of daisies and crowned her with it, proclaiming her queen of the flowers. She was overcome with joy.

Thanks to the Christmas box, Geneviève's depression lifted, and she found herself able to pray again. She spent much of the rest of her time and energy focusing on her cockroaches and their races. They had now become pets of a sort and were clustered around her even when no bread crumbs were in sight. Félix in particular seemed to want to be with her, and she sometimes discovered him lodged in the hollow of her arm.

But her health remained a constant worry. One morning she awoke with chills, excruciating chest pain, and a high fever. One of the guards summoned a doctor, who instead of examining her, stood in the doorway of her cell and questioned her about her symptoms. She told him she thought she was probably suffering from a recurrence of pleurisy, a lung disease that she had contracted when she first arrived at Ravensbrück. For the next two days, she was given medication. Although the doctor's visit couldn't have been more cursory, she was stunned that he actually came: "I can't get over the fact that anyone cared!"

A few days later, she received another surprise. A woman guard handed her a letter, the first she'd received since she arrived at Ravensbrück. When she saw the handwriting on the envelope, postmarked from Switzerland, she burst into tears: It was her father's. Her hand shaking, she opened the envelope and read Xavier de Gaulle's "simple, short sentences, which were filled with immense tenderness."

Xavier told her how he and his wife had escaped to Switzerland, one step ahead of the Gestapo, and brought her up to date on other members of the family. Marie-Agnès Cailliau de Gaulle, his sister and

Geneviève's aunt, who had been with Geneviève at Fresnes, was now imprisoned at a subcamp of Buchenwald. Pierre de Gaulle, his youngest brother, was also being held at Buchenwald. Roger, Geneviève's brother, was fighting with the Free French forces.

The letter was in German, to satisfy Nazi censors, and seeing the words brought back memories of the German folk songs Geneviève's father had taught her as a small child when the family was living in the country's Saar region. Singing those songs now, she further celebrated the letter's arrival by giving her cockroaches an extra ration of crumbs.

The next day, the same woman guard handed her, without explanation, several boxes of Vitamin C and calcium phosphate. They were from Switzerland, and Geneviève was sure they'd been sent by her father. She was almost as excited by the boxes as she was by the vitamins themselves, which she hoped would help heal the scurvy-caused open sores all over her body. Using the scissors Anna had given her, Geneviève carefully cut up the boxes into tiny rectangles, which, with a pencil stub, she transformed into a pack of cards with which she played solitaire.

The arrival of Xavier de Gaulle's letter coincided with another upsurge in official German interest in Geneviève's welfare. In mid-January 1945, Fritz Suhren paid her a visit to ask about her health. When she told him of her recent attack of pleurisy, she had the feeling he already knew about it. A few hours after he'd left, a woman guard came to tell her to pack up her things because she was being transferred to another cell. As she waited for Geneviève to finish collecting her belongings, the guard noticed Félix at Geneviève's feet. With a look of disgust, she raised her foot and crushed him. For a moment, Geneviève was sorry—Félix and the other roaches had provided her with some of her few moments of mental escape in the Bunker—but her regret soon passed. It was time to move on.

Her new cell was one flight up and flooded with sunshine. "Without question, I am feeling better, thanks to the calcium and the light," she wrote. Later that day, she was taken to the courtyard for a walk. This time, the sky was blue and the air bracing. A wave of exhilaration washed over her: "I have the feeling that I am emerging from a deep dark cave. I no longer feel indifferent about whether I live or die. I want to see my loved ones again, see another spring in Paris, see the trees in bloom."

Yet even though Geneviève's new quarters were immeasurably better than her previous surroundings, the view from her window was a persistent reminder of Ravensbrück's hellishness. She looked out on the wall separating the camp from its crematorium, a squat concrete building where the bodies of inmates were burned. When she had arrived at the camp, it was in operation only twice a week and just a few hours each time. Now, however, noxious smoke belched from its chimney twenty-four hours a day, emitting an "intolerable odor" and, depending on which way the wind was blowing, drifting into her cell. When she mentioned it to Anna, the older woman said there were so many bodies being burned now that a second crematorium had been built. One of them, still unable to keep up with the volume, had recently exploded. As she handed Geneviève her soup, Anna said with a sigh, "They're all going to die."

IN MID-FEBRUARY, SUHREN AGAIN paid Geneviève a call. This time, she thought, he seemed a little less arrogant. He announced that two men were coming to ask her a series of questions, which she must answer as accurately and candidly as possible. Just as he finished his instructions, the men arrived. One was in civilian clothes; the other, who was younger, was in uniform but with no SS insignia on display. Geneviève had the impression he was a doctor. When they asked her how she'd been treated, she didn't mince words. With her usual candor, she told them about "the terrible trip in the cattle cars, the anguish of being stripped naked, the dogs, the beatings, the terror . . . the progressive destruction of what constitutes a human being, depriving her of her dignity and her most basic rights."

Although the men made no comment about her blistering observations, the younger man seemed incensed by her poor physical condition—her open sores, ulcerated corneas, and skin-and-bones body. After escorting her to the SS infirmary for a chest X-ray, he expressed indignation at "the terrible state of my lungs" and the fact that nothing had been done about them. After all the tests and questions, she was returned to her cell, bewildered by "this completely surreal experience" and having no idea what it meant.

The inexplicable interrogations continued. A week later, she was summoned to appear before a high-ranking Gestapo official at the camp's administrative offices. She was surprised by his courteous treatment of her, which included the use of her name rather than her identification number. He began by telling her he had been stationed in Paris for several months early in the war and had many fond memories of it, to which she responded that she had no fond memories of the Gestapo men she'd encountered there. Hearing that, he briskly moved on to her Resistance activities with Défense de la France. "I did my best to minimize my role, and though he kept pressing, I steadfastly refused to reveal any of my comrades' names," she wrote in her journal. She sensed, in any event, that he wasn't really intent on getting new information from her and that his questioning was merely a formality.

His secretary transcribed Geneviève's deposition, and when she'd finished, the official left after instructing Geneviève to read and sign it. As she was doing so, the secretary began speaking to her in French, saying that she, too, had been in Paris and adored it. "Would you mind very much inscribing something in French in my journal?" she asked Geneviève. "Just a few lines, in remembrance of our meeting?"

Dumbfounded, Geneviève had no idea how to respond. Perhaps, the secretary suggested, she could write down the first few lines of a song by the woman's favorite French cabaret singer, Lucienne Boyer, the doyenne of Paris nightlife. Geneviève obliged, jotting down the beginning of Boyer's best-known song: *"Parlez-moi d'amour, dites-moi les choses tendres . . ."* ("Speak to me of love, whisper me sweet nothings.") Underneath, she inscribed Lucienne Boyer's name, then her own.

Still puzzling over the oddity of the session, Geneviève returned to her cell. For some time, she had suspected that all these strange goings-on might be a prelude to her being released from Ravensbrück, but she had tried hard to tamp down any such hope. This latest episode, however, made her think again. Unable to sleep that night, she decided to collect her most important possessions and put them in one place: the doll and her other Christmas gifts, a small pouch containing the needles and scissors Anna had given her, her makeshift deck of playing cards, and her calcium and vitamin C tablets.

It was just as well she did. Soon after dozing off in the predawn darkness, she was awakened by a woman guard, who burst into her cell, turned on the light, and shouted, "On your feet! Get dressed, and be quick about it!" Without another word, she handed Geneviève a pile of clothing—a navy blue dress with white stripes, a pair of sandals, and, unbelievably, the coat she'd been wearing when she'd arrived at Ravensbrück the year before.

In minutes, Geneviève was dressed. She wrapped herself in her Christmas shawl before putting on her coat, then placed her prized items in a large square of fabric she'd been saving and knotted it. She left her prison uniform, cup, and spoon on the bed and walked out of the cell, feeling, as she did so, that "I'd spent entire years there, living several lives within its walls." As she was escorted to the Bunker's office, she spied Anna, who lifted the handkerchief Geneviève had given her and waved a discreet goodbye.

In the office, two SS officers and a female guard were waiting. With them was another prisoner, a wizened, skeletal woman with a shaven head who seemed "absolutely ancient." Years later, Geneviève would describe the woman as "looking like Gandhi at the end of his life." She was thirty-eight-year-old Virginia d'Albert-Lake, the American who had supported Jeannie Rousseau's rebellion at Torgau and had been sent with Jeannie and the other French rebels to the punishment camp at Königsberg.

The two women exchanged glances, and Geneviève took Virginia's hand. Flanked by the SS officers and woman guard, they walked together down the steps of the Bunker and across the camp's parade ground. It was snowing, and the wind felt like ice, but Geneviève was oblivious to the cold. As she and the others passed through Ravensbrück's main gate, she turned around and glanced at the stooped silhouettes of prisoners beginning their early morning labor. Turning back, she continued walking, hand in hand with Virginia, just as dawn was breaking. It was, Geneviève later wrote, "the dawn of hope."

ALTHOUGH GENEVIÈVE AND VIRGINIA had been freed from Ravensbrück, they had no guarantee of a safe journey out of the hellhole that Germany had become. Along with their guards, they boarded a train in the village of Fürstenberg, at the same station where they'd disembarked the year before. By evening, the little group was in the smoldering ruins of Berlin, leveled after months of relentless Allied air raids. Picking their way across bomb craters and piles of rubble, the two women and their guards were caught in a raid themselves and finally found shelter in a subway station filled with fallen timbers.

Eventually they discovered a Berlin railway station whose trains were still running and caught a military transport to the south. They were joined in their compartment by a young, heavily bemedaled Luftwaffe pilot, who, despite the presence of the SS men, engaged Geneviève in conversation. When he asked why she was in Germany, she described the horrors of what she and Virginia had endured and predicted that the Reich was on the brink of defeat. "Very proud of his country, he tried in vain to persuade me that the Germans, despite appearances, were going to win the war," Geneviève recalled. "Had they not conquered all the capitals of Europe?" As a matter of fact, no, she replied. They hadn't vanquished London, had already been evicted from Paris, Brussels, and most of their other conquests, and were on the verge of losing their own capital. After that, the pilot didn't say another word.

After a week of dodging Allied bombs in Berlin, Munich, Ulm, and Stuttgart, Geneviève and Virginia finally arrived at their destination—an internment camp in Liebenau, a small town in the rolling hills of northwest Germany. The camp, which, unlike Ravensbrück and the other German concentration camps, abided by Geneva Convention rules governing the treatment of prisoners of war, had been set up to house citizens of Allied countries who'd been living in Germany at the start of the conflict. It provided its inmates, most of them women and children from Britain and the United States, with comfortable living conditions, including good medical care and plentiful food, supplemented by frequent parcels from the International Red Cross.

Put to bed in the camp's hospital, which was largely populated by American and British prisoners of war, Geneviève and Virginia began a long, slow process of physical and psychological healing while the Red Cross and German authorities negotiated the terms of their release from German custody.

Virginia's liberation from Ravensbrück was largely due to the relentless efforts of her mother, Edith Roush, the headmistress of a private school in St. Petersburg, Florida. Learning from her son-in-law of her daughter's arrest, she had bombarded high-ranking officials in the International Red Cross and U.S. government, including Secretary of State Cordell Hull, with letters urging them to secure Virginia's release. At Hull's direction, the State Department asked the Swiss government to find out where Virginia was.

Eventually, her case was turned over to a section of the War Department dealing with the escape and evasion of captured U.S. troops. In late January 1945, with Virginia's status still uncertain, the headquarters of General Dwight D. Eisenhower, the supreme commander of Allied forces in Europe, became involved, facilitating the prisoner of war exchange that resulted in Virginia's freedom. Her mother died of leukemia in mid-April 1945, before the two could be reunited.

For her part, Geneviève believed and insisted until the end of her life that Charles de Gaulle had nothing to do with her own release. There's no question that her uncle had ignored Heinrich Himmler's first offer in October 1944 to exchange Geneviève for a German prisoner, believing it would be wrong to show favoritism toward a family member while other French citizens were being held in concentration camps. But that decision came at a great emotional cost. Élisabeth de Miribel, de Gaulle's secretary in London and Algiers, recalled how, on one occasion when he talked to her about Geneviève, his eyes filled with tears.

By early 1945, de Gaulle had changed his mind. Red Cross officials had told him of their fear that Geneviève, along with other members of de Gaulle's family held by the Germans, would be moved by Nazi die-hards to Hitler's stronghold at Berchtesgaden, to be used as hostages in a last-ditch fight to the death. An International Red Cross official informed the German Red Cross of de Gaulle's anxiety about his niece, adding that the general "particularly requested she should be sent to Switzerland and treated in a sanitarium." Heinrich Himmler, still intent on his phantasmal campaign to persuade Allied leaders to agree to a separate peace, authorized the release of both women.

On April 20, 1945, after more than a month at Liebenau, Geneviève was finally allowed to leave Germany. In the back seat of the Red Cross car transporting her to Switzerland, she savored the balminess of the early spring day and the beauty of the pastoral landscapes she passed—row after row of flowering fruit trees, picturesque villages, Lake Constance shimmering in the sun—all of them untouched by war.

Once they'd crossed the border into Switzerland, the driver stopped at the first town they reached so that Geneviève could call her father. They reunited late the following night in the small town of Winterthur, both so emotionally overcome they could barely speak. Even though Geneviève had made great strides in recovering her health at Liebenau, she was still desperately thin, and Xavier had difficulty disguising his shock at her appearance.

Geneviève herself was beset with conflicting emotions—her overwhelming joy to be free vying with her trepidation over the fate of the sisterhood she'd left behind in Ravensbrück. As Germany continued to disintegrate, it was, to say the least, a well-founded fear.

Chapter 10

....

Saving the Rabbits

IN DECEMBER 1944, TWO MONTHS BEFORE GENEVIÈVE DE GAULLE
and Virginia d'Albert-Lake were released from Ravensbrück, the
camp's main priority underwent a dramatic and murderous change.
Previously, its chief goal was to exploit the labor of its prisoners. But
with the Third Reich close to collapse and many if not most of its factories destroyed by Allied bombs, inmates and their work had become
superfluous. The priority now was to kill them all as fast as possible.

Hundreds of Ravensbrück prisoners were already dying each week
from starvation and disease, while hundreds more, mostly the sick and
elderly, were being eliminated by the old ways of killing: injections and
shooting. But those methods couldn't possibly get rid of all the camp's
current inmates, much less the huge influx of newcomers currently
swamping it. And sending prisoners to the gas chambers at Auschwitz
was no longer an option.

On January 12, 1945, the Russians launched a massive offensive,
smashing Germany's Eastern Front and pushing into Poland. They
were now approaching Auschwitz and other death camps located in
that country. To erase the evidence of mass murders at Auschwitz,
Himmler ordered the destruction of its gas chambers and the evacuation of its prisoners to other camps, putting Ravensbrück officials in a
double bind. Not only were they prevented from sending inmates to be

killed at Auschwitz, they were now flooded by Auschwitz's female prisoners.

Toward the end of January, the first of some seven thousand women, most of them Jews, arrived from Auschwitz. They joined more than twelve thousand other recent arrivals from Poland, who were neither Jewish nor political prisoners. They were women and children from Warsaw, who were forced to leave the city when German forces laid waste to it after crushing an uprising by the Polish resistance. The Germans dispatched them to Ravensbrück.

At least forty thousand women were crammed into a camp supposed to hold no more than ten thousand. Actually, SS officials had no idea of the real number because, with the collapse of Ravensbrück's bureaucracy, identification numbers were no longer being issued. Women entered the camp and died without anyone even recording their names.

13. — *Elles étaient 40.000...*

"There were 40,000 of them": Violette Lecoq's portrayal of the vast number of prisoners at Ravensbrück in 1944-45, showing a line extending far beyond the horizon.

All the blocks were so choked with prisoners that it was physically impossible to fit any more in. To house the enormous overflow, a huge rectangular canvas tent was erected on a marshy piece of land at the camp's far end. It was divided into two sections—one with dozens of four-tier bunkbeds, the other an empty space. The "floor" consisted of a thin layer of straw.

So many women were packed into the tent that within days of its assembly, there was no more space. There were a few makeshift latrines, no mattresses or blankets, and very little food or water. Virtually none of its occupants had anything warm to wear. Not surprisingly, outbreaks of dysentery and typhus soon followed.

In February 1945, a new group joined the throng—the surviving remnants of the band of Frenchwomen who'd been sent to the Königsberg punishment camp the previous November. Most of them, including Virginia d'Albert-Lake, were already half dead from malnutrition, dysentery, tuberculosis, and a multitude of other diseases.

If they had remained at Königsberg, they would already have been liberated by Russian troops. On January 30, the Red Army had been three miles from Königsberg, and their guns could be heard in the camp. Panicked, its SS guards fled, and the women prepared to welcome their liberators.

On February 1, troops did arrive, but they turned out to be SS men from Ravensbrück, dispatched to bring the women back. "It was clear that the men were in a desperate hurry," Virginia d'Albert-Lake recalled. "They acted like brutes being tracked down by hunters. They knew they were finished—but they still had us on whom to mete out their vengeance and despair." She and the other prisoners were force-marched for six days back to Ravensbrück; several died along the way.

The survivors were thrown into the tent, where the already horrendous conditions had worsened since the onset of winter. Women's bodies lay everywhere, the dead mingled with inmates still barely clinging to life. The only space Virginia and several of her friends could find was a small area next to one of the tent's walls, where they huddled together.

For almost two weeks, she lay in the filth of the tent, having contracted dysentery herself. "I saw all my friends around me growing weaker and weaker—and I knew that I was like them. . . . In the eve-ning, we curled up against a body still warm, but in the morning you could hug a corpse. The bodies were not removed until much later."

Then, on February 25, a guard shouted, "Will the American who was at Königsberg come immediately!" Virginia was taken away and her lice-infested hair shaved off. For the first time in months, she was allowed to take a shower, then was given a new set of clothes, including a warm coat. Three days later, she was summoned to the Bunker office to join Geneviève de Gaulle. If she hadn't been plucked out at that point, she almost certainly would have died.

TO DEAL WITH THE out-of-control situation at Ravensbrück, Hein-rich Himmler dispatched Johann Schwarzhuber, who had been in charge of the gas chamber at Auschwitz, to the women's camp to launch a mass killing operation. At a time when most other gas chambers had been shut down by the Reich because of the approach of Allied troops, Ravensbrück became the only concentration camp to add one in the last months of the war. It had become, officially, an extermination cen-ter.

In December 1944, the gas chamber was installed in a large con-verted storeroom next to the camp's crematorium. Specialists who'd been trained at Auschwitz were sent to implement Himmler's order, and the camp began killing inmates at a breakneck pace. Several times a day, SS guards rounded up fifty or sixty women and ferried them the short distance to its entrance. A second crematorium was added, but even that wasn't enough to dispose of all the bodies. The thick, mal-odorous smoke that poured from the twin chimneys permeated not only Geneviève de Gaulle's Bunker cell but the entire camp and its surroundings, reaching as far as the village of Fürstenberg.

When the extermination operation began, its primary targets were the old, weak, and sick, which by then comprised the majority of Ra-vensbrück's population. So many inmates had fallen seriously ill that several barracks had been transformed into additional infirmary blocks, and that's where the trucks collecting women for the gas chamber headed. Every afternoon, camp authorities would announce roll calls for selected blocks, which would then be surrounded by SS guards. The inmates who were still ambulatory stood at attention outside, while those too weak to move remained in their beds. The selections were made by Johann Schwarzhuber; Hans Pflaum, the SS supervisor of the daily labor "slave market"; and a doctor named Adolf Winkelmann. Fritz Suhren was often there as well. Once the victims had been chosen, they were loaded aboard the trucks, which disappeared to the east of the camp.

A French prisoner named Claire Davinroy recalled being assigned to a painting work detail one day near a block filled with tuberculosis patients. She and the others in her detail watched in horror as trucks roared up to the block to collect the women inside from their beds.

As she was hustled outside by Hans Pflaum, a small, dignified elderly woman looked straight at Davinroy and her co-workers. "My name is Madame Guillot," she called out, then repeated, "My name is Madame Guillot." "I assume she wanted us to know," Davinroy later said, "that on that day, Madame Guillot—a woman, not a cipher—was going to die."

In the last months of the war, Pflaum divided his time between selecting prisoners for ordinary work details and deciding who was next to die. One of the most hated and feared of all the SS men and women at Ravensbrück, he was known for his extreme brutality. Germaine Tillion called him "the unspeakable beast."

Germaine, who kept an eagle eye out for her mother, did her best to keep Émilie Tillion away from the clutches of the sadistic Pflaum and the other SS agents of death. Aware that the elderly Émilie was in great danger, Germaine persuaded her Czech friends in Ravensbrück's offices to change her age in the camp records from sixty-nine to under sixty. But there was nothing she could do to alter her mother's white hair and wrinkled face. The two were not housed in the same block, but Germaine managed to spend a considerable amount of her time with Émilie. She deputized several women in her wide circle of friends, principally Anise Girard, to be on the lookout for Pflaum and to whisk Émilie into hiding whenever there was a selection.

Hans
Pflaum

One day in February 1945, Germaine was drafted for another of her rare work stints—a much sought-after assignment to the outdoor gardening detail. Not only was the labor relatively undemanding, but the Polish inmate who served as foreman was known for her lenient treatment of the women who worked under her. The group's current assignment was to dig an outdoor air raid shelter, but as long as there were no guards around, she allowed her workers, who also included Anise Girard and twenty-year-old Béatrix Gontaut-Biron, to take it easy. "She would walk up and down above the shelter, saying from time to time, 'Work, ladies, work,'" Béatrix recalled. "But her heart wasn't really in it."

Béatrix and the others spent much of their time chatting and dozing, but as soon as the foreman spied an SS man or woman in the distance, her directive—"Work, ladies, work"—became much more emphatic, and the workers grabbed their shovels and dug with vigor. As soon as the coast was clear, the detail fell back into its usual torpor.

On this February day, the foreman caught sight of a group of SS men advancing toward several barracks located behind their digging site. *"Raus! Raus!"* shouted a voice in the distance. With new urgency, the foreman called out, "Work, ladies, work! You have to look busy, because with them, you never know."

Suddenly, the foreman's deputy, a young Polish woman named Irenka, came running toward them to announce that a selection for the gas chamber was taking place in Blocks 27, 28, and 29 and that all their occupants were being brought outside. Germaine turned pale: Her mother was in Block 27. She rushed over to Irenka and whispered in her ear. "Count on me," the young Pole said. "I know the blockova of 27." She hurried away to the chaotic scene unfolding behind them. "It lasted, I believe, thirty minutes, which seemed like thirty centuries to us," wrote Béatrix Gontaut-Biron. "Human language is insufficient to describe what we saw."

Women were screaming, moaning, and crying for help. Some were running away from the squadron of policemen and guards come to round them up. Just then, a man on a bicycle—Hans Pflaum—sped past the work detail and toward the frenzied crowd.

"Please, ladies, work!" the foreman pleaded, her voice trembling. "Otherwise he'll come here!" As her detail followed her orders, Pflaum turned his attention to one of the women trying to flee. He pursued her on his bicycle, a riding crop in his hand. When he caught up with her, he threw the bicycle aside and whipped and beat her bloody, then hurled her on the ground. "Like a ferocious beast," Béatrix remembered, "he picked her up, shook her, dragged her, hit her with his fist, threw her down again, and repeatedly kicked her." Now unrecognizable, she lay there unmoving.

Having completed his mission, Pflaum got back on his bicycle and rode away, as trucks bearing several dozen inmates headed for the gas chamber. Just then, Irenka approached the workers, with Émilie Tillion by her side. Germaine hurried to her mother and enfolded her in her arms. Once again, Émilie had cheated death.

WHILE THIS RUSH TO kill had thrown the camp into a paroxysm of fear and terror, it also served as a signal to inmates that the end of the war was fast approaching and that if they could hold on just a bit longer, they might still have a chance of survival. In these last few months, there was a deadly race at Ravensbrück, pitting the Germans' determination to destroy all evidence of their crimes against the resolution of women to stay alive and bring their would-be executioners to justice.

In this all-out battle, one of the inmates' most crucial weapons was the heightened resolve of a growing number to band together to protect and save one another—not just those who were their compatriots but also women from other countries. When a group of Frenchwomen, accused of some wrongdoing, was denied food for three consecutive Sundays, they received so much bread from others throughout Ravensbrück that they were unable to eat it all. Women of nationalities considered most in danger of being gassed were concealed by others in various hiding places that had been created around the camp, including in makeshift attics in various barracks, between the ceiling and the rafters.

But of all the rescue efforts, none was more breathtakingly audacious than the campaign in early February 1945 by inmates throughout the camp to save the lives of the young Poles who'd been crippled by medical experiments earlier in the war. More than any other group, the Polish "rabbits," living proof of one of the Nazis' most horrific scientific atrocities, were thought to have no chance of survival.

As the Red Army came closer to Ravensbrück and the camp's administration began destroying incriminating records, Dr. Karl Gebhardt sent an order, approved by Heinrich Himmler, to Fritz Suhren ordering the execution of the rabbits. It was time to get rid of the evidence of the crimes against humanity that Gebhardt, who oversaw the experiments, and his henchmen had committed.

Of the seventy-four rabbits operated on, more than sixty were still alive, although none had fully recovered from their wounds. Early in 1944, they had been moved to Block 32, joining several other groups of prisoners slated to be executed before the war's end. Besides Germaine Tillion, Anise Girard, and the other French *Nacht und Nebel* resisters, there were several hundred female soldiers belonging to the Red Army, most of them medical personnel, who were captured during Germany's 1941 invasion of Russia. As members of the Soviet military, they should

have been dealt with as prisoners of war, but Ravensbrück officials refused to do so. In fact, they treated them even more savagely than inmates of other nationalities, though they failed to break their spirits.
Throughout, the Russians remained a disciplined unit. "In the camp,
we were strong—we Soviet girls," one remembered.

The rest of the camp had been made aware of that discipline one
Sunday in the summer of 1943, when Fritz Suhren ordered all inmates
to march along the camp's parade ground singing German songs.
When the Russians appeared, marching in perfect military parade step,
they delivered a full-throated rendition of a Red Army fighting song.
"They walked into the center of the square, young faces and shaven
heads, with their heads up high," observed a Czech inmate. "Everyone
froze on the spot. They walked as if they were parading on Red Square
in Moscow, not in a Nazi concentration camp."

When the young Polish women took up residence in Block 32, they
were greeted warmly by both Russian and French contingents, but the
French formed especially close relationships with them. Indeed, Anise
Girard said after the war that several of the Poles, including Nina
Iwanska, were among her best friends at Ravensbrück. Along with
other French inmates, Anise looked out for the Polish rabbits' welfare,
including efforts to acquire additional food, warm clothing, and medical supplies for them. Above all, the French were on constant guard for
signs of a German move to eliminate them.

That sign appeared on the evening of February 4, 1945. The Poles
received an order from the camp's administration not to leave the barracks for roll call early the next morning; they were to remain inside
until further notice. That same night, Anise Girard received word from
administrative staffers that a double ration of alcohol had been ordered
for the SS guards assigned to the camp's firing squad. There was no
doubt that a large-scale execution was imminent.

"A total and unimaginable silence followed the departure of the
messenger who brought the news," recalled Wanda Wojtasik, one of
the rabbits. "Everyone in the block wept. . . . We knew we were to be
completely exterminated." In tears, several of the Poles began to prepare for their last night, brushing their hair, putting on clean clothes,

distributing their meager possessions to their French and Russian comrades, and writing letters to their loved ones. These, too, they handed to the French and Russians, with instructions to send them on to Poland if their friends survived the war.

But their fatalism was not shared by a large number of their compatriots, who were determined to fight back. They were joined in their resolve by their French and Russian barrack mates, who argued that the time had come for the collective escape of the rabbits. The congestion in the camp was so great and the atmosphere so chaotic, they said, that if the operation was planned properly, the rabbits could slip out of the block and take indefinite refuge in hiding places without being detected. From experience, the French, Russian, and Polish plotters knew that the roundup would probably take place at the morning roll call. That gave them just a few hours to prepare.

Throughout the night, they held feverish meetings to come up with a workable plan, dispatching couriers to the blockovas and leaders of other barracks to ask for their help. The inmates of several barracks had constructed crawl spaces between the ceiling and roof of their blocks. That night, they removed the wood planks covering those improvised hiding places to make them ready for their new occupants. In blocks that were raised above the ground, boltholes were prepared in the space between the ground and barracks floor. In the infirmary blocks, inmate doctors readied hiding places under the beds of patients, notably in the typhoid block, which the SS never entered.

As the night progressed, "an incredible, unheard-of thing happened," recalled Dziuba Sokulska, another of the rabbits. "The whole camp decided we were to be saved." Nina Iwanska shared that same sense of wonderment: "Everyone at Ravensbrück seemed to agree on one thing: 'The war is about to end, and there's no way we're going to let you die now.'" Dozens of inmates offered to spirit the Poles to their hiding places, while dozens more, among them several Frenchwomen, prepared to take the Poles' places in line during the roll call.

Czech administrative clerks, meanwhile, prepared to facilitate the smuggling of the Poles into work gangs by exchanging their registration numbers with those of women who had died. In order to make sure the rabbits would be provided with food, the inmate heads of blocks in which they would be hidden decided not to report future deaths within their barracks so that the rabbits could be given the dead women's rations.

By 4 A.M. on February 5, several hours before dawn, everyone was ready. The first contingent of Poles slipped out the back windows of their block, aided by other inmates, while their stand-ins—mainly Russians and French—prepared to fill the gaps in the roll call line as soon as the siren blared.

Just as it did, the inmates heard murmurs from the far end of the camp. Then a voice shouted, "They're coming for them!" In the distance, the women saw a phalanx of SS men, accompanied by dogs and led by Fritz Suhren, striding toward them. In the hands of one was a piece of paper—presumably a list of the Polish women to be rounded up. At that moment, additional SS guards moved into position on the parade ground while a green truck pulled up at its side.

Watching the death squad approach, the French and Russian women shouted, "End of call!" At that prearranged signal, thousands of prisoners broke ranks and scattered, some yelling, "We won't let you take them!" Pandemonium reigned as guards charged into the massive throng with their dogs, whips, and truncheons, trying to restore order.

It was then that the powerful floodlights illuminating the square suddenly went out, plunging the huge space into darkness. Hardly an accident, it was another key part of the escape plan drawn up the night before, carried out by Red Army members who worked as electricians in the camp and were in charge of operating the floodlights.

As screams and shouts reverberated throughout the parade ground, the rest of the rabbits took advantage of the bedlam engulfing the camp to escape from their block. Most jumped out the back windows, while others, unable to walk, were carried out by their rescuers. Before they were whisked away, they removed the badges from the front of their prison dresses that specified their nationality and identification number. They were then escorted to their assigned boltholes, with the most seriously disabled tucked away in the contagious wards of the infirmary and the blocks' crawl spaces.

When the sun finally rose that day, disorder still ruled in Ravensbrück, and it continued to do so over the next days and weeks. Each day, the same volunteers took the place of the missing rabbits during the morning roll calls, and each night, as Wanda Wojtasik remembered, "the lights always went out. It was the darkness and the infernal racket that made it impossible for them to count us or see who was missing. The Germans made an all-out effort to defeat us, holding extra head-count roll calls, closing all the camp thoroughfares so as to catch us in their net. The watchword 'They're after the rabbits' was understood by everybody, and the alarm was raised many times a day. Almost everyone took part in that fearful game of hide-and-seek."

Astonishingly, until the end of the war, the rabbits remained untraceable. "In theory, it should have been possible for the administration to order all of the prisoners out to the roll call square (presumably during the daytime to prevent electrical issues from interfering), search the assembled women and their emptied barracks, and remove the rabbits by force," wrote the historian Regina Coffey. "However, in practice, the camp was in such a state of constant confusion that an orderly inspection of the entire premises was effectively impossible."

Making the search even more difficult was the fact that large transports of inmates were leaving Ravensbrück each day en route to other camps. A number of the rabbits, after being provided with new identification numbers by inmate clerical workers, were smuggled into some of the transports just before they left.

For more than three months, the entire camp remained united in its determination to keep the rabbits safe, its inmates willing to risk their own lives to ensure their survival. No one denounced or informed on them. To save these young Poles, the women of Ravensbrück had in effect risen up in open rebellion against the Germans.

But that fierce resistance only intensified the SS's campaign to exterminate as many of them as possible. Now, in the "fearful hide-and-seek" noted by Wanda Wojtasik, every inmate at Ravensbrück was a target.

Chapter 11
....

"I Want to Look My Death in the Face"

O N MARCH 1, 1945, THE FRENCH N/N PRISONERS IN BLOCK
32 were put on the list for a transport leaving the next day for Mauthausen, a camp on the Danube River in Austria. It was the latest in a series
of convoys dispatching thousands of prisoners from Ravensbrück to
other German concentration camps to reduce its calamitous over-
crowding.

The thousand-plus women assigned to the Mauthausen transport
had no idea what to make of their destination. They knew about the
horrors of Auschwitz, but they had heard nothing about Mauthausen.
Fixated on the danger facing her mother at Ravensbrück, Germaine
Tillion, for one, was not averse to going there, thinking she might have
a better chance of protecting Émilie, and she managed to get her mother
added to the roster. Also on the list were several dozen other French
prisoners, including Jacqueline d'Alincourt.

As horrific as Ravensbrück was, Jacqueline was wary of being sent
elsewhere, recalling the half-dead condition of the Frenchwomen from
Königsberg after their forced march back to the camp. As she and the
hundreds of others scheduled to make the trip headed to the Bunker,
where they were to spend the night before leaving the following morning, she waited until the nearest guard to her was otherwise occupied

Émilie
Tillion

and slipped back to her barracks, where she, along with several other women who'd managed to escape, hid for the next twenty-four hours.

That night, Anise Girard huddled next to Émilie Tillion in a large concrete chamber in the Bunker, surrounded by others on the transport list, many of them weeping from exhaustion, hunger, and fear. As she looked around the room, Anise was not nearly as sanguine as Germaine about what awaited them at Mauthausen. Most of the women she saw belonged to groups that were already under sentence of death, including all the N/N prisoners from Western Europe. Even more ominous was the presence of hundreds of Romany women and their children. Members of the Roma, an ethnic group of traditionally itinerant people, they had long been treated as outsiders in Europe. The Nazis classified them, like the Jews, as racially inferior and enemies of the state and had set out to exterminate them.

But Anise could not share her fears with Germaine, who had just been taken away from the Bunker suffering from an infected abscess in her jaw. She'd been so ill when she arrived that a Czech friend named Anicka, working as an inmate guard, pulled strings to send her to the infirmary.

At dawn the next day, Anise, Émilie, and the other women on the Mauthausen list were ordered to line up in rows of five on the road outside the Bunker. Linking arms with Émilie, Anise set off with the others toward the main gate. Suddenly, a woman she didn't know rushed to her side, dragged her out of the line, and hustled her to a secluded space between two barracks several hundred feet away. Awaiting her was the Czech guard, Anicka, who tied a red armband around Anise's arm, signifying that she, too, was an inmate guard, and whispered to her, "Run off and hide in your barracks! They're going to gas you at Mauthausen!"

With that, Anicka disappeared, and Anise hurried toward her barracks. After just a few steps, she stopped. What about Émilie Tillion? Germaine had entrusted her to Anise's care, and she couldn't run off and abandon her. She turned back to the square where the rows of women were still proceeding to the gate. Keeping pace as she moved along the edge of the throng, she finally spotted Émilie and darted forward to grab her and pull her out of line. She ran with the older woman to the perimeter of the camp, then waited a few minutes before taking her back to Block 27, where several Frenchwomen still remained.

Later that day, after the transport had left and it was safer to move around, Anise went to the infirmary to see Germaine and explain what had happened. But she was unable to do so—Germaine was too sick to see anyone, she was told—and she had to settle for asking one of the inmate doctors to pass on the information.

As appalling as the morning had been, however, it couldn't compare to the horrific news she received that afternoon. Word spread that a roll call of everyone in the camp was to be held in a few hours—the first gas chamber selection in which all the inmates at Ravensbrück would be at risk. But the priority targets, as Anise knew, remained the sick and the elderly, which included both Germaine and her mother.

There was nothing Anise could do about Germaine at the moment, but she was determined to save Madame Tillion. Hurrying to Block 27, she took her aside and urged her to evade the roll call by hiding in the crawl space between the barrack's ceiling and roof. Looking up at the ceiling, Émilie smiled and said, "You must be joking. I'm not going up there." Distraught, Anise pleaded with her to follow her advice, saying that she and a friend could easily hoist her up. The alternative—showing up at the roll call—was unthinkable.

It was then that Émilie Tillion took charge of her life. Taking the hands of her daughter's closest friend in hers, she said gently, "My darling, I want to face my destiny. I don't want you to hide me." Years later, an emotional Anise described the moment: "She was very serene but very determined. She wouldn't listen to any of my arguments." As they talked, Anise remembered an earlier conversation with Madame Tillion. "There is one thing that would really displease me," she told Anise, "and that would be to die suddenly, without seeing myself die. I have always looked my life in the face. I want to look my death in the face." If death came calling, she was determined to meet it head-on.

Still, even though the odds were long, Anise was determined to do everything in her power to protect Émilie. As thousands of terrified women assembled in rows on the parade ground, she recruited a Frenchwoman named Sylvie to help her with her plan. Anise had heard that Dr. Adolf Winkelmann, who was in charge of making the selections, was partial to choosing women with pale, drawn faces, so she and Sylvie pinched and slapped Émilie's cheeks, as well as their own, to turn them pink. She encouraged Émilie to walk at a fast, sprightly pace and produced a head scarf to cover her white hair.

Just then the siren sounded, and a female guard shouted, *"Appel!"* ("Roll call!") *"Raus! Raus!"* The lines of women began to move, marching past the fat, bloated Winkelmann, whose face, one inmate said, was that of a "professional killer." He was surrounded by a group of Ravensbrück officials, including several other doctors and Fritz Suhren. On either side of the parade ground, SS men pointed machine guns at the women as they walked past.

When their turn came, Anise and Sylvie, both of whom were tall, placed the much shorter Émilie Tillion between them and linked arms, marching quickly toward Winkelmann. Standing ramrod straight, Anise tried to block Émilie from Winkelmann's view. But as they moved past the Germans, he separated himself from those around him, pushed through the line of women, and pointed at Émilie.

Pretending not to notice, Anise hurried on, clutching Émilie's arm. "He had hardly made this gesture," Anise remembered, "when police-women from the camp arrived and took Madame Tillion away. My heart stood still. I couldn't move. I was so stunned that, for a moment, I didn't even know where I was." All around her, women were scream-ing, crying, and pushing. She was forced to move on, unable to focus her mind on anything.

Off to the side, Madame Tillion, who had waved and smiled at her stricken friends as she was marched away, now stood in the crowd of those "marked down to die," surrounded by a large group of SS men, machine guns at the ready. Finally collecting her thoughts, Anise thought of approaching a nearby group of women who, like her, had survived the inspection and ask them to help her try to get Émilie away. But the idea was suicidal, and she knew it. Her only alternative, she thought, was to join Émilie and die in the gas chamber with her. She decided against that, too.

"Afterward," she wrote, "I said to myself that if Madame Tillion had seen me arrive voluntarily in this column, she would have been absolutely horrified. In any case, it was too well guarded; I would not have succeeded. But I didn't try it either. I was afraid. I felt like a cow-ard, all the more so because my cowardice was based on reason and logic."

Her head swimming, torn between opposing impulses, she finally decided her first priority must be to get word to Germaine about what had happened. Focused as she was on Émilie's fate, Anise didn't stop to think that the danger facing Germaine that morning was every bit as grave as that which confronted her mother.

After the mass roll call, Winkelmann, accompanied by two other doctors, would sweep through the infirmary, inspecting ward after ward and selecting many of their occupants. Alerted beforehand, the Czech guard Anicka had raced to the infirmary to protect Germaine.

Anicka knew that Margarete Buber-Neumann, a noted German journalist and writer and member of the German resistance, was recov-ering from an illness in the infirmary's ward for privileged prisoners. Buber-Neumann, known as Grete, had been at Ravensbrück since 1940 and had worked at one time as the assistant to Johanna Langefeld, then head of the camp's female SS guards, who was later dismissed for what Nazi authorities considered her lenient treatment of inmates. Of all Germaine Tillion's friends at Ravensbrück, Grete Buber-Neumann was one of her closest.

Grete was lying in her bed when a window in the ward was opened from the outside and Anicka climbed in. She told Grete that a search of the infirmary was imminent and that Germaine must be hidden as soon as possible. Grete hurriedly arranged with friendly medical personnel to bring Germaine to her ward, which contained just one other inmate. After being carried in, the barely conscious Germaine—who, weighing less than eighty pounds at that point, was as diminutive as a child—was put at the foot of Grete's bed and hidden by the same blankets that covered Grete.

When Winkelmann and the other two doctors entered the ward, Grete placed her feet atop Germaine. In his inspection of the room, Winkelmann recognized Grete and stopped at her bed. He asked her how many patients were currently there. "Only two of us," she replied. He glanced around again. Then, beckoning to his colleagues, he left.

At five o'clock that afternoon, another visitor appeared at the window in the ward. Anise Girard had just discovered where Germaine was, and she came to tell Grete the dreadful news about Madame Tillion. "Anise's face appeared at the window, frozen with horror," Grete Buber-Neumann remembered. She explained to Grete in German what had happened. Then, spying Germaine, she exclaimed, "Germaine, your mother has been taken to the gas chamber!" Germaine sprang from the bed, screaming, "My mother! My mother!" Her voice trembling decades later as she described the scene, Anise said, "That night was the worst of my entire life. I suffered terrible agonies of guilt and remorse and I could hardly bear to think of Germaine."

Although she was still very sick, Germaine devoted the next several days to contacting her many inmate friends in the camp's administration to try to track her mother down and see if there was any possibility she might still be alive. Told that condemned women were often kept in the *Jugendlager*, a small camp next to the gas chamber, for one or more days before they were killed, she searched desperately for anyone who might have seen Émilie there.

On three consecutive days, she sent letters to her mother, along with small packages containing bits of food and medicine. One of the letters read: "My darling *maman,* We hope to see you again this evening or tomorrow, after so much anxiety. . . . Take care of your health and look alert and cheerful. . . . I am better. . . . I kiss you so, so hard."

The letters were delivered to the holding camp. On March 8, Micky Poirier, the only Frenchwoman to work as a secretary in the camp offices, returned the letters and packages to Germaine, none of which had been opened. Only then could she accept the terrible truth: Her mother was dead. She never learned the exact time and date of Émilie Tillion's gassing, but it was assumed she died on the night of her selection or the following morning.

The news plunged Ravensbrück's French community into mourning. Beloved for her grace, warmth, wit, and wise counsel, Émilie had been especially popular with younger prisoners, who considered her a surrogate mother. Paulette Don Zimmet would later describe her as a "beautiful, radiant, great spirit who made such a lasting impact on our lives."

For weeks afterward, Germaine was in despair. Her grief was made worse by an agonizing sense of guilt: She had not been present where she felt she should have been—at the selection. She could have tried to protect her mother, maybe even save her, and if that failed, she could have accompanied her to the gas chamber.

The woman who had inspired her compatriots at Ravensbrück to keep their spirits up, to join forces and do everything they could to survive, now thought longingly of dying. By March 15, Germaine's physical condition had dramatically worsened. Her fever spiked to 106 degrees, and her doctor friends suspected she had developed septicemia—a poisoning of the blood from her infected jaw—that could lead to a shutdown of vital organs. There was not much they could do to combat it.

For hours, she found herself in a delirious state during which she surveyed the landscape of her life—"a panoramic view where facts and arguments moved on their own with the ease of a dream." She was ready to embrace death, she decided. It lay waiting for her, "the whole Atlantic of death, ready to rush in and engulf me if I allowed it. Like a diver, I felt immersed in it. There was a sweetness in its presence." But in the end, despite death's allure, she reluctantly turned away from it. "That night, I decided to live," she wrote, "after great deliberation and with some indifference." Her fever broke, and she began to recover.

While the murder of the most important person in her life robbed Germaine Tillion of an essential part of her being, it also sparked a tremendous rage and an obsession with collecting all the material she could on the executioners of Émilie Tillion and so many thousands of others. Her approach was no longer measured and scientific, as it had been when she first began her anthropological study of Ravensbrück. Now the mission was fueled by a desire for vengeance, to let the world know what these beasts had done and bring them to justice.

As the days passed and the killing campaign intensified, Germaine and Anise moved around the camp, avoiding Hans Pflaum and his men while feverishly collecting data, most of it coming from inmate office personnel, some from onsite inspection. "During this last period of the camp, that of methodical extermination, I kept a day-to-day diary of the most essential facts," Germaine wrote. Her explicit, detailed notes—considerably more than she had taken during her previous months in the camp—recorded, among other things, the daily numbers of deaths by gassing and other methods, the names of many of those exterminated, particularly heinous examples of the guards' brutality, and even the vast amounts of money being looted by the SS. As evidence of the mass executions, she observed that the population of the camp had declined precipitously over the previous couple of weeks.

The campwide selection for the gas chamber that claimed the life of Émilie Tillion opened the floodgates. No longer confined to barracks whose occupants were ill, selections were now made in ordinary blocks, even the blocks of privileged prisoners, at any hour of the day or night. The killing had reached its peak, and residents of nearby villages com-

30. — *Sélection pour les gaz. Rameaux 1945...*

"Selection for the gas chamber"

plained not only of the unrelenting smoke from the camp's crematoriums but of the inundation of ash in the lake bordering Ravensbrück.

In her diary throughout March, Germaine noted *"la chasse, la chasse"* ("the hunt"). Another French inmate, Dr. Loulou le Porz, referred to *"la chasse à l'homme"* ("the manhunt") in her journal. Squads of SS men roamed the camp, grabbing inmates at random. A man possessed, Hans Pflaum ran after women trying to get away, grabbing their clothes and pulling them down, then yanking them up by the scruff of their neck. "It became dangerous to be out on the Lagerstrasse," le Porz remembered. "They would appear with a lorry, and you'd be taken. We certainly went out as little as possible."

Béatrix Gontaut-Biron, who had become quite adept at eluding the SS dragnet, was more reckless, continuing to venture out occasionally with one or more of her friends. The last time she and the others did so, it almost cost them their lives. In her memoir, she noted the terrifying details of the chase:

—"Over there!" a voice howls.
—"Quick, quick!" Hanka says. "We have been seen."
—"Halt!"

—We turn right to throw them off and circle around a block. Suddenly I see the air raid shelter. We find ourselves deep in the shelter, our hearts pounding.

—"Do you think we were seen?"

—"Surely, you heard the SS men screaming?"

—"Yes, but did they see us come in here?"

—In the darkest place of the shelter, we wait without even daring to breathe. Up above us, footsteps. They're looking for us. If they find us here, we're done for.

—Hours go by. "Hush, listen!"

—Nothing. We're safe.

Although considerably more cautious than Béatrix, Jacqueline d'Alincourt found herself constantly on the run as well. On March 2, she and four friends from her barracks had hidden in its crawl space to avoid the Mauthausen transport. They were still there when the gas chamber selection took place.

When they crept down the following morning, they discovered that because of their disappearance, they were no longer on the block's roster and therefore were no longer entitled to food rations, bunk space, or medical attention. In effect, they were homeless—a calamity that greatly increased their risk of apprehension, not to mention starvation. Fortunately, the blockova took pity on them. She could not give them food, she said, but if they managed to locate rations by other means, she would look the other way and not turn them in.

Other Frenchwomen came to their aid. While some gave them part of their own rations, an inmate who worked in the kitchen clandestinely set aside a pail of soup for them each day, which others picked up and left outside their barracks. "We went to fetch it," Jacqueline recalled, "but it was not easy. A group of inmates reduced to a famished pack of dogs attacked us. The jug was knocked over, and the soup disappeared into the ground. After that, we had to have people accompany us."

Since they were no longer considered part of the camp's population,

Jacqueline and her friends were also barred from work details, which made them even more vulnerable to being captured. "Constantly on the alert," Jacqueline wrote, "each morning we thought up all sorts of strategies to escape the hunt: jumping out of the windows, hiding in the drop ceiling of the block, or under the bunk beds. Our survival depended on the speed of our reactions."

At one point, she was given precious breathing space by a Polish friend who lived in one of the barracks for privileged prisoners. Each day, for about two weeks, Jacqueline entered her friend's barracks through a window and sat quietly in a corner for one or two hours. But then one of the other occupants of the block began asking questions about why she was there. "My only recourse was to make myself scarce," she observed, "which I did, through the window, with the greatest speed possible."

In late March, another friend came to the rescue, arranging to have Jacqueline admitted to her block and to register for a regular work detail. Although very weak from illness and hunger, she became a woodcutter in the forest near the camp, the only Frenchwoman among Russian peasants with whom she could not communicate.

FOR HUNDREDS OF WOMEN at Ravensbrück, April 1, 1945—Easter Sunday—was a day of death. For some of its French inmates, though, it offered the first hint of hope of life after the war.

As many as twenty-five hundred prisoners had been gassed in the week leading up to Christianity's most important holiday. More than three hundred fifty, including some fifty Frenchwomen, were killed on Easter Sunday alone. As one truck after another left for the gas chamber on April 1, having picked up its requisite number of victims from their barracks, the terrified survivors watched from the windows of their blocks. "We could see they were clearing us out," Loulou le Porz observed. "We were isolated, forgotten by the entire world. People knew nothing about us. They didn't know where we were."

A stunning rumor making the rounds of the camp claimed other-

31. — *La voie du ciel...*

"The Path to Heaven": Inmates on their way to the gas chamber. Note the flames of the crematorium in the background.

wise. Someone insisted she saw a white truck with a red cross painted on its side in front of the camp's entrance. Most of her fellow inmates dismissed the idea, pointing out that rumors of their imminent liberation had circulated for months, and nothing had come of them but disappointment and heartache.

Then, later that day, camp authorities issued a new order: All French inmates were to line up the following morning at the camp's main gate. The same thought occupied everyone's mind: Could the rumor actually be true?

EVEN AT THAT LATE date in the war, Allied leaders remained steadfastly opposed to the idea of rescuing concentration camp prisoners. If anything, their opposition had grown even stronger. The headquarters of General Dwight D. Eisenhower's Allied Expeditionary Force

(SHAEF) issued a statement calling on prisoners of all nations "to stay put, await the arrival of Allied forces and be prepared for orderly repatriation." Until Germany surrendered, those inside the camps were on their own.

To anyone remotely aware of the reality inside the camps—and Allied authorities were among those who knew—the statement made no sense. Stay put? Orderly repatriation? Preposterous ideas, both of them. There was no time to lose: Hitler had vowed that no inmates must be found alive, and many in the Red Cross and other humanitarian agencies feared he would order the destruction of the camps within days. At Ravensbrück, a Norwegian inmate wrote to the Swedish Red Cross, "Prisoners are starving, and living skeletons are wandering around. They are bound to die in a short time, and if they don't die naturally, they are disposed of in a camp whose terror no words can describe."

Although they were fighting a steep uphill battle, Count Folke Bernadotte and the Swedish Red Cross continued to press for a full-blown rescue operation, spearheaded by a squadron of buses and military vehicles and manned by volunteers, that would drive from Sweden through German-occupied Denmark and into Germany. Bernadotte had already collected considerable information about the location of the camps and the numbers and nationalities of the prisoners in them. But he could do nothing without Heinrich Himmler's approval, and Himmler, who was operating behind Hitler's back in trying to organize a separate peace with the Allies, was wavering.

That Easter weekend, Bernadotte flew to Germany for a second meeting with Himmler, who wanted Bernadotte to act as an intermediary between him and Eisenhower and inform the Allied supreme commander of Himmler's wish to negotiate an immediate armistice on the Western front. In return, Bernadotte pressed Himmler to give his rescue operation permission to enter the camps. His primary focus, he told Himmler, was saving the Frenchwomen at Ravensbrück.

At that point, Bernadotte had no idea that another Red Cross entity, the International Red Cross (IRC) in Geneva, had already done what he had not yet been able to accomplish. The IRC had persuaded Himmler to release three hundred French prisoners at Ravensbrück in exchange for the release of three hundred German civilians held in France.

For years, the International Red Cross had shown virtually no interest in the welfare or fate of those held in Nazi camps. But now, with the war almost over and Germany clearly on the ropes, the Swiss, hoping to repair their own tarnished image resulting from their earlier cozy relationship with the Nazis, didn't want their rival neutrals, the Swedes, to get all the recognition for their campaign to save concentration camp prisoners.

So yes, as it happened, there *was* a white Red Cross truck parked outside Ravensbrück's main gate on Easter Sunday. The following morning, several buses would arrive, all of them from Switzerland.

UNAWARE THAT THE RUMOR was true, the Frenchwomen in Ravensbrück spent the night of April 1 in alternating states of excitement and fear. Was this another selection ploy, a way of getting them to assemble quietly on their way to the gas chamber? Or could this in fact be the prelude to what they'd dreamed of since arriving there?

Early the next morning, the camp's two thousand–plus French prisoners stood at attention while Hans Pflaum walked slowly along the rows, selecting inmates. As they watched one of the camp's most savage executioners make his choices, so horribly reminiscent of gas chamber selections, the women struggled to remain calm.

Pflaum initially selected about four hundred women; from that group, he picked three hundred. They were dispatched to the showers and returned in new clothes with no identifying marks on them—no triangles or registration numbers. They were then sent to Block 31. Throughout this process, not a word was said about the reason for it.

"For the rest of us, the call was over," Béatrix Gontaut-Biron recalled. "The whole thing was curious, and each of us wondered what it meant." Among those not chosen were the French N/N prisoners and a group of about fifteen inmates who came from aristocratic and noble families or were the wives or other relatives of prominent French military and government leaders. That list included Jacqueline d'Alincourt and Béatrix Gontaut-Biron and her mother.

Early the following morning, those on the list of the chosen were escorted through the camp's main gate and past the camp's administration building and the houses occupied by SS officials and guards. Looking down the road, they saw a line of white trucks, each painted with a huge red cross, half hidden in a pine grove several hundred yards away.

Grouped around the trucks were soldiers in khaki uniforms, whose sleeves sported badges with the word CANADA. They were Canadian prisoners of war who, under the agreement between the International Red Cross and Himmler, were to be freed in order to drive the trucks to Switzerland. When the Canadians saw the wraithlike figures approaching them, several of them wept. "When I saw them crying," said one of the women, "I began to think that this was real." Two days later, the women arrived in Switzerland, and on April 15, they returned to France. Among those waiting at Paris's Gare de Lyon to greet the first group of freed Ravensbrück deportees was General Charles de Gaulle.

Those who were left behind, meanwhile, struggled with conflicting emotions. "I am ashamed to confess that a pang of envy and bitterness entered my heart," Béatrix Gontaut-Biron wrote. While happy for those who'd been freed, Germaine Tillion noted what she called a "grotesque selection in reverse." For selection to the gas chambers, the SS initially chose the elderly, sick, and others who were considered useless. For those to be liberated, the SS picked the women they thought looked the healthiest and most presentable as the first ones to appear before Allied authorities, the public, and the press.

For the more than fifteen hundred Frenchwomen still at Ravensbrück, the manhunts and executions continued.

Chapter 12

Racing Death

In EARLY APRIL 1945, JACQUELINE D'ALINCOURT FELT HER LIFE
slipping away. "My beloved little Mama, I'm so afraid of dying here," she
wrote her mother, "but I believe it's going to happen. Oh, Mama, I had
hoped for so long to see you again. . . . Dear Mama, I love you so much."

To evade the gas chamber selections, Jacqueline had been working
for several weeks as a woodcutter. Racked by dysentery and burning
up with fever, she could barely stand, much less work. One afternoon
in the forest, she sank to her knees and thought, "It's over." Reaching
into her pocket, she took out a piece of paper and a pencil and began
the letter to her mother. But she was so consumed with despair she
couldn't finish it.

When she returned to the camp that evening, in a state of imminent
collapse, she encountered a French friend who worked in the infirmary.
Taking one look at her, the friend went to the infirmary and stole an
authorization allowing her to stay in her block and not report for roll
calls or her labor detail. For two weeks, Jacqueline lay motionless on
her straw pallet, as if in hibernation. Several other friends, only slightly
better off than she, worked hard to keep her alive. They talked and sang
to her, gave her water, fed her bits of their own pathetically small rations, and attempted not to fall into despair themselves.

Their liberation still seemed incredibly remote, even though they'd heard that American and Soviet troops were closing in on Berlin, just fifty miles from Ravensbrück. By the second week of April, the Americans had reached the Elbe River, seventy-seven miles west of the German capital, while the Red Army was massing on the Oder River, ready to attack Berlin from the east. On April 17, when the Russians began their massive assault, Ravensbrück's inmates could clearly hear the thunder of their artillery.

A number of other extermination and concentration camps had already been liberated, some of them more than six months earlier. The Red Army had freed inmates at Treblinka, Belzec, and Sobibor—death camps in Poland—in the summer of 1944 and had taken Auschwitz in January 1945. American troops, meanwhile, liberated the Buchenwald, Dachau, and Bergen-Belsen concentration camps in mid-April 1945. In late April, only Ravensbrück and a handful of other camps remained in Nazi hands. But despite their proximity to the women's camp, neither the Americans nor the Russians would consider the idea of sending troops to rescue or protect its inmates. General Eisenhower refused to move any of his men beyond the Elbe, and the Red Army was otherwise engaged in Berlin.

Even so, Ravensbrück authorities were readying the camp for its end. On April 14, the nearby Siemens factory was shut down, and the inmates working there were marched back to the main camp. Secretaries and SS officials built bonfires to burn documents and prisoners' files, and inmates' valuables were carted away.

The killing, however, went on unabated.

FOR COUNT FOLKE BERNADOTTE, April 21 marked his final throw of the dice. He set out on what he knew would be his last trip to Berlin, to find Heinrich Himmler once more and persuade him to authorize the release of Ravensbrück's French prisoners. He was well aware of the dangers involved in traveling to the chaotic war zone that Germany had become; during his previous trip there, his vehicle had been attacked by Allied planes, and he and his party had had to dive into a nearby ditch to escape the gunfire.

Traveling by ferry and train, Bernadotte finally located Himmler, who was holed up at a military clinic about sixty miles from Berlin. Eisenhower had already rejected Himmler's proposal for a separate peace, and Bernadotte feared the worst when he sat down to confer with the SS chief. To his amazement, however, Himmler didn't seem upset by the setback; he still believed that once Hitler was gone, the Allies would see himself as the man to deal with. Even more astonishingly, he not only agreed to Bernadotte's plan to rescue Ravensbrück's French inmates but told the Swedish official he could take all the women held there, including the Jews.

Bernadotte was shocked to realize he'd just been given permission to launch one of the largest prisoner rescues of World War II. But the time available to do so was ebbing fast: The Germans were expected to cut off access to roads leading to Ravensbrück within days, if not hours. To the Swedish Red Cross in Stockholm, Bernadotte dispatched an urgent SOS to round up as many buses and trucks as possible and put them on the road immediately. That night, dozens began the long, treacherous trip south.

LATE ON THE NIGHT of April 22, three weeks after the exodus of the first group of Frenchwomen, Ravensbrück authorities issued an order directing the remaining French inmates to assemble the following morning on the parade ground. The order, "which most of us had lost hope would ever come, burst like a bomb throughout the camp," one prisoner remembered. She and her compatriots would not learn until later that this last-minute rescue was in danger of imploding before it even began.

Early the next morning, Captain Hans Arnoldsson, the Swedish commander of the mission, appeared in Fritz Suhren's office to present him with Himmler's order authorizing the Frenchwomen's departure. To Arnoldsson's astonishment, Suhren refused to accept the order, claiming he'd just received a countermanding directive from Berlin, issued by Hitler himself, who was furious at Himmler for making the secret deal. According to the new order, Suhren declared, he was to retain all prisoners at the camp and liquidate them as Allied troops approached.

For more than an hour, Arnoldsson and Franz Göring, a Gestapo official who was serving as Himmler's emissary, engaged in a furious argument with Suhren, who refused to back down. Finally, Göring called Himmler, who ordered the Ravensbrück commandant to do as he'd been told. Suhren reminded the SS chief of his previous orders to kill the Polish rabbits and all N/N prisoners from Western Europe. Those commands were no longer valid, Himmler replied. He informed Suhren he had given permission to the Swedes to take all Ravensbrück prisoners, no matter their nationality or race. At long last, Suhren gave in.

Unaware of the behind-the-scenes Sturm und Drang, the French prisoners stood at attention on the parade ground, clutching their few belongings and still reluctant to believe that their long nightmare might actually be coming to an end. After a wait of several hours, the first identification number was called, and the woman who answered to that number approached a table where Hans Pflaum and other SS men were seated. A guard tore the ID number and triangle from the sleeve of her prison uniform. It was then that the prisoners allowed the excitement they'd tamped down to bubble to the surface. They were still in prison rags, but one by one, they were reclaiming their identities—a string of numbers no longer.

More than an hour into the lengthy process, Germaine Tillion followed Anise Girard to the table. The day before, Germaine had collected all the information about Ravensbrück that she'd secreted for more than a year in hiding places in her barracks and other spots throughout the camp—notes from the early months of her anthropological study, lengthy diary entries about the killing spree in the winter and spring of 1945, and the identities of the camp's main SS officials and guards, encoded in recipes. Before the Frenchwomen assembled that morning, she distributed the various bits of intelligence to Anise Girard, Jacqueline d'Alincourt, and several other friends to smuggle out.

Hidden in the pocket of her own prison dress was an undeveloped roll of film containing photos of the mutilated legs of several of the Polish rabbits. They'd been taken months before by other Polish prisoners, with a camera stolen from the luggage of a convoy of newcomers to Ravensbrück. The Poles had given the film roll to Germaine as another integral piece of the evidence she'd amassed of the war crimes committed by camp officials.

Both Germaine and Anise passed through the SS gauntlet without question. A few minutes later, though, a guard brought a temporary halt to the operation. Waving a sheet of paper, he shouted, "The women whose names I am going to call must step out of the ranks." He read out fifteen names, among them those of Jacqueline d'Alincourt and Béatrix Gontaut-Biron and her mother. It was the same group of inmates with aristocratic names or close relationships with prominent French leaders who had been rejected during the selection of the first French convoy in early April.

Stunned, Jacqueline, who was barely able to walk, left the line with the others as the long column of their compatriots resumed its march to the SS table, then filed out the main gate. On the other side of the gate, tall, fair-haired men wearing grayish-green uniforms approached them. Thinking they were Germans, a few of the first women they encountered pushed them away in terror. "It took me a moment to realize," said one, "that the blue-and-yellow emblem on the soldiers' shoulders and caps was the Swedish flag." Another woman recalled, "They kept asking us if we were nervous or afraid of the long, dangerous journey ahead. They had no way of knowing that for years we had faced death every moment of every day."

Amid the ecstasy of her compatriots, Anise Girard was growing more and more concerned: She didn't see Jacqueline d'Alincourt anywhere. When she questioned some of those who had been behind her and Germaine in line, she learned that Jacqueline and the others had been ejected from the column. Before boarding a bus, she took aside a young Swedish officer who seemed to be one of the leaders of the rescue, told him what had happened, and made him promise to track down her missing friends.

———

AS THE CONVOY CARRYING their comrades pulled away from Ravensbrück, the women who'd been left behind had recovered from their
initial shock and were now enraged. Guessing rightly that they were
being held as hostages, they gathered to decide how to fight back. Their
first step was to send a three-woman delegation, one of whom was Jacqueline, to the office of Dorothea Binz, the head of the SS female
guards, to demand an explanation.

Binz, Jacqueline recalled, "was stupefied by our audacity. How dare
we try to speak to her? 'We are keeping you as hostages,' she told us.
'You will be executed if we have any problems with you.'" Binz walked
away, then paused. Turning back to the women, she said their lives
would be spared if they all signed a declaration certifying they had
been well treated at Ravensbrück. No, the women exclaimed. That was
out of the question! Her face crimson with fury, Binz threw them out of
her office.

The delegation next paid a call on Suhren, who tried to spin their
continued detention as a favor to them. He assured them they would be
released eventually but that it would come in the form of an exchange
with captured German officers. They were of a higher status than the
other Frenchwomen who'd been freed, he said, adding that when they
were finally released, they would travel in private cars rather than
buses. As he talked, it became increasingly clear that Suhren was taking
a page from Himmler's playbook, hoping to use these women, all with
illustrious family names, as possible bargaining chips for himself with
the Allies.

Meanwhile, the Swedish officer who'd been approached by Anise
remained behind at Ravensbrück that night to prepare for the next convoy of buses due to arrive the following morning. Given a room in one
of the houses assigned to SS guards, he awoke in the morning to find a
sheet of paper slipped under his door. It was a list of the names of the
Frenchwomen who'd been pulled at the last minute from the earlier
convoy, as well as those of several British prisoners whom Suhren was
also trying to hide.

The officer immediately took the list, whose source was never identified, to Suhren. Thrusting the paper in the commandant's face, he
declared, "I know these women are here! I demand that you produce
them!" Suhren replied he didn't know what the Swede was talking
about. Summoning Hans Pflaum, Suhren gave him the list and ordered
him to investigate. An hour or so later, Pflaum returned and announced
that the women were no longer there. They had disappeared from the
camp's roster, most likely sent in a convoy to another camp—an event
that, due to Ravensbrück's bureaucratic chaos, apparently had never
been entered in the records. The Swedish officer rejected Pflaum's explanation. According to Jacqueline, he "got nasty, threatened Suhren
and Pflaum, and in the end was able to wrench us into freedom."

That afternoon, the Frenchwomen on the list lined up for the third
time on the camp's parade ground to undergo processing. A new transport had been announced earlier in the day, and for the next several
hours, hundreds of other inmates had assembled in the square and then
disappeared through the gate.

Without a word, Hans Pflaum and another SS officer approached
the Frenchwomen and led them through the main gate. In agonized
silence, they followed the two men down the road bordering the nearby
lake. A few minutes later, they came to a fork. To the left was the gas
chamber; to the right, a large, joyful throng of women milling about in
the countryside several hundred yards away. The column paused for a
moment. Then the second SS officer pointed to the right. "You are
free," he said.

In a daze, the French hostages headed slowly toward the crowd of
women, most of them Belgian and Dutch, who were waiting for the
next convoy of rescue vehicles to appear. "To walk in the country for
the first time in three years without guards seemed to us unreal," wrote
an inmate named Maisie Renault. "The other women were sitting on
the grass, singing and laughing. It was a holiday atmosphere, as if we
all were taking part in an immensely enjoyable picnic."

Quietly sitting off to the side were two women no one recognized.
The younger of the two was emaciated and clearly very ill—"a half-

dead stick doll of a woman," someone later described her—while her older companion was trying to make her as comfortable as possible.

They were Jeannie Rousseau, the ringleader of the strike at Torgau, and her closest friend, Germaine de Renty, who, along with Virginia d'Albert-Lake, were among the handful of survivors of the Königsberg punishment camp. The two had been imprisoned in the Bunker since November 1944, after they'd escaped from Königsberg in a truck filled with dead and dying women and had been caught by the SS trying to hide in Ravensbrück. After undergoing several days of interrogation, accompanied by beatings, Jeannie and Germaine had been shut away in a cell in the Bunker, where they were given half rations and forced to clean latrines throughout the building, as well as engage, as Jeannie put it, in "other terrible work."

Already sick from tuberculosis when she arrived there, Jeannie was rapidly wasting away. Her only nurse was Germaine, who had been at her side since their arrival at Ravensbrück in August 1944. "I owe her my life," Jeannie would later declare. "With no medication, she somehow kept me from dying. She was always there, comforting me. Too young to be my mother, she was my vigilant, loving, beloved elder sister."

In mid-April 1945, the two women received word of the Red Cross convoys and their rescue of French prisoners. But, sequestered in the Bunker as they were, it appeared that neither their compatriots in the camp nor the Swedish Red Cross mission were aware of their presence there. One of Jeannie's lungs had collapsed, and she knew that if she had any chance of survival, she had to leave now.

So on April 23, when she heard from a female guard in the Bunker that another convoy was on its way, she summoned up all her remaining strength and unleashed a storm of invective at the guard. "I decided I must intimidate her," she later told an American journalist. "I knew it was my only chance. So I said to her, 'You will be in terrible trouble after the war ends. They know I'm here. They will come after you and find you, and punish you!' " The ferocity of her verbal assault had its desired effect: Both women were allowed to leave.

Early that evening, a shout rang out—"There they are!"—and hundreds of women, abandoning their bags and parcels, rushed toward the road, crying, screaming, and cheering, as a line of white trucks flying the Red Cross flag appeared around a bend in the road. Captain Hans Arnoldsson led the convoy. He climbed out of the first truck and raised his hand to ask for quiet as the women swarmed around him. Noting that it would be dark soon, he said it was too dangerous for the trucks to travel at night and that it might be better for the women to go back to the camp and spend one last night there.

He was interrupted by a loud, passionate storm of protest. They'd rather die than return to the camp, the women shouted. Couldn't the trucks drive a few miles farther into the countryside and let them sleep there? "You won't be very comfortable," Arnoldsson warned— a statement that elicited gales of laughter. After the hell they'd been through, the women told him, sleeping outdoors would seem like paradise. Capitulating, Arnoldsson and the drivers began helping the women into the trucks.

As the vehicles headed away from Ravensbrück, their occupants were awash in emotion. "Is it joy? Is it sadness? Is it both?" Béatrix Gontaut-Biron wondered. "Some of us laugh; others cry. I was in tears as I looked back at the tall gray chimney of the crematorium, thinking of all my friends and comrades—my sisters—who had not made it out with us."

A few minutes later, the trucks stopped for the night in a forest, where an improvised camp was set up. "I couldn't sleep or speak," Jacqueline d'Alincourt remembered. "I walked alone in the woods, taking in deep breaths of fresh air, far from the pestilence of the camp, from the flames of the crematorium." Looking up at the stars twinkling through the branches of the trees, she couldn't imagine a more beautiful night.

INITIALLY INTENDED TO RESCUE only Scandinavian prisoners from Nazi concentration camps, the Swedish Red Cross mission, under the command of Count Folke Bernadotte, ended up saving almost sixteen thousand prisoners from more than a dozen countries. The operation was launched on March 9, 1945, when Bernadotte persuaded Himmler to allow some eight thousand Norwegian and Danish male prisoners to be brought to the Neuengamme concentration camp for future rescue, which took place over the next several weeks.

The second-largest group to be saved consisted of more than six thousand women, many of them Jews, from Ravensbrück. A little more than fifteen hundred of that number were French. The Ravensbrück mission ended on April 28, five days after the group that included Jacqueline d'Alincourt was whisked to safety. The roads to the camp had indeed been closed shortly after that convoy's departure, but the Swedes managed to locate and commandeer a fifty-car freight train, which departed on April 25, taking another three thousand–plus Ravensbrück inmates to freedom.

THAT SAME DAY, THE first Swedish Red Cross convoys from Ravensbrück began arriving at the small Danish town of Padborg, on the border between Germany and Denmark. In her memoir, Béatrix Gontaut-Biron recalled the euphoria she and her compatriots felt when crossing the border:

—"So we've really left Germany?" we ask our driver in disbelief.
—"Yes."
—"So we have left hell," we say. "No more prison! No more beatings! No more terror!"
—I am afraid to dream. "Pinch me," I say, and the others cry with joy. We have left Germany.

In Padborg, Germaine Tillion remembered, the women were taken to a hospital, where they spent the night in "clean beds with crisp white sheets and blankets" and were given their first substantial nourishment—a thick white soup whose ingredients included milk and a little sugar. To Germaine, "it was pure happiness to drink something hot in which there was a little milk!"

Early the next morning, the women in Germaine's convoy were taken to the Padborg railway station. Denmark at that point was still under German occupation, but the Third Reich's hold on the country was extremely tenuous, as was evident in the extraordinary reception awaiting the Frenchwomen at the station. Word had spread quickly through the town that they had arrived, and the platform was packed with what seemed like the entire population of Padborg, bearing flowers, sweets, cakes, perfumes, and soap as gifts for "the poor wretches that we were—skeletons dressed in rags," Germaine remembered. "The welcome was indescribable."

After the women boarded their train, it remained in the station for several hours. Most of those in the crowd stayed, too, continuing to celebrate the women's release until the train pulled out. As she sat by the window, Germaine gazed out at another train headed in the opposite direction, which was stopped on a platform about twenty feet from theirs. It was filled with a German regiment, apparently traveling back to Germany to fight in the war's last gasp there. She locked eyes with an SS officer on the train, his face pale with rage as he stared at her. "He was helpless to do anything about us," she observed. "In his fury, I saw his defeat and our victory. It was the most beautiful gift I have ever received."

As the women's train crossed Denmark, its passengers saw people gathered at several of the stations through which it passed, held back by German soldiers guarding the platforms but pressing forward as far as possible, cheering and waving at the women as their train flashed by. The convoys' Danish journey ended in Copenhagen, where the Frenchwomen in their care boarded a ferry to Malmö, a bustling port city in the far south of Sweden.

Once they boarded the ferry, all vestiges of German control were gone. The ferry's crew served the women the first real meal they had eaten since arriving at Ravensbrück, doing it "with so much respect and courtesy that we were in awe," Jacqueline d'Alincourt wrote.

She sat on the deck with several of her friends, savoring the beauty around her—the sea sparkling in the sunlight, the splash of the waves, even the seagulls following in the ferry's wake. She and her companions began throwing crumbs of bread at the gulls. "There was as much as they wanted, as much as we wanted," she marveled. "How was that possible? We were coming from a world where one crumb of bread meant everything."

For Jacqueline d'Alincourt, it finally hit home. She had survived hell, and a new life was beginning.

AT ABOUT THE SAME time that the Frenchwomen arrived in Sweden, Ravensbrück authorities began their evacuation of the camp. Most of the ten thousand–plus inmates still there were organized into columns and forced to march northward. When the Red Army finally liberated Ravensbrück on April 30, more than two thousand women were found there, most of them barely clinging to life.

The forced march was an exercise in misery and chaos. Hundreds of women collapsed and died on the road, while hundreds more escaped, hoping to be rescued by approaching Allied troops. Also fleeing were many if not most of the SS men assigned to guard them.

As the inmates were marched out of the camp, they saw Fritz Suhren and Dorothea Binz, their eyes red-rimmed and their faces covered with soot, throwing pile after pile of documents on an enormous bonfire in front of the camp's administration building. Shortly afterward, Suhren was on the run, too. He had lost the women he had planned to use as his bargaining chips with the Allies, but there was one hostage left—an SOE agent known as Odette Churchill, who had been captured in France while working as a courier for a French sabotage network. Odette, whose real surname was Sansom, had become the lover of the SOE operative Peter Churchill, the network's head. Initially, the two had been based in Cannes, but when their network there was penetrated by the Gestapo, they moved to the Annecy area of Haute-Savoie, in the French Alps.

Both of them were arrested in April 1943, and Odette was sent to

Ravensbrück, where she claimed that she was married to Churchill and that he was Winston Churchill's nephew. Although neither assertion was true, Fritz Suhren accepted their veracity, in the belief that he had added another potentially valuable hostage to his list.

Like Geneviève de Gaulle, Odette Churchill was kept in solitary confinement in the Bunker. On April 30, 1945, Suhren came to her cell, telling her to gather her things and be prepared to leave the following morning. She was taken in a van to a Ravensbrück subcamp at Malchow, about fifty miles northwest of Ravensbrück, which had been designated by Himmler as a last-ditch SS stronghold.

By the time Suhren reached Malchow on May 2, the stronghold, such as it was, had disintegrated and the Red Army was just a few miles away. Suhren ordered Odette into his black Mercedes and set off with her in search of American troops, with whom he hoped to cut a deal.

When they finally encountered a U.S. infantry regiment, Suhren got out of his car and said in broken English to the soldier who confronted him, "I have with me Frau Churchill. She is related to Winston Churchill, the prime minister of England." At that point, Odette stepped out of the car and said, "And this is Fritz Suhren, the commandant of the Ravensbrück concentration camp. Please take him as your prisoner."

Chapter 13

Homecoming

INSIDE PARIS'S GARE DU NORD, THE MOOD WAS ELECTRIC. A LARGE crowd had gathered in the railway station's cavernous central hall, with its iron pillars and towering glass roof, to welcome back the first prisoners liberated from Ravensbrück. Presiding over the occasion was General Charles de Gaulle himself.

The date was April 15, 1945. The war in Europe was not yet over—it would last another three weeks—but the arrival of this first transport of French concentration camp survivors was a welcome sign that victory was indeed on its way.

At 11 A.M., a train pulled into the station and huffed to a stop. The excited murmurs of the onlookers, many carrying bouquets of lilacs and other spring flowers, crescendoed as they scanned the train's windows, searching for loved ones. Abruptly, the clamor died away, replaced by a shocked silence. Staring back from the train were faces that all looked the same, wrote the *New Yorker* correspondent Janet Flanner: "Faces that were gray-green, with reddish-brown circles around their eyes, which seemed to see but not to take in."

These were the three hundred women, judged by the SS to be the healthiest and most presentable inmates, who were released from Ravensbrück in early April. Eleven of them had died en route to Paris. A young American diplomat who had joined a group of officials meeting the women at the French border described them as "a convoy of martyrs, frightfully mutilated, skeleton-like." The sight of them, he said, "was a terrifying spectacle."

A stunned Charles de Gaulle shook hands with a woman leaning from a train window. But as she did so, she spied another man standing near the French president. She pulled her hand from de Gaulle's grasp and, pointing at the man, screamed, *"C'est lui!"* It was her husband. He had no idea who she was.

After the women were helped off the train, the throng circulated among them in a fevered search for mothers, daughters, sisters, wives. "There was almost no joy," Flanner noted. "The emotion was nearer to pain. Too much suffering lay behind this homecoming, and it showed in the women's faces and bodies."

She observed the reunion of a smartly dressed man with his sister who before the war had been an elegant society matron and now was a "bent, dazed, shabby old woman." When he asked her where her luggage was, she silently handed him "what looked like a dirty black sweater fastened with safety pins around whatever small belongings were rolled inside."

Until that April morning, virtually no one in France had any inkling of the atrocities endured by their compatriots who had been deported to German concentration camps. "No one had thought they would return in this state," Geneviève de Gaulle observed. "People imagined they would return like prisoners of war." Although the provisional government had been receiving reports about the camps' horrors for several months, it had suppressed the information for fear the news would spark panic on the part of the deportees' families.

Months earlier, the government had set up a new department—the Ministry for Prisoners, Deportees, and Refugees—to organize and oversee their homecoming. Having expected a slower, less tumultuous return, it was totally unprepared for the mass evacuation of the camps that began in April and the tens of thousands of survivors who would swiftly follow this first transport, most of them in terrible health, many on the brink of death. One French newspaper "has had the disagreeable courage to say what thousands of prisoners' families know is the truth: the ministry functions, as it has functioned from the start, with inefficiency and confusion," Flanner reported.

Throughout the months to come, there was a flood of complaints about official neglect of deportees arriving in Paris, with no one at the train stations to greet them, to arrange transport to hospitals or their homes, or to help them begin the complicated bureaucratic process of repatriation. Families, left in the dark about the whereabouts of their relatives, swarmed the stately Hotel Lutetia, which had been designated as the reception center for returning camp inmates. Inside the hotel, hundreds of photographs and lists of missing prisoners were tacked onto panels in the lobby and halls. Dazed former inmates reporting to the Lutetia were besieged at its entrance by an onslaught of anguished family members, begging the newcomers to look at the photos they were holding and see if they could recognize the faces of those in the images.

"The hubbub overwhelms us, and we have the impression of having landed on an unknown planet," said one Ravensbrück survivor about her arrival in Paris. "We have only one thing in mind: to get news of our family and our home. But we are drawn into a tunnel that we have to follow to the end."

THAT FIRST GROUP OF women to be freed from Ravensbrück was brought directly to France by the Swiss Red Cross. The thousands of women liberated from the camp later in April by the Swedish Red Cross, including Germaine Tillion, Anise Girard, and Jacqueline d'Alincourt, were allowed to begin their recovery in the peace and tranquility of Sweden. According to Germaine, her two-plus months there were like being in an airlock—a compartment between two environments with different air pressures, allowing a person to decompress from the first before entering the other.

When the women first arrived at the port of Malmö, they underwent rigorous physical examinations and then were quarantined for two weeks, to guard against the spread of typhus and other infectious diseases they might have brought in with them. But unlike the quarantine they'd endured at Ravensbrück, this was largely a joyful experience.

For the first several days, they were housed in the city's Museum of Natural History, where they were given mats with paper sheets and woolen blankets and assigned sleeping spaces in various galleries. Anise Girard remembered bedding down between the legs of a giant mounted giraffe. After being supplied with combs, mirrors, soap, and other toiletries, the women were taken to a huge dressing room, "a veritable Ali Baba's cave, filled with new clothing of all sorts, to choose a dress and coat according to our fancy," one woman recalled. "We shed our convicts' outfits and became human beings again!"

They completed their quarantine at a school in the center of Malmö. On May 8, hearing a cacophony of shouts and cheers outside, they rushed to the window and saw a large crowd of Malmö residents along the fence surrounding the school. They had gathered there to let the former prisoners know that the war in Europe was officially over. Prohibited from leaving the school, the women joined the celebration by opening all the windows and serenading the crowd with a rousing rendition of "La Marseillaise."

Once they were released from quarantine, they were dispersed to rest homes and hospitals throughout Sweden for several more weeks of rest and treatment, beginning the long process of restoring their bodies and psyches before returning to France. Germaine and Anise were among three hundred women dispatched to the city of Gothenburg, a major seaport on Sweden's west coast.

Still struggling with grief and guilt over her mother's death, Germaine spent most of her time there pursuing her mission to bear witness to the truth of what had happened in Ravensbrück. She was particularly obsessed with documenting the fates of individual inmates, like the dignified elderly woman who'd repeatedly shouted to Germaine's friend, Claire Davinroy, on her way to the gas chamber, "My name is Madame Guillot!" "It was an absolute duty for me to try to find all these names, all these dates," Germaine would later write, "so that

Madame Guillot and the many other women like her would not be en-gulfed in silence and oblivion."

In Gothenburg, she conducted extensive interviews with virtually all her compatriots there, questioning them about various details of their time at Ravensbrück, including the dates of their arrival, their identification numbers, and the names and approximate numbers of the other women in their convoys. "Thanks to them, even before my repa-triation to Paris, I was able to reconstitute an almost complete list of the train convoys leaving France for Ravensbrück, along with the names and numbers of the transported victims," she observed. "I also found out the names of the factories and other labor camps where some of them were later shipped. Above all, I began compiling a list of the dead, with the names of witnesses who saw them die."

BY MIDSUMMER 1945, MOST of the Ravensbrück deportees in Sweden had returned to France. That, of course, had been their dream since being pitchforked into the hell of the camp. Still, for many, the prospect of being separated from their campmates—the women whose friend-ship had helped them survive, who had shared their experiences and understood their horrors in a way no one else possibly could—was another trauma with which they were forced to cope.

Irrevocably changed, they now had to go back, separately, to a world whose ways they had forgotten. Each of them hoped that the idealistic vision of home to which they had clung in the camp— "a world where we would be respected by all, well treated, loved, and understood," as one of them said—would turn out to be the case. For many, if not most, it wasn't.

But there was one notable exception: Jacqueline d'Alincourt, who was one of the last of the Ravensbrück women to leave Sweden. Al-though greatly debilitated when she arrived there, she made a surpris-ingly speedy recovery. "The older women had the most difficult time," she later said. "Those of us who were in our twenties, as long as we didn't have a serious disease, recovered quite quickly."

Instead of going home, Jacqueline decided to stay on to help with the repatriation of the rest of her compatriots. Appointed the head of social services for an official French government mission organizing the women's return, Jacqueline traveled throughout Sweden to the various hospitals and rest camps where they had been sent. She checked on their living conditions and whether their needs were being met. She also made sure they were getting mail from home, and when it was time for them to leave, she arranged their departures, including accompanying them to train stations and airports. "Life is interesting [and] full of surprises," she wrote Claire Chevrillon, her close friend and former Resistance colleague. "But then when you are just out of Ravensbrück, everything seems like a fairy tale. My dear, we think we are living in a dream!"

Jacqueline finally left Sweden in early August, embarking on a weeklong road trip with Swedish friends through Denmark, Germany, the Netherlands, and Belgium. She arrived in Paris late on the night of August 15. No members of her family lived there, and she was unsure where to go. Taking a chance, she asked her traveling companions to drop her off at the apartment of Claire Chevrillon's parents on boulevard Saint-Germain. She doubted they would be there. It was, after all, August—the month when many Parisians decamped from the city for vacations in the country or at the seaside. When she rang the bell, it was Claire who opened the door. The two fell into each other's arms.

The following evening, Jacqueline took an overnight train north, heading for her family's country estate in northeastern France. Early the next morning, she was met by her sister Ghislaine in the bustling city of Niort, and the two boarded the local train that would take them to their ancestral village. As the train chugged along, Jacqueline remembered the agonizing last time she'd been home almost two years before—to see her family once more before she was arrested. She recalled how her mother had cried when she said goodbye at the little station on the edge of her family's property, and how her little sister Monique had insisted on one more kiss before letting Jacqueline go.

Now, just a few miles from the village, the train circled the woods where, as a child, Jacqueline had played with her brothers and sisters.

A couple of minutes more, and the station on the estate, looking like a toy in the midst of the fields surrounding it, popped up on the horizon. Jacqueline assumed the train would pass the station and proceed to the one in the village. Instead it slowed down. "What's happening?" she asked Ghislaine, who smiled without replying. When the train came to a stop with a loud screech and Jacqueline looked out the window, she got her answer.

Hundreds of people were massed outside, waiting for her. As she and Ghislaine left the train, one of their brothers and a childhood friend rushed forward, lifted her off the ground, and carried her toward the enormous crowd, comprising the populations of two neighboring villages. She later discovered that when her telegram announcing her return had arrived from Paris the previous day, the constable of the closest village to her family's house had spread the word to everyone there, as well as to the residents of a village nearby. "I disappeared under an avalanche of flowers presented to me with great ceremony by all the associations," she recalled. "I had to shake hundreds of hands and kiss hundreds of cheeks streaming with tears, since everyone was crying (here, we always cry, whether it's a funeral or a wedding)."

She burst into tears herself when she was greeted by her beloved maternal grandfather, whom she had been sure she would never see again. Her mother was not there; she was taking care of one of Jacqueline's sisters, who had just had a baby. But her other siblings accompanied her as she, arm in arm with her grandfather, led a lengthy procession down the road to her family's ancestral village, whose houses were all decked out with flags. Church bells rang out as she laid the flowers she had been given at the foot of the stately stone war memorial in the village square. Standing next to her was her little sister Monique, now a teenager, whose smiling face she had constantly brought to mind during her worst moments at Ravensbrück. Jacqueline was the only member of her immediate family to suffer retribution at the hands of the Germans; in her extended family, there was one other casualty—an uncle—who had died in a German concentration camp.

She, her grandfather, and her siblings, along with the villages' dignitaries and a number of other invited guests, continued on to the Rochebrochard family estate, where a giant cross of Lorraine, the symbol of Charles de Gaulle's Free French, had been outlined in flowers in the manor's courtyard. The celebration continued with a champagne toast to her safe return. Jacqueline d'Alincourt's homecoming could hardly have been more idyllic. "I felt I was soaring on a cloud," she later wrote. Most of her friends from Ravensbrück, however, had diametrically opposite experiences.

GERMAINE TILLION HAD RETURNED to France in early July, aboard a military transport plane carrying dozens of Ravensbrück survivors, some of them still in fragile health, who were cared for by a Swedish nurse during the flight. Soon after takeoff, the nurse announced that they were now flying over Germany. While several of the women rushed to the plane's small portholes to look out, Germaine lay on a stretcher, a handkerchief over her eyes. When the nurse asked her if she was all right, Germaine waved her away. "She was leaving her mother there," said Maisie Renault, a friend and fellow survivor. "She was upset, and I think she wanted to hide her tears."

At Ravensbrück, Germaine often dreamed of the first thing she would do if and when she returned to Paris: go to a café with her mother and order a glass of milk and a boiled egg. But her mother was dead, and so was her maternal grandmother, who had lived with Germaine and Émilie Tillion in the family house in Saint-Maur-des-Fossés and died six months before Germaine's return. No loved ones were there to greet her when she returned; her only other close relative—her sister, Françoise—was still trapped in Japanese-occupied Indochina with her family.

Germaine was met at the airport by Jacques Lecompte-Boine, a friend who had worked with her in the Museum of Man network and who later formed a major Resistance intelligence group of his own. When he took her to her house in Saint-Maur, she found it a wreck. The water pipes had burst the previous winter, and when they thawed in the spring of 1945, the house was flooded and the furnishings ruined.

Before they left, the Germans had looted all the family's valuables, including her father's priceless collection of antique musical instruments.
Germaine was overwhelmed for a time by how much she had lost in
the war: loved ones, her house, and the fruits of eight years of work
that represented "the most creative part of my life"—her study of the
Chaouia tribes in the mountains of Algeria.

For a year and a half, Germaine had urged her fellow inmates at
Ravensbrück to band together and do everything they could to survive. Continuing to live, she repeatedly said, would be their ultimate
act of resistance against the Germans. Against all odds, she and many
others had succeeded in doing so.

But now that they had cheated death, what else was there? The extraordinary energy and determination that had fueled their battle to
live was depleted, and Germaine Tillion, like so many others, was on
the brink of total collapse. "Liberation was a terrible thing," she would
later write. With the threat gone, "the vital springs of our being were
broken."

"For me, it was a nightmare," she added. "There was no joy . . . at
least in my case, there was none. For months after our liberation, I was
in extreme darkness." For a time, she was so crushed by despair that
she could barely move. On the rare occasions that she went out, she
was exhausted after taking just a few steps. "I remember that when I
walked to the Métro station, I sometimes had to sit on the pavement for
a few minutes because I couldn't go any farther."

But despite the darkness, she kept working. In addition to her investigation of Ravensbrück, she became deeply involved in another act of
remembrance—the documentation of the activities and achievements
of her colleagues in the Museum of Man network. After the war, each
Resistance network and movement was required by the government to
produce detailed records of its members and the work they had done to
defy the Germans. The information was then used to determine their
eligibility for government recognition and financial aid, including pensions. An "administrative liquidator," usually a leader of the group,
was appointed to oversee the lengthy process.

Jacques Lecompte-Boine, who was named the liquidator for his network, offered to perform the same function for the Museum of Man group. Germaine politely but firmly turned him down. As the only leader of her network still living, she said, it was her responsibility to do so. No one else knew her comrades' history and the scope of their achievements as intimately as she.

It's interesting to note that until Germaine came back from Ravensbrück, she had never heard the term "network." Nor was she familiar with the term "resistance" as the generic name for anti-Nazi activities in France. During the early and middle years of the war, no one had yet come up with such descriptive labels. Indeed, her own group had no official name during the two years of its existence. In her final report to the government, she was the one who christened it the Museum of Man network.

After weeks of working on the dossiers of the group's leaders and agents, Germaine submitted her report to the government, which granted official recognition to the network. But the effort took a significant mental and physical toll. Focusing on the lives and deaths of its members, many of whom had been friends of hers, "caused me terrible pain," she said, "so terrible that I could never bring myself to do what I wanted to do—write a definitive history of the network."

LIKE MANY DEPORTEES, ANISE Girard returned to a family steeped in sadness. Few of the Ravensbrück women had had the good fortune of Jacqueline d'Alincourt, whose loved ones had largely escaped the horrors of war. A sizable number of them had come home to discover that their husbands, sons, and other relatives had been killed in battle, been executed by the Nazis, or died in concentration camps.

As it happened, Anise's greatest worry during the war—that her father would not survive German detention—proved to be unfounded. He returned from Dora, a subcamp of Buchenwald, whose inmates were forced to dig underground tunnels and build subterranean factories under exceptionally brutal conditions. François, one of Anise's younger brothers, had joined the Resistance after the arrest of his sister and father. He, too, was captured by the Gestapo and sent to Buchen-wald but managed to survive.

But another of her siblings did not. Shortly after she arrived in Swe-den, Anise discovered that her twenty-four-year-old sister, Claire, had been shot by the Germans on August 27, two days after the Allies liber-ated Paris.

Unlike her father, mother, and siblings, Claire Girard had not been heavily involved with the Resistance. Raised to be independent and think for herself, she followed a very different path in life than her other family members. She loved living in the country, and as a little girl, she decided she wanted to become a farmer. In the fall of 1939, she enrolled in France's National School of Agriculture in Rennes, the only woman in her class. After graduating, she received on-the-job training on three farms in different regions of France.

At the age of twenty-two, Claire was hired by a large cooperative in Paris to manage a hundred-acre farm near the village of Welles-Perennes in the Oise, a verdant area about twenty-five miles north of Paris. Initially doubtful about her youth and gender, villagers and workers on her farm were gradually won over by her passion and agri-cultural skills.

Her first brush with the Resistance came in February 1944, when an American fighter plane crash-landed in a nearby field and its pilot was hidden on a neighboring farm. Claire, who had studied for a year in Britain, spoke good English, and several villagers with ties to the Resis-tance asked for her help in communicating with him. She did so, visit-ing him several times, providing him with civilian clothes, and acting as the liaison between him and members of the escape line that eventu-ally smuggled him out of the area. Although Claire apparently never joined a Resistance group herself, she continued to help Resistance members in the region who, on several other occasions, sheltered peo-ple on the run from the Germans.

In late August 1944, when the liberation of Paris was imminent, she traveled to Paris to be with her family and friends. After celebrating the march of Allied troops into Paris on August 25, she was anxious to return to her farm and accepted a ride two days later from two members of the French Forces of the Interior (FFI), former Resistance fighters now under the command of Charles de Gaulle and the Free French. After they escorted her home, she had promised to give them several kilos of potatoes and other vegetables to distribute to nearby maquis groups.

As their car neared the farm, it suddenly came upon a German roadblock on a bridge spanning the Oise River. The Germans manning it pulled Claire and her companions from the car and took them to a farm, where they staged a kangaroo trial, charging the three with terrorism and sentencing them to death. They were dragged to the edge of a nearby wood, and as the Germans raised their machine guns, Claire and the FFI men ran. She and one of the men were cut down. The other escaped.

When Anise returned home in July 1945, the pall of Claire's senseless death still enveloped her once voluble, lively family. "When we met, it was difficult for any of us to speak," she remembered. "My father never talked about what he had been through. And we never discussed any of this with my mother. Why make it worse?

"The only person I communicated with was my brother," she added. "Neither of us could sleep during the first months of our return, so we talked at night, with the feeling that we were speaking the same language."

During the first years of the war, Anise's mother, Germaine, had been a member of the Comet Line, hiding Allied airmen in her home until couriers from the escape line could smuggle them out of Paris and across France to neutral Spain. After her husband and Anise were captured by the Gestapo, Germaine gave up that activity. Claire Chevrillon, Jacqueline d'Alincourt's friend, then recruited her to work as a coder for messages sent by the Free French headquarters in Paris to London.

"She needed a distraction from her agonizing worry about her husband and daughter," Claire wrote. "Though she was obviously older than I, there was something girlish about her laugh, which rang out at the least provocation, and something very touching about her efforts to participate in our strange, brain-twisting work in which a mistake of one letter could render a message unintelligible." But Claire could see that Germaine's mind was elsewhere, which led to mistakes that "slowed us down. She decided not to stay on, but our friendship continued long afterward."

For much of the war, Germaine Girard remained in a terrible emotional state. From the time her children were little, she had encouraged them to take chances and think for themselves. They had followed her lead. When Anise wanted to join the Resistance, her mother had provided her with the link to the intelligence network she joined. Already guilt-ridden and grieving, Germaine was sent over the edge by Claire's murder and suffered a nervous breakdown.

In February 1946, an employee of a government commission preparing an official history of France during World War II interviewed Louis, Germaine, Anise, and François Girard at their home. She found Louis Girard "to be quite old and diminished by his long period of deportation" and Germaine Girard to be "broken by the family trauma." She described François as "somewhat listless." Although the woman said nothing about Anise, she, too, had been shattered by Claire's death and her father's and brother's suffering, not to mention her own.

Although she had been in better physical shape than most of her fellow Ravensbrück inmates when she returned, Anise, like Germaine Tillion, found herself totally depleted in body and spirit. Once a dynamo of energy, she could no longer ride a bicycle or climb a hill.

Not long after she came back, she traveled to Switzerland to try to regain her health. Once there, she began to figure out a way to rebuild her life. Her partner in that effort was Geneviève de Gaulle.

AT THE TIME OF her friends' release from Ravensbrück, Geneviève had been gone from the camp for two months. After reuniting with her father in early March, she had stayed with him and his wife at their home in the Swiss capital of Bern for just four days before heading back to France and the person in her family to whom she felt closest: Charles de Gaulle.

As much as she loved her father, there had long been an emotional distance between them; that was never more true than following her return from Ravensbrück. Since her childhood, Geneviève had always sought to protect him from worry and pain, which made it impossible for her to tell him about the atrocities of the camp.

Her uncle, who had invited her to visit as soon as he found out she'd been released, was the only person in whom she could confide. She stayed for a month at the villa that he and his wife, Yvonne, were renting in Neuilly, an exclusive residential suburb of Paris. During late-evening conversations and long Sunday walks in the countryside, she poured out her heart to him. "He was about the only person I've ever talked to like that," she said years later. "There were things that for me were practically unspeakable but . . . that I told Uncle Charles. We really had, I must say, moments of very great intimacy."

She described the savage beatings she had endured, her struggle to retain her sanity during her months in the Bunker, the gnawing hunger, the executions of friends, the horrific medical experiments performed on the young Polish inmates. As she talked, she saw tears in de Gaulle's eyes, which sometimes spilled over and ran down his face. "To hear her recount the details of her detention in that horrible death camp plunged my father into a sadness . . . from which he had a difficult time recovering," de Gaulle's son, Philippe, later said.

In turn, de Gaulle opened up to her, describing the challenges he had encountered during the war to convince Allied leaders and the people of France to accept his leadership and the extraordinary difficulties the country now faced in its struggle to recover. In their mutual exchanges during their month together, he and Geneviève formed an even tighter bond than before. "For Charles de Gaulle, Geneviève was like a daughter," observed Michel Anthonioz, Geneviève's oldest son.

Invigorated by the month she spent with her uncle, she ignored the advice of doctors to rest. Early in the war, her mission had been to convince her fellow resisters that de Gaulle was the right leader for the country. Now it was to inform the public of the brutal reality of the concentration camp experience and the pressing need to help the deported women of the Resistance recover from their physical and emotional wounds.

In the early summer of 1945, Geneviève embarked on an extensive lecture tour throughout France and Switzerland. One of her first stops was in Gentilly, a southern suburb of Paris, where she filled a four-hundred-seat movie theater. "Everyone was enthralled by her," a local journalist wrote. "The account she gave of her captivity, the calmness of her thought, the accuracy and natural nobility of her words, went straight to the heart of the men and women seated before her."

During her tour, Geneviève launched a fundraising campaign to bring ailing French deportees to Switzerland for extended stays. Thanks to her efforts, enough money was donated to provide more than five hundred former prisoners with lengthy respites in rest homes throughout the country over the next several years.

At one of her stops in Switzerland, Geneviève ran into Anise Girard, who was still convalescing there. Even though Anise had been instrumental at Ravensbrück in saving Geneviève from the sadistic SS officer who had repeatedly beaten her, the two young women had been in different barracks and didn't know each other well. But when they met again in Switzerland, they formed an instant rapport, and Geneviève invited Anise to join her for the rest of her tour.

"We went to churches and spoke to youth groups," Anise recalled. "Like her uncle, Geneviève had a gift for speaking. Actually, she was even better than he was." At night, the two shared a room, and because neither could sleep well, they often talked through the night, telling each other the stories of their lives before and during the war. Because of the need for secrecy, members of the Resistance had tended to be closemouthed about their personal histories, even with those with whom they formed close wartime friendships. That secrecy often extended to disclosure of their real names.

Both of Anise's parents had come from eastern France, near the Swiss border, and Anise invited Geneviève to spend some time at the farm of some of her cousins. There she tried to teach her friend to milk a cow, which, according to Anise, turned into a complete disaster. Thanks to their time together, she said, she and Geneviève "became extraordinarily close and remained forever linked."

That deep friendship soon included Germaine Tillion, who also came to stay with Anise's extended family in eastern France. In early 1946, Germaine, Anise, and Geneviève spent a week together at a chalet in the Swiss ski resort of Verbier, which they shared with Élisabeth de Miribel, Charles de Gaulle's secretary. The women spent considerable time outside, taking long walks and frolicking in the snow; the rest of the time, they talked. "For days and nights, I listened to their stories," Miribel wrote. In her journal, she observed, "The way in which they speak of Ravensbrück, with a pitiless lucidity but without a shadow of hatred, overwhelms me. . . . From these three physically exhausted women emerges a great strength. It is not about them that they speak, but about the depths of human suffering. Their testimony would be unbearable if it were not imbued with great peace. They seem to me to have gone to the other side of things."

The three Ravensbrück survivors came away from their time together in Switzerland with a newfound sense of energy and purpose. From then on, they were inseparable. When she visited Paris, Geneviève stayed with Germaine Tillion in the home to which she eventually moved. "I had my own room there," she said. "I lived there when I wanted, as often as I wanted, for as long as I wanted."

Not long afterward, the three would come together again, this time with hundreds of other women from Ravensbrück. They would join forces to help one another heal and then find ways to transcend the horror of their experience and turn it into something good for themselves and the world.

Chapter 14

"This Powerful Friendship"

ÉMILIE TILLION HAD ALWAYS THOUGHT AHEAD. THROUGHOUT her imprisonment at Ravensbrück, she bolstered the spirits of her comrades, especially the younger ones, by urging them to look beyond the awful present and focus on the prospect of a new life after the war. Then, in late 1944, Émilie began meeting secretly with a few other inmates to plan the creation of a postwar organization to provide support for Ravensbrück survivors, honor those who had died, and bring to the public's attention the accomplishments and sacrifices of women in the French Resistance.

Sadly, none of the women in that group survived the conflict, but their leadership inspired others, notably Geneviève de Gaulle, to transform their dream into reality. As soon as they returned to France, the women of Ravensbrück realized they couldn't rely on anything or anyone else to help them put their lives back together. Once again, they had to turn to one another.

It was clear that the provisional government, overwhelmed by the problems of a bankrupt, war-ravaged country, was not going to be the source of much aid. Support for the survivors of concentration camps, while important, was low on its priority list. And, as the women knew, any funds that were made available would likely go first to male deportees.

After the war, the French public's perception of resisters was over-whelmingly male, an attitude that did not reflect reality. As it happened, the provisional government's groundbreaking decision in 1944 to grant French women the right to vote was made in response to the important role women had played in defying the Germans. With many French-men either in German prison camps or not yet demobilized from the army after the country's capitulation in the summer of 1940, women had stepped in to help create some of France's first Resistance net-works. When the men came back, they took over most of the leader-ship roles, but women performed much of the essential work. They acted as couriers, collected intelligence, transported arms, escorted Al-lied pilots caught behind enemy lines to safety, and hid other Resis-tance members in their homes, among other vitally important tasks.

Yet following the war, they were treated as an afterthought. Indeed, the French were encouraged by Charles de Gaulle and male Resistance leaders to believe that it was "an entirely male affair, with many men who had claimed to be in the Resistance but who in fact had done noth-ing strutting down the streets with their medals," one Ravensbrück survivor remarked.

Ignoring the fact that de Gaulle's own niece had distinguished her-self in its activities, he and his followers insisted that the only notewor-thy members of the Resistance were those who had engaged in armed struggle with the Germans, whether as soldiers in the Free French army or at home specializing in sabotage and other forms of open con-frontation. In November 1940, de Gaulle created the Compagnons de la Libération, an elite group of those deemed heroes in the fight for French liberation during the war. By the conflict's end, 1,038 persons were deemed worthy of the honor. Of that number, only six were women.

That same blinkered view also applied to members of the Resis-tance caught by the Nazis and sent to prisons and concentration camps. Women accounted for more than twenty percent of the political pris-oners held by the Germans—some ten thousand in all—but with few exceptions, their experiences were excluded from histories of the pe-riod. As the French historian Annette Wieviorka has written, "Reading the wartime memoirs of Charles de Gaulle, one would never know that French women were among those deported and subsequently repatriated." He only talked about "sons."

By forming an all-female activist organization, the *résistantes* who'd been deported were giving notice that they would not retreat into the shadows. In the words of the American historian Debra Workman, they "had voluntarily taken the same risks as men in defense of their country, had suffered the same brutal punishments, and now had united to care for one another and obtain [the] rights and recognition that they had legitimately earned."

This demonstration of female solidarity was revolutionary for its time. After the war, France remained a conservative, patriarchal country; although women now could vote, they were still regarded as second-class citizens. By asserting their authority, the women of Ravensbrück were staking a claim to the right of women to take charge of their own lives.

THE NEW GROUP, CALLED the Association Nationale des Anciennes Déportées et Internées de la Résistance (National Association of Former [Female] Deportees and Internees of the Resistance), was established in July 1945. Known as ADIR, it had its roots in another, smaller women's organization, the Amicale des Prisonnières de la Résistance (Friendship of [Female] Prisoners of the Resistance, abbreviated APR), a group of several hundred *résistantes* who had been imprisoned in Paris by the Germans but who, for various reasons, had not been deported by the time of the city's liberation. After they had been freed, the women decided in the fall of 1944 to band together to prepare for the return of the thousands of female Resistance members who *had* been deported to concentration camps.

When Irene Delmas, APR's leader, met Geneviève de Gaulle during Geneviève's lecture tour in Switzerland in the early summer of 1945, she told Geneviève what she and her group had done and offered to withdraw to the sidelines. Geneviève, however, insisted that APR join forces with the camp survivors to create ADIR. Composed exclusively of women resisters who had been imprisoned either in Nazi concentration camps or French and German prisons, the organization quickly became "the principal cornerstone on which most female political deportees rebuilt their postwar lives," Debra Workman wrote.

During its fifty years of existence, ADIR's membership list included about five thousand women, the majority of whom had been at Ravensbrück. In its first newsletter, Claire Davinroy, ADIR's newly elected general secretary, stated its purpose: "to preserve the feeling of sisterhood from the camps that was so intense that any woman who was in them feels closer to us than certain members of our own family." The name of their newsletter, *Voix et Visages* (*Voices and Faces*), Davinroy added, was meant to evoke the community created in the prisons and camps by "voices coming through walls and fences, through cracks and pipes" and by the "emaciated faces who were known only by their first names."

In another article in that first issue, Geneviève de Gaulle wrote to her fellow members, "A look, a squeeze of the hand, a memory: our camaraderie from the past continues. This is our strength, as it was in prison or in the camp, this powerful friendship. We need to give and receive it in order to rise to this new task."

In addition to Claire Davinroy, Geneviève enlisted Germaine Tillion, Anise Girard, and other women who'd been regarded as leaders at Ravensbrück to help in the organization of ADIR. The situation was urgent, and the challenges facing the organizers herculean.

The most immediate crisis was the extremely poor health of about sixty percent of returning women prisoners, all requiring prompt medical attention. More than a quarter had life-threatening infectious diseases, such as typhus and tuberculosis; some came back with multiple afflictions. At its rue Guynemer headquarters, ADIR opened a clinic, offering the services of seventeen doctors free of charge. In addition to the more serious illnesses, the organization's medical personnel treated a host of other ailments, among them anemia, upper respiratory problems, bouts of crippling fatigue, skin diseases, loss of bone calcium, and vitamin deficiencies.

The most seriously ill women received long-term care at ADIR's network of twelve convalescent homes scattered throughout France and Switzerland. On average, patients spent four to six months in the homes, although some stayed more than a year. ADIR paid all costs, which were subsidized by private donations, largely from Switzerland and the United States. The brainchild of Geneviève de Gaulle, the subsidized care was provided to more than one thousand survivors in the five years of their operation. Geneviève made frequent visits to check on the women's progress.

"Without question," Debra Workman wrote, "the work of ADIR helped to prevent the repatriation crisis from escalating into a catastrophe"—at least where women were concerned. Male survivors did not get the same level of support. Not until 1953, eight years after the war's end, did the French government attempt to come up with a comprehensive plan to care for the health of the nation's male deportees. By then, more than a third had died as a direct result of the savagery of their treatment in the camps. Among the roughly forty thousand men and women who'd returned, some two to three thousand died within a couple of months of their liberation—the vast majority of them men.

ADIR continued providing medical assistance to its members for more than a decade after the war was over. "On more than one occasion, hospital administrators called the offices of the association, saying, 'We have one of yours here,'" noted an article in *Voix et Visages*. "Always the reply was, 'I will grab my hat and be right there.'" In November 1952, a Ravensbrück deportee with no family to care for her suddenly fell ill. Her doctor informed ADIR she needed full-time observation. For the next three months, women who'd been with her at the camp took care of her day and night until she recovered.

Healthcare was just one of the many services ADIR offered returning prison and camp survivors, whether they were countesses, shop assistants, or factory workers. A good number found themselves destitute, with no home or family to take them in; they were temporarily housed at a 150-bed shelter set up at the group's headquarters. ADIR also supplied members with clothing, furniture, bedding, cookware, and dishes. It organized its own employment service, finding jobs for members, more than half of whom had never worked outside their home before, as telephone operators, babysitters, cooks, cleaners, saleswomen, and in other positions. Women who wanted to develop new job skills were provided with retraining opportunities and educational grants.

Even as it dealt with survivors' health and material needs, ADIR also put considerable emphasis on helping them cope with the deep emotional trauma most of them had suffered. Only at 4 rue Guynemer could many find the love and understanding they needed to come to grips with their nightmarish wartime experiences. It became their sole refuge, a haven of moral support.

"We were beings apart," explained Micheline Maurel, a Ravensbrück survivor. "We descended from another planet." Another survivor remarked, "I came back very nervous and irritable, hypersensitive to the slightest annoyance. This state of mind was not understood by most people. It was accepted only by my old comrades from Ravensbrück." A third deportee, who went to work in an office shortly after she returned, recalled feeling like a foreigner around her office colleagues. "They laughed and joked and made plans for their lives. I remained silent and alone. Their dynamism, their joie de vivre had no meaning for me. They couldn't understand why I didn't feel the way they did. It was as if a spring were broken."

She and other survivors had the sense that the people around them, like most of the French population, were anxious to forget the war, with all its misery and internal strife, and focus solely on the future. France had not yet faced the reality of its own official collaboration with the Nazis; as a result, the stories of those who did resist and who suffered for it were often unwelcome. "Enough of cadavers! Enough of torture!" a French book editor was reported to have exclaimed in rejecting the manuscript of a deportee. "Enough of stories of the resistance! We need to laugh now."

Every Monday afternoon, ADIR hosted a tea party at its headquarters to give its members a chance to share confidences with one another. These teas, which in effect were group therapy sessions, were extremely popular. One of their most highly sought-after participants was Germaine de Renty, Jeannie Rousseau's close companion who had helped save her life during their time at Königsberg and Ravensbrück. Considerably older than most ADIR members, Germaine became a mother figure to a number of them, listening to their stories, advising them, comforting them, and helping them look beyond the horrific past and to see the possibility of a better life. "If Germaine was everything to me," Jeannie Rousseau said decades later, "for our companions she was an inspiration, a model, and very often the main source of help." In effect, Germaine de Renty, in Paris, had assumed the role that Émilie Tillion had played at Ravensbrück.

IN APRIL 1944, GERMAINE and her husband, Robert, had sent their fourteen-year-old daughter, Claude, away from their Paris apartment to stay with family friends on a farm in Normandy. She was still grow-ing, they said, and they wanted her to have access to the nutritious foods available there, like eggs, milk, and vegetables, that were almost impossible to find in Paris.

Five months later, after the liberation of Paris, Claude received a shocking phone call from her twenty-one-year-old sister, Christiane: Two weeks earlier, their parents had been arrested and deported to Germany. It was then Claude realized they might well have had an-other motive for getting her out of Paris—to keep her safe from the fate that lay in store for them. Although she had long suspected that Christiane was a member of the Resistance, she had no idea that their parents had been involved, too.

Returning to her family's apartment at 78 rue Mozart, in Paris's af-fluent 16th arrondissement, Claude lived alone until after the war ended. Christiane was still in hiding; their sister Ghislaine was married and expecting a baby in another part of France; and their brother, Yves, was in the French army.

Like other French citizens seeking news of their deported loved ones, fifteen-year-old Claude haunted the corridors of the Lutetia Hotel, showing photos of her parents to any returning survivor she came across and asking if he or she had seen them. No one had. Then, out of the blue, in early May, Claude received a letter from her mother. She had been liberated the week before, Germaine wrote, and was now in a Swedish hospital. She would return home as soon as she had recovered enough to travel. In fact, she was spending most of her time at the bedside of Jeannie Rousseau, who, when she arrived in Sweden, weighed less than seventy pounds, had a collapsed lung, and was close to death from pneumonia and tuberculosis. When Jeannie asked a doctor to cable her parents that she was still alive, he warned, "Don't get their hopes up."

Germaine stayed with Jeannie until she was out of danger. Later, in Switzerland, she was informed of the death of her husband, who'd ended up at Dora, the same slave labor camp in Germany in which Anise Girard's father was imprisoned. Within four months of his arrival, Robert de Renty was dead, his emaciated corpse thrown onto a funeral pyre with the dozens of other workers who had succumbed that day.

Germaine had long feared that Robert, who was several years older than she, would not survive the war. She, on the other hand, was determined to do so, repeatedly telling Jeannie in the camps, "I have to go back to raise my daughter." She and Claude were reunited in Paris on a warm June day in 1945. Although her face was gaunt and her body still painfully thin, Germaine had regained, in her daughter's words, "an almost normal appearance." But the appearance of normality was deceiving.

For a number of years after the war, Germaine never directly told Claude about what she had endured at Ravensbrück, Torgau, and Königsberg. "She only spoke with her friends who'd been there," Claude observed. "It was a reflex among all the deportees: They only spoke to each other, because what they were saying was unspeakable and unimaginable to everyone else."

From snippets of conversation Claude overheard during telephone calls and visits from her mother's Ravensbrück friends, she was able to piece together some of the barbarities the women had endured—the torture and squalor; the hunger, extreme cold, and relentless disease; the deaths of friends; the bouts of despair. But when Germaine was alone with Claude, "she showed no sign of sadness and was a master of her emotions," her daughter said. "She created a barely perceptible distance for herself. There were moments of silence, a sort of recurrent absence, a suspension of time that I was not authorized to disturb."

Germaine's behavior provided Claude with additional clues about her mother's time at Ravensbrück and the other camps. When she went to Germaine's bedroom one morning to wake her up shortly after her return, she found her lying on the floor next to her bed. "I can't sleep in a bed," she told Claude. "It's much too soft." (Later, she explained that at Ravensbrück, she had slept in a barracks with two other women on a two-foot-wide wooden board.) Claude also noticed how Germaine would wash potatoes but never peel them, and had an obsession about never throwing anything edible away.

As was true of other Ravensbrück survivors, Germaine's reluctance to talk about the camp stemmed in part from her feeling that virtually no one in her social circle had any desire to hear what she had to say. One evening shortly after her return, she and Claude attended a dinner party with old friends. During their pre-dinner conversation, the other guests congratulated her on the courage she had shown during the war and complimented her on how attractive she looked now. It was clear from her elegant appearance, one young woman said, that "life in Ravensbrück was not nearly as terrible as we've been told."

Germaine stared at her for a moment. "Every night in the barracks, we carried the bodies of the women who had died that day into the washroom," she icily declared. "And every morning, when we went to the washroom, we had to step over these bodies, with their eyes already eaten by rats." At that point, she rose, motioned to Claude to follow her, and left the apartment.

"With these few words, she had restored the honor of her comrades who had died of misery and of hunger," Claude later wrote. "Faced with this denial of the reality of the camps, which risked disturbing these people's tranquility, she stood up and freed herself from the conventions of her former life."

Bolstered by what Claude called her audacity, Germaine de Renty was a different woman from that night on: "She had left in Ravensbrück the rules of her past existence, the prejudices of her social class, her conformity to the idea of how a woman from that class should act. She essentially said, 'I lived through the worst, I survived, I can and will live from now on as I want.'"

Germaine refused, for example, to follow the custom in French social circles dictating that widows wear black for an extended period of time. The only occasion for which she donned black was for a memorial mass said for her husband. Instead, she favored dresses in cheerful light colors, signifying her celebration of life, not death.

In her determination to find new meaning for her own life, she withdrew almost entirely from Paris high society, refusing all invitations with politeness but firmness and "even a little edge of contempt." Aside from members of her extended family, the only prewar acquaintances she spent much time with were those who had either been in the camps or who lost someone close there.

But her main focus remained her fellow Ravensbrück prisoners. She not only counseled her fellow deportees at the weekly teas but made herself available in the evening for calls from those who needed immediate emotional support. In the words of Jeannie Rousseau, Germaine "invented help by telephone."

Now in her late forties, Germaine de Renty emerged as a key figure in ADIR's operations. In addition to her counseling work, she assisted its members in applying for honors, pensions, and other benefits that the government eventually granted to certain wartime resisters. It was a long, arduous, frequently infuriating process, primarily due to the belief on the part of more than a few government officials that women resisters didn't deserve the same benefits as men.

Even as she worked on behalf of others, Germaine herself was denied benefits or other compensation. Like many of her comrades from Ravensbrück, she faced the problem of making a living. Having never held a job in her life, what could she possibly do?

For her, the only solution, she decided, was to offer room and board to students from the Sorbonne and other institutions of higher education in Paris. At the top of her list were American students in the French capital for their junior year abroad. In the fall of 1949, one of those she welcomed was a smart, privileged twenty-year-old from Vassar named Jacqueline Bouvier.

Years later, the future Jacqueline Kennedy would describe her time with Germaine and Claude de Renty as the happiest year of her life. Germaine was everything Janet Auchincloss, Jacqueline's own mother, was not—warm and nurturing, with a gentle sense of humor. She became a sort of surrogate mother for Jacqueline, urging her to have faith in herself and follow her dreams. While Janet was fixated on the expectations and demands of society—the right dress, the right party, the right husband—Germaine had long discarded such societal restrictions and prejudices. In their many conversations, she encouraged Jacqueline to refuse to allow anyone around her to dictate how she should behave.

Having experienced the depths of ugliness and depravity during the war, Germaine made a point of seeking out beauty in everyday life. It was another viewpoint that she passed on to her young American charge, infecting her with a passion for French furniture, textiles, ceramics, and other decorative arts—a love that came from years of visiting museums and poking around antiques shops and flea markets. Every week, Germaine would organize an expedition for the two of them—a personal seminar that would prove to be more valuable to Jacqueline and her future than any of her formal classes in French literature or art history at the Sorbonne.

In addition to these outings, Germaine accompanied Jacqueline on tours of the Marais, the Latin Quarter, and other Paris neighborhoods, describing in detail their histories that in most cases spanned hundreds of years. She emphasized the importance of protecting such a rich cultural heritage and talked about the deep respect the French had for what they term their *patrimoine,* their inheritance, which helped ensure that old buildings were restored and preserved.

When Jacqueline Kennedy became First Lady of the United States in 1961, the lessons she had learned from what she called her "apprenticeship" with Germaine bore abundant fruit, first in her campaign to restore the White House and then in her lifelong campaign to weave historic preservation into the fabric of American life.

Her close bond with Germaine and Claude de Renty remained strong for the rest of her life. After John F. Kennedy was assassinated in 1963, Germaine became a mainstay and sounding board for her. After Jacqueline married Aristotle Onassis, they kept an apartment in Paris, and when she was there, she frequently saw Germaine and Claude. At one point, Onassis called Germaine, telling her Jacqueline was not well emotionally and asking if his wife could come visit her. Jacqueline did so, seeking Germaine's counsel at a "time in her life when she really needed it," Claude recalled.

When Jacqueline Kennedy Onassis died in May 1994, both Germaine and Claude were invited to the funeral. At ninety-three, Germaine was too infirm to attend. "She firmly demanded that I go, to replace her," Claude wrote. "She told me, 'I want to be close to her in my thought and your presence.'"

After the funeral, Claude went for a walk in Central Park, just as she'd done several times with Jacqueline over the years. She thought about how she would never be able to talk to her again about one of their favorite subjects: "the extraordinary influence my mother had on both our lives."

Chapter 15

Finding Love

O N THE DAY BEFORE JACQUELINE D'ALINCOURT WAS ARRESTED in September 1943, she was scheduled to meet with a tall, lean, dark-haired BCRA agent she knew only as Gustav. A contact between the two had been arranged a few weeks earlier, but when she'd approached him at the prearranged meeting place, he signaled to her with a faint nod not to come any closer. Later she discovered he'd been with a courier who had been compromised.

Gustav was arrested in the roundup that followed Jacqueline's capture, and he and she caught sight of each other again at Gestapo headquarters. Although she'd never actually met him, she was overjoyed to learn from Claude Serreulles, who replaced Jean Moulin as de Gaulle's representative to the Resistance, that Gustav, too, had survived incarceration in a concentration camp, in his case Buchenwald.

Days after Jacqueline's rapturous homecoming at her family's estate, Serreulles and his wife invited her to dinner at their apartment in Paris. Gustav, whose real name was Pierre Péry, was there, too. Handsome and charming, with an infectious sense of humor, he immediately captivated Jacqueline—an attraction heightened by his offer to accompany her to the Hotel Lutetia and guide her through the administrative labyrinth of repatriation. Having returned three months before, he was a master at filling out the necessary papers and forms.

Two weeks later, he and she were engaged to be married.

Jacqueline was hardly alone in finding love almost immediately following her return. After so much grief, there seemed to be an urgency on the part of young Ravensbrück survivors to find and claim personal happiness as part of their healing. Claude de Renty recalled accompanying her mother to a dizzying succession of weddings soon after the war. Like Jacqueline, most of Germaine's younger comrades married men who had been resisters, too.

Pierre Péry had been among the throng of young Frenchmen who fled to London early in the conflict to join de Gaulle's forces. He was already familiar with the British capital, having attended high school there. From childhood, his main passion had been aviation. Returning to France after school, he completed flight training in the French air force but was grounded after suffering a serious head injury in a crash landing.

When the war broke out, Pierre was working for Air France in London; within days, he had returned to France to join the French army. Several months after the country's capitulation, he escaped, crossing the Pyrenees on foot, only to be arrested by Spanish police. After more than a month in a Spanish prison, he finally made his way to the Free French headquarters in London, where he was recruited by the BCRA, de Gaulle's sabotage and intelligence agency.

At the beginning of 1943, he parachuted back into France, where he became part of Jean Ayral's BCRA air operation, overseeing parachute drops of agents and equipment in the unoccupied zone. He later was assigned to intelligence work at Jean Moulin's headquarters in Paris.

Four months after Pierre's arrest in September 1943, he was deported to Buchenwald. He swiftly emerged as one of the leaders of resistance activities within the camp, which culminated in an uprising of prisoners shortly before it was liberated by American troops.

When he met Jacqueline at the Serreulles' apartment, he had just accepted an offer from Air France to work in its New York office. A few days after the dinner, he confided to a close friend that he'd met "a woman whom I'm going to export to America—but before that, I'm going to marry her." Two weeks later, he told Jacqueline about his new job in the United States and asked if she would come with him. "Why not?" she replied.

Their wedding took place in November 1945, in the same little village church where Jacqueline had married Joseph d'Alincourt six years before. The members of the couple's wedding party, including the priest who married them, were all concentration camp survivors. Geneviève de Gaulle served as Jacqueline's maid of honor.

GENEVIÈVE, FOR HER PART, had already met the love of her life. They'd been introduced the previous summer at a luncheon organized by her father to honor Swiss residents who had worked with the French Resistance. It didn't take long for Bernard Anthonioz—known for his intellect, energy, wit, and a perpetual mischievous glint in his eye—to win Geneviève's heart.

The son of a French sculptor who lived in Geneva and was an influential member of the French community there, Bernard had attended the University of Lyon but returned to Switzerland when the war broke out and became active in aiding the French Resistance. In addition to helping smuggle French Jews into Switzerland, he was the editor of *Cahiers du Rhône*, an influential literary journal launched in 1942 that printed poetry and essays calling for defiance of the Nazis. Traveling frequently to France's unoccupied zone to collect manuscripts from French writers, including the poets Louis Aragon, Paul Claudel, and Paul Éluard, he also distributed the journal throughout southern France, focusing on Lyon and the region surrounding it.

After the luncheon, Bernard and Geneviève began spending considerable time together. They had much in common, including their commitment to the Resistance and their love of culture and history. But Bernard had another quality that endeared him to this serious, determined young woman—his ability to put her at ease, draw her out, and make her laugh.

At one point that winter, when Germaine Tillion and Geneviève were spending a few days together at a Swiss chalet, Bernard came to visit. *Cahiers du Rhône* was planning to do a special issue on Ravensbrück, he said, and he wanted both of them to write pieces. As she observed the interaction between him and Geneviève, Germaine realized that he clearly had another reason for dropping in to see her friend. To give them privacy, she announced she was going out for a couple of hours of skiing. "I boldly set off on skis, without really knowing how to ski, to give them some time together," she recalled.

After several months of seeing Bernard, Geneviève was sure she wanted to marry him, but he never brought the subject up. Shy and reserved before the war, Geneviève had emerged from it as a bold, forthright leader, and she decided to take the lead now. During a walk in the country in January 1946, she proposed to Bernard. Decades later, their son Michel noted with amusement that "Dad took three days to think things over" before accepting.

On May 28, 1946, Geneviève and Bernard were married in a quiet civil ceremony in Bossey, a French village near the Swiss border that was the Anthonioz family's ancestral home. The following day, they celebrated their marriage at a Catholic mass in Geneva's Basilica of Notre Dame. Charles de Gaulle was there, as were Germaine Tillion and a number of other Ravensbrück survivors. When Germaine was introduced to de Gaulle, she said with a smile, "I've heard a lot about you." He replied, "I've heard a lot about you, too."

MEANWHILE, THE FLOOD OF weddings continued. A week after their marriage, Geneviève and Bernard Anthonioz cut short their honeymoon to attend the wedding of Anise Girard and André Postel-Vinay. Like Jacqueline d'Alincourt and Pierre Péry, the two had met at a dinner party. It's unclear whether the hosts of Jacqueline's dinner were matchmaking, but there's no question that that was the case with Anise and André. "My wedding was like out of a novel from the last century," Anise later recalled with a laugh. "It was very much an arranged marriage."

In 1943, when Anise was imprisoned at Fresnes, her mother met André's formidable sister, Marie-Hélène Lefaucheux, who, with her husband, Pierre, was a major figure in the Resistance in Paris. The couple's apartment, a popular gathering place for Resistance leaders, also served as the headquarters for an organization that sent food packages to resisters in Paris prisons and jails.

Anise's mother, who belonged to the group, occasionally read to her fellow members the spirited messages of defiance Anise had managed to smuggle out to her. After listening to one of them, Marie-Hélène exclaimed, "Oh, but Mrs. Girard, she sounds like she would be perfect for my brother, André! But I have a very important caveat. He only likes blondes." Germaine Girard assured her there was no problem: Her daughter was indeed a blonde.

Soon after Anise returned home in the summer of 1945, Marie-Hélène invited her to dinner. She felt out of place—"like a hair in the soup," she said—at this gathering of prominent political and military figures, several of whom were war heroes. But she noticed one young man there who was as quiet and reticent as she. He introduced himself as André Postel-Vinay.

As it turned out, the war record of Marie-Helene's thirty-four-year-old brother was as illustrious as that of any of the other guests. Indeed, the year before, he had been named a member of the Compagnons de Libération, the exclusive group deemed by the Free French to be heroes in the fight against the Nazis.

A junior government official before the war, André Postel-Vinay had fought in the battle for France and was captured. After escaping from a German prison camp, he joined a Resistance network of former military intelligence officers that passed intelligence to the British. The following year, he became a leader in a far-flung escape line called the Pat O'Leary network, which smuggled stranded Allied soldiers and airmen out of occupied France and across the Pyrenees to Spain.

Betrayed by a double agent at the end of 1941, Postel-Vinay was arrested and sent to La Santé prison in Paris. He was consumed with worry that the Gestapo would find an address book he had left behind in his room filled with the coded names of his Resistance contacts, and would succeed in breaking the code. Fearing that his comrades would think he had betrayed them and that he might indeed do so if he were tortured, he attempted suicide by jumping off the catwalk outside his third-floor cell.

Astonishingly, although his spine and legs were fractured in the fall, he survived. After undergoing several operations, he was hospitalized, encased in plaster from his shoulders to his ankles, for six months at Paris's La Pitié Hospital. As André recovered, his sister, afraid the Germans would execute or deport him, sent word to him in the hospital that he should feign insanity. He did so, cutting his wrist and severing an artery, which earned him another operation and a transfer in August 1942 to a mental hospital, where he underwent a series of psychiatric examinations.

At the end of the tests, the German psychiatrist conducting them told him: "Mr. Postel-Vinay, you may be a good patriot but you are not crazy at all." When he left the room, André, dressed in plain clothes and limping badly, followed him out at a distance. Noticing that the German sentries paid no attention to him, he kept walking—out the door of the hospital and down its long driveway. Two weeks later, the Pat O'Leary escape line spirited him out of France, first to Gibraltar and then to London.

Joining de Gaulle's civilian cabinet there, André became deputy director general of the Caisse Centrale de la France Libre, which served as Free France's treasury ministry. When the Free French moved to Algeria in 1943 and became France's provisional government, André was named to the government's Consultative Assembly, in effect its main legislative body. When he met Anise, he was a key figure in de Gaulle's postwar administration, serving as director of the government body responsible for aid to France's overseas territories.

Notwithstanding his august credentials, Anise recognized a kindred spirit in André. Like her, he was bold, audacious, and headstrong, refusing to let anything stop him in his pursuit of what he thought was right. "When I met him, I understood immediately that he was the man of my life," she said, "and that gave me a lot of strength and a desire to live."

AT ONE OF THE weddings of her mother's Ravensbrück friends, Claude de Renty overheard a guest, in a whispered conversation with another, applaud the "courage" of the bridegroom for marrying the bride, adding, "After what she suffered, will she be able to have children?" When Claude told her mother about the comment, Germaine de Renty responded with an exasperated shrug: "These people don't understand." Of her young friends, she said, "They will give life as a new proof of their strength and to taunt those who wanted them dead."

Germaine was right. Eleven months after Anise Postel-Vinay's marriage, she gave birth to a son. The month before, Geneviève de Gaulle Anthonioz had done the same. Geneviève "had a second son a few years later, and then I did," Anise remembered. "And then she had a little girl, and not long after that, I had a little girl. And then Geneviève had another little boy and then after that, I did, too. I couldn't do anything but imitate Geneviève. We always laughed about that."

Geneviève de Gaulle Anthonioz with
her four children, c. 1958

As it happened, Jacqueline Péry d'Alincourt had beaten them both in the baby derby. In August 1946, nine months after her wedding, she gave birth in New York to a daughter, whom she named Violaine, her nom de guerre. After Violaine's birth, Jacqueline sent a cable to Geneviève: THE FRUIT OF OUR LOVE SALUTES HER GODMOTHER.

Even though Jacqueline outwardly seemed to have recovered from her ordeal at Ravensbrück, she had underlying medical issues that prompted her doctor to warn against having a child as quickly as she did. "It was crazy, considering my health," she said, "but it was a wager in favor of life." Two years later, her uncertain health became more of a problem when she had her second daughter, Marie-Claire. After a difficult pregnancy, she feared she might not survive the birth and decided to go back to her childhood home in France for the delivery, which was arduous and required a long period of recovery for both mother and daughter. But Jacqueline never regretted the decision she and Pierre had made to have children. Giving birth, she said, "was a miracle."

Jacqueline Péry d'Alincourt with
her daughter Violaine

For many of the women, having children was like being reborn themselves. "Until then, I felt like a traveler in a foreign country, interested, satisfied, but not like the others who lived there," Geneviève observed. It was only by giving life, she said, that life was truly given back to her. "Maternity," she added, "was the antidote to all that we had experienced in deportation." As Isabelle Anthonioz, Geneviève's daughter, put it, happiness for her mother was "to bring children into the world and [in doing so], to perpetuate a life that was almost brutally extinguished."

Echoing that view, Jacqueline Marié, who had been with Germaine de Renty and Jeannie Rousseau at Ravensbrück and Torgau, said that starting a family "was life beginning again for me. It represented a new act of resistance—against my demons and those who tried to kill me. It was a tangible sign that we had emerged victorious from the war." Jacqueline, who married Guy Fleury, a childhood friend of her brother's, had five children within eight years.

For Jacqueline Fleury-Marié, as for many of her fellow survivors, her family included not only her husband and offspring but the other women from Ravensbrück, whom she considered her "real sisters." To Isabelle Anthonioz, her mother's friends—Germaine Tillion, Anise Postel-Vinay, and Jacqueline Péry d'Alincourt, among others—were "my second family": "We were, my brothers and I, witnesses to the force that united these women . . . the warm tenderness they had for one another at Ravensbrück, where, without this fraternity, they could not have survived."

Germaine Tillion, who never married, was at the center of this sisterhood, as she had been at Ravensbrück. The godmother of Geneviève's youngest son, Germaine "had a special place in our family," Isabelle Anthonioz said. She and her brothers loved Germaine's "radiance, her sense of humor, her storytelling, and the way she addressed us as equals. We took immense pleasure in having her in our lives."

Chapter 16

....

Bearing Witness

O N A FRIGID SUNDAY IN DECEMBER 1946, GERMAINE TILLION boarded a train at the Gare du Nord and headed back into the belly of the beast. Sixteen months had passed since her liberation from Ravensbrück. Now she was returning to Germany to fulfill the vow she and fellow survivors had made: to bear witness to the savagery they and their dead comrades had suffered and to bring those responsible to justice.

At a time when Germaine's young friends from the camp were marrying, having children, and finding some measure of personal happiness, she remained fixated on her search for the truth about Ravensbrück. In the words of the German historian Bernhard Strebe, that quest "obsessed her from her first steps in captivity and never left her again."

Indeed, she had made it her official occupation. When she'd returned to Paris in the summer of 1945, the French government's National Center for Scientific Research (CNRS), which had subsidized her last two years of study of the Chaouia tribes, suggested she resume her work in the mountains of Algeria. Pointing out she had lost all her research notes at Ravensbrück, she asked that she be allowed instead to continue her investigation of what she called European "decivilization"—to "try to understand how an educated European people like the Germans could have sunk into such dementia." The CNRS agreed to sponsor the project.

While recuperating in Switzerland later that summer, Germaine began to write a seventy-seven-page essay, "À la Recherche de la Vérité" ("In Search of the Truth"), an account of what she'd learned about Ravensbrück during her eighteen months there and in her research afterward. Her extensive interviews of other survivors in Sweden would be at the center of the study, along with the documents and notes she had smuggled out of the camp. They included the list she had made of SS officers and guards, which she'd encoded as recipes, and a batch of official records handed over to her by Czech, German, and Polish friends who'd worked as secretaries and filing clerks in the camp's offices. Among them was a file called "Mittwerda," ostensibly referring to a fictional camp by that name but in fact a list of women sent to the gas chamber. Germaine's accumulation of Ravensbrück records, while relatively small, was far more extensive than the holdings of anyone else, including those of Allied war crimes investigators.

In the summer of 1946, Germaine's essay was published, together with shorter essays by other deportees, in a book entitled *Ravensbrück*. After it was rejected by French publishers, who were already shying away from books about France and World War II, a small Swiss publishing house, founded by the eminent critic and writer Albert Béguin, took it on.

A seminal work, *Ravensbrück* was one of the first analytical studies of the Nazi concentration camp system, combining Germaine's personal observations with scientific analysis, which established, among other things, that prisoners were gassed at Ravensbrück and that the camp, by providing slave labor for German industry, was a major money-making venture for Heinrich Himmler and other leading Nazis. The book's publication, however, didn't bring an end to her inquiry. She considered the 1946 edition a first draft and continued her research over the next four decades, traveling to archives throughout Europe and the United States to uncover new information. Two updated versions of the book would be published in 1973 and 1988.

On December 1, 1946, Germaine was taking a break from bearing public witness. She was on her way to the German city of Hamburg as an official observer of the first Ravensbrück war crimes tribunal. It was bitingly cold when she boarded the train at the Gare du Nord. Winter had not yet officially begun, but the temperature across almost all of Europe had already plunged to below zero—a harbinger of what would turn out to be one of the harshest winters in modern European history. The next morning, from her sleeping compartment, Germaine looked out on "a desolate vision of Germany, dominated by snow-covered ruins and children begging along the tracks."

At two-thirty that afternoon, the train pulled in to the Hamburg station, located in a city center almost completely obliterated in a 1943 Allied bombing blitz called Operation Gomorrah that had lasted ten days. Heavy snow, falling through the station's shattered glass roof, covered railway platforms, and the air was thick with coal dust.

Over the next several weeks, as Germaine made her way from her hotel to the tribunal and back again, she witnessed Hamburg residents' desperate daily struggle for survival—foraging on rubble-strewn streets for pieces of coal and bits of potato, searching for shelter from the cold and snow and finding it only in bombed-out cellars. It was a searing experience for her. So, as it turned out, was the trial itself.

BY THE TIME THE Hamburg tribunal began, dozens of trials of accused Nazi war criminals had already taken place. The best known was the trial of the Third Reich's key military and political leaders in Nuremberg from November 1945 to October 1946. An international military tribunal, it was presided over by judges and prosecutors from the four Allied powers occupying Germany—the United States, the Soviet Union, Britain, and France.

Less widely publicized were twelve additional tribunals at Nuremberg, conducted by U.S. military authorities and focusing on the war crimes of members of various Nazi professional elites, including judges, doctors, industrialists, and lesser military and SS commanders. In addition, trials were held for SS commandants, guards, and other officials at the major concentration camps. The main Auschwitz trial took place in Krakow, Poland, near where the camp was located, while the Dachau and Buchenwald trials were conducted by U.S. Army officials inside the camps themselves. Both Dachau and Buchenwald had been liberated by American troops and were located within the U.S. occupation zone.

Ravensbrück, however, was a unique case. Since it had been liberated by Soviet troops and was inside the Soviet-controlled sector of Germany, by rights the trial of those who worked there should have been conducted by the Soviets. But Joseph Stalin's government, for complicated political reasons, wanted nothing to do with it. Instead it was handed over to the British, the rationale being that many of the Germans at Ravensbrück had fled to the British zone to avoid being captured by the Soviets.

Although British military authorities accepted the task, they showed little enthusiasm in doing so. They, like the rest of the world, knew almost nothing about what had happened at Ravensbrück and didn't consider the crimes committed there to be a major investigation priority. While the atrocities of Dachau, Buchenwald, and other concentration camps liberated by the Western allies had been extensively documented by journalists, photographers, and newsreel cameramen, the Soviets had allowed no outside observers into Ravensbrück.

Even before it began work, the small British team assigned to investigate Ravensbrück atrocities faced major obstacles. For one, it didn't have enough members to conduct a thorough inquiry, and few of those on its roster had much legal experience. John da Cunha, who later would become an eminent British barrister and judge, recalled how he came to work in the unit. A twenty-two-year-old army tank commander, da Cunha, who had studied law at Cambridge, had been seriously injured in Normandy shortly after D-Day; in the midst of his recuperation he was summoned to the War Office and told he was being sent to Germany to work on war crimes trials. The only question he was asked was whether his injury was an abdominal one. When he replied no, he was told, "Good! You can eat the disgusting German food then. Off you go to war crimes."

Once they began work, da Cunha and his colleagues were confronted with even thornier problems. Unlike in the investigations preceding the Nuremberg trials and those at the other camps, they could find almost no physical evidence of war crimes at Ravensbrück. The Nazis were meticulous record keepers, and when most of the other camps were liberated, Allied forces discovered huge stacks of files documenting virtually every detail of their operation. They included lists of prisoners who'd been gassed or executed by other means, as well as those who had been victims of medical experiments. Located as well were the names of the Germans responsible for committing those crimes.

That was not the case for Ravensbrück, which was liberated much later than most of the other camps. Its commandant, Fritz Suhren, and the SS men and women under him had enough time to destroy virtually all physical records containing details of their crimes. Few documents remained, other than those smuggled out by Germaine Tillion and other inmates.

As a result, the British investigators had to base their case almost entirely on the testimony of Ravensbrück survivors. For six months, they traveled throughout Europe, visiting ten countries and interviewing potential witnesses. Travel at that point was still monumentally difficult; road, railway, and electricity networks in much of Europe had suffered serious damage during the war and still had not been completely repaired. Such difficulties, coupled with the small size of their team, limited the scope of the investigators' efforts. Of the several thousand Ravensbrück survivors, they interviewed slightly more than one hundred.

During the war, only a handful of British women had been imprisoned at Ravensbrück; as a result, most of those on its war crimes team had never heard of the camp before beginning their work. In piecing together what had happened there, it would have made sense for them to consult French officials, considering the fact that some eight thousand Frenchwomen had been imprisoned at the camp. But they never did so. Nor did they approach Germaine Tillion, who at that point was arguably the world's leading expert on Ravensbrück. There's no indication they even knew she existed.

Germaine never revealed, at least publicly, how she felt about being overlooked. But she made no secret of her disapproval of many other aspects of the British conduct of the trial, including the adoption of English common law as its judicial underpinning. According to common law, criminal defendants are to be judged on an individual basis, and there must be objective evidence, provided by prosecutors and witnesses, of defendants' guilt.

This was a very different standard from the one applied at most of the other war crimes trials, all of which dealt with the torture and murder of not just one individual but thousands—in some cases, millions—of them. In these tribunals, a chain of responsibility was established, and everyone in the chain, from top Nazi officials to camp commandants to lowly guards, was held responsible for the crimes. At Ravensbrück, as at other camps, "for each agony, there was a collaboration of several assassins," Germaine Tillion pointed out.

To illustrate that point, she described the brutal chain of circumstances leading to the death of one young French inmate, a professor of literature whom Germaine identified only as Claire. "First, she was cruelly bitten and mangled by a dog. Who set the dog on her? We do not know, but he was Claire's first assassin. She went to the infirmary, where she was denied treatment. Who refused her? We don't know for sure, probably [the chief nurse Elisabeth] Marschall. The second murderer.

"Her wounds did not heal, and she was sent to the Jugendlager. Who sent her? We don't know—probably Pflaum or Winkelmann. The third murderer. Now that she was among the ranks of the condemned, who kept her from fleeing—a guard or one of the police? Possibly both. The fourth murderer. At the Jugendlager, Claire refused to swallow the poison [Vera] Salvequart had given her, and Salvequart, with the help of others, beat her senseless with a club and finally killed her.

"For this one victim, there were five bands of murderers. For all the others killed, there were the same assassins, or some like them; every victim was killed and rekilled. We were all caught up in a terrifying cycle, with an assassin waiting at every turn."

The four "murderers" named by Germaine were among the twenty-two defendants initially selected by the British for the first of what would be seven Ravensbrück trials. The lead defendants were to be Fritz Suhren and his right-hand man, Hans Pflaum, the brutal head of the camp's labor detail. Among the others joining them in the dock were five doctors and one nurse, several of whom had participated in the experiments on the Polish rabbits. But Dr. Karl Gebhardt, the mastermind of the experiments, was not among them. He and his assistant, Dr. Herta Oberheuser, were to be judged by the Americans at the Nuremberg doctors' trial, which would begin on December 9, 1946, just four days after the start of the Hamburg tribunal.

By then, the list of Ravensbrück defendants had dwindled to sixteen. Four were judged to be too ill. Two others—Suhren and Pflaum—had set off a tsunami-strength shock wave by escaping from captivity the month before. They, along with hundreds of other alleged Nazi war criminals, had been held at Neuengamme, a former concentration camp near Hamburg where some forty thousand prisoners from across occupied Europe had died during the war.

Before the escape, the young English colonel commanding the Neuengamme camp had announced his intention to turn it into a model penal institution, in an effort to rehabilitate the men in his charge. "You don't straighten out men with a cudgel," he told a French journalist who was writing a story about the camp. "What we need to do is to change their mentality." Showing her around, he took her to a building where inmates charged with war crimes were making wooden toys in their cells, to be sent "as gifts to the little poor children of England at Christmas."

As it turned out, the security of the prison camp proved to be as relaxed as its treatment of war criminals. The escape of Suhren and Pflaum, unsurprisingly, was an enormous embarrassment for the British. Germaine was stunned. "How was such an escape possible?" she wrote. "Was it simply negligence? Or was external complicity involved?"

Those questions were just the first of many she would pose over the next eight weeks.

THE TRIAL, WHICH BEGAN on December 5, was held at the Curio-
Haus, a stately building in downtown Hamburg that had been a favorite prewar meeting place for artists and intellectuals and was one of the
few structures largely unscathed by the bombings. Germaine was at the
trial only because the French survivors of Ravensbrück had insisted
she attend. Initially, British authorities had decreed that no deportee
could be present for the entire trial; those called as witnesses were allowed to attend during and after their testimony. Outraged by their
exclusion, members of ADIR and the Amicale de Ravensbrück, a
smaller, Communist-dominated group of camp survivors, insisted that
at least one of their number be accredited as an official observer. The
British finally gave in, and the groups designated Germaine to represent them.

As she entered the small courtroom, she was momentarily blinded
by sharp, intense flares of light. They came from the flashbulbs of cam-
eras in the hands of news photographers, who were darting around the
room. Once her eyes adjusted to the bursts of light, Germaine saw the
photographers' targets—the sixteen defendants, seated in two rows on
raised benches, each with a black number on a white card around his or
her neck. Surrounding them were several armed British guards.

Germaine recognized most of the nine men and seven women sitting directly opposite her. Johann Schwarzhuber, now the lead defendant, the SS official in charge of the Ravensbrück gas chamber. Adolf
Winkelmann, the doctor who had condemned Germaine's mother to
die. Dorothea Binz, the head female guard who delighted in bludgeon-
ing and whipping inmates to death. Gustav Binder, the SS foreman
who took the same pleasure in killing inmates assigned to his sewing
workshop. Elisabeth Marschall, the head nurse, who helped select
women for the gas chamber. Vera Salvequart, originally a prisoner,
later in charge of the Jugendlager infirmary, who murdered countless
prisoners with injections and poison.

Germaine carefully studied each of them. She found it impossible to
square their appearance in the courtroom with the terrifying appari-

The sixteen Ravensbrück defendants, on a raised
platform, listen to testimony, December 1946.
Their German defense attorneys are seated
below them.

tions she remembered, strutting around in their black-and-gray SS
uniforms, with their whips, clubs, dogs, rifles, and revolvers. These
people looked so *ordinary*! The men in suits and ties; the women in
dresses, a couple of them wearing fur coats. That same thought would
cross the minds of other observers at the trial: A journalist would later
write that the women in the dock "might have stepped out of a bread
line in any German city."

The women looked better than the men, Germaine decided. They
appeared healthy and strong and obviously cared about their groom-
ing, some of them sporting lipstick and new hairstyles. The men, on
the other hand, appeared diminished: Winkelmann, once grossly fat,
had lost a great deal of weight, and Schwarzhuber kept his eyes cast
down much of the time.

As Germaine examined them, several stared back at her. "Elisabeth
Marschall looks me in the eye and is clearly angry," she wrote, noting
that if she, Germaine, had done that at the camp, "it would have gotten
me into trouble." Winkelmann gazed at her "with bullish eyes," while
at one point Schwarzhuber raised his head and looked straight at her.

"He has a smarter expression," she noted. "I wonder what he is think-ing."

Finally the judges entered and the trial began. There were eight judges in all. Seven were military officers—five British, one French, and one Polish. They would hear the testimony, decide the verdict, and pass sentence. The eighth, a Briton who was an actual judge and wore the customary black robe and white wig, presided over the trial and advised his colleagues on substantive and procedural judicial matters.

Sitting below the judges' raised platform were the British prosecu-tors. Across from them were twelve German defense lawyers, ten of whom were being paid by the British for their services. As witnesses, the prosecution would call twenty-two Ravensbrück survivors, most of them French and Polish. For the defense, forty-one witnesses would testify—"almost twice as many as those representing [the defendants'] many thousands of victims," Germaine noted.

Day after day, Germaine's former comrades came before the court to describe the horrors they had suffered and witnessed. Violette Lecoq, a French nurse who had worked in infirmary wards for tubercular and mentally ill patients, testified about the numerous medically induced murders she'd seen in both.* She also described watching Dorothea Binz, whom she called "the ogress of Ravensbrück," set her Alsatian dog on a young Russian prisoner, who was fatally mauled, "much to the great amusement of the ogress herself."

Another Frenchwoman, twenty-four-year-old Irène Ottelard, asked the court if she could approach the defendants' dock after being asked to identify Vera Salvequart, whom she had accused of killing several of her friends. Irène, who suffered from glaucoma, testified she had seen one friend being dragged into a room at the Jugendlager infirmary, followed by Salvequart, who was carrying a hypodermic needle. She heard her comrade scream, "Irène, they are killing me!" Minutes later, she was dead. Another friend, Irène testified, was given a white pow-der in a honey supplement by Salvequart and died the next day. Given

* The dozens of sketches Lecoq had drawn depicting the inmates' hellish existence were introduced by prosecutors as evidence at the Hamburg trial.

permission to stand close to the defendants, Irène proceeded slowly along the dock, peering at each of them. She finally stopped in front of Salvequart and pointed her index finger a few inches from her face: "It's her!"

In an attempt to undermine Irène's testimony, Salvequart's defense lawyer swore in another survivor, who testified that Salvequart had been known to help inmates on occasion. The lawyer then accused Irène of showing ingratitude to a woman "who actually saved your life, who gave you supplements of bread and honey several times." The prosecutor, Germaine reported, offered no rebuttal to the lawyer's assertion. "It's times like these when you feel very much alone," she wrote. "It's heavy on your heart because you know the truth. We received the ersatz honey supplement once a month, and it was in this honey that on a number of occasions, Salvequart put in her poison."

The harsh cross-examination of Irène Ottelard was the first of many such interrogations of prosecution witnesses by the defendants' attorneys, who browbeat the witnesses in an effort to impugn their testimony. When former inmates recounted instances of torture or killings, for example, defense lawyers demanded to know the exact date and time of the incidents, as well as the exact kind of weapon used. If the witnesses couldn't remember, the defense used that fact to try to cast doubt on their stories. No one, including members of the prosecution team, seemed to show any concern for the fact that the prosecution witnesses, several of whom were still in fragile mental and physical health, were struggling with the trauma of reliving the nightmare from which they had only recently escaped.

Shocked by the hectoring, Germaine wrote, "The criminals, taking advantage of the scruples of the British justice system, have become the accusers and have made it seem that the victims are the guilty ones. Nobody is there to represent the victims." The justices, she added, were being inundated with confusing and inaccurate information.

Aline Chalufour, a French lawyer assisting the Ravensbrück prosecutors, would later agree with Germaine, writing that the German lawyers' "insinuation of derogatory facts made it appear that the witnesses were suspected if not accused." Chalufour went on to say that "one sometimes had the impression that the conduct of the trial overlooked the overall Nazi plan to exterminate those who resisted them."

Germaine was also highly critical of what she considered the slapdash, negligent nature of the trial preparations of the British war crimes team, particularly in its selection of prosecution witnesses. Citing the case of Gustav Binder, the murderous SS foreman, she wrote that she personally knew several former inmates who had been present in his workshop when he killed one of their comrades. But the only prisoner who testified about his crimes had never been assigned to his workshop, which made that testimony hearsay.

Even more outrageous in Germaine's view was the prosecution's handling of the case against another defendant reportedly responsible for many deaths—Margaretha Mewes, the head guard of the Bunker. Only one witness—Odette Sansom, the former SOE agent who'd been held as a hostage in the Bunker by Fritz Suhren—was called to testify against Mewes. She accused the guard of mistreating her but said nothing about Mewes's culpability for crimes against other inmates.

As it happened, Germaine had brought to Hamburg a deposition from a German inmate who had witnessed Mewes's poisoning of eleven prisoners in the war's final days. The statement had been submitted to the French war crimes service in July 1945, and Germaine was given a copy. As soon as she'd arrived in Hamburg, she asked to be provided with a copy of the file of witness statements that the British had distributed to those involved in the proceedings. She was told that no more copies were available. "If I'd been able to see this file as soon as I'd arrived," she wrote, "I would have immediately noticed the absence of the Mewes document, which I could have handed over. There still would have been plenty of time to summon the witness to testify in court."

That never happened. Instead, the court was given no sense of the crimes Mewes had committed and no idea that the Bunker was Ravensbrück's center of terror, where the most severe punishments were meted out and where prisoners were taken just prior to being shot.

From the beginning of the trial, Germaine had taken detailed notes of each day's proceedings, sending them back to her comrades in Paris, who eventually would reprint them in the ADIR newsletter. As the tribunal continued, her anger and frustration over what she considered its failures became increasingly apparent in her notes. When she returned to Paris for a weeklong break at Christmas, she met with Geneviève de Gaulle, Anise Postel-Vinay, and other ADIR leaders, who made clear they shared her indignation. Even though the trial was still under way, these other women decided they'd had enough.

On January 15, 1947, with the tribunal in its sixth week, Geneviève and Anise appeared at a press conference in Paris convened by ADIR and the Amicale de Ravensbrück. Joining them was the Amicale's head, Marie-Claude Vaillant-Couturier, a former photojournalist and prominent Communist *résistante* who spent more than a year at Auschwitz before being transferred to Ravensbrück. A friend of Germaine, Geneviève, and Anise, Marie-Claude had testified at the first Nuremberg trial, electrifying the court with her vivid eyewitness account of Jews being sent to the gas chamber.

In "carefully measured tones," as *The Manchester Guardian* put it, the three women criticized the way the Ravensbrück trial was being conducted, declaring that British trial procedure and rules of evidence were "quite unsuitable" and noting that the court "concentrated on detailed evidence against the individual rather than the overall camp system." Such "excessive meticulousness of British justice," the women said, prevented an understanding of the systemic nature of Nazi war crimes and their chain of responsibility.

Raising another issue that Germaine had mentioned, Geneviève, Anise, and Marie-Claude argued it was unfair to expect witnesses to remember details such as exact dates and the kinds of weapons used against them: "Because the witness cannot give with accuracy that information, a doubt will remain in the mind of the tribunal." They added that the prosecution, as well as the judges, "failed to understand the trauma of the atmosphere in which prisoners lived," observing that at one point, a judge suggested to a witness testifying about the cruelty of a female guard that she should remember it was the guard's duty to keep her, as a prisoner, in line.

Meanwhile, while Anise was publicly excoriating the British, her husband, André Postel-Vinay, engaged in a bit of behind-the-scenes diplomacy, suggesting to British authorities they might consider reaching out to a French expert on Ravensbrück, namely Germaine Tillion.

In a letter to Brooks Richards, a friend of his and the press attaché at the British embassy in Paris, André noted "the very complete and very serious documentation" that Germaine had gathered about Ravensbrück and urged him to encourage the British prosecutors in Hamburg to consult with her.

Richards took André's message to heart. Forwarding it to an official in the war crimes section of the British Foreign Office, he noted that the press conference had received extensive and sympathetic coverage from several major British and French newspapers and made clear that he thought the Frenchwomen's complaints should be taken seriously. "I assume we will receive a written protest in the next few days," he added, "but it would strengthen our position if in this interval the military authorities could do everything to please Miss Tillion."

His advice, however, was not followed. On February 3, barely a week after Richards sent his dispatch, the Hamburg trial ended and the judges announced their verdicts. Eleven of the defendants were sentenced to death, including Johann Schwarzhuber, Adolf Winkelmann, Dorothea Binz, Gustav Binder, Elisabeth Marschall, and Vera Salvequart.*

The other five, including Margarethe Mewes, were sentenced to prison. All of them, in the eyes of Germaine and most of the other Ravensbrück survivors, were as guilty of murder as those sentenced to die. "The court procedures . . . excluded the possibility of justice," Germaine wrote. "Let us be clear: the verdict is the consequence of the bits of truth that have been brought to light by the trial. But it is not the truth." After finishing a final report to her comrades in Paris, she left Hamburg. "It was a horrible time for me," she recalled.

Immediately after her departure, she made no public mention of how upset she was. But Geneviève de Gaulle Anthonioz did not follow

---

* On the day the verdict was announced, Winkelmann died of a heart attack. Some speculated he had killed himself, but an autopsy was never performed.

her example. On February 28, Geneviève, who was seven months pregnant with her first child, delivered an anguished, angry speech at Paris's Marigny Theatre, denouncing both the trial and the verdict. In her view, the way the British had conducted the trial had reduced the suffering and deaths at Ravensbrück to the status of a "trivial incident."

"What we had experienced was inexpressible," Geneviève declared. "How, in two months, was it possible for those who had lived ignoring this horrible reality, to imagine it all of a sudden?" The British-run court was incapable of doing so, she said. It couldn't see Ravensbrück for what it was—an insane world totally disconnected from reality.

Geneviève had hoped that the trial would educate the public about what had happened at Ravensbrück, just as the principal Nuremberg tribunal had done in its revelation of the Nazi leaders' crimes against humanity. But in her opinion, the public had no better idea of the horror of the place than before the trial was held.

Even more hurtful to her and other Ravensbrück survivors was the fact that no one really seemed to care. "It's this indifference that has affected us more painfully than any of the atrocities. Our comrades who died, of whom nothing remains, had the right to get justice! We're not talking here about hatred and revenge. We experienced something else under the Baltic sky. It was outrage, a call for justice. It is this feeling of justice and indignation that we would like to see all the honest people of the world adopt."

In fact, there was considerable truth in Geneviève's complaint of waning interest and support in bringing Nazi war criminals to justice. Even as British authorities geared up to stage six more Ravensbrück trials, sentiment was growing in official circles in the West to stop the investigation of war crimes and even to consider the release of those who'd been convicted and were now in prison. According to proponents of this view, it was time to put aside the past—World War II—and focus on the future—the Cold War. In this topsy-turvy postwar world, allies had become enemies and vice versa. Once one of the Big Three, the Soviet Union was now the West's main foe in the struggle against Communism, and the newly established government of West

Germany, which was pushing hard for the release of Nazi criminals, was a pivotal ally.

The United States led the charge in that effort, with Britain following in its wake. On December 2, 1946, the British and Americans merged their German areas of occupation, and a few months later, U.S. officials announced plans to suspend requests for the extradition of Nazi war criminals. During a debate in the House of Lords, Lord Jowitt—who as the lord chancellor was in charge of British courts— agreed with the idea of letting bygones be bygones, declaring that "the infinite extension of trials is neither an interesting nor a desirable objective." Winston Churchill, who as prime minister had called for the execution of Nazi war criminals, agreed with Jowitt's sentiment, saying, "Revenge is endless and . . . most burdensome. Avenging justice is, of all politics, the most harmful."

Despite this dramatic shift in sentiment, the British decided to go ahead with the Ravensbrück trials. With the backing of their government, French survivors became much more forceful in their approach regarding the new tribunals, successfully pressuring the British to allow them to designate a certain number of witnesses.

ADIR made an urgent appeal to its members to come forward with written testimonials. In an article in *Voix et Visages,* Germaine Tillion reminded her fellow deportees of the lenient sentences imposed on Margarethe Mewes and four other defendants in the first trial. "This must not be repeated in the ones to come," she said.

She gave her comrades detailed instructions about how to structure their statements: "You must explain very clearly and with great precision the circumstances in which you saw the accused commit a criminal act. You may not have seen the deed yourself; it may have been told to you by one of your comrades who is now dead. In this case you must give the name of the comrade in question, and indicate everything you know about her (her sincerity, her personality, and, in general, anything that can authenticate her judgment)."

A good number of survivors did as they were asked, but their testimony made little difference. The new trials, which were held in 1947 and 1948, were greatly hampered by the reluctance of officials in the American and British governments to cooperate, particularly where the extradition of former Ravensbrück officers and guards was concerned. Just twenty-two defendants were put on trial over the course of these six proceedings. Of the thousands of SS officials, guards, and others who worked at the camp over the six years of its existence, only thirty-eight (counting the original sixteen defendants) were brought to justice. Of that number, nineteen were executed, sixteen imprisoned, and three acquitted.

Of the three Ravensbrück doctors tried at Nuremberg, two—one of them Karl Gebhardt, the mastermind of the experiments on the rabbits—were executed. The third, Herta Oberheuser, was sentenced to fifteen years in prison, which was soon commuted to ten. She, along with hundreds of other convicted Nazi war criminals, was quietly given her freedom in the early 1950s.

The Ravensbrück survivors were hardly the only ones to decry what they considered a gross miscarriage of justice. Numerous other critics lashed out at what they termed the hypocrisy of the Western allies in devoting a vast amount of time, money, and effort into prosecuting and trying Nazi war criminals, only to grant them clemency a few years later.

HOWEVER, THE SAGA OF tracking down Ravensbrück criminals and bringing them to trial was not yet over. In the early spring of 1949, Fritz Suhren and Hans Pflaum, who'd been on the run since their escape more than two years before, were discovered working as waiters in a Munich beer garden. The former Ravensbrück commandant and his confederate had been trafficking in American dollars on the side, which had attracted the attention of U.S. authorities.

After they were taken into custody, they were told by an American interrogator how lucky they'd been to have escaped arrest until then: "People like you are no longer judged as harshly as they were right after the war." Suhren and Pflaum were further reassured by the fact that the British, who still retained jurisdiction over Ravensbrück war crimes, had made it clear they were done with putting perpetrators on trial.

What they hadn't bargained for was Britain's decision to turn their case over to French authorities who, at the prodding of the Ravensbrück survivors, aggressively intervened and asked that it be assigned to France. On May 6, 1949, the French began official extradition proceedings, requesting U.S. authorities to transfer custody of Suhren and Pflaum to the French war crimes unit in Germany as soon as possible, "due to the importance of the individuals and the fact there is an interest in trying them in the French zone."

The Americans didn't respond for almost a month, and then only to say they would keep Suhren and Pflaum in detention until a decision was made. Finally succumbing to a steady drumbeat of French pressure, they surrendered Suhren and Pflaum to French custody in the early fall of 1949.

On February 13, 1950, Fritz Suhren and Hans Pflaum went on trial in the baroque palace of the princes of Baden-Baden—a gaudy replica of Versailles—in the town of Rastatt, on the Rhine River near the German-French border. A lengthy investigation by the French preceded the trial, with French survivors, along with former prisoners from Poland, Germany, Belgium, and the Netherlands, playing major roles in the inquiry.

Fifty-nine witnesses—thirty-three for the defense and twenty-six for the prosecution—were called. Among those on the prosecution's roster were Germaine Tillion, Geneviève de Gaulle Anthonioz, Anise Postel-Vinay, and Marie-Claude Vaillant-Couturier, all of whom testified at length about the barbarism they had experienced and witnessed.

Throughout the trial, Geneviève studied the two defendants closely. "Pflaum is what one would expect of a subordinate SS man: thick and vulgar but not stupid," she wrote. "Certainly a good performer, who still shows slavish respect for his former commander. Suhren is in another class. The former commander is slim, confident, and sarcastic, with an intelligent face and red hair. Neither he nor Pflaum seems to have any feeling of guilt. They are perfect civil servants who for years have received nothing but advancement and praise and who no doubt think that today they are being treated unfairly."

In her testimony, Germaine Tillion described in harrowing detail her witnessing Pflaum chasing down prisoners and clubbing them to death. "He stood out for his brutality," she said. Suhren, on the other hand, was "the consummate technician of scientific extermination, accomplishing at his leisure all the plans for killing. . . . He was the head of the whole organization, responsible for everything that happened at the camp." She added, "I consider him one of the truest, greatest, most indisputable criminals of this world."

As vivid as Germaine's testimony and that of other witnesses was, however, there was one key piece of evidence that sealed Suhren's fate. In his pretrial interrogations and during the tribunal itself, the former commandant had never denied the existence of a gas chamber at Ravensbrück. But he claimed that by the beginning of 1945, when it was first used, he had been relieved of his duties as head of the camp, exempting him from responsibility for the gassing of thousands.

When Germaine and her comrades were liberated in April 1945, one of the records she smuggled out, the one she titled "Mittwerda," was a list of the names of almost five hundred women designated to be sent to the gas chamber. The date of the memo was April 6, 1945. The signature of the official authorizing the women's deaths was that of Fritz Suhren. "Suhren had defended himself very skillfully, and it was Germaine who managed to find the only list that we have of gassed women that he signed with his hand," Anise said. It proved to be his death knell.

The tribunal's French and Dutch judges found Fritz Suhren and Hans Pflaum guilty of war crimes and crimes against humanity. On June 12, 1950, they were executed by a French firing squad.

Chapter 17

"The Lapins Are
Coming"

I N THE AUTUMN OF 1943, TWENTY-ONE-YEAR-OLD ANISE GIRARD
had promised her twenty-year-old Polish friend Nina Iwanska that if
Anise survived Ravensbrück, she would do "everything in my power
to bring your story to the attention of the world." A bold promise, to
be sure, but one that, in the early 1950s, Anise was determined to keep.

When Ravensbrück authorities set out in February 1945 to kill Nina
and the other Polish prisoners whose legs had been mutilated by Nazi
doctors, Anise and dozens of other camp inmates helped them evade
the SS dragnet. Having been given the identification number of a dead
prisoner, Nina was smuggled out a month later in a transport of inmates bound for an aircraft factory several dozen miles from Ravensbrück. Shortly after arriving there, she managed to slip away from a
labor column, but not before a guard spotted her and shot her in the
right arm; luckily it was a flesh wound. After traveling for several days,
she found a job at a farm near Hamburg, where she identified herself as
Maria Ivanova, a Ukrainian evacuee who'd been living in the German
Baltic city of Stettin.

Several weeks later, Allied troops arrived, and Nina, with her fluent
French, became an interpreter for a French doctor at a displaced persons' camp near the German-French border. At one point during the
eight months she spent there, she wrote a long letter to Anise Girard in

which she described her dreams for the future. First, a hospital stay of several months to regain the full use of both of her legs, after which "I will be able to swim, to walk in the sun and enjoy myself. While I'm in hospital, I will receive lots of letters from you about the beauty of life, and after a while I will have news that you are coming to Poland. And then all will be as we have planned—sitting around an open fire in the evening and talking about all that is to come."

Sadly, none of Nina's dreams were realized. In early 1946, she returned to Poland, which she found to be a frightening, dangerous place. Despite the fact that Poland had played a key role in the Allied victory, it had lost its independence and was now under Soviet control, thanks to the acquiescence of British prime minister Winston Churchill and U.S. president Franklin Roosevelt. Like the Nazis, Stalin and the puppet Polish government he installed in Warsaw regarded members of the wartime Polish resistance as enemies of the state and treated them accordingly.

Desperate to leave, Nina reached out to Anise and ADIR. In March 1946, through diplomatic channels, Anise succeeded in bringing her and several other Polish rabbits to Paris for medical treatment. After undergoing surgery on her butchered leg, Nina remained in Paris, taking classes at the Sorbonne and working part time for ADIR. That operation—and a later one at Beth Israel Hospital in Boston—provided some relief. But her wound was so grievous that it never completely healed. Unable to hold a full-time job, Nina was crippled and in pain for the rest of her life.

For Anise, Nina's presence in Paris was a constant reminder of the mission she had promised to undertake. Having wound up its effort to bring the Ravensbrück criminals to justice, ADIR, Anise argued, must now throw itself into a new fight—to demand recognition and reparations from the postwar German government for Nina and the other rabbits.

Soon to join Anise as a partner in that quest was an elegant, vivacious New York socialite named Caroline Woolsey Ferriday. Together, the two women would set in motion an extraordinary, drama-filled campaign that would last ten years and would indeed, as Anise had pledged, spark the attention of the world.

CAROLINE FERRIDAY CAME INTO ADIR's orbit thanks to Jacqueline Péry d'Alincourt, who had arrived in New York with her new husband in early 1946. The large French community there instantly fell in love with this well-born, attractive young couple who, as Resistance heroes and concentration camp survivors, seemed to have emerged straight from central casting.

They were particularly popular with an organization called France Forever, founded in New York in June 1940 to support de Gaulle and the Free French. Many in the group were French expatriates, but it also contained a fair number of Americans, Caroline Ferriday among them.

The tall, dark-haired heiress, a fixture in the upper reaches of New York society and an ardent Francophile, waylaid Jacqueline as soon as she'd arrived at a reception in the couple's honor at the French consulate in New York. "We embodied for her the miracle of France's resurrection," Jacqueline recalled. "She asked me about what had happened during the war. She wanted to know everything, to understand everything." The two swiftly formed a close friendship, and Jacqueline became a frequent guest at Caroline's New York apartment and her seventeenth-century Federalist country house on ninety-six acres in Connecticut's rural Litchfield County.

As Jacqueline quickly learned, forty-three-year-old Caroline Woolsey Ferriday was a force of nature, the latest in a long line of activist, strong-willed women on her mother's side of the family. Firmly entrenched in old New York social circles, Caroline's mother, Eliza Woolsey, and her three sisters traced their roots to an ancestor born in the Dutch settlement of New Amsterdam, which became New York City in 1664. The four sisters were all staunch abolitionists who had served as nurses in the Union Army during the Civil War.

Caroline, whose father was a wealthy businessman with Louisiana roots, grew up in Manhattan, attending the Chapin School and making her debut in 1920. From then on, however, she refused to pursue what was considered the proper role for a young woman in her milieu— marriage to a socially acceptable man—and instead, with her mother's blessing, became an actress on Broadway. Mentored by Julia Marlowe, a close friend of Eliza Woolsey Ferriday and the most celebrated Shakespearean actress of her day, Caroline landed roles in several productions, including *The Merchant of Venice* and *A Midsummer Night's Dream,* in which she played the lead part of Helena. She also appeared in *Victoria Regina,* a hit play about Queen Victoria starring Helen Hayes.

As it turned out, though, Caroline cared far more about France than she did Broadway. Her father, who died when she was ten, had spent several years in Paris as a child, and he had passed on his passion for the country to his daughter. By 1939, when World War II broke out, she had left the theater behind and was working as a volunteer at the French consulate, spending much of her time raising money to aid French orphans. Soon after she met Jacqueline, she asked what she could do to help ADIR. That query led to her formation of a group called the American Friends of ADIR, which she headed. "From that moment," Jacqueline said, "Caroline would stand by our side as our sister."

A master at staging society fundraising events, including the annual April in Paris ball in New York, Caroline collected large amounts of money over the next few years to assist ADIR in financing its many activities. Through Anise Postel-Vinay, whom she met during one of her trips to Paris, she had become friends with Nina Iwanska and Helena Piasecka, another Polish rabbit who had moved to Paris and then to the United States in the late 1940s.

In the years to come, after signing on to Anise's campaign to seek justice for the Poles, Caroline would recruit three other New Yorkers— a prominent doctor, a whiz-kid former Nuremberg prosecutor, and the editor of one of America's most influential magazines—as collaborators in the venture. The German government, which had stonewalled the effort until then, had no idea of what was about to hit them.

———

THE FOUNDATION FOR THE campaign had been laid in 1950 by Marie-Hélène Lefaucheux, Anise Postel-Vinay's sister-in-law, who had played matchmaker for Anise and Marie-Hélène's brother. The sole woman in France's delegation to the new United Nations, Marie-Hélène was an ardent supporter of women's rights and a co-founder of the U.N.'s Commission on the Status of Women, which she headed from 1948 to 1953.

In 1950, she noted the fact that a small group of women who had been victims of Nazi medical experiments during the war were now in Paris hospitals and needed financial support to pay for their care. She introduced a resolution in the United Nations calling for the West German government to pay them compensation, declaring that "this is a serious humanitarian problem that cannot be neglected."

In response, the U.N. ordered an investigation, which turned up the names of more than two hundred concentration camp survivors throughout Europe who were possible victims of Nazi experiments. With the support of the French, British, and American delegations, it approved a resolution urging the Germans to "consider the most complete reparation possible" for those on the list.

After months of negotiations, the German government, which had accepted responsibility for making amends to victims of Nazi crimes, announced in 1951 it would provide a one-time payout, but only for survivors of medical experiments who could prove they were in urgent need. Following more intense prodding from France, Britain, and the United States, the Germans agreed two years later to provide compensation for all such victims.

That decision spurred the U.N. to conduct an even more thorough search for those who'd been subjected to such experiments. Aiding the investigation were the French and U.S. branches of ADIR, which sought the names of victims through newspaper advertisements and other means. This time, more than five hundred names made the list.

Among those who finally received small amounts of money were

Nina Iwanska in Paris and Helena Piasecka, who lived in Cleveland, Ohio. In 1957, Caroline Ferriday invited Helena to spend a few days at her Connecticut country house. During their visit, Caroline asked her guest about her sister, Wladyslawa Karolewska, known as Dzunia, who also had been a victim of the Ravensbrück experiments and who now lived in Poland. Had Dzunia used her compensation to pay for anything but medical expenses? Helena looked quizzically at her hostess and said, "But Dzunia didn't get anything." She added that none of the rabbits living in Poland had been compensated, even though a number of them had filled out U.N. questionnaires in 1951 and 1953.

Caroline discovered that Helena was right. The German government had refused to provide aid to anyone living in countries that did not have diplomatic relations with Germany—specifically, the Soviet Union and its Eastern European satellites. The U.N. Human Rights Office told her that a number of women in Poland had indeed filled out the questionnaires but that Bonn had refused to act and there was nothing the U.N. could do. When Caroline argued otherwise, she was told that if ADIR persisted in making the claims, it would have to assume the responsibility of being the Polish women's sole lobbyist. So be it, Caroline responded. "As I left the U.N. that morning," she recalled, "my arms filled with questionnaires to be filled out, I in no way considered all the surprises that the future had in store for us."

Within days, ADIR had launched a full-throated campaign calling for pensions to be awarded to the rabbits, whom they referred to as *lapins* (the French word for rabbits). In a letter seeking support from the French president Guy Mollet, Caroline wrote, "Abandoned, sick, physically and morally diminished, the victims of pseudo-medical experiments are at the end of their resistance. Never in history has there been a more monstrous crime. Never did a more just cause need a champion."

In addition to sending questionnaires to the fifty-four *lapins* in Poland, ADIR notified the Polish government of its effort. It also contacted an association of Polish concentration camp survivors, which had already launched its own effort, thus far unsuccessful, to persuade German authorities to grant reparations to the Ravensbrück victims.

Once Caroline had received translated copies of the *lapins'* completed questionnaires, along with graphic photos of their injuries, her
interest in helping them became a compulsion. Before then, despite the
florid language in her letter to the French president, she had had only a
vague knowledge of what had happened to them. Immersed now in the
ghastly details, "I became obsessed by the horror of what these girls
had to suffer," she said. "It became essential that the public learn what
had been done to them and be told that, despite such crimes, the German authorities were refusing to help them."

The Polish survivors' association had already sent to the Bonn government the latest documentation supplied by the *lapins*. It also had
urged Bonn to consider, given the lack of diplomatic relations between
Germany and Poland, inviting the International Red Cross to mediate
the matter. Again, the Germans said no, notwithstanding the fact they
were paying out millions of dollars annually in various kinds of restitution to other concentration camp victims.

In effect, the question of aid to the *lapins* had become a political
football in the rapidly intensifying Cold War. Poland was a Communist-
controlled country, and West Germany was not about to give money to
people it considered Communists, even though the vast majority of
Polish citizens did not approve of their government and were neither
party members nor sympathizers.

For months, ADIR tried to change Bonn's mind, dispatching a constant flow of letters to German officials and other opinion makers and
asking influential French government ministers and other politicians to
intervene on the *lapins'* behalf. Nothing worked. Despite the prestige
of several of ADIR's leaders, it remained a small organization, unaf-
filiated with the French government or a political party and thus lacking political influence of its own. When the German chancellor, Konrad
Adenauer, himself rejected ADIR's request in July 1957, Anise Postel-
Vinay and Caroline Ferriday realized the days of behind-the-scenes
lobbying were over. It was time to tell the world what was going on.

Caroline came up with the idea of bringing several of the Polish
women to the United States for medical treatment. After three major
hospitals on the East Coast agreed to participate in her venture, she set

out to raise funds for it, approaching foundations, other institutions, and wealthy friends. She had little success. Then one day, a relative suggested she get in touch with Dr. William Hitzig, a well-connected internist in Manhattan. "You know who he is," Caroline was told. "He's the doctor who took care of the women from Hiroshima."

Caroline's relative was referring to an event that had occurred two years earlier and had triggered international headlines—a visit to the United States by a group of young Japanese women who'd been disfigured and maimed in the atomic bombing of Hiroshima. Hitzig had played a major role in arranging the visit, whose purpose was to provide the women, dubbed the Hiroshima Maidens, with treatment of their scars and deformities. Although embroiled in political controversy, the project, which was hailed by the American College of Surgeons in 2020 as "a potent symbol of goodwill and understanding between two former enemies," was greeted at the time with widespread public enthusiasm.

To Caroline, the parallels between the Hiroshima Maidens and the Polish *lapins* were blindingly obvious. She immediately phoned Hitzig's office for an appointment.

AN INTERNIST WITH FORMIDABLE diagnostic skills who specialized in cardiovascular disease, Hitzig was renowned for his roster of famous patients, including Haile Selassie, the former emperor of Ethiopia; the Indian statesman V. K. Krishna Menon; and other world leaders. At the same time, he was known for his warm bedside manner and a willingness to make house calls, even for not-so-famous patients.

Over the years, Hitzig had become friends with another of his notable patients—Norman Cousins, the editor of *The Saturday Review of Literature*. A lively weekly magazine that focused on literary and cultural issues as well as current events, *The Saturday Review* was widely read by New York and Washington movers and shakers. But it also had a devoted clique of readers throughout the country.

The son of Russian Jewish immigrants, Cousins combined journalism with political activism. A vocal critic of America's use of the atomic bomb, he was the mastermind behind the idea of bringing disfigured young female victims of Hiroshima to the United States for treatment. The Eisenhower administration, eager to avoid any hint of liability for what had happened to the victims of the bombing, opposed Cousins's venture, claiming America bore no responsibility for the catastrophic damage that had resulted.

Cousins, who believed his country was indeed responsible, went ahead with his campaign. While the government might not have had sympathy for the bomb's victims, it was soon apparent that the American people did. Responding to a flood of stories in *The Saturday Review* and other media outlets, Cousins received some twenty-five thousand letters expressing support for bringing the women to America. After several of the Maidens appeared on a popular CBS television program called *This Is Your Life,* its viewers donated an astounding $55,000 to the project.

Cousins had recruited Bill Hitzig, who was on the faculty of Mount Sinai Hospital in New York, to be in charge of the young women's plastic and reconstructive surgery and other medical procedures. In all, the Mount Sinai surgical team performed more than one hundred operations on the twenty-four women over a year and a half.

On a December day in 1957, Hitzig met with Caroline Ferriday. He listened carefully to her detailed account of the *lapins'* story, examined the photos she had brought, and peppered her with "a thousand questions." At the conclusion of his interrogation, he picked up the phone and called Norman Cousins.

The next day, waiting on a huge red couch in Cousins's office, Caroline was far more nervous than she'd been at her meeting with Hitzig. When Cousins joined her, he said almost nothing as she began her account of the experiments, showing him testimony by the *lapins* at the Nuremberg doctors' trial and reading to him a couple of letters, including one that ended, "If the international authorities could see what was done to us, perhaps their hearts would be touched. . . . We are reaching the extreme limit of our strength. Perhaps the best solution for us would be to die." Caroline told Cousins she hoped he would consider intervening on the Polish women's behalf, perhaps even bringing some of them to America as he had done with the Hiroshima Maidens.

Although impressed with Caroline's eloquence, the editor wondered if her claims of the extreme atrocities the Poles suffered were exaggerated. After all, he wrote later, "atrocity stories and war invariably march together—not always on solid ground." Was there actual proof to back up what she said? He wanted to see all the documents she had, as well as detailed information on the current condition and needs of the *lapins*. She said she would deliver the material the following morning.

She did so, depositing on his desk a stack of papers at least a foot high. It was all the documentation Cousins could have wished for, containing case histories of every one of the surviving Polish *lapins,* as well as photos, articles, medical reports, and protocols. As he pored through the material that day and night, Cousins found himself profoundly shaken. It was, he later wrote, like peering "into the bowels of hell."

He decided to bring the matter up with a committee of experts who had overseen the Hiroshima Maidens project, among them doctors, writers, and foundation executives. When he distributed the case studies among them, he wrote, "I could see a somewhat pained here-we-go-again expression on some of their faces." But when they began to read, those expressions quickly changed: "One of the members bit her lip, a look of incredulity on her face. Another looked as if he had just seen a truck hit a child."

Meanwhile, Caroline waited for news. Two weeks had passed, and she had heard nothing from Cousins. Had this become another dead end? Then late one morning, the phone rang; Norman Cousins's secretary was calling. "Can you provide us immediately with the names and current addresses of all the *lapins?*" she asked. "Mr. Cousins is flying to Warsaw tomorrow." Stunned by the news, Caroline later learned that the Hiroshima Maidens committee had unanimously authorized a campaign to help the rabbits and directed Cousins to fly to Poland as soon as possible to begin planning it.

With Hitzig, Cousins, and the committee on board, it was time to add the last crucial member of the team. While the others would focus on stirring up public opinion, Benjamin Ferencz would work behind the scenes, putting pressure on the German government. He had already proved to be a master of doing exactly that.

WHEN HE WAS IN his nineties, Ferencz still had vivid memories of the day that "a very nice young lady named Caroline Ferriday showed up at my office in the Pan Am building with an interesting plea." A lawyer, Ferencz had specialized since the war in winning compensation from the Germans for Jewish victims of Nazi persecution. Caroline told him about the *lapins,* "poor Catholic girls who have been stripped of everything. They were clearly victims of persecution but they were excluded because they live in Poland."

Ferencz replied that Germany had indeed made it clear it would not send money to a Communist country, and public sentiment in America was inclined at the moment to endorse that view. What she was proposing was "a mission impossible on its face," he said. He paused a moment. "As it happens," he added with a grin, "I like missions impossible."

Benjamin Ferencz had proved the truth of that statement all his life. His parents were Romanian Jews who had emigrated to New York when Benjamin was a baby. Barely five feet tall, he grew up in the city's rough-and-tumble Hell's Kitchen neighborhood, where his father worked as a janitor. Although he didn't speak or read English until he was eight years old, he proved to be a pint-sized prodigy, winning acceptance to a prep school for the City College of New York, then graduating from Harvard Law School in 1943.

After Harvard, Ferencz enlisted as a private in an artillery battalion with the U.S. Third Army, landing on Omaha Beach four days after D-Day and fighting across France into Germany. Toward the end of the conflict, he was transferred to a new unit created to investigate war crimes. As U.S. forces began to liberate Dachau and other concentration camps, his job was to race to the camps during the first few days of liberation and collect their records, gathering as much evidence as he could about the crimes committed there as well as about those responsible. His findings would serve as the basis for later war crimes trials.

Following the war, Telford Taylor, the lead prosecutor for the twelve Nuremberg trials of Nazi elites, recruited Ferencz to head a unit assigned to scour the official German records in Berlin to supplement evidence gathered elsewhere. One day, a researcher for Ferencz discovered files of top-secret reports about special SS units called *Einsatzgruppen* (Special Action Groups), whose assignment was to murder civilians in the Soviet Union and Eastern European countries soon after they were invaded by German troops.

Even before the fighting ended in Poland in 1939, squads of these extermination units had entered the country to kill those considered enemies of the Reich, including Jews and members of the Polish intelligentsia, clergy, and nobility. In towns and villages across Poland, the squads' targets were taken to the main square or marketplace and shot. Similar massacres occurred in Soviet territory after the Reich attacked that nation in June 1941.

More than a million civilians, most of them Jews, were killed by the *Einsatzgruppen* in the early years of the war, in effect launching the Holocaust even before the extermination camps were built. And until Ferencz's researcher dug up the records of these actions, apparently no one outside Germany was aware that they existed.

When he was informed of the find, Ferencz urged Telford Taylor to schedule another trial at Nuremberg for the leaders of the murder squads. Initially Taylor said no. Public and official interest in Nazi war crimes was rapidly waning, he said, and there was no way the U.S. government would provide more money and staff for a new trial. Ferencz refused to accept that rationale. "You have to put on a new trial!" he exclaimed. "This is outrageous! I have a million dead people on my hands. You can't let these murderers go free." For a moment, Taylor said nothing. Then he asked, "Can you do it in addition to your other work?" When Ferencz replied, "Sure," Taylor said, "You're it."

At the age of twenty-seven, Benjamin Ferencz, who had never tried a case in his life, became chief prosecutor for what turned out to be the biggest murder trial in history. Twenty-two SS officers, several of them generals, were put in the dock. All of them were found guilty. If it hadn't been for Ferencz, they almost certainly would never have been brought to justice.

Once the Nuremberg trials ended, Ferencz remained in Germany for several years, working to get restitution for Jewish victims of the Nazis. His specialty was obtaining compensation from large German industrial conglomerates, like Krupp, Siemens, and I.G. Farben, for Jewish prisoners who had been used as slave labor.

When Caroline Ferriday approached him in December 1958, he had returned to New York and was a partner in Telford Taylor's law firm. Intrigued by Caroline's "mission impossible," he agreed to join her campaign, working in tandem with her and Cousins, whom he already knew. The latter two would be the public faces of the effort, pitching the project to the American people as a desperately needed humanitarian initiative, while Ferencz would be in charge of lobbying the German government. Together the three would act, in Cousins's words, "as a hot poker to prod some consciences." Their beginning moves, he added, "would heat up the coals."

FOR NORMAN COUSINS, VISITING Warsaw in the winter of 1958 was, to say the least, an eye-opening experience. Thirteen years after the end of the war, the Polish capital remained a shattered city. "Not since I had been in Berlin in 1948 had I seen so many empty shells of buildings," Cousins later wrote in *The Saturday Review*.

Neither Poland nor any other Eastern European satellite of the Soviet Union had been allowed to accept postwar economic aid from the U.S.-sponsored Marshall Plan, aimed at jump-starting the recovery of war-ravaged Europe. While most of Western Europe was now thriving thanks to American aid, a beggared Poland had been thrust into the shadows.

That sense of being forgotten hung over Cousins's visit. As he prepared for an initial interview with two of the *lapins*, the Polish interpreter assigned to him by the U.S. embassy warned him, "Don't be surprised if you have some difficulty in exchanging views with these ladies. You must remember that the outside world has shown very little interest so far in what has happened to us. Germany today is the most prosperous nation in Europe, but this country, which Germany over-ran and razed, is still struggling to get back on its feet."

She went on, "We love our freedom. I think we have proved that. But there is the feeling that people on the outside don't really care very much. You will probably find this feeling especially strong among these women, who are still waiting for help after fifteen years."

Cousins explained about the Hiroshima Maidens' visit to America and how he and his associates wanted to do something similar for the Polish women. He'd come to Warsaw to find out from them what kind of help they needed. The interpreter shook her head. "I'm afraid it will be of no use. These ladies have used up all their hope. . . . You must understand how strange it will sound to them when someone comes from the U.S. and holds out his hand. I honestly don't think they will believe what you say is real."

She was right, at least initially. When he met with the two women, they expressed their deep frustration over being ignored by the German government, even as Bonn was compensating other concentration camp victims. "If the Germans pay us—as they are now paying others—this will not cause our serious illnesses to disappear," one of them said. "But it will at least relieve us of the terrible indignation we feel that no one cares. Some of us are ill, very ill, and may not live much longer. We would like to see justice done before we die."

Cousins told them he was determined to do everything he could to make that dream a reality. He outlined his idea of bringing them to the United States for a lengthy visit. One aim of the trip, he said, would be to provide medical treatment to help alleviate their pain and other physical problems resulting from the surgeries. But just as important, perhaps even more so, would be to give them the chance to meet the American people and tell them their story. That, Cousins implied, might be the key that unlocked everything.

As he talked about what the women might possibly accomplish in America, Cousins felt the atmosphere in the room shift from doubt to subdued excitement. The two women were now leaning forward in their chairs, intent on what he was saying, and even the interpreter was considerably more animated than she had been before. Yes, the women said, they might consider doing what Cousins suggested.

Cousins then met with the leaders of the Polish association of concentration camp survivors, who approved the plan to bring some of the *lapins* to the United States. The next step, they all agreed, would be to appoint a committee of Polish doctors to examine the women and decide which ones might be helped by further surgical and medical treatment. After this initial screening, Dr. Hitzig would travel to Warsaw to consult with the doctors and meet the *lapins* himself. At that point, a final decision would be made about whether to proceed with the trip, and if it was approved, who would participate.

Cousins's advisory group began preliminary planning in New York, sorting out the myriad details involved in such a large, complicated venture, from finding American surgeons and other doctors to treat the Polish women to locating families across the country who would take them in as guests for several months. Not to mention, of course, raising enough money to pay for it all.

But before the committee could put its plans in motion, the *lapins* themselves would have to give their approval, as would Poland's Communist government. Caroline Ferriday, now a member of Cousins's committee, was given both of those assignments. They were formidable, but Cousins had no worries about her succeeding. Caroline, he said, "had an almost magical gift of inspiring confidence."

Arriving in Warsaw a couple of weeks before Hitzig's visit, Caroline Ferriday lived up to Cousins's expectations. In her interactions with the *lapins*, she made it clear she had come as a friend, not as a Lady Bountiful. As they got to know her, it became apparent that she viewed them not as a group of victims to be pitied but as individuals with extraordinary stories of courage and accomplishment. She asked them about their lives and met their families. "Dear Miss Caroline," one of them later wrote to her. "You have won our hearts immediately through your kindness. . . . We are moved by your dedication on our behalf."

After several days of arduous discussions with Polish officials, they, too, endorsed the plan. Under its then leader, Wladyslaw Gomulka, the country's Communist government had begun to allow its citizens certain freedoms, such as traveling abroad, listening to foreign broadcasts, and participating in cultural visits with the West.

Of Caroline's visit, Cousins later wrote, "Her first few days in Warsaw were not without their difficulties, but after a while the project began to move. At the end of her first week there, we received a cable saying that the Polish authorities were cooperative and gracious and that our prospects were excellent."

IT WASN'T UNTIL MUCH later that William Hitzig confessed to Norman Cousins that he had had serious doubts about the feasibility of the Ravensbrück venture. Even as his plane touched down in Warsaw in the spring of 1958, those uncertainties were still plaguing him. Hitzig feared that unlike the Hiroshima Maidens project, which dealt with the catastrophic damage of nuclear warfare, the suffering of a relatively small group of women at the hands of the Nazis was not an important enough issue to warrant a campaign like the one they were considering.

It took him two weeks to change his mind. By then, Hitzig, who knew almost nothing about Poland before his trip, had learned many things about it. He discovered, above all, that the Nazis' butchery of the Poles had extended far beyond their heinous treatment of the *lapins;* as he noted to Cousins, it could be found in "every nook and cranny of Poland." More than six million Poles, half of them Jews, had died during the war—the largest number of wartime deaths per capita of any country in the world.

During his time in Warsaw, Hitzig was reminded daily of those horrors as he walked among the smashed façades of almost every old building standing in the city and during his casual contacts with some of its residents—"everyday people in all walks of Polish life who still suffer emotionally from both Nazi occupation and from the ruthless Stalinist domination that followed."

Unlike other Eastern European nations, Poland had for centuries been Western in its outlook. During World War II, nearly two hundred thousand Polish military personnel—air force, army, and navy— fought in British uniforms on the Allied side. Back home, Poland's Home Army proved to be the most effective resistance movement of any of the Nazi-occupied countries. Yet after Churchill and Roosevelt ceded control of Poland to Stalin at Yalta, the West turned its back on the Poles.

In Hitzig's consultations with Polish surgeons and other doctors, he realized how pro-Western virtually all of them were. As he got to know them better, several opened up to him about "their own personal harassment as servants of the state and of the relentless role that [the Soviet Union] played directly and indirectly in their lives."

Hungry for closer ties to the West themselves, his Polish colleagues emphasized how important it was for the *lapins* to go to America "to represent not only their own cause but that of their countrymen who had shared similar and, in some cases, even more tragic fates." When Hitzig told the head of the association of concentration camp survivors that the proposed campaign was "but a drop in the ocean" in the effort to improve Polish-American relations, the man disagreed. "Not at all," he said. "It's like a river flowing into the ocean."

Hitzig finally came to agree. "Our project," he wrote Cousins, "has suddenly become urgent to me as a way of spreading the gospel at this unique moment in world history. . . . I am now convinced that [it] deserves our full-hearted and active support."

He and his Polish colleagues spent more than a week examining the fifty-four *lapins* who appeared before them. It was an emotionally and physically stressful experience for all the women, and most dissolved in tears as the doctors poked and prodded them. Caroline Ferriday was on hand to comfort them and to press Hitzig and the other doctors to be less clinical and more aware of how difficult it was for these women to relive the savagery of the experiments.

In addition to the loss and atrophy of leg muscles and bones, the women had a wide array of other physical infirmities and diseases stemming from their surgeries and imprisonment, among them nerve tumors, infections, spinal deformities, cardiac problems, osteomyelitis, hepatitis, hypertension, arthritis, and tuberculosis. No surgery could heal their mutilated legs, Hitzig concluded, but a number of their other ailments could be treated successfully. At that point, though, his main concern was their psychological well-being. After witnessing the emotional collapse of many of them during the examinations, he worried about how they would react when they arrived in America.

On Hitzig's last night in Poland, he staged a lavish farewell banquet at Warsaw's grand Bristol Hotel, one of the few buildings in the city's center to escape destruction during the war. Among the guests were Caroline, the Polish doctors, and, of course, the *lapins,* who in the eyes of an astounded Hitzig seemed to have undergone a mass personality change. They were lighthearted and buoyant, laughing, talking, teasing one another and Caroline, and clearly enjoying every minute of the festive evening. "You would have been amazed," Hitzig wrote Cousins. "You would never have believed these were the same women I saw the day before, reliving with heartbreaking tears the savagery of Ravensbrück."

The Polish survivors of Ravensbrück surgical experiments reunite in Warsaw in 1958.

Of the fifty-four *lapins* in Poland, thirty-five were tentatively chosen to make the trip to America. About half were married, and almost all were now in their mid- to late thirties. Among them were three doctors, two dentists, two pharmacists, one university professor, and several secretaries and other office workers. The majority, however, were unable to work full time because of their disabilities. Those who were not selected were either too lame or ill to travel or could not commit, because of family and other obligations, to spending several months away from home.

Before returning to the United States, Hitzig stopped off for a few days in Paris. There, one last surprise awaited him. As he entered the Gare des Invalides, about to take a train to the airport for his flight back to New York, an attractive blond woman approached him. "You are Dr. Hitzig?" she asked in French-accented English. "I am Anise Postel-Vinay, and I do the same work in Paris that Caroline Ferriday does in your country."

Anise invited him to come for a few minutes to her family's apartment, which was nearby. Ignoring his protests that he didn't have enough time, she picked up his bags, took him home, and introduced him to her four children. Within minutes, he was totally captivated by "this exciting, dynamic young woman" who had appeared out of nowhere. In his report to Cousins, he described her as "a breath of fresh air as she talked about her work in the underground during the occupation of France." At the end of his short visit, he told Cousins, "I felt as if I'd known her all my life. . . . As long as I'm alive, I will remember 'Danielle.' It is my earnest hope that she will come to America to join the Lapins."

Anise never made it to the United States, but her brief encounter with Hitzig convinced him that she was the real mastermind behind the *lapins* project. Without Anise's "courage and genius," he felt, it would never have gotten off the ground.

IN NEW YORK, MEANWHILE, Norman Cousins launched the first salvo in his campaign to stir up public interest in the upcoming visit. In a

June 1958 article entitled "Dialogue in Warsaw," he told *Saturday Review* readers about his trip to Poland to meet these brave women whose legs had been mangled by Nazi doctors at Ravensbrück and who had failed thus far to win compensation from the German government. They "are still alive and are still waiting to be helped," he wrote. "The world, in forgetting the horrors that were detailed at the Nuremberg trials, has also forgotten the victims. It is a mark of my own forgetfulness or ignorance or both that I did not know of the existence of this problem until very recently."

Giving his readers a graphic look at what the *lapins* had endured, he wrote about one of them, Dzunia Karolewska, who had testified at Nuremberg. "After the first surgery, the incision was so deep that I could see the bone itself," she said. "When I was sent back to the barracks, pus flowed from my leg and I was unable to walk. I was called again to the hospital one week later. My friends had to carry me there. A second operation was performed." Then another, followed by another. Dzunia was subjected to six surgeries in all.

In his piece, Cousins mentioned the possibility that Dzunia and the other women might travel to the United States for treatment. Left unstated was the fact that a considerable amount of money needed to be raised before that could happen. But *Saturday Review* readers had no trouble reading between the lines. Within a month, they had contributed some $6,000, more than enough to cover initial planning costs.

Four months later, in an article entitled "The Lapins Are Coming," Cousins thanked readers for their "electrifying generosity." He also noted that the outpouring of support from across the country included offers of many other kinds of aid, from the services of doctors, clinics, and hospitals to clothing and footwear provided by department stores and shoe companies.

The women, Cousins said, would probably arrive in New York before the end of the year and, after a few days of medical exams and sightseeing, would split up and travel to twelve cities, where families would host them for the next couple of months. Committees in the cities were developing programs tailored to the needs and interests of each guest, including medical care and social and cultural activities.

Throughout the article, Cousins gave his readers a glimpse of his Machiavellian approach to get what he wanted—for example, the use of a Pan American Airways plane to transport the *lapins* from Poland to New York. Pan Am had already agreed to lend one of its aircraft for the venture, but to do so, it needed authorization from the Civil Aeronautics Board, the federal agency in charge of regulating airlines. Because international travel was involved, the request to the CAB had to go through the State Department.

Instead of making the request himself, Cousins enlisted the help of a Michigan congressman of Polish descent, who in turn recruited eleven of his colleagues who were also Polish Americans. The twelve representatives signed a letter to the State Department asking for its approval. Three days later, the request was denied.

Refusing to accept the decision, the Michigan congressman asked a State Department representative to come to his office to explain. When the staffer arrived, the congressman put him on the phone to Cousins. "He was most cordial and sympathetic," Cousins wrote, "but said the department feared that a favorable decision in this case would open up the floodgates of requests from needy and worthy people around the world." Cousins pointed out that he was not asking the government to provide free transportation. Pan Am was doing so, "and if there was any problem of a future floodgate, this was a risk that Pan Am was willing to take."

Cousins further reminded the official that another body in the State Department—the U.S. embassy in Warsaw—was enthusiastic about the venture and had already issued visas for the women. "The effect of the department's decision might be to annul the entire project," Cousins added. "Is that its wish? Was the State Department taking into account the high visibility that the cancellation of the project might have throughout the world?"

Implicitly acknowledging defeat, the staffer invited Cousins to prepare an appeal and said he would pass it on to the appropriate officials. Not leaving anything to chance, the *Saturday Review* editor recruited Senator Jacob Javits of New York and two of his senatorial colleagues to phone high-level officials at State with their endorsement. The next day, the Michigan congressman called Cousins with the welcome news that the State Department had reversed itself "and was very happy to give its go-ahead to the Civil Aeronautics Board."

As the date approached for the *lapins'* arrival, Cousins and Benjamin Ferencz gave the German government one final opportunity to settle the question of compensation for the women before launching an all-out public relations blitz that would, among other things, target its refusal to do anything to help them. "The silk glove must precede the mailed fist," said Ferencz, whose lobbying of German officials up to that point had been as fruitless as that of ADIR.

In early December 1958, Cousins called a press conference in New York. Also present was the Polish ambassador to the United States, who read a statement from his government saying it welcomed Cousins's campaign to win redress for the *lapins*. A few days earlier, Cousins had urged German authorities to reconsider their opposition, assuring them that the main purpose of the upcoming visit was humanitarian in nature.

Foreseeing trouble, the German government's press office suggested that an emissary be dispatched to speak with Cousins, and the German embassy in Washington urged Bonn to consider establishing a contingency fund of more than $20,000 for medical treatment for the women while they were in the United States. Its existence could be kept secret, the embassy said, and no money would be disbursed until officials saw how the Polish women's visit was playing out.

Again Bonn said no. It was in control of the situation. Or so it thought.

Chapter 18

"They Are No Longer Alone"

ON A MID-DECEMBER MORNING IN 1958, THE FIRST AMERICAN civilian aircraft ever to land in Poland was parked just outside the Warsaw terminal. The Pan American World Airways plane, its tail displaying the stylized blue globe of Pan Am's logo, seemed an apt symbol for the U.S.-Polish expedition about to begin.

Inside the terminal, twenty-seven women waited nervously to board the aircraft and begin a six-month journey that would take them from the skyscrapers of New York to cities across the United States and end at the U.S. Capitol in Washington.* Joining them was Norman Cousins, who couldn't resist accompanying the *lapins* on the initial leg of their history-making trip.

It was the first flight for virtually all the women, whose excitement was tinged with anxiety as they awaited takeoff. When a stewardess explained the ditching procedure in case of a plane malfunction over the Atlantic, a few giggled uncertainly. One, however, responded with a scornful laugh. "There's nothing to worry about," Jadwiga Dzido-Hassa declared. "The sharks would stick up their noses and turn away

---

* Eight additional *lapins,* who for various reasons couldn't leave Poland in December, would join the group in the United States two months later.

from our skinny legs. We'd have to beg them to pay any attention to us."

Her quip was greeted with gales of laughter, and the women's anxiety began to ebb. Within minutes, Cousins wrote, "there was no longer anything restrained about their smiles. When they laughed, it was a pure reflection of their enjoyment of the moment."

Hours later, when the pilot announced that the aircraft was flying over the United States, the women rushed to the windows to peer out at the snow-covered landscape of Maine. After getting her first glimpse of America, one turned away from the window and saw Cousins watching her. She smiled. "I am very, very happy," she told him.

From the moment of their arrival at New York's Idlewild Airport, the *lapins* were swept up in a whirlwind of events that didn't end until they left the city a few days later. They were met by an impressive welcoming committee, including the Polish ambassador to the United States and high-ranking New York City officials, as well as Caroline Ferriday and William Hitzig. After a brief press conference, covered by reporters and photographers from New York and national news outlets, they were bundled into limousines and taken to midtown Manhattan, decked out in its magical holiday best. They oohed and aahed at the twinkling lights along Fifth Avenue, the Christmas tree and twirling skaters at Rockefeller Center, and the exquisite window displays of Christmases past at Bergdorf Goodman and Saks Fifth Avenue.

Interspersed with their sightseeing were medical exams at Hitzig's office, a visit to the United Nations, various receptions in their honor, and a meeting on the steps of St. Patrick's Cathedral with Francis Cardinal Spellman, arguably America's best-known and most influential Catholic prelate. Spellman's remarks praising the courage and fortitude of these Catholic women and underscoring the horrors of what they'd experienced were extensively covered by the media, as were most of their other activities while in Manhattan. The result was a flurry of front page headlines in *The New York Times* and several of the city's other major dailies, as well as numerous wire service stories reprinted by newspapers across the country.

Of course, none of this news coverage was an accident. It had been orchestrated by Cousins, Caroline Ferriday, and other members of their committee, who had spent the previous twelve months planning the *lapins'* visit. The publicity blitz was aimed primarily at the West German government.

One of the trip's main goals was to pressure West Germany into granting compensation to the *lapins*—a strategy that Cousins wanted to keep as quiet as possible. Still trying to nudge the Germans into cooperating, he suggested publicly that Bonn was edging closer to an agreement. "An attempt is being made, which we are convinced is genuine, to find a way around the previous difficulty: i.e., the fact that no diplomatic relations exist between Bonn and Warsaw," Cousins told his *Saturday Review* readers. "That Germany would soon like to make a meaningful moral gesture seems clear. There is definite movement on this issue."

In fact there were no signs of any such movement. The Bonn government had hired a Chicago public relations firm to monitor the American and international press coverage of the venture and to help handle its response. Initially, both the PR firm and German officials believed that public and press interest in the *lapins* would quickly dissipate once they'd left New York. Bonn made clear to Benjamin Ferencz that regardless of Cousins's optimistic public statements, it had not shifted its position.

A FEW DAYS BEFORE CHRISTMAS, most of the women said goodbye to their New York hosts and headed off to spend the holidays and the next two months with families in twelve cities: Philadelphia; Baltimore; Buffalo; Birmingham, Alabama; Detroit; Boston; Fall River, Massachusetts; Cleveland; Denver; Tampa; Phoenix; Los Angeles; and San Francisco.

The selection of a particular city for each woman was based on her medical needs and personal interests. Most of the women staying in New York and Boston were slated to undergo surgery on their legs at Manhattan's Mount Sinai Hospital and Boston's Beth Israel Hospital. Another woman, who had tuberculosis, was sent to the National Jewish

Hospital in Denver, which was internationally renowned for its treatment of tuberculosis patients. The rest of the Polish women, though, were found to be in better health than had been expected. Most of them received extensive dental work, but other than that, their medical care turned out to be minimal.

For most of the women, living with American families was the best part of their trip. No longer was the spotlight on their collective wartime suffering or their status as victims. In those private homes, they were accepted for who they were at that point in their lives: individuals with unique personalities, interests, and talents.

Joanna Szydlowaska, a sculptor and jewelry maker, spent most of her time in New York and San Francisco, where she visited museums, shops, and galleries and learned the art of enameling. Anna Zieleniec, an illustrator of children's books, took advantage of Southern California's balmy climate to sketch and paint outdoors. Maria Kuzmierczuk, a doctor and one of the most grievously wounded of the *lapins*, was supposed to undergo surgery at Mount Sinai in New York. Although she spent most of her time there over the next two months, it was not as a patient. Announcing she wanted "no more tinkering" on her leg, she studied new techniques in radiology being developed at Mount Sinai, including the use of radioisotopes.

Caroline Ferriday, who hosted Maria and two other Polish women at her New York apartment, wrote that "little by little, we could see a change taking place in these women who were marked not only by the instruments of Gebhardt but by a wound much more difficult to heal: a fundamental mistrust which had become their only weapon. They learned that friendship is not an illusion and that there were people in the world ready to help them, love them, and take on the fight alongside them."

THE POLISH WOMEN WERE not alone in benefiting from this cross-cultural exchange. Ann Horvitz was a case in point. In her midthirties, Ann was a homemaker who lived with her husband and four young children in Scottsdale, Arizona, an affluent suburb of Phoenix. Few of

Ann's friends and acquaintances there knew that she had formerly led a very different kind of life. A native New Yorker and graduate of Vassar, she had worked during World War II as a counterintelligence analyst for the Office of Strategic Services (OSS), America's intelligence and sabotage agency, in Washington, London, and Rome.

To Ann, it seemed an eon ago, but even as she focused now on home and family, she never lost interest in what was going on in the rest of the world. So when she and Lorraine Frank, a Scottsdale friend who was also a Vassar alumna, heard that the Cousins committee was looking for hosts for the Polish women, they both volunteered.

As the date of their guests' arrival approached, however, Ann began having second thoughts. She and Lorraine knew nothing about the women they were hosting except their names—Krystyna Wilgat and Janina Sterkowicz—and their professions—university professor and gynecologist/obstetrician.

Krystyna, a professor of geography and geology at the University of Lublin, would stay with the Horvitzes. Ann would not learn until later that her soon-to-be houseguest was one of the most celebrated of the *lapins*. As Krysia Czyz, Krystyna had been the mastermind behind the daring campaign that she, Nina Iwanska, and two other young Poles had launched at Ravensbrück to inform the world about the Nazi medical experiments through letters written in invisible ink.

Growing increasingly nervous about having a stranger in her home for an extended period, Ann, together with Lorraine, decided they would limit their hosting duties to one month and give other friends the opportunity to house the women for the second. After Ann and her husband, Wayne, picked up Krystyna from the Phoenix airport, she wondered, during the tense, awkward drive home, whether she could handle even a week.

Although warm and gracious, Krystyna spoke no English, and Ann had been counting on her own expertise in French to "keep the conversational ball rolling." To her horror, the only French word she could remember at the airport was *bonjour*. "Our twenty-minute ride was one of the longest periods of my life," she recalled.

By the following night, however, a "minor miracle" occurred, and

Ann's French began to return. "By the end of the week, there was no subject I couldn't tackle, admittedly with atrocious grammar and an even worse accent—but we were communicating!" In fact, they were talking nonstop. Krystyna wanted to learn some English, but, according to Ann, "she and I had so much to say to each other that we never had the willpower to stick to English for long when we could do so much better in French." Within days, the stranger "had become a member of our family."

The close bond that developed between the two women was partly due to their mutual fascination with Arizona's extraordinary landscape, particularly the iconic canyons and rock formations that dot much of the northern part of the state. But they also had in common a deep love for and attachment to home and family.

One weekend shortly after Krystyna's arrival, Ann and her husband took her to see the Petrified Forest, a national park in northeastern Arizona noted for its extraordinary fossilized trees dating back more than 200 million years. Krystyna "was almost beside herself with excitement at the wonders all around her," Ann remembered, but at dinner that night, she became quiet and seemed depressed. When Ann asked if anything was troubling her, Krystyna blurted out that she was sorry her husband wasn't there: It was their tenth wedding anniversary, and she wished she could be with him. She had been reluctant to come to America for such a long time, she added, but he and their four children had persuaded her to do so. She missed them terribly.

After listening to her story, the Horvitzes presented her with an anniversary gift: a phone call to her family in Lublin. Placing an international call in the 1950s was time-consuming and expensive—at least $10 (more than $100 today) for three minutes. On the day the call was placed, Krystyna was up at five in the morning, making a detailed list of all that she wanted to say to her family during those precious minutes.

The Horvitzes' kindness further cemented their friendship with their Polish guest. As the end of Krystyna's first month with them approached, Ann realized that both she and Lorraine Frank had made a mistake in their advance planning: "Far from looking for other people to take over the host role, we found we wanted our guests to stay on with us."

At the same time, she and Lorraine worked to limit the number of social engagements on Krystyna's and Janina's schedules. Deluged with invitations from women's clubs and other groups, the Polish women felt overwhelmed; their hostesses played the role of gatekeeper, accepting only a select few invitations on their behalf. They did agree to a couple of interviews with local media, knowing, as Ann wrote, "that a major objective of their trip was to remind the American public that they were forgotten victims of Nazi brutality."

For the rest of their visit, the women and their hosts mostly did what they wanted. Ann and Krystyna chose to go exploring. Among their favorite outings were hikes along an ancient trail bordering the Gila River that served from prehistoric days as the main road to the Pacific, and into the forbidding Superstition Mountain Range, where a host of nineteenth-century gold prospectors had lost their lives in their search for the mythic Lost Dutchman Mine.

For Ann, the high point of those two months was a weeklong car expedition she took with both Polish women into the wilds of the Navajo Nation, the largest land area held by a Native American tribe, occupying more than twenty-seven thousand square miles in northwestern New Mexico, northeastern Arizona, and southeastern Utah. A Navajo guide escorted them on a four-hour jeep ride into Canyon de Chelly, noted for its breathtakingly sheer red-orange sandstone cliffs and its ruins of indigenous tribal dwellings that dated back more than a thousand years.

On their way home, Ann and Krystyna climbed Sunset Crater, an extinct volcano that last erupted a millennium before. It was during this excursion that Krystyna opened up to Ann, telling her about the Nazis' butchery of the *lapins'* legs and her own role in revealing the atrocity to the world. "It was the first time I had heard the story," Ann remembered. "None of us wished to pry, and we never asked Krystyna or Janina direct questions about their experiences."

When Krystyna left in March 1959, the Horvitzes felt bereft. "I couldn't begin to name the rewards which Wayne and I derived from

Krystyna's visit," Ann wrote the following year in an article in Vassar's alumnae magazine. "But three stood out: an insight into her world, a glimpse of our own world as others see it, and above all the opportunity to know a rare human being whose courage and remarkable sense of values are seldom equaled. We all missed her when she left, right down to our three-year-old who had started by resenting her and ended up following her around like a puppy."

Both she and Krystyna were determined to keep their friendship going. "We correspond voluminously," Ann wrote. "Best of all, there is another chapter to come"—a trip planned by the Horvitzes the following summer to visit Krystyna and her family in Lublin.

Other American hosts voiced similar sentiments. In a letter to Norman Cousins, Mary Myers, who housed two Polish women in Los Angeles, wrote, "As I told each goodbye, a very real part of me dissolved and went along. It could not be otherwise. As their lives were enriched by the goodness of others, so my life has been doubly enriched by them."

The Polish women, for their part, expressed deep appreciation for the kindnesses shown them. One told Jeanne Benenson, a colleague of Cousins who was the executive director of the project, "I don't know how to say it right, but I feel a new kind of electricity running through me." Another wrote to Caroline Ferriday, "From the persons with whom we are living and from those we meet, we are continually receiving so many proofs of their sincere friendliness that to the end of my life, I am supplied with food for the soul. I regained my faith in people."

IN MARCH, THE SECOND contingent of Polish women, among them Nina Iwanska, arrived in New York. After a few days of sightseeing, they scattered throughout the country, most of them ending up in states with balmy winter weather, like Florida, California, and Arizona. Their compatriots from the earlier group joined them there, where they all were treated to a couple of weeks of total relaxation—swimming, sunbathing, and in general enjoying themselves.

Their final expedition before they returned to Poland was a three-week cross-country bus jaunt in May, starting in San Francisco and ending in New York City, with numerous stops along the way, including Disneyland (where they were guests of Walt Disney himself), the Grand Canyon, Las Vegas and its casinos, Dallas, Memphis, and, most important as it turned out, Washington, D.C.

The tour generated press attention at every stop, continuing the steady stream of news stories and features about the *lapins'* visit that had appeared in newspapers, magazines, and television news broadcasts throughout the country since they first arrived in America five months before. Increasingly, the coverage focused on the refusal of the West German government to provide compensation to them. *Look* magazine published a scathing article eviscerating the Germans for their inaction. In an editorial, *The Washington Post* declared that "justice for the 'Lapins' is a major obligation" for the Germans, adding that the women's visit "has brought public opinion pressure upon the German government with some success." As the *Oakland Tribune* saw it, "Surely there is an unbalanced scale of justice being used in this case. Reparation to the Ravensbrück Lapins ought to be the responsibility of those who, while repudiating their 'collective guilt,' insist upon their collective remorse for the atrocities committed by Hitler in the name of the German people."

Members of the public were speaking up, too. *The New York Times* ran a letter to the editor from a reader named Samuel Weiss, who wrote that "the Germans perpetrated these inhuman acts. Wouldn't you think they would come forward freely and provide any funds necessary to ameliorate the agony which these Lapins live with?" In a letter to the German ambassador, Albert Shaft, a Philadelphia doctor, declared, "It is disgusting to learn that the present German government has taken [this] position. . . . [It is] an insult to individuals of intelligence and good will."

Even though the German government's strategy to ignore the issue, hoping it would fade away, was clearly not working, it remained obdurate in its refusal to provide compensation. In a meeting with a Foreign Ministry official in Bonn, Benjamin Ferencz was told that "it did not pay financially or politically to incite strong American public reaction against Germany on an issue of this kind." Informing Cousins that he had been shut out, Ferencz wrote, "Only the highest level in the Foreign Office could bring about a serious reconsideration, and I must therefore throw the ball back to you for action."

Speaking a few months earlier about his and Cousins's strategy in dealing with the Germans, Ferencz had said, "The silk glove must precede the mailed fist." The "silk glove" approach had clearly failed. It was now time for the "mailed fist." The first blows would come from members of the U.S. Congress.

WHEN THE TOUR BUS arrived in Washington, the Polish women discovered they'd become front page news in the nation's capital. Prodded by the Cousins committee, the Washington press corps was paying close attention to the issue of Germany's refusal to provide reparations. So, too, were a growing number of senators and representatives. Dozens of them attended a luncheon in the women's honor sponsored by Senator Jacob Javits of New York and held in the Senate dining room. Some of the legislators were of Polish descent, while others represented large Polish populations in their districts or states. Several were chairmen of influential congressional committees, including Representative Clement Zablocki of Wisconsin, chair of the House Foreign Affairs Committee, and Representative Emanuel Celler of New York, chair of the House Judiciary Committee.

As the women discovered, the luncheon was just the opening act of a major PR offensive. After the lunch, the women were escorted to the gallery of the Senate chamber, where Senator Frank Carlson of Kansas called his colleagues' attention to their presence. That was the cue for well over an hour of senatorial tributes to them and emphatic criticism of the West German government. One by one, senators rose to speak. Some were lions of the chamber, like Javits; his New York colleague, Kenneth Keating; and Montana's Mike Mansfield, soon to become Senate majority leader. Others were rising congressional stars, like Wisconsin's Eugene McCarthy, a future Democratic candidate for president. Yet another was Thomas Dodd of Connecticut, who'd served as the deputy U.S. prosecutor at the main Nuremberg tribunal, during which he'd cross-examined some of Nazi Germany's top leaders.

But the most passionate address came from Edmund Muskie of Maine, whose father had emigrated from Poland in 1903. "For nearly ten years, various groups and individuals have attempted to persuade the government of West Germany that it has an obligation to these courageous women," Muskie said. "Nothing has happened. How can it be that even now, a decade and a half after the end of the war, we are still far from having achieved justice for these victims of some of the most inhuman actions on record?" He added, "All America has been touched by the story of these ladies. We demand that West Germany provide a prompt and just settlement of their claims."

Faced with criticism from some of America's top congressional leaders, several of whom played key roles in deciding which countries received U.S. aid, the West German government began to rethink its refusal to provide recompense. Two days after the women's congressional visit, the German embassy in Washington sent a $27,000 check to the Cousins committee to help defray the costs of their medical care in the United States. A nice gesture, Cousins replied, but it was not enough: The *lapins* wanted what they had been requesting for years: ongoing pension payments like those paid to other victims of Nazi medical experiments.

In early June 1959, the women boarded a Pan Am flight in New York for their return to Poland. Caroline Ferriday, who saw them off, wrote in *The Saturday Review* about the striking changes she had noted in their appearance and demeanor over the past six months. "These were rested, well-groomed, outgoing, and self-confident women who got on that plane," she observed. "Their departure has left a void, but it in no way means the end of our work. Quite the contrary!"

The committee's pressure campaign continued. "On several occasions, we went as a group to Washington, giving testimony in both the

Senate and the House," Caroline recalled. "Letters were written, articles were published, and the cause we had adopted was not allowed to fall into oblivion for a moment."

Ferencz, meanwhile, was on the phone to the German ambassador several times a week. "We'll keep on marching," he told the ambassador at one point, "and we're going to continue to hammer the hell out of you until you take a more moral position." According to Ferencz, after months of lobbying, the ambassador finally came around to his point of view, calling the lawyer into his office and showing him a telegram he had sent that morning to Bonn. "The gist of it," Ferencz said, "was 'This is not a legal matter, it's not a financial matter, it's a political matter. And I'm telling you these women are ruining the reputation of Germany in ways we'll never recover from. You need to satisfy them.' "

But while the ambassador and several other officials in the German Foreign Ministry were now advocating a settlement, the Finance Ministry, which was directly responsible for reparations, was still opposed. Indeed, Ferencz was told during a trip to Bonn that ministry officials had put out the word he was a Communist and that no money should be paid out to the Polish women because it would be used for "nefarious Communist purposes." In response, Ferencz offered to recuse himself and have the International Red Cross handle the negotiation and distribution of reparations.

The wrangling continued until the spring of 1960, when Bonn finally conceded defeat. At a meeting of the German cabinet, a statement was read into the record noting that "a short time ago, the Polish women were in the American senate and received a warm reception as victims of Hitlerism. America is today still deeply aroused about this matter. We have not only a political but also a moral duty to help in this instance." That same day, the Bundestag, Germany's legislature, voted to pay compensation to each of the *lapins*.

Despite the fact that the International Red Cross agreed to mediate, it took another eighteen months—and several more rounds of negotiations—before the deal was finalized and payment was made. Initially, the German government offered lump sums ranging from 2,000 to 25,000 deutsche marks ($500 to $6,250 in 1960 dollars), depending on the severity of each woman's injuries. The Cousins committee, the Polish Red Cross, and the women themselves rejected the offer. Both sides finally agreed to the range proposed by the International Red Cross: 25,000–40,000 deutsche marks (roughly $65,000–$105,000 in today's dollars). Most of the *lapins* received the maximum amount.

The settlement was not all they wanted—they had initially requested monthly pensions—but it still was a major victory. A miracle, Caroline Ferriday called it. "In a divided world, men and women of different nationalities and faiths have made common cause," she wrote in *Voix et Visages*. "They have voluntarily undertaken to rectify a scandalous injustice and, despite all the difficulties, have spent their strength and their assets so that the rights of the weak are recognized and the wrong righted.

"The new year [of 1962] brings to our friends in Poland, not only the material aid which was refused so unjustly and for so long, but also the conviction that their suffering has finally been recognized, that the German Government has admitted the crimes of its predecessors. For each lapin of Ravensbrück, the future looks a little less dark, because our dear lapins know today that they are no longer alone."

There was more good news for the Polish women. In the mid-1950s, one of them had alerted ADIR that Herta Oberheuser, the Nazi doctor found guilty at Nuremberg for her involvement in the experiments on them, was practicing medicine in Stocksee, a small town in northern Germany, after her 1952 release from a German prison. With the help of the British Medical Association, who called Oberheuser's return to medicine "an affront to the honour, morals, and ideals of medical practice," ADIR launched a campaign to have her medical license taken away. In 1960, the government of the state of Schleswig-Holstein permanently revoked her license and shut down her practice.

In the months and years to come, the triumphant ten-year crusade to win justice for the *lapins* would receive considerable public attention. Most of the credit for its success would go to Caroline Ferriday and Norman Cousins, who was singled out by *The New York Times* as the main figure in the effort in its front-page story about the German settlement. In *Lilac Girls*, her bestselling 2015 novel about the Polish rabbits of Ravensbrück, Martha Hall Kelly makes Caroline Ferriday her central character.

Unquestionably, both Cousins and Caroline played key roles in the campaign, which would not have succeeded without them. But it's also important to note that it would never have been launched at all if it hadn't been for Anise Postel-Vinay and her promise to make good on her pledge to Nina Iwanska. Never in the public eye, she and ADIR worked behind the scenes throughout the effort. Only once—during her encounter with Dr. William Hitzig—did Anise step out of the shadows, to let Cousins's partner know that she and her French comrades from Ravensbrück were the ones responsible for its creation. Hitzig had no trouble believing it. As he had written Cousins several years before, without Anise's "courage and genius," the project would never have gotten off the ground.

Chapter 19

"Watchmen in the Night"

O N A LATE SPRING MORNING IN 1987, A YOUNG AMERICAN journalist stood for a moment in front of the door of a Paris apartment, then rang the bell. A tall, elegant woman, her snow-white hair pulled back in a French twist, opened the door and invited her in.

World War II and the French Resistance were very much in the news that year. Klaus Barbie, the Gestapo chief in Lyon who was responsible for the murder of Jean Moulin and thousands of other Resistance members, as well as untold numbers of Jews, had been found in Bolivia and was extradited back to Lyon in 1983 to face trial. It finally took place in May 1987.

Maia Wechsler, a correspondent for *U.S. News and World Report,* was dispatched to Lyon to cover the trial's first days and provide material for a story to be written by the American newsmagazine's Paris bureau chief. But she was eager to produce a story of her own—a feature on a Resistance survivor. An acquaintance put her in touch with a woman regarded as a heroine of that time—sixty-eight-year-old Jacqueline Péry d'Alincourt.

Initially nervous about interviewing this icon, Maia listened, enthralled, as Jacqueline recounted one story after another, beginning with her first days in the Resistance and continuing through her agonizing time at Ravensbrück. "We talked for hours," Maia recalled,

"and then Jacqueline said, 'You must come back again tomorrow.' "
When she returned, Jacqueline picked up where she had left off, the
stories spilling out, again for hours.

Maia did write an article, but that was hardly enough: Jacqueline
d'Alincourt's risking everything, including her life, in her passionate
fight for justice and freedom had struck a chord. "It was so much in line
with where I came from," Maia remarked. "That was how I was taught
to view the world. I said, 'I want to make a movie about her one day.' "

BORN AND RAISED IN Gary, Indiana, Maia Wechsler was brought up
by Jewish parents who were deeply engaged in the 1960s civil rights
movement and other campaigns for political and social justice. Burton
and Fredrica Wechsler, among their other activities, played a major
role in the 1968 election of Richard Hatcher as the first black mayor of
Gary (and, as it happened, the first black mayor of any sizable American city). The Wechslers' house was a frequent meeting place for various activist groups, including the ACLU, the NAACP, and the local
branch of Dr. Martin Luther King, Jr.'s Southern Christian Leadership
Conference. When public school teachers went out on strike in Gary,
Maia's father, a lawyer, took her with him to picket alongside her own
teachers outside her school.

While caught up in social activism as a child, she also had another
passion—ballet—and from the age of twelve, she devoted much of her
energy and time to dance classes and performances. After her junior
year in high school, she left for New York to pursue her dream of becoming a ballerina. At the age of eighteen, however, she broke her
ankle, and despite many months of work to rehabilitate it, she was
never able to dance on pointe again.

Devastated, Maia continued to take classes and perform with small
dance companies in New York. "I just could not let it go," she said. But
during this period, she also enrolled in French courses at Columbia
University. The language was not new to her; she had taken French
classes since middle school. She performed well in the courses, and in
the summer of 1980, she registered for a Columbia summer program in

Paris. "It was the first time I dared to leave New York and my ballet training," she said. "It turned out to be the most liberating summer ever." She fell in love with the language and with Paris, which gave her the impetus to give up ballet and return to school.

Having earned her GED several years earlier, Maia enrolled at Barnard College in New York. She then returned to Paris for a year abroad in 1981, immersing herself in studies about France during World War II, particularly the Vichy government's deportation of the country's Jews. Her closest friend during this time was a Duke University student named Paul Farmer, who, less than a decade later, would become world renowned for his work providing healthcare to the poorest of the poor around the globe. "He was the smartest person I'd ever met, and the most selfless," Maia recalled. "He had already committed himself to saving the world. He became very significant in my life. I began to feel I needed to live up to his example and that of my parents."

After her year in Paris, Maia went back to Barnard and finished her degree. In 1983, she returned to France and was hired as an editorial assistant at *Passion*, a trendy English-language magazine about life in Paris. Less than a year later, she became its managing editor. She enjoyed working there but eventually decided she wanted a more substantial journalistic career. "I remember Paul came to visit once," she said, "and I almost felt I had to apologize for where I was working."

In late 1986, Maia was hired by *U.S. News and World Report*. Not long afterward, she encountered Jacqueline Péry d'Alincourt—an event that would change her life.

SINCE THE EARLY POSTWAR YEARS, Jacqueline had faced what seemed like an endless series of personal crises. Her good fortune after her liberation from Ravensbrück—the idyllic reunion with her family and her whirlwind romance and marriage to Pierre Péry—deserted her not long after she and Pierre moved to New York in 1946 and she gave birth to her first daughter.

"She wanted a baby, but she was not ready in her body and probably in her mind," her granddaughter, Aline Corraze de Ziegler, observed.

"She couldn't sleep, she was having a lot of nightmares. Life was very, very hard for her." Still extremely weak, Jacqueline became pregnant again soon after the arrival of her daughter, and she and Pierre moved back to France for her second child's birth. Both the pregnancy and birth were difficult, and the health of mother and newborn was fragile for many months.

In a letter to Germaine Tillion, Jacqueline poured out her anguish about her weakened physical condition and the difficulties she had in taking care of her daughters: "I feel completely powerless to protect them, too tired to raise them." At the same time, her husband's health began to deteriorate rapidly, in large part because of the torture and other horrific treatment he'd endured at Buchenwald. He also was suffering from the aftereffects of the traumatic brain injury he'd sustained in a plane crash during his prewar training as an army pilot. "He says I am essential to him, that he cannot breathe without me," Jacqueline told Germaine.

Eventually, Pierre was forced to stop working. "Doctors told me I had to take responsibility for the family, and at that time I didn't believe them," Jacqueline later said. "I thought to myself: I experienced a miracle when I left Ravensbrück alive. Now we'll have another miracle by healing Pierre. But we couldn't cure him. It was as if his life was going out like the flame of a candle, disappearing little by little."

Forced to get a job to provide for her husband's care and her children's livelihood, Jacqueline, who had no professional training or experience, had little luck in the beginning. She worked as a temporary employee for a number of companies and associations, often as a translator. Gradually, though, the jobs became more substantive. She was hired for a public relations position at an international transportation association, which initially "terrified me." She discovered, however, that she was not only very good at it but thoroughly enjoyed what she was doing. "It was excellent for me in all respects," she later said. "I found that when you have a professional job, you are forced to put your other concerns on hold. It was the best possible way of gaining psychological strength."

She later was hired as an executive at an association that promoted

French companies and products abroad. For the next fifteen years, she traveled the world, including many trips to the United States. It was a fulfilling and demanding position, and it proved to be her lifeline when she was hit by two tragedies. In 1964, Pierre Péry died at the age of fifty-four. Ten years later, Jacqueline lost her younger daughter, twenty-six-year-old Marie-Claire, in a car accident on Long Island, New York, where Marie-Claire and her American husband had been living.

For some forty years after the war, Jacqueline had largely tucked her wartime memories away in the back of her mind. She still was close to Resistance friends like Geneviève de Gaulle and Germaine Tillion—and with Claire Chevrillon, with whom she had worked in Paris during the war. They and several others had banded together to give her emotional support when she lost Pierre and Marie-Claire. She also had made a couple of trips to Ravensbrück, joining other former deportees from all over Europe to lay wreaths outside the camp's walls to honor their dead comrades. But she never talked publicly about what had happened to her. Instead she focused on making a living.

Then, shortly after she retired from her job in 1984, Jacqueline received an invitation from Scripps College, a private liberal arts school for women in Claremont, California, to speak to its students about her experience in the Resistance and at Ravensbrück. At first she thought about turning the offer down. "I couldn't imagine what I could say and how to say it," she remarked. "It is really difficult to return to that time. It's like finding yourself in front of a wall: behind the wall, something terrible is waiting for me, and I have to go there, in order to show it to you. And I have to say the unspeakable."

She was finally persuaded to accept by Claire Chevrillon, to whom, soon after Jacqueline's return from Ravensbrück, she had given a written description of her time there. Claire had kept it, and now she brought it out and gave it back to her friend. "People have to know this, Jacqueline," she said. "It's your duty to tell them."

After her appearance at Scripps, the floodgates opened. For the rest of her life, Jacqueline Péry d'Alincourt dedicated herself to what she called "the duty of memory," bearing witness to the horrors of what she and her fellow *résistantes* had endured and emphasizing the continuing importance of joining forces and standing up against evil. She wrote articles, made radio and television broadcasts, and addressed audiences at schools, universities, cultural centers, and other groups and institutions in France and abroad.

It was soon after Jacqueline launched this new phase of her life that she met Maia Wechsler, forming a friendship that would last until her death more than twenty years later. "What I came to understand was that she had a desperate need to speak," Maia said. "I became her designated listener because I wanted to know everything about her. I felt a need to tell her story."

The year after her first interviews with Jacqueline, Maia had returned to the United States and married Edward Hernstadt, a young American she had met in Paris. While her husband attended law school at the University of Pennsylvania, she got a job as a reporter for New Jersey's *Trenton Times*. Her long-term objective, though, remained the same: to make a documentary film about Jacqueline and her circle of friends from Ravensbrück. "She talked a lot about the closeness of these women—how important they'd been to each other's survival and how important they were to each other now."

As a first step toward her goal, Maia enrolled in a New York University course on documentary film theory. Her teacher, a Frenchwoman, loved her idea and encouraged her to write a proposal, which she did. Having no experience in film production, she set out to get some, assisting on various documentary projects, including working as an assistant editor on a film by the Academy Award–winning documentarian Barbara Kopple.

In 1992, Maia realized she couldn't wait any longer. Jacqueline and her friends were now in their seventies and eighties, and although most were in relatively good health, who knew how long that would last? Early the following year, accompanied by her husband, she flew to Paris to see Jacqueline and tell her about her idea for a film. Over lunch, she mentioned that after their stay in Paris, she and Ed were planning to visit Ravensbrück. Jacqueline asked if she could go with them. Maia was stunned: "I said it would be the dream of my life if she would come."

In her earlier trips to Ravensbrück, Jacqueline and her comrades had never actually entered the camp itself. After the Russians liberated it in 1945, they had turned it into a Soviet army camp that was off-limits to everyone but Soviet military personnel. But after the Soviet Union's fall in 1991, its army began pulling out of Eastern Europe, including its bases in East Germany, where Ravensbrück was located.

When Jacqueline, Maia, and Ed arrived there one morning in March 1993, Russian soldiers were in the midst of packing up, and the visitors, accompanied by an East German archivist, were allowed to enter the camp. For the first time in almost fifty years, Jacqueline, aided by an ivory cane, walked past the gates, across the giant square where the daily wartime roll calls had been held, and into the interior of the place that, for her, had been hell on earth.

Although the barracks had been torn down, their concrete foundations were still in place. Jacqueline identified the location of the quarantine barracks, where she and the camp's other prisoners were first sent. With the help of the archivist, she eventually found Barracks 31, where she and Geneviève de Gaulle had slept on a straw pallet together, and the clothing workshop, where Geneviève had come close to death and where Jacqueline had surreptitiously made the little doll to comfort her when Geneviève was a prisoner in the Bunker.

Somber but composed, Jacqueline talked to Maia, Ed, and the archivist about her experiences in the camp. Maia said, "It was a day of memory for her and a day of discovery for me."

OVER THE NEXT SEVERAL YEARS, Maia spent considerable time in Paris with Jacqueline, meeting and getting to know other Ravensbrück survivors. She filmed an interview with Jacqueline and put together a preview reel, complete with archival footage, to show potential investors. Even for experienced documentary filmmakers, finding financial backers is more often than not a slow, frustrating grind. For a novice like Maia, the effort was particularly challenging.

One day, in the midst of her search for funds, she had a phone conversation with an old New York friend of hers who was working in Los

Angeles as a writer for a new television series called *Star Trek: Voyager*—the latest spinoff of the extraordinarily successful franchise. When she told her friend about the film, he said, "Come to L.A. and I'll have a fundraiser for you. I'll invite all my friends on the show."

At the cocktail party he gave, one of the guests was Kate Mulgrew, the star of the series. Mulgrew played Captain Kathryn Janeway, commander of the Starfleet starship the USS *Voyager*—the first time the franchise featured a woman as the lead character. Over the series's seven-year run, Kathryn Janeway became a hero to girls all over the world, including New York congresswoman Alexandria Ocasio-Cortez, Georgia activist and political leader Stacey Abrams, and Samantha Cristoforetti, an Italian astronaut who in 2015 tweeted a photo of herself aboard the International Space Station in a *Star Trek* uniform.

After Maia showed her preview reel at the party, Mulgrew approached her. "I love what you're doing, and if I can help you, I will," she said. Maia recalled that Mulgrew "gave me a few thousand dollars then and there, and about eight months later, she had a sit-down dinner party for me at her home and invited all the show's producers and other leading actors." At the dinner, Mulgrew spoke about the importance of Maia's project and urged her co-workers to provide the funds to make it. They did—"and that's how I financed the film. The money from all my *Star Trek* supporters at these two events got me through the rest of production."

With that infusion of funds, Maia could now turn her full attention to shooting the film. One of her first tasks was to decide which former *résistantes* besides Jacqueline she would focus on. She spent some time at the weekly meetings of ADIR, which, even though its membership had dwindled considerably in recent years, was still functioning. What particularly impressed her was the ongoing activism of its members. Unlike many male war veterans' groups, whose gatherings were largely devoted to rehashing the past, the survivors of Ravensbrück, while still bearing witness to their shared history, were also fighting for social and economic justice in the present and for the future.

"No one better than us, the deportees, knows what it's like to be deprived of the deepest rights of a human being, to be treated like noth-

ing, to be controlled, to be humiliated," Geneviève de Gaulle Anthonioz declared at one ADIR annual meeting. "We will fight to protect
others who are in that same situation until we no longer draw breath."
She and others in the group focused on those who had been most forgotten in modern society—the poor, the homeless, the elderly, children, refugees.

Maia was struck by the tight bonds that linked all the women, but
she was particularly fascinated by the closeness between Jacqueline,
Geneviève, Germaine Tillion, and Anise Postel-Vinay. There was a
special warmth and tenderness that united them, almost as if they were
actual sisters. Her film would focus on the four of them, Maia decided.
She already knew a great deal about Jacqueline; now she had to explore
the lives of the other three.

WHEN MAIA WECHSLER MET Germaine Tillion in the 1990s, Germaine, then in her late eighties, had long been regarded as one of the
most influential public intellectuals in the country. Known as "the
moral conscience of twentieth-century France," she was still extremely
active, writing and speaking about the value and dignity of every
human being and insisting on telling truth to power.

Her renown stemmed largely from her involvement in the fierce
national debate in the 1950s and '60s over the French-Algerian conflict,
which began when Algerian nationalists launched an armed uprising in
1954 against their French colonial masters. Because of her prewar work
in Algeria, the French government asked Germaine to investigate conditions there. She found the country in a state of near collapse, with
poverty and hunger endemic among its population, along with an upsurge of anger, hopelessness, and alienation.

In an effort to improve the life of the Algerian people, Germaine
persuaded the government to authorize the creation of a national network of social centers, aimed at providing basic education, job training, and health services. The centers, which she ran, eventually
numbered several dozen, with more than four hundred employees. In
1955, when all-out war erupted between the Algerian National Libera-

tion Front (FLN) and French military forces, the social centers were caught in the murderous cross fire: The FLN murdered several center workers, while the French military arrested and tortured a good number of them.

In 1957, Germaine wrote a book analyzing the social and economic reasons for the conflict that was tearing France apart. It became an immediate bestseller and made her a major public figure. A year later, French officials asked her to return to Algeria as part of an international committee inspecting the prisons and prisoner of war camps in which Algerian fighters were being held. She was profoundly shocked by what she discovered: the widespread use of torture by the French military. Even worse was the fact it had been officially sanctioned by the French government.

She immediately condemned what she called the Gestapo-like interrogation techniques being practiced in Algeria. "Unlike what happened in 1942," Germaine wrote, "it is now our people who are arresting, monitoring, and torturing. These are my compatriots, my loved ones, with whom I have always felt solidarity. . . . And yet what is happening before my eyes is obvious: they are using the same practices as those of the Nazis." As *The New York Times* pointed out, "hers was one of the first and loudest voices to protest French torture."

At the same time, Germaine also condemned FLN terrorism, unlike many leftist intellectuals who, led by Simone de Beauvoir and Jean-Paul Sartre, defended the rebels' tactics. "The survivor of Ravensbrück refused to excuse torture or murder or atrocities by anyone," wrote one observer. "She had witnessed more than enough barbarism for one lifetime."

Harshly criticized by both sides—the intellectuals and those supporting the government's tactics—Germaine, fearless as usual, made no apologies. "I am always on the side of those who are under attack," she said. "I am on the side of those who receive the blows." Regardless of whether a war was just or unjust, she declared, it was never permissible to torture a person or massacre civilians. Years later, she told a friend, "Today, I still love my country, perhaps even more than I did before, but if I find something wrong that it's doing, with all my strength I will try to prevent it."

Germaine's unflagging condemnation of the use of torture was credited by some political observers with helping to sway a large segment of French public opinion toward supporting independence for Algeria. Among the prominent figures with whom she conferred was Charles de Gaulle, who at that point was in retirement but was considering running again for president of France. "If God wants me back in service, I will take this matter seriously," he told Germaine. He lived up to his pledge. After taking office again in 1958, de Gaulle authorized negotiations that in 1962 brought an end to the eight-year war and formalized the status of Algeria as an independent nation.

During that period, Geneviève de Gaulle Anthonioz, too, had become a moral conscience for France. In her quiet, understated way, she mounted a crusade seeking economic and social justice for the poor and homeless of her country and elsewhere.

In 1958, shortly before that effort began, Geneviève had joined her uncle's government as an official in the newly created Ministry of Culture, led by André Malraux. She also had become the president of ADIR. When she was asked to visit a recently erected encampment of homeless families in the working-class Paris suburb of Noisy-le-Grand, she had no intention of taking on any more responsibilities.

But all that changed once she saw the occupants of the corrugated tin shacks that lined the muddy paths of the makeshift camp. Everything about the place and the people reminded her of Ravensbrück. "When I entered this large shantytown, at the end of a mud road, I thought of the camp," she recalled. "Of course, there were no watchtowers, no SS sentries, no barbed and electrified enclosure, but this landscape of low, undulating roofs from which gray smoke rose was a place separated from life."

On that freezing day, there was no heat or light. Garbage was everywhere, and children played next to an open sewer. Adults wandered around the camp with the same empty eyes and gaunt features as Ravensbrück inmates. "The expression that I read on [these] faces was the one that I had read a long time before on the faces of my comrades in deportation. I read the humiliation and despair of a human being struggling to maintain his dignity."

Also familiar were the rank odors of garbage, human waste, and unwashed bodies. "I recognized the smell immediately," she wrote. "It was the way I smelled at Ravensbrück, the way everything smelled. Suddenly I was back there. . . . When you are scarred as I was, there are certain things you can never accept again."

Geneviève quit her job in the government and from then on devoted most of her time to a crusade to improve living conditions in the Noisy-le-Grand camp. She later headed an international movement called Aide à Toute Détresse (ATD), aimed at eradicating poverty throughout the world. Today, that organization, now called ATD Fourth World, operates in twelve nations in Europe; the United States and Canada; seven countries in Latin America; and nine in Asia and Africa.

In a 1962 article in *Voix et Visages*, Geneviève called on her fellow survivors to join in her fight to help those excluded and forgotten by the rest of society. "Our past struggles and suffering give us more duties than rights," she wrote. "Duties toward our country, duties of solidarity with those who undergo ordeals similar to those we have endured."

While Germaine Tillion's and Geneviève de Gaulle Anthonioz's activities were very much in the public eye after the war, Anise Postel-Vinay was, as usual, working behind the scenes. In addition to her efforts on behalf of the Polish rabbits, she had replaced Germaine as the foremost researcher into the deportation of French women resisters, as well as Nazi war crimes at Ravensbrück. When Germaine began focusing on Algeria, Anise, helped by others, completed Germaine's work on that project and played a major role in the 1973 and 1988 updates of her classic work, *Ravensbrück*.

Germaine's and Anise's vast documentation of the Frenchwomen's experiences became the underpinning for an extraordinary book called *Les Françaises á Ravensbrück*. Published in 1964, the book combined their research with collective testimony from hundreds of survivors, "providing as complete and accurate a vision of the deportation of French women as possible," in the words of one survivor.

In the book, the French survivors described in detail how they risked death to defy the Germans. "For us," they declared, "the camp was not only a symbol of destruction. It was also the symbol of a struggle. Caught up in this relentless machine, we carried on the fight by joining forces, withstanding brutality and debasement, and crippling Nazi production in all sorts of ways. We knew that as long as we were alive, we continued to be one of the elements of the immense battle that was taking place in France."

At about the same time the book was published, Anise became one of the first voices to speak out against revisionist historians who in the 1960s had begun to raise questions about the Holocaust. Some denied it had ever happened, while others took issue with various aspects of it.

In 1968, the French historian Olga Wormser-Migot claimed that, contrary to the testimony of concentration camp survivors, there were never any gas chambers in the camps located in Germany, like Ravensbrück and Mauthausen. In the early 1970s, Robert Faurisson, a French literature professor at the University of Lyon, upped the ante, writing a number of scholarly articles and letters to French newspapers contending that gas chambers had never existed at Auschwitz or elsewhere. He called the Holocaust a forgery staged by Jewish conspirators.

Anise, who had never recovered emotionally from Émilie Tillion's death in the Ravensbrück gas chamber, was outraged. For several years, she traveled to government archives throughout Europe, unearthing documents and statements from, among others, German, Polish, and Czech survivors who had worked in the camp's administrative offices and could testify to the existence of the gas chamber.

She added her evidence to that of historians from Germany, Israel, and elsewhere to debunk the claims of Faurisson and other deniers. Their work, published first in German and then in French (as *Les Chambres à gaz: Secret d'état*), was one of the first books countering the deniers.

———

AS MAIA LEARNED MORE about the four women's lives, she repeatedly asked herself, "What would I have done? Would I have had the courage to follow their lead?" Years later, she said, "They became for me a kind of barometer, setting this incredibly high bar of integrity, action, morality, courage, and resolve."

For three years she conducted interviews with them, separately and together, usually at their homes. Germaine's two houses—one in Saint-Mandé, a leafy, affluent neighborhood just east of Paris, and the other a summer cottage on the south coast of Brittany—were favorite gathering spots. Warm and ebullient, Germaine loved to entertain, welcoming visitors of all kinds, from college students to heads of state. But her friends from Ravensbrück occupied a special place in her heart.

During her time with the four women, Maia paid close attention to their interactions. Germaine and Geneviève seemed completely comfortable with each other, bantering back and forth and often engaging in mutual teasing. During one session, Germaine, talking about the beginning of French resistance to the Germans, vehemently declared, "France in 1940 was unbelievable! There were no men! Women began the Resistance." Sitting next to her, Geneviève, her eyes twinkling, let a moment pass. Then she said with a slight smile, "Well, there were a few." Germaine sputtered a bit, then joined in the laughter that followed.

That sense of ease extended to their relationships with Anise and Jacqueline. "We have a very great need for one another," Geneviève explained to Maia. "Something exists between us that cannot be compared to any other bond. Yes, I do have friends who were not deported. Very good friends, in fact. But what we have is something else entirely."

No one but a fellow survivor could fully appreciate the immense scale of the horror they experienced during the war, nor could anyone else understand how haunted they remained by Ravensbrück. Often, when Anise was asked about the circumstances surrounding Émilie Tillion's death, she would begin to speak in a voice choked with emotion and then break down in tears. "Sorry," she apologized when she abruptly stopped talking about Émilie during an interview with Maia. On another occasion, she said to her, "Excuse me. I wrote this down for you, and I'll give it to you later. I can't talk about it." According to Jeannie Rousseau, Anise "has always borne the guilt of Émilie Tillion's death. She has not forgotten it for one second."

In an interview with a journalist more than a decade later, Anise said, "I thought that as I got older, the shadow of what I went through would fade and I would forget a little. But it's been the opposite: Seventy years after my return, this past is more and more present in me. I lost the ability to sleep like a child during the war, and I never found it again. I often have the same nightmare: The Gestapo are chasing me. But I run so fast that I wake up."

For other survivors, insomnia and nightmares were also common, long-lasting afflictions. When a woman asked Jacqueline if it was possible to forget Ravensbrück, she replied, "Every night for a long time, I woke up screaming because of my dreams. And even awake, I would suddenly be overwhelmed by visions so terrible that I couldn't hold back a cry." In 1949, Germaine wrote to Anise, "I dream almost every night of the dead, or of being killed, or of someone being killed in front of me."

Maia once asked Jacqueline if she and the others ever talked among themselves about the horrendous things they experienced at the camp. "They're always very present," Jacqueline replied. "But what we talk about now are memories that are linked to friendship and tenderness or incidents that are humorous or ridiculous or a little absurd. Not the things that endangered our lives or the deepest parts of our being. It would be unbearable for us if we spent our time talking about these horrors. We had to fight against them in order to breathe, to be able to exist. We had to fight against them to rebuild our lives." The women's ceaseless activism, Maia concluded, helped them manage that pain and those scars.

During interviews with Maia, the women occasionally acknowledged their growing concern about the rise of right-wing populism throughout Europe—an unsavory stew of authoritarianism, xenophobia, racism, antisemitism, and intolerance toward groups like refugees and other immigrants. It reminded them of the Nazis.

"The world must pay attention to this contempt and negation of 'the other,'" Geneviève said. "Sometimes I say we are a bit like watchmen in the night. We feel the need to warn that this attitude—to despise human beings we consider inferior—is how we ended up with places like Auschwitz and Ravensbrück." But she and the others still held out hope, based on their own solidarity at Ravensbrück, that justice would prevail. "Our time there taught me a lot about the horror of which men are capable," Jacqueline observed. "But it also taught me a lot about the extraordinary courage and dedication of people, too. Even when we were subjected to every possible way to destroy us, we refused to allow that to happen and were able to resist."

Germaine echoed that view. To Maia, she emphasized that "we don't have a pessimistic, black vision of humanity. Of course, there are terrible people in the world, but there is also so much greatness, so much nobility that exists. That's the message we want to get across. Yes, we have worries, but we also have hope."

FOURTEEN YEARS AFTER MAIA WECHSLER first met Jacqueline Péry d'Alincourt, she completed her film. Narrated by Kate Mulgrew, *Sisters in Resistance* was shown at numerous film festivals in the United States and France and won several awards. PBS broadcast it in 2003, as did one of the major French television networks. Maia went on to make several more well-received, award-winning documentaries.

Jacqueline, who, in Maia's words, had "stuck by me" throughout the long process of making the film, was by her side when it was released, traveling with her to festivals and other venues to promote it. In effect, she became part of Maia's family, which now included two young children. She often visited Maia, Ed, and the kids in their apartment in lower Manhattan, sleeping in a room designated as the family's library, with its floor-to-ceiling bookshelves and a rolling ladder to reach the highest ones. "She loved it," Maia remembered. "She would often read

Jacqueline Péry d'Alincourt and her granddaughter
Aline Corraze de Ziegler peering inside the
Ravensbrück building where Jacqueline spent
several harrowing months as a laborer in a sewing
workshop, 1999

late into the night." When the family moved to Brooklyn in 2004, she came there, too, visiting at least twice before her death in 2009.

"I think about Jacqueline all the time," Maia said in 2024, more than two decades after *Sisters in Resistance* was released. "She and the others have never left me. To be in their presence was the greatest honor I've ever had. I've never lost the feeling of how fortunate I was to meet them and tell their story."

Together with Maia's parents, they're her role models, she added, reminding her that "no matter how isolated we are, how few in numbers we are, we must act" to resist oppression. "I feel an obligation to show up. If I don't show up and nobody else shows up, then who will fight injustice? That's part of me now, thanks to them."

Chapter 20
·······

*"This Beautiful Piece
of Art"*

WHEN THE PLAYWRIGHT KIRK BOETTCHER TALKED TO FRIENDS in 2014 about the project he was currently working on, he braced himself for the inevitable, incredulous response: "Wait a minute. You're working on a musical about . . . the Holocaust?"

"Yeah."

An uncomfortable silence, then the next question: "Is it funny?"

"No, it's not funny. It's an opera, or it's actually an operetta. I guess there are some jokes in it, though."

Another uncomfortable silence, followed by "Is there dancing?"

"Yeah, there's dancing."

Boettcher, who was serving as the dramaturg, or literary adviser, for several performances of the operetta in question at the University of Southern Maine, wrote in its program: "I would be a wealthy man if I had twenty dollars for every time I have had this conversation over the course of the last year. As uncomfortable or morbidly comic as the exchange may be, it explains so clearly why this beautiful piece of art remained hidden away from the world for so many years."

"This beautiful piece of art" was Germaine Tillion's *Le Verfügbar aux Enfers*, the operetta-revue she wrote inside a packing crate at Ravensbrück in the fall of 1944. Just before Germaine and the other survivors left the camp the following April, she handed over the tiny

notebook containing the 118-page manuscript to Jacqueline d'Alincourt, who smuggled it out and stored it with her other possessions at
her family's home after the war. There it stayed until the late 1940s,
when Jacqueline discovered it after she, her husband, and their small
daughter returned to France from New York. She gave it back to Germaine, who tucked it in a cupboard at her apartment in Saint-Mandé. It
remained there for the next fifty years.

Germaine apparently had no second thoughts about putting the
manuscript away. It had accomplished its purpose in the camp—to lift
her fellow inmates' spirits and allow them to forget for a moment the
rapidly escalating horrors of their existence. In the postwar years, Germaine had other things to focus on: recovering her mental and physical
health, finishing her study of Ravensbrück, calling to account those
responsible for its atrocities, and fighting for human rights in Algeria
and elsewhere.

But for her and her fellow deportees, there was another, arguably
more compelling reason for burying *Le Verfügbar*. The women still
bore the emotional scars of the public's lack of interest in the awful
reality of Ravensbrück, with some people claiming that conditions
couldn't possibly be as harrowing as they said. The survivors feared
that a work employing humor and irony in its description of life within
Ravensbrück's walls would be regarded as making light of what they
had endured and play into the hands of those who denied, among other
things, the existence of a gas chamber there.

In 1987, ADIR's newsletter, *Voix et Visages*, reproduced a few
paragraphs from *Le Verfügbar*'s prologue, noting that if an anthology
of humor in the camps were ever published, Germaine's operetta
"would be its finest jewel." Sadly, the newsletter went on, such a work
would probably never be produced because of the fear that "laughter
might come across as a desecration of the millions of victims." Even
though "humor is a form of courage . . . there is also fear of being totally misunderstood."

And then, in the spring of 2004, Roselyne de Ayala, an editor at a
small literary publishing house in Paris, reached out to Nelly Forget,
Germaine's assistant, with a request. Ayala explained she was working

on a book about the manuscripts of noted women writers and wanted to include two pages on Germaine: one with her biography, the other reproducing a page from one of her manuscripts. At that point, the ninety-seven-year-old Germaine, while still mentally alert, was physically frail and relied on Nelly, who had known her for almost fifty years, to handle most requests dealing with her writing and archives. Nelly found a page of typescript from the manuscripts of one of Germaine's books that contained numerous corrections in her handwriting.

After the page was photographed, Nelly came up with another idea. Almost twenty years younger than Germaine, she had not been involved in the wartime Resistance; she had met Germaine in Algeria in the mid-1950s and had worked with her in setting up the social centers there.

Although she was close to several members of the Ravensbrück sisterhood, Nelly Forget didn't view *Le Verfügbar* as they did. More than half a century had passed since it had been written: enough time, she thought, to bring it out into the open. Nelly told Ayala it might be more interesting for her to use a page, all of it in Germaine's handwriting, from a manuscript she had composed at Ravensbrück. The editor agreed to look at it.

A few days later, having examined the manuscript, Ayala called Nelly. She not only wanted to feature one page from it in the book she was currently editing. She wanted to publish *Le Verfügbar aux Enfers* in its entirety.

Her proposal was met with consternation by Anise Postel-Vinay and other survivors close to Germaine, several of whom urged her not to allow it. Nelly Forget, however, was very much in favor of doing so. She had recently read *Le Verfügbar* for the first time while staying with Germaine at her summer cottage on the coast of Brittany. It was, Nelly remembered, "an unforgettable evening." A storm was raging outside, with the wind howling, lightning flashing, and giant waves submerging a dike in the distance. The wild weather formed a suitably dramatic backdrop for what she was reading—"a literary and musical work that overwhelmed me with emotion. I was transported from the outset, sharing the laughter and the anguish, the challenges and the hopes of the characters."

When Nelly told Germaine she thought *Le Verfügbar* should be published, the older woman offered no objection. It undoubtedly helped that she was well acquainted with Ayala's publishing house, Éditions de La Martinière, which had produced *L'Algérie aurésienne*, a book of her photographs of the tribespeople she had studied in the mountains of Algeria in the 1930s. The photos, along with notes describing the landscape and descriptions of the region, had been left behind in her home in Paris during the war.

Le Verfügbar was published in April 2005. Not long afterward, Jean-Luc Choplin, the new general director of one of Paris's most storied theaters, saw it in a bookstore window as he was strolling by. He recalled that a friend had recently read it and recommended he do the same. After buying it, "I devoured it in one night," he said. He was mesmerized by Tillion's "extraordinary capacity to laugh at tragedy in order to survive," calling her work "a glorification of the best of humanity at a time when humanity was at its worst." That night, he decided to stage *Le Verfügbar* as part of his first season as general director of the Théâtre du Châtelet. An unorthodox choice, to be sure, but then Jean-Luc Choplin was an unorthodox cultural leader. His appointment a few months before had stirred considerable outrage in certain artistic circles in Paris, who considered him a renegade, unfit to take charge of the Châtelet.

Built in 1862, shortly before France's Belle Époque period, the theater—a jewel box containing twenty-five hundred red velvet seats, chandeliers, and a gilded interior—swiftly became one of the city's temples of high culture. Particularly noted for its dance programming, it was for a time the Paris base of Sergei Diaghilev's famed Ballets Russes, with its corps of legendary dancers, including Vaslav Nijinsky and Anna Pavlova. The ballet *Afternoon of a Faun*, which boasted Nijinsky as its star and Claude Debussy as composer, made its debut there, as did Maurice Ravel's *Daphnis et Chloé* and Erik Satie's and Jean

Cocteau's *Parade*. Among the many other composers and conductors who appeared at the Châtelet were Pyotr Tchaikovsky, Gustav Mahler, and Richard Strauss.

By the end of the twentieth century, however, the Châtelet's trend-setting days were over. For the previous several decades it had focused on presenting concerts and opera performances, but it was having increasing difficulty attracting sufficiently large audiences.

When Jean-Luc Choplin was named its director in late 2004, he was determined to shake up its programming, offering instead an eclectic array of popular yet sophisticated works ranging from classical to contemporary—from opera to rap, from ballet to American musicals. "I dreamed that this theater would once again become a place dedicated to magic," he said, "by offering shows accessible to all and bringing together exceptional performers. . . . My goal was to abolish borders, not to give in to elitism, to confinement."

Choplin himself had had an eclectic, wide-ranging career. After working as the director of a French ballet company and the administrator of dance at the Paris Opéra, he had become a senior vice president of Disneyland Paris, and in 1995 he moved to Los Angeles as creative vice president of the overall Disney company. In 2002, he was named chief executive of the Sadler's Wells theater in London, which he left to come to the Châtelet.

Choplin's appointment was widely panned by French theater critics, who were aghast at his championing of popular culture and gave him the nickname of Mickey—after the famous Disney cartoon mouse. In a scathing article, the newspaper *Le Monde* condemned what it called his scandalously lowbrow tastes and accused him of being "a dangerous defender of the entertainment world."

Unfazed by the criticism, Choplin cemented his reputation as a cultural iconoclast by choosing as one of his first projects an operetta set in a concentration camp. Despite its subject matter, he did not regard *Le Verfügbar* as a "solemn text." He saw it as both "deep and light," "tragic and funny," and "able to provide joy at a time when everything else seemed to be in darkness."

In 2004 Germaine had turned over official control of her written works and other papers to the Association of Friends of Germaine Til-lion, a group set up by family members and close friends. Choplin asked for the association's permission to produce *Le Verfügbar* for the first time onstage. After considerable discussion, his request was granted, although not without some hesitation on the part of Anise Postel-Vinay and the few other women still alive who had been with Germaine at Ravensbrück.

Choplin planned to stage three performances of *Le Verfügbar* near the end of the Châtelet's 2006–2007 season, to coincide with Ger-maine's hundredth birthday on May 30, 2007. That gave him and his team a little less than two years to grapple with the many significant obstacles facing them in bringing this sixty-year-old work to life.

High on the list of challenges was the fact that *Le Verfügbar* had never been performed onstage; indeed, Germaine had not written it for that purpose. In the words of the French composer Christophe Mau-dot, she had meant it "to be dreamed—as a way to escape through one's thoughts, to rediscover one's homeland through music and memories, in order to survive." Now Choplin, Maudot, and the other collaborators had to figure out a way to make this operetta-revue, with its dialogue and songs from a bygone era, come alive for a modern au-dience, taking a respectful approach while at the same time underscor-ing its black humor.

A twenty-seven-year-old playwright named Géraldine Keiflin was chosen to adapt the text. A graduate of the Sorbonne and an actor by training, she met with Germaine to discuss the ideas she had in mind for changes. During their conversation, Keiflin started to read a pas-sage from the original text when Germaine interrupted her and com-pleted it. "She knew the whole thing by heart," Keiflin recalled.

Keiflin and the production's thirty-two-year-old director, Bérénice Collet, were keenly aware of the minefields involved in this produc-tion. "Could we put this on a stage and expect the audience to laugh and applaud?" Collet later said to an interviewer. "It was a question that really worried us." She and Keiflin worked closely with Anise Postel-Vinay to try to defuse any possible problems.

Christophe Maudot, who had been selected to adapt the musical part of the work, had to cope with an arguably even greater challenge: the total lack of a score. While Germaine had provided lyrics for the songs, her only guide to their melodies were references to borrowed musical works; she would often write, "according to the tune of . . ." Some of her references were very vague; others were instantly recognizable.

In his musical detective hunt, the forty-three-year-old Maudot was aided by the work of Nelly Forget, who, months earlier, had embarked on her own search to identify the tunes Germaine had had in mind. With the help of Anise and Jany Sylvaire-Blouet, a professional singer of light opera who also had been at Ravensbrück, Nelly eventually identified fifteen of the twenty-six musical numbers. Maudot came up with several more. For the few that remained unknown, he composed music in the style of the period that would complement the lyrics.

While working on the score, Maudot also had to wrestle with the question of what kind of instrumentation to use. Not surprisingly, Germaine had made no reference to which instruments might accompany the songs, since the work would never be performed at Ravensbrück. Now Maudot needed to decide whether the musical numbers should be sung a cappella or with accompaniment, and if the latter, which instruments should be used?

Maudot opted for an orchestra, but one in keeping with the stark, minimalist setting of *Le Verfügbar*. Unlike other Nazi camps, Ravensbrück had had no orchestra of prisoners. But if it had, Maudot wondered, what kind of musical instruments would have been available to them? He knew about the railroad cars filled with goods from occupied Europe that Germaine and other prisoners unloaded. What sort of instruments would have been aboard? Certainly not large ones like pianos or harps, but smaller ones, like violins, cellos, flutes, clarinets, and trumpets, were possible. With that in mind, Maudot decided on a ten-person orchestra using a variety of smaller instruments.

Another issue was the casting of the operetta's characters. As Maudot saw it, Ravensbrück's French prisoners encompassed three generations: young girls in their teens and early twenties; women like Germaine, in their thirties and forties; and older women, like Émilie

Tillion. The decision was made to cast performers in a similarly broad age range. The soloists, six in all, were professional singers, most in their thirties and older. The chorus was made up mainly of teenagers, some from the Maîtrise de Paris, a precollege music school, and others from two regular high schools in Paris. The dancers, also teenagers, came from municipal conservatories in the city. Combining the appearance and voices of young amateurs with those of professional artists did give the production a certain verisimilitude. But it also was done to make *Le Verfügbar* more appealing to young people in the audience who would have little or no knowledge of the events on which it was based.

The production's three performances were set for June 2 and 3, 2007. As the dates drew near and the performers rehearsed in a studio hall at the theater, Anise Postel-Vinay sat in the back of the hall, watching and listening intently. It was the first time since Ravensbrück that she had heard the songs. "There are surely lots of things that people will not understand," she told Catherine Simon, a journalist from *Le Monde* who was writing a story about the Châtelet production. "If people misunderstand, if they think that in the end we had a good laugh at Ravensbrück . . ." Anise sighed, and her voice trailed off. Also voicing concern was the historian and philosopher Tzvetan Todorov, president of the Germaine Tillion Association, who said the production had the almost impossible job of "avoiding trauma without minimizing the horror."

Marceline Loridan-Ivens, a prominent writer and filmmaker who had been deported to Auschwitz, was even more pointed, bluntly declaring that the production was probably doomed to fail. "Simply put, those who have not been in that situation . . . do not have the imagination to know what it was like," she told Catherine Simon. Staging the macabre humor of the deportees was almost impossible, Loridan-Ivens added. To succeed, the performance had to rise to the level of such theater masterpieces as *Cabaret* or Bertolt Brecht's *Threepenny Opera*. "Otherwise," she said, "it's shit. At worst, it will be boring."

Nelly Forget, for her part, shrugged off such doubts and worries. Having worked closely with the Châtelet team on the adaptation, she now attended the production's rehearsals. "The schoolgirls, like the singers, have managed to put themselves in the shoes of their characters," she told Simon. "The message is alive."

About to turn one hundred, the woman at the center of this Sturm und Drang had scant awareness of what was going on. "She is not always able to follow what we say to her or what we read to her," Anise Postel-Vinay wrote a friend. "What remains . . . is her gentleness, her goodness, her beneficial love which she still offers to every human being who approaches her."

Paying a call on Germaine at her apartment in Saint-Mandé, Catherine Simon found her lying down, her eyes half closed, on a sofa in the living room, near a bay window that looked out over the Bois de Vincennes. "Would you like a glass of milk, Kouri?" asked Anise, who visited her cherished friend almost every day. Nodding, Germaine took a sip, then closed her eyes.

She was too debilitated to attend the performance, so on May 28, two days before her birthday and five days before *Le Verfügbar* was to be staged, Jean-Luc Choplin, Christophe Maudot, Bérénice Collet, and others on their team brought the production to her. Several soloists sang excerpts from their numbers, and Germaine appeared energized by their perforrmance. According to Choplin, she seemed "lucid" and "strong," and she mouthed the words as the soloists sang. In a short conversation with Choplin, she told him she had often gone to the Châtelet as a girl and had vivid memories of seeing the Ballets Russes. To Maudot's delight, she signed the score of his musical adaptation.

"She seemed very moved," recalled the operetta's music director, Hélène Bouchez. "It was an incredibly emotional moment—both for her and for us."

ON JUNE 2, JUST before the curtain rose on *Le Verfügbar*'s first performance, Anise Postel-Vinay emerged from the wings and took center stage at the Châtelet. "The operetta you are going to see this evening is quite unique," she told the standing-room-only audience. Explaining its genesis, she described the growing despair of Ravensbrück inmates in the fall of 1944. "Our hope has become very tenuous. Germaine Tillion is worried. . . . We must continue to try to laugh at our lamentable state, she says; it is our only salvation. She will help us. She invites us to write something cheerful with her, an operetta that reflects our miserable condition but with pieces of music as comforting as possible. Let's not feel sorry for ourselves, she says. Let's write, let's sing!"

The curtain rose on a minimalist set, with barrack bunk beds at the back of the stage and an upside-down sign on a pediment above declaring WORK WILL MAKE YOU HEALTHY, a sly allusion to Auschwitz's infamous motto "Work Will Set You Free." The Naturalist, wearing a frock coat, peered out at the audience and began to explain the strange new species of life he has just discovered, while the *Verfügbaren* he was describing, seated on raw wooden benches flanking him, stared at him in puzzlement and then with derision.

From the start of the show, it was clear that Jean-Luc Choplin's gamble had paid off. Members of the audience were mesmerized by the performance, tapping their feet to the often rollicking music, laughing at the caustic humor and caught up in the *Verfügbaren*'s poignant longing for freedom and their fear that it would never come. When the show came to an end, the audience sat silent for several moments in total darkness. Then the house lights came up, and the theater exploded in applause. At that moment, a huge portrait of Germaine Tillion was lowered onto the stage. As one, playgoers rose to their feet in a crescendo of cheers, many with tears streaming down their faces.

The reaction of critics was equally glowing. *Le Monde,* the newspaper that had decried Choplin's appointment at the Châtelet, called *Le Verfügbar* "witty and imaginative" and "a formidable monument to hope." *Telerama,* a weekly French cultural magazine, dubbed it "dizzyingly brilliant," while Agence France Press praised "its strength and singularity" and termed it "a complete success."

Danielle Dumas, the former editor of the theater magazine *L'Avant-Scène,* declared that *Le Verfügbar* was "a masterpiece" and the "best show of the season." Bemoaning the fact that it was limited to three performances, she urged that it be widely and frequently staged in the future, "to celebrate memory and fraternity and to remind us not to despair of the human race."

That's exactly what happened. Over the next decade, *Le Verfügbar* was performed at dozens of venues, most of them in France. It was staged in a variety of ways, from productions involving large casts and full orchestras to a two-person cabaret performance. Arguably the most powerful of all occurred at the place where *Le Verfügbar* was created—Ravensbrück itself.

IN APRIL 2010, ANISE POSTEL-VINAY once again found herself sitting in the rehearsal hall of the Châtelet Theatre, talking to young cast members of *Le Verfügbar*. They were taking time out from rehearsals for their historic one-time performance at Ravensbrück, in commemoration of the sixty-fifth anniversary of the camp's liberation.

The teenage girls listened intently as the eighty-seven-year-old Anise described how the operetta was created and the key role it played in lifting the spirits of the tight-knit band of French prisoners at the camp. "You know," she said, "we could only survive Ravensbrück because of the friendships we had with one another. It really was a matter of life and death."

Many of those involved in the original staging in Paris, including Christophe Maudot, Bérénice Collet, and several of the soloists, were to reprise their roles in the new production, which was to be co-presented in a concert version by the Châtelet Theatre and the Ravensbrück Concentration Camp Memorial. But its young singers and musicians, whose casting added an intriguing element to the project, were all new to it. Half of them were French, the other half German. Members of the chorus came from high schools in Berlin and Paris, and the orchestra was composed of members of the Young Philharmonic of Brandenburg, a town west of Berlin.

In the week before the performance was to take place, emotions ran high, especially among the dozen-plus French survivors of Ravensbrück who were to attend. For some, it would be their first journey back since the camp's liberation. Making the trip even more fraught was the knowledge that the operetta would be staged on the huge open square where they and other inmates had been forced to stand for hours during the agonizing morning and evening roll calls.

Then, two days before the performance, catastrophe struck. Just as the Paris-based cast, crew, and survivors prepared to board a plane for the short flight to Berlin, the flight was canceled. So was virtually all air traffic across Europe. The massive eruption of a volcano in Iceland, spewing clouds of ash and gases over the continent, was responsible for the largest air traffic shutdown since World War II.

When word came that the concert was to be canceled, the young performers broke down in tears. The Châtelet staff, however, was determined to find a way to get them there. After hours of calling everyone they could think of in positions of authority, they persuaded French military officials to lend them a couple of buses for the trip to Germany—a seventeen-hour journey that would get them to Ravensbrück just hours before the performance.

While the French participants were en route, the young German performers arrived by train at the railway station in the town of Fürstenberg—the same station where the prisoner transports to Ravensbrück had ended their journey. The choir and orchestra members then set off by foot on the same path that the women they would soon portray in *Le Verfügbar* used to get to the camp. Inside Ravensbrück's gates, a guide noted to the German students that they were now standing on the vast square where the daily roll calls were held and where prisoners were routinely whipped, beaten, and attacked by dogs. The concert would be staged there the following day.

As one German student walked, wide-eyed and troubled, around the camp, she asked herself how she, as a German, would have responded if she had been alive during the war. "Would I have gone along with this terrible thing?" she said to a French journalist. "To be honest, I really don't know."

On the morning of the performance, the French contingent, exhausted from seventeen hours on the road, finally arrived. After two hours of sleep, they took part in a quick rehearsal. Early that afternoon, they, along with their German counterparts, staged a passionate, moving concert rendition of *Le Verfügbar*, which brought many members of the audience, including a number of former Ravensbrück inmates from all over Europe, to tears. Among those overcome with emotion was Claude du Granrut, whose mother, Germaine de Renty, had barely survived the camp. Claude had come with her granddaughter, Pauline, to bear witness and pay tribute to what she called the "courage, fortitude, and solidarity" of her mother and the others in standing up to the Nazis.

Also in the audience was Christine Holden, an American historian whose specialty was European women's history, with an emphasis on the Holocaust. Holden was mesmerized by *Le Verfügbar*. Her fascination with it led four years later to its staging at a most unlikely venue— the University of Southern Maine, where she taught.

A STATE UNIVERSITY WITH campuses in and near Portland, the University of Southern Maine boasted a vibrant theater department. Holden gave a copy of *Le Verfügbar* to Meghan Brodie, a theater professor, who was as captivated by it as Holden had been. "It was such a brilliant, dark comic rendering of these women's experiences," Brodie said. "What an incredible act of resistance—especially when you consider that Germaine Tillion at any moment could have been killed if the Nazis had found her notebook. Hers was the kind of quiet bravery that is rarely acknowledged. . . . It became my passion project."

Determined to direct *Le Verfügbar*, Brodie, backed by her department, encountered a host of challenges, among them the commissioning of an English translation. Once that had been done, money had to be raised. Brodie then had to acquire permissions from the Germaine Tillion Association, the Châtelet Theatre, and several other French entities, all of which took several months.

When those details had been settled, Brodie turned to the operetta itself, reducing the sizable cast to eleven members and deciding that, unlike previous productions in France and elsewhere, the Naturalist would be played by a woman. "My thought was that there were no men in the camp. If the operetta [had been] read out loud [at the time], women would be playing all the roles. It was written by a woman presenting her idea how these women would be seen and understood. So I very much felt this should be an all-female cast."

Four months before the April 2014 production, the cast began an intensive immersion course in the Holocaust, as well as learning about the Nazis' persecution and murder of non-Jewish civilians in concentration camps. "It was clear to me that the students' education about the Holocaust was almost nonexistent," Brodie said. They also knew virtually nothing about the German camps. "We undertook a mass reading campaign together—a lot of women prisoners' autobiographies and other accounts of their lives—so they would have a better understanding of the characters they played." It helped that the cast members, who were in their late teens and early twenties, were the same age as some of the inmates they were playing. "It added to their sense of identity," Brodie observed.

While the university's student body was predominantly white, there was considerable diversity in students' social, economic, and religious backgrounds, as well as in their gender and sexual orientation. "We had some Jewish students in the operetta, but we also talked about the reasons why every single cast member seated around that table could have ended up in the camp, whether it was for their sexuality or their heritage or their politics or their disability. I think that helped them put themselves in the shoes of these women. It made it personal. They understood that they were telling the women's stories for posterity. This was a different kind of acting experience—a form of witnessing."

The cast members' commitment to representing their characters as realistically as possible included making dramatic changes in their own appearance. On their audition forms, Brodie asked if they would be willing to cut their hair short or shave their head. She made it clear, she later said, that it was not a requirement for being cast and that if they said yes, they could change their mind at any time before the actual performances.

They all agreed to do it. Half of them had their heads shaved; the other half cut their hair. "By doing that, they had an experience similar to that of the women in the camps," Brodie remarked. "It was voluntary, but it still felt like an assault. We talked about our hair and how important it is for women, about sexuality, about our bodies. They viewed what they had done as a tribute to the women they were portraying. It was their way of saying that the women's stories were now embodied in them. For some, it took many months for their hair to grow back, but no one regretted it."

For everyone involved, the four months leading up to the production, as well as the eight performances themselves, were a grueling, emotional experience, but none felt it more keenly than the young women in the cast. At the end of each performance, they gathered together backstage and cried. "I was crying too," Brodie said. "I think part of it was grief reflecting the story they were telling. But it also reflected the solidarity of those young women onstage in that moment. They were a community and will remain one for the rest of their lives. That's one of the most powerful facets of theater—creating something together that stays with you. They had built the same bonds that the women in the camp had built." During the rehearsal process, "one would say to the other, 'Are you cold? Take my sweater.' Or 'You're not feeling well? I'll do this for you.' I don't think they were even aware of it, but I saw how they much they had become invested in one another."

Production of Germaine Tillion's operetta/revue
Le Verfügbar aux Enfers at the University of
Southern Maine, April 2014

According to Brodie, the production succeeded beyond her wildest expectations. Christophe Maudot, who had advised her throughout the process, came from France, as did representatives of the Tillion Association. "People who had never come before to see one of our plays—veterans of the war, folks from the Jewish community and those with French ties—a lot of different groups of people were there," she said. "Their response was overwhelmingly positive."

Ten years later, Brodie was still in touch with most of the students with whom she worked on *Le Verfügbar*. "Every time I see or hear from them, we inevitably talk about that production. It is one of the most remarkable artistic experiences of my life without a doubt. It's one of the most transformative experiences I've had as a director. I really do believe it was life-changing for everyone involved."

Epilogue

O N A WARM, SUNNY DAY IN MAY 2015, ANISE POSTEL-VINAY TOOK her place in the front row of dignitaries assembled on the plaza in front of Paris's Panthéon. In the plaza's center were four coffins draped with French flags—the latest additions to the array of national heroes interred in this neoclassical white marble shrine.

The day before, members of the Republican Guard, the ceremonial regiment that acts as guard of honor at important state occasions, had escorted the coffins through the streets of Paris. Traffic was stopped for hours, and thousands of people lined the sidewalks and watched from balconies as the slow, stately cortège passed by. The pomp and panoply underscored the importance that the French attach to burial in the Panthéon—the highest tribute possible for those considered the country's greatest heroes.

Until 2015, only seventy-one people had been judged worthy of the honor. Among them were France's most illustrious scientists, writers, generals, and statesmen. They included Voltaire, Victor Hugo, Jean-Jacques Rousseau, Émile Zola, Alexandre Dumas, and Pierre Curie.

Almost without exception, they were male. That fact was reflected in the carved inscription over the Panthéon's massive doors: AUX GRANDS HOMMES LA PATRIE RECONNAISSANTE (For Great Men, a Grateful Country). But on this day, two women would join Marie Curie, the

sole female to be singled out for the honor. They were Anise Postel-
Vinay's closest friends: Germaine Tillion and Geneviève de Gaulle.

Sound and light show at the Panthéon
in Paris, May 27, 2015

Anise listened closely to French president François Hollande's tribute to the four honorees, all of whom had played significant roles in the
French Resistance.* At the end of his speech, Hollande, in a rhetorical
flourish, addressed the souls of the four. "Take your place here!" he
declared. "It belongs to you!"

At first, Anise Postel-Vinay did not agree. As the last survivor of
her tight-knit circle of friends,† the ninety-two-year-old Anise had
been pursued for interviews by the news media after the announcement
of Germaine's and Geneviève's selection. Asked for her reaction,
Anise told one interviewer, "I was stunned. I said to myself, 'My God,

---

*   The other two were Pierre Brossolette, a journalist and Resistance leader, and Jean
Zay, a former French minister of education who had been murdered by the Nazis.

†   Geneviève de Gaulle had died in 2002 at the age of eighty-one; Germaine Tillion in
2008, just before her 101st birthday; and Jacqueline Péry d'Alincourt in 2009, at eighty-
nine.

now that they are at peace, each in her own little cemetery, why are we going to disturb them?" To another journalist, she said, "It was very unsettling to me that Germaine and Geneviève, my great old friends, were going to be 'pantheonized.' I wondered why they didn't leave them alone. It just didn't seem very important to me."

In reality, the women's families had made it clear they didn't want their bodies removed, so the coffins at the Panthéon contained only soil from their grave sites. But that fact did not obviate the main point of Anise's argument. Neither Germaine nor Geneviève had sought glory, nor did they ever consider themselves heroes. "I don't like the word 'heroism,'" Geneviève had once said. "And I don't think that we should seek to have a great life or grand destiny. I think we should simply seek to do what is right."

As Anise saw it, Geneviève and Germaine would have laughed and made gentle fun of the idea of receiving this honor, just as they had done when they received earlier, lesser accolades. In 1998, Geneviève was the first woman to be awarded the Grand Cross of the Legion of Honor, the highest level of France's most prestigious order of merit. Two years later, Germaine became the second woman to receive the Grand Cross, which Geneviève presented to her at Germaine's house in Saint-Mandé.

That same year, Geneviève bestowed on Jacqueline Péry d'Alincourt the Grand Cross of the Order of Merit, the second-highest state decoration after the Legion of Honor. At the beginning of the ceremony, Geneviève said with a smile, "Look at us, poor people that we are, with our ribbons and our medals. When we were shivering in our convict outfits, could we have imagined this moment when, after having pronounced the ritual words, my Jacqueline, I will present you with this Order?"

Anise, for her part, had made it a point to refuse honors and decorations. "She was offered them all," Germaine said of her friend. "Her Resistance comrades agreed that if anyone was heroic, it was she. But she said she didn't want them." Until the end of her life, Anise minimized what she had done in the Resistance, calling it "an anonymous story among millions of others."

She was hardly alone. After the war, many *résistantes* played down the importance of their own wartime achievements even as they emphasized the overall significance of women's contributions to the Resistance. Even Marie-Madeleine Fourcade, the only woman to head a major Resistance network, felt constrained to minimize what she had done. When asked by a postwar interviewer to describe herself, she made no mention of the war and instead ticked off the following attributes: "the wife of an officer, the mother of a family, a member of no political party, and a Catholic."

François Hollande's selection of two Ravensbrück survivors for inclusion in the Panthéon was meant to upend France's traditional historical narrative of the Resistance: that men were chiefly responsible for its creation and achievements and that they alone had suffered. The choice of Germaine Tillion and Geneviève de Gaulle Anthonioz argued and proved otherwise.

But Hollande's decision was meant to do more than honor these two women. The selection of Germaine and Geneviève, he said, was also aimed at "remembering the contributions of all the other women, most of them anonymous, who helped save the country and spent the postwar years in the shadows." At the same time, though, he mentioned three other Ravensbrück survivors by name—Anise Postel-Vinay, Jacqueline Péry d'Alincourt, and Marie-Claude Vaillant-Couturier— calling them "sublime" and "sisters of suffering and hope."

Sisterhood. That was the key.

Germaine and Geneviève entered the Panthéon accompanied in spirit not only by Anise, Jacqueline, and Marie-Claude but by all the women of the Resistance. But those singled out at the ceremony all belonged to the Ravensbrück sisterhood. Refusing to surrender to savagery and terror, they had demonstrated the extraordinary power of solidarity in fighting for freedom and justice. "Female heroes are not limited to one great individual," observed Geneviève's biographer Frédérique Neau-Dufour. "They come in numbers."

In honoring their defiance of evil, Hollande also emphasized that what they had done had resonance for today. He noted the rise of right-wing populism throughout much of the world and its similarities to the fascism of the 1930s. "History is not nostalgia," he said, "but a lesson to be learned. Each generation has a duty of watchfulness."

In the last years of Germaine Tillion's life, Anise remembered, "she was obsessed with this problem of evil. If such a thing had been possible in Germany, a neighboring, civilized country, how could we think that it could not happen again?" Speaking of the French use of torture in Algeria, Germaine herself once said, "What we stigmatized a few years earlier among the Nazis, France, which is a liberal, democratic country, used in its own way—proof that no people are safe from infection."

In the end, Anise came to accept the value of her friends' inclusion. She did so not only because they were representing their comrades as well as themselves but also because of their work as "watchmen in the night," underscoring the importance of vigilance in combating present and future evil.

Quentin Girard, a correspondent for the French newspaper *Libération,* was one of the many journalists to interview Anise at the time. The day after their first meeting, he accompanied her to a symposium focusing on the latest Panthéon heroes. As they walked past the Panthéon, Anise stopped for a moment and read aloud the words engraved over the door: "For Great Men a Grateful Country." She looked at Girard. "Now," she said, "they must add 'For Great Women' too."

Acknowledgments

....

*T*HE *SISTERHOOD OF RAVENSBRÜCK* IS MY TENTH BOOK OF HIStory. In coming up with ideas for my previous books, I have often chosen subjects that had some connection with the books that came before them. *Sisterhood* is no exception: Its roots lie in the the two narratives that immediately preceded it, both of them about history-making yet relatively unknown women in the French Resistance. In effect, it is the third volume of a trilogy, something that I had no thought of doing when I began work on the first one eight years ago.

The initial book—*Madame Fourcade's Secret War*—explored the wartime exploits of Marie-Madeleine Fourcade, whose identity as the only woman to head a major Resistance organization in occupied France has long been ignored by historians.

The second—*Empress of the Nile*—focused on another unsung figure: Christiane Desroches, a young Egyptologist at the Louvre who belonged to the trailblazing Museum of Man network. Even though my book on Christiane focused more on her amazing postwar archaeological career than her resistance efforts, I remained fascinated by the wartime organization to which she belonged—a group of intellectuals led, at least at the beginning, by women. One of them was the brilliant young anthropologist Germaine Tillion.

In the course of my research, I also became intrigued by yet another forgotten woman—a French countess named Germaine de Renty, one of Marie-Madeleine Fourcade's wartime agents and a survivor of Ravensbrück, who after the war hosted Jacqueline Bouvier Kennedy during her junior year abroad in Paris. As I explored Germaine's life, I discovered that she and a number of other Frenchwomen at Ravensbrück had come together to defy the Nazis there. The most prominent leader of that group turned out to be none other than Germaine Tillion.

This, I realized, was another remarkable story about the French Resistance that has remained largely untold. While the number of books about French *résistantes* has skyrocketed in recent years, they have focused almost exclusively on their subjects' activities and achievements during the war. Almost none, including *Madame Fourcade's Secret War*, paid much attention to what happened to the women afterward, particularly to the large numbers—more than ten thousand—who were captured and sent to various German prisons and concentration camps. Even less attention has been given to the fact that a good number of the women continued to resist the Germans in the camps, particularly at Ravensbrück.

In telling that story, I decided to focus on four of the group's leading members: Germaine Tillion and her friends Geneviève de Gaulle, Anise (Girard) Postel-Vinay, and Jacqueline Péry d'Alincourt. In doing so, I was able to draw on a wealth of resources, including the powerful accounts that each woman wrote about her nightmarish experiences at Ravensbrück. I also learned much from biographies of three of them: Jean Lacouture's and Lorraine de Meaux's portraits of Germaine Tillion; Frédérique Neau-Dufour's and Paige Bowers's assessments of Geneviève de Gaulle; and François Berriot's biography of Jacqueline Péry d'Alincourt.

Another key resource was the videos and transcripts from interviews with these women by the American filmmaker Maia Wechsler for her remarkable documentary *Sisters in Resistance*. Maia's lengthy conversations with the women, conducted separately and together over several years, explored in great detail their courage and the hellishness of their existence at Ravensbrück, as well as their prewar and postwar lives and their relationships with one another. In these poignant, revealing exchanges, the "sisters" come to brilliant life.

I owe a particular debt of gratitude to Maia, not only for these wonderful conversations but for sharing with me her experience in working on the documentary, along with her vivid memories of the women and their profound impact on her life. I highly recommend her excellent film, which is available for a small rental fee at vimeo.com/ondemand/sistersinresistance.

I am also immensely grateful to Aline Corraze de Ziegler, Jacqueline Péry d'Alincourt's granddaughter, and Meghan Brodie, director of the only American performance of Germaine Tillion's *Le Verfügbar aux Enfers*, for their insights into the sisterhood and its far-reaching influence. Many thanks, too, to Christian Bromberger, president of the Germaine Tillion Association in Paris, and to Geneviève Zamansky-Bonnin, the association's secretary general, for their generous assistance.

I also thank Franck Veyron, head of the archives at the Bibliothèque de documentation international contemporaine (Library of International Contemporary Documentation) in Nanterre, France, and his staff for their help. BDIC is the repository for the archives of ADIR, the association of female concentration camp and prison survivors, which include the videos and transcripts of Maia Wechsler's film and issues of ADIR's newsletter *Voix et Visages*—all indispensable resources for this book.

Thanks, too, to the archivists at the U.S. Holocaust Museum in Bowie, Maryland, for their guidance in consulting the Caroline Ferriday papers and other manuscript collections with a bearing on the book's subject. As I've said before, librarians and archivists are the preservers of history and civilization, and their selfless approach to the work they do is nothing short of heroic.

I could not have written this book—and the two that preceded it—without the counsel and collaboration of my partner and friend, Dorie Denbigh-Laurent. Dorie was involved in every aspect of research and writing *Sisterhood*, from spending long days in the archives at Nanterre to contacting and interviewing sources to translating and analyzing numerous broadcast and print interviews and other resources. Her contribution has been incalculable.

Working on *Sisterhood* has been a total joy, thanks in large part to having the brilliant Susanna Porter as my editor. It's impossible to overstate how much I owe to Susanna and the rest of the Random House team—among them Tom Perry, who recently retired as deputy publisher—for their enthusiasm, support, and encouragement. They are the best.

So is Gail Ross, who has been my friend, agent, and champion for more than thirty years. My debt to her is immense—never more so than in our early discussions about whether I should write *Sisterhood*. She was the one who persuaded me to do it, and I couldn't be happier with the result.

And finally my thanks to the two most important people in my life—my husband (and sometime co-author), Stan Cloud, and our daughter, Carly. I love you both more than I can say.

Notes

....

PROLOGUE

3   "For a child, it was like a wonderland": Interview with Aline Corraze de Ziegler.

3   "living things": François Berriot, *Chronicles of Resistance and Deportation: Jacqueline Péry d'Alincourt and Her World* (West Kennebunk, Maine: Androscoggin Press, 2021), 6.

3   "They looked like perfectly ordinary old women": Interview with Aline Corraze de Ziegler.

4   "true Resistance heroes": Ibid.

4   "We committed ourselves to fight": Jacqueline Fleury-Marié, *Résistante* (Paris: Calmann-Lévy, 2019), 9.

CHAPTER 1: "SOMETHING MUST BE DONE"

6   "There is no such thing as an uncivilized people": Jean Lacouture, *Le Témoignage est un combat: Une biographie de Germaine Tillion* (Paris: Seuil, 2000), 24.

6   "impatient to decipher the riddles": Ibid., 11.

8   "my initial sympathy": Ibid., 37.

8   "tales of travel": Ibid., 45.

8   "they were very sorry": Ibid., 46.

9   "If nature had given me a Cyclops eye": *Germaine Tillion, in Her Own Words*, film documentary, Germaine Tillion Association, Paris, 2016.

10 "accepted wholeheartedly": Lacouture, *Témoignage*, 43.

10 "narrow-minded nor thieves": Ibid., 49.

11 "The shock, the disgust": Geneviève de Gaulle Anthonioz and Germaine Tillion, *Dialogues* (Paris: Plon, 2015), Loc. 227, Kindle edition.

11 "To ask for an armistice": Lacouture, *Témoignage*, 63.

11 "how essential my country's dignity": Ibid., 68.

11 "something must be done immediately": Ibid., 69.

12 "Something has been broken in this country": Jean Guéhenno, *Diary of the Dark Years 1940–1944* (Oxford: Oxford University Press, 2015), 20–21.

12 "a boiling fury": Lacouture, *Témoignage*, 71.

13 "a defiant gesture": Laura Spinney, "The Museum Director Who Defied the Nazis," *Smithsonian*, June 2020.

13 "the country is not with you": Lacouture, *Témoignage*, 81.

14 "a big brain": David Schoenbrun, *Soldiers of the Night: The Story of the French Resistance* (New York: Dutton, 1980), Loc. 2462, Kindle edition.

15 "I will go mad": Agnès Humbert, *Résistance: Memoirs of Occupied France* (London: Bloomsbury, 2008), 38.

15 "At the time of the great French collapse": Robert Gildea, *Fighters in the Shadows: A New History of the French Resistance* (Cambridge, Mass.: Belknap Press of Harvard University Press, 2015), 470.

16 "What we wanted to do in 1940": Interview transcripts, Maia Wechsler, *Sisters in Resistance*, film documentary, Women Make Movies, 2000, ADIR archives, BDIC.

17 "It was," one British historian remarked: Barbara Mellor, "Bold Defiance in Nazi Paris," *Today*, BBC Radio, September 26, 2008.

17 "transformed itself into a veritable spider's web": Spinney, "Museum Director."

18 "For me, there is one word": Humbert, *Résistance*, 331.

18 "Although [the network's members] were serious people": Schoenbrun, *Soldiers of the Night*, Loc. 2584, Kindle edition.

19 "We did not slink about in cloaks and daggers": Ibid.

19 "I think that if our network had survived": Ibid.

20 "They all died as heroes": Humbert, *Résistance*, 167.

20 "an unbearable pain and impotent anger": Lacouture, *Témoignage*, 106.

20 "I had a revolver": James Knowlson, "Samuel Beckett's Biographer Reveals Secrets of the Writer's Time as a French Resistance Spy," *Independent*, July 23, 2014.

21 "I was the head of the *réseau*": Interview transcripts, Maia Wechsler, *Sisters in Resistance*.

CHAPTER 2: "HOLD ON!"

22 "Freedom was one of my mother's great principles": Anise Postel-Vinay, *Vivre* (Paris: Grasset & Fasquelle, 2015), Loc. 2, Kindle edition.

23 "We worked in the morning": Ibid.

23 "a tall, blond, attractive woman": Wolfgang Benz and Barbara Distel, eds., *Dachau Review 1: History of Nazi Concentration Camps; Studies, Reports, Documents*, vol. 1 (Dachau: Verlag Dachauer Hefte, 1988), 211.

23 "I didn't enjoy myself at all there": Postel-Vinay, *Vivre*, Loc. 49, Kindle edition.

23 "I was rebellious": Interview transcripts, Maia Wechsler, *Sisters in Resistance*.

23 "I thought our high schools had appalling methods of education": Ibid.

24 "was the first big disappointment of my life": Postel-Vinay, *Vivre*, Loc. 74, Kindle edition.

24 "do something": Ibid.

25 "We wanted to free ourselves": Anne and Claire Berest, *Gabriële* (Paris: Stock, 2017), Loc. 754, Kindle edition.

25 "She seemed so rebellious and sure of herself": Ibid., Loc. 1125, Kindle edition.

25 "Conversations with her": Ibid., Loc. 1267, Kindle edition.

26 "Francis took all her attention": Ibid., Loc. 1311, Kindle edition.

28   "They would bring all this information to me": James Knowlson, *Damned to Fame: The Life of Samuel Beckett* (New York: Simon & Schuster, 1996), 282.

29   "It was a task for which I was wholly unfitted": Benz and Distel, *Dachau Review 1*, 213.

29   "My descriptions of the guns": Ibid.

30   "had a hard time taking security measures seriously": Lynne Olson, *Madame Fourcade's Secret War: The Daring Young Woman Who Led France's Largest Spy Network Against Hitler* (New York: Random House, 2019), 202.

30   "We have no experience of clandestine life": Lynne Olson, *Last Hope Island: Britain, Occupied Europe, and the Brotherhood That Helped Turn the Tide of War* (New York: Random House, 2017), 169.

34   "incredible joy": Postel-Vinay, *Vivre*, Loc. 119, Kindle edition.

34   "massively important, mysterious man": Benz and Distel, *Dachau Review 1*, 213.

35   "At a time when most of the French": Alan Riding, *And the Show Went On: Cultural Life in Nazi-Occupied Paris* (New York: Alfred A. Knopf, 2010), 143.

36   "visceral, terrible fear": Postel-Vinay, *Vivre*, Loc. 140, Kindle edition.

36   "Either my death warrant had been countermanded": Benz and Distel, *Dachau Review 1*, 215.

36   "The loneliness was unbearable": Postel-Vinay, *Vivre*, Loc. 155, Kindle edition.

36   "I believed him": Alison Rice and Germaine Tillion, "'Déchiffrer le silence': A Conversation with Germaine Tillion," *Research in African Literatures*, Spring 2004, vol. 35.

37   "The two months I spent [at La Santé]": Marie-Laure Le Foulon, *Le Procès de Ravensbrück: Germaine Tillion; de la vérité à la justice* (Paris: Cherche Midi, 2016), 35.

37   "keep in touch with time": Tzvetan Todorov, ed., *Germaine Tillion: Fragments de Vie* (Paris: Seuil, 2009), 191.

39   "an outrageous lie": Benz and Distel, *Dachau Review 1*, 219.

39   "This seemed to amuse him": Postel-Vinay, *Vivre*, Loc. 220, Kindle edition.

40   "In this abyss of absence": Lorraine de Meaux, *Germaine Tillion: Une certaine idée de la résistance* (Paris: Perrin, 2024), 192.

40   "For a brief moment, we looked at each other": Interview transcripts, Maia Wechsler, *Sisters in Resistance*.

40   "It's the only way to hold on": Lacouture, *Témoignage*, 126.

CHAPTER 3: "WE ARE HERE TO BE KILLED"

42   "I don't know if it was because": Postel-Vinay, *Vivre*, Loc. 257, Kindle edition.

42   "I thought it must be Germaine Tillion": Ibid., Loc. 272, Kindle edition.

42   "She made me talk about myself": Ibid.

43   "felt what animals probably feel": *Germaine Tillion, in Her Own Words*, film, Tillion Association, 2016.

48   "To maintain the prosperity of [Himmler's] business": Germaine Tillion, *Ravensbrück* (Garden City, N.Y.: Anchor Books, 1975), 40.

49   "My experience in Algeria": Todorov, *Germaine Tillion*, 12.

50   "We called Anise 'the great Danielle'": Interview transcripts, Maia Wechsler, *Sisters in Resistance*.

50   "You are a Frenchwoman": "William Hitzig, Report to Norman Cousins," October 20, 1958, in *Congressional Record*, April 16, 1959, Caroline Ferriday collection, U.S. Holocaust Museum archives.

51   "losing Heydrich is the equivalent": Benz and Distel, *Dachau Review 1*, 224.

52   "was soaked with odorous black and red slime": "Janina Iwanska," *Chronicles of Ter-*

ror, *1939–1945*, November 6, 1945, zapisyterroru.pl/dlibra/publication/1441/edition/1424/content.

52 "Of all those who underwent the operation": Letter from Nina Iwanska to Anise Girard, undated, Caroline Ferriday collection, U.S. Holocaust Museum archives.

53 "but I would feel the consequences": "Janina Iwanska."

CHAPTER 4: "KEEPER OF THE FLAME"

58 "I was almost paralyzed with grief": Tillion, *Ravensbrück*, xvii.

58 "Unlike most of us": Henry Samuel, "Diary of Nazi Survivor Turned into an Opera," *Telegraph*, June 2, 2007.

58 *"Voyage exultant!"*: Lacouture, *Témoignage*, 167.

58 "She didn't seem to feel any sadness": Mechthild Gilzmer, "Il était une fois Ravensbrück," in Philippe Despoix et al., eds., *Chanter, Rire, et Résister à Ravensbrück: Autour de Germaine Tillion et du Verfügbar aux Enfers* (Paris: Seuil, 2018), 80.

58 "well-behaved little girls": Anthonioz and Tillion, *Dialogues*, Loc. 684, Kindle edition.

59 "looking like figures in a painting": Ibid., Loc. 14, Kindle edition.

59 "Nothing is more terrifying than a complete mystery": Tillion, *Ravensbrück*, 49.

59 "By explaining these mysteries": Anthonioz and Tillion, *Dialogues*, Loc. 23, Kindle edition.

59 "amazed and filled with admiration": Ibid., Loc. 140, Kindle edition.

59 "The first thing she did": Ibid., Loc. 1248, Kindle edition.

60 "I don't like the word 'heroism'": Paige Bowers, *The General's Niece: The Little-Known de Gaulle Who Fought to Free Occupied France* (Chicago: Chicago Review Press, 2017), xiv.

60 "She would say, 'Yes, I am a de Gaulle'": Ibid.

60 "I was very unhappy about it": Frédérique Neau-Dufour, *Geneviève de Gaulle Anthonioz: L'Autre de Gaulle* (Paris: Cerf, 2015), Loc. 479, Kindle edition.

61 "quiet resistance": Ibid., Loc. 494, Kindle edition.

61 "almost as twins": Ibid., Loc. 568, Kindle edition.

61 "psychological resilience": Ibid., Loc. 598, Kindle edition.

62 "I felt as if I'd been burned": Ibid., Loc. 685, Kindle edition.

64 "You're always talking about patriotism": Bowers, *General's Niece*, 50.

66 "Back then, women still had the mentality": Dominique Veillon and Françoise Thébaud, "Hélène Viannay," *Clio*, January 1995.

66 "We looked at each other": Ibid.

66 "Even in the resistance": Bowers, *General's Niece*, 54.

67 "with great skill and conviction": Neau-Dufour, *Geneviève de Gaulle Anthonioz*, Loc. 991, Kindle edition.

67 "independence of spirit": Bowers, *General's Niece*, 55.

67 she decried as "nonsense": Anthonioz and Tillion, *Dialogues*, Loc. 154, Kindle edition.

67 "It was Geneviève de Gaulle who completely converted us": "Jacqueline Pardon," Les Amis de la Fondation de la Résistance, memoresist.org/temoignage/jacqueline-pardon/.

68 "We had the physicians' directory": Bowers, *General's Niece*, 58.

69 He "couldn't kill me": Ibid., 59.

70 "Do you maintain that these documents are real?": Ibid., 61.

70 "I wanted them to know": Neau-Dufour, *Geneviève de Gaulle Anthonioz*, Loc. 1102, Kindle edition.

71   "Where is Geneviève de Gaulle?": Bowers, *General's Niece*, 68.

72   "I was amazed to discover": Geneviève de Gaulle Anthonioz, *The Dawn of Hope: A Memoir of Ravensbrück* (New York: Arcade, 1999), 63–64.

72   "As each name was shouted out": Anthonioz and Tillion, *Dialogues*, Loc. 1418, Kindle edition.

73   "To my comrades": Neau-Dufour, *Geneviève de Gaulle Anthonioz*, Loc. 1271, Kindle edition.

74   "Hummingbirds are very, very fragile": Anthonioz and Tillion, *Dialogues*, Loc. 670, Kindle edition.

75   "she very quickly became the privileged comrade": Ibid., Loc. 1311, Kindle edition.

75   "She was standing on a stool": Neau-Dufour, *Geneviève de Gaulle Anthonioz*, Loc. 1537, Kindle edition.

75   "Here's Geneviève de Gaulle!": Anthonioz and Tillion, *Dialogues*, Loc. 154, Kindle edition.

76   "our inspiration": Berriot, *Chronicles of Resistance*, 40.

CHAPTER 5: THE SEVENTH CIRCLE OF HELL

77   "I don't think our friendship can be described": Interview transcripts, Maia Wechsler, *Sisters in Resistance*.

77   "was even stronger than blood ties": Ibid.

79   "We grew up very close to our mother": Berriot, *Chronicles of Resistance*, 76.

79   "We weren't expecting anyone": Ibid., 65.

80   "marked like cattle": Interview transcripts, Maia Wechsler, *Sisters in Resistance*.

81   "We knew that men of good will": Douglas Porch, *The French Secret Services: From the Dreyfus Affair to the Gulf War* (New York: Farrar, Straus and Giroux, 1995), 185.

82   "served as the umbilical cord": Berriot, *Chronicles of Resistance*, 79.

84   "two amazing girls": Daniel Cordier, *Alias Caracalla* (Paris: Gallimard, 2009), 915.

84   "the epitome of intellectual independence": Berriot, *Chronicles of Resistance*, 20.

85   "both Cordier's educator and a surrogate father figure": Julian Jackson, "Daniel Cordier Obituary," *Guardian*, November 23, 2020.

85   "We could easily have used two or three times the number": Berriot, *Chronicles of Resistance*, 23.

86   "Thanks to the many comings and goings": Ibid., 92.

86   "They couldn't go to a hotel": Ibid.

86   Jacqueline's "wonderful energy": Claire Chevrillon, *Code Name Christiane Clouet: A Woman in the French Resistance* (College Station: Texas A&M University Press, 1995), 104.

86   "It was necessary for me to smile": Berriot, *Chronicles of Resistance*, 35.

87   "If there had been any bridle": Philippe de Vomécourt, *An Army of Amateurs* (New York: Doubleday, 1961), 126.

87   "Danger stalked us everywhere": Berriot, *Chronicles of Resistance*, 35.

87   "There have been sentimental entanglements": Chevrillon, *Code Name Christiane Clouet*, 111.

88   "Instead of thinking about winning the war": Cordier, *Alias Caracalla*, 452.

88   "I looked at them constantly": Berriot, *Chronicles of Resistance*, 81.

89   "with the radiant image of my little sister": Ibid.

91   "I will not speak": Interview transcripts, Maia Wechsler, *Sisters in Resistance*.

91   "the cruelest punishment of all": Berriot, *Chronicles of Resistance*, 38.

91   "I was always taught": Ibid., 56.

92 "Then climb on the chair": Ibid., 69.

92 "I felt a great weight of anguish fall away": Ibid., 97.

94 "If someone steals from you": Neau-Dufour, *Geneviève de Gaulle Anthonioz*, Loc. 1454, Kindle edition.

95 "until she saw blood": Sarah Helm, *Ravensbrück: Life and Death in Hitler's Concentration Camp for Women* (New York: Anchor, 2016), 215.

95 "you literally felt a wind of terror": Tillion, *Ravensbrück*, 68.

95 "The pain of the cold was so intense": Berriot, *Chronicles of Resistance*, 34.

96 "It was really like Dante's seventh circle": Interview transcripts, Maia Wechsler, *Sisters in Resistance.*

96 the daily "slave market": Berriot, *Chronicles of Resistance*, 68.

96 "One could be killed at any time": Tillion, *Ravensbrück*, 8.

97 "The SS overseer yelled at us": Berriot, *Chronicles of Resistance*, 100.

CHAPTER 6: "THE MAQUIS OF RAVENSBRÜCK"

99 "I have never experienced such strong demonstrations": Fleury-Marié, *Résistante*, 172.

99 "We absolutely needed to care for one another": *Germaine Tillion, in Her Own Words*, film, Tillion Association, 2016.

99 "'Take it,' she'd tell me": Interview transcripts, Maia Wechsler, *Sisters in Resistance.*

99 "I experienced the worst at Ravensbrück": Neau-Dufour, *Geneviève de Gaulle Anthonioz*, Loc. 1454, Kindle edition.

100 "I would slip them to my friends": Interview transcripts, Maia Wechsler, *Sisters in Resistance.*

100 "radiant spiritual beauty": Paulette Don Zimmet, "C'est à vous que je songe, Madame Émilie Tillion," *Mémoires des déportations 1939–1945.*

100 "all sorts of ideas": Ibid.

101 "lessons in history": Issa Eschebach, "Créer son propre lieu social," in Despoix et al., eds., *Chanter, Rire, et Résister à Ravensbrück*, 25.

101 "Often, it was only a single murmur": Berriot, *Chronicles of Resistance*, 92.

102 "These books were our escape": Ibid., 60.

102 "Coming from a nation that had not known captivity": Helm, *Ravensbrück*, 251.

103 "Once again, we rolled them!": Antoine de Meaux, *Miarka* (Paris: Phebus, 2020), 162.

103 "would do nearly anything to get out of this category": Donald Reid, "Germaine Tillion's Operetta of Resistance at Ravensbrück," *French Politics, Culture & Society*, Summer 2007.

104 "The status of *Verfügbar*": Tillion, *Ravensbrück*, 15.

104 "We had to resist their efforts": Reid, "Germaine Tillion's Operetta."

104 "It was," said one of the evaders: Ibid.

105 "the queens of irregularity": Béatrix de Toulouse-Lautrec, *J'ai eu vingt ans à Ravensbrück: La victoire en pleurant* (Paris: Perrin, 1991), 278.

105 "very Gallic taste for chaos": De Meaux, *Miarka*, 155.

105 "You know, my name is not Jacquier": Ibid.

CHAPTER 7: "TO LAUGH IS TO RESIST"

106 "We all helped one another": Benz and Distel, *Dachau Review 1*, 229.

107 "Listen, ladies!": Paulette Don Zimmet, "Bobard-Tant-Pis" et "Bobard-Tant-Mieux," *Mémoires des déportations 1939–1945.*

107 One of them would shout "France": Donald Reid, "Re-mémoration et créativité dans *Le Verfügbar aux Enfers*," in Despoix et al., eds., *Chanter, Rire, et Résister à Ravensbrück*, 115.

107 "They were like a breath of free France": Reid, "Germaine Tillion's Operetta."

107 "had a tendency to talk about things": Neau-Dufour, *Geneviève de Gaulle Anthonioz*, Loc. 1575, Kindle edition.

107 "And with whom are we washing today?": Interview transcripts, Maia Wechsler, *Sisters in Resistance*.

107 "that made us laugh a lot": Ibid.

108 "an extraordinary propensity to laugh": Julien Blanc, "Humour et résistance chez Germaine Tillion: Rire de (presque) tout," in Despoix et al., eds., *Chanter, Rire, et Résister à Ravensbrück*, 37.

108 "took pleasure in composing little witty texts": Ibid., 43.

108 "one of a small group who knew how to ridicule": "Helene Lajeunesse," *Visages et Voix*, October 1955, ADIR archives, BDIC.

108 "We laughed to prove to ourselves": Fleury-Marié, *Résistante*, 86.

108 "we must find a way to laugh": Julien Blanc, "Humour et résistance," 103.

109 "Our work was sometimes very hard": Don Zimmet, "Bobard-Tant-Pis" et "Bobard-Tant-Mieux."

109 "I felt," she later said: Christine Holden, "Joie de (Sur)Vivre: Germaine Tillion's Artistic Representation of Experiences in Ravensbrück Concentration Camp in the Operetta 'Le Verfügbar aux Enfers,'" *International Journal of Conflict & Resolution*, Spring 2017.

110 "I fell asleep every night": Nelly Forget, "Témoignage sur l'improbable parcours d'un manuscrit," in Despoix et al., eds., *Chanter, Rire, et Résister à Ravensbrück*, 101–102.

110 "deep awareness of the musical canon": Holden, "Joie de (Sur)Vivre."

111 "a model camp with all the comforts": Lacouture, *Témoignage*, 160.

111 "There is another slump": Françoise Carasso, "Styles de Germaine Tillion: Pertinence et impertinence," in Despoix et al., eds., *Chanter, Rire, et Résister à Ravensbrück*, 63.

111 "a large piece of pink bacon": Paulette Don Zimmet, "Un Gros Morceau de Lard Rose, Translucide, Fumant," *Mémoires des déportations 1939–1945*.

111 "There was always a profusion of exotic meats": Ibid.

113 "The beauty of *Le Verfügbar aux Enfers*": Holden, "Joie de (Sur)Vivre."

113 "We marched in step singing verses": Claire Mestre and Marie Rose Moro, "Une Pensée et un engagement: Entretien avec Germaine Tillion," *L'Autre*, vol. 5, no. 1, 2004.

114 "not to mess up and get caught": Toulouse-Lautrec, *J'ai eu vingt ans à Ravensbrück*, 278.

CHAPTER 8: "WE WON'T MAKE YOUR BOMBS!"

116 "You'll never make it to Germany": Virginia d'Albert-Lake, *An American Heroine in the French Resistance: The Diary and Memoir of Virginia d'Albert-Lake* (New York: Fordham University Press, 2006), 216.

118 "Germaine meant everything to me": Jeannie Rousseau de Clarens, "In Memoriam: Germaine de Renty," *Voix et Visages*, July-August 1994, ADIR archives, BDIC.

118 "Dante could not have imagined": Fleury-Marié, *Résistante*, 86.

119   "we realized that if we were to be saved": D'Albert-Lake, *American Heroine*, 224–25.

119   "wore ridiculously fashionable dresses": Helm, *Ravensbrück*, 296.

120   "Ravensbrück was by this time divided": Ibid., 312.

121   "We were actually treated like human beings": D'Albert-Lake, *American Heroine*, 239.

121   "At the time, we did not think twice": Fleury-Marié, *Résistante*, 117.

122   "You are mad, little ones!": Toulouse-Lautrec, *J'ai eu vingt ans à Ravensbrück*, 220.

122   "We have brothers, fathers, husbands": Ibid., 221.

123   "had put a match to a fuse": D'Albert-Lake, *American Heroine*, 240.

123   "The war is nearly over": Ibid., 241.

123   "We have gone through so many difficult years": Helm, *Ravensbrück*, 315.

123   "I was convinced somebody had to do something": Ibid.

124   "They were going to kill me": David Ignatius, "After Five Decades, a Spy Tells Her Tale," *Washington Post*, December 28, 1998.

125   "Absolutely not!": Fleury-Marié, *Résistante*, 120.

125   "It often happened that we made mistakes": Ibid.

125   "It was hard labor": Helm, *Ravensbrück*, 325.

126   "This frail woman was indomitable": Rousseau de Clarens, "In Memoriam: Germaine de Renty."

CHAPTER 9: "THE DAWN OF HOPE"

129   "had a story, a first name": Neau-Dufour, *Geneviève de Gaulle Anthonioz*, Loc. 1658, Kindle edition.

129   "How are you feeling?": De Gaulle Anthonioz, *Dawn of Hope*, 48.

129   "the kind of assassin": "Le Procès de Ravensbrück," *Voix et Visages*, November 1946.

129   "Very poorly, thank you": De Gaulle Anthonioz, *Dawn of Hope*, 48.

129   "Yes, I can see": Ibid., 49.

130   "Starting immediately, you'll be assigned": Ibid., 51–52.

130   "As you well know": Ibid., 53.

131   "a poor, humble person": Ibid., 54.

132   "like the queen of England": Helm, *Ravensbrück*, 279.

133   "Clearly I was no longer a part": De Gaulle Anthonioz, *Dawn of Hope*, 56.

133   "a true moment of happiness": Ibid., 6

134   "No one will be there to help": Ibid., 5–6.

135   "Obviously, if they're planning to kill me": Ibid., 9.

135   "God was strangely absent": Neau-Dufour, *Geneviève de Gaulle Anthonioz*, Loc. 1789, Kindle edition.

135   "Who are you?": De Gaulle Anthonioz, *Dawn of Hope*, 18.

136   "I was," she said, "thoroughly astonished": Ibid., 25.

137   "Your friends sent it to you for Christmas": Ibid., 35.

138   "a very, very precious treasure": Interview transcripts, Maia Wechsler, *Sisters in Resistance*.

138   "Even in my dungeon cell": De Gaulle Anthonioz, *Dawn of Hope*, 35.

139   "I can't get over the fact": Ibid., 47.

140   "Without question, I am feeling better": Ibid., 70.

140   "I have the feeling that I am emerging": Ibid.

141   "intolerable odor": Ibid.

141   "They're all going to die": Ibid., 71.

141   "the terrible trip in the cattle cars": Ibid., 75.

142   "the terrible state of my lungs": Ibid., 77.

142   "this completely surreal experience": Ibid.

142   "I did my best to minimize my role": Ibid., 78.

142   "Would you mind very much": Ibid., 79.

143   "On your feet!": Ibid., 81.

143   "I'd spent entire years there": Ibid., 82.

143   "absolutely ancient": Ibid.

144   "the dawn of hope": Ibid., 83.

144   "Very proud of his country": Neau-Dufour, *Geneviève de Gaulle Anthonioz*, Loc. 1878, Kindle edition.

146   "particularly requested she should be sent": Helm, *Ravensbrück*, 457.

CHAPTER 10: SAVING THE RABBITS

149   "It was clear that the men": D'Albert-Lake, *American Heroine*, 297.

149   "I saw all my friends around me": Ibid., 308.

150   "Will the American who was at Königsberg": Ibid., 313.

151   "My name is Madame Guillot": Ariane Laroux, *Déjeuners chez Germaine Tillion: Peintures et dialogues* (Lausanne: L'Age d'Homme, 2008), 44–45.

151   "the unspeakable beast": Tillion, *Ravensbrück*, 100.

152   "She would walk up and down": Toulouse-Lautrec, *J'ai eu vingt ans à Ravensbrück*, 301.

152   "Work, ladies, work!": Ibid., 304.

153   "Count on me": Ibid., 305.

153   "Please, ladies, work!": Ibid., 306.

155   "In the camp, we were strong": Helm, *Ravensbrück*, 216.

155   "They walked into the center of the square": Ibid., 216–17.

155   "A total and unimaginable silence": Ibid., 446.

156   "an incredible, unheard-of thing happened": Ibid.

156   "Everyone at Ravensbrück seemed to agree": "Janina Iwanska."

157   "They're coming for them!": Helm, *Ravensbrück*, 446.

157   "End of call!": L'Amicale de Ravensbrück et l'association des déportées et internées de la Résistance, *Les Françaises à Ravensbrück: Un grand témoignage collectif sur la déportation des femmes* (Paris: Gallimard, 1965), 225.

157   "We won't let you take them!": Helm, *Ravensbrück*, 446.

158   "the lights always went out": Ibid., 447.

158   "In theory, it should have been possible": Regina Coffey, "You Must Live and Show to the World What They Have Been Doing Here: The Survival of the 'Rabbits' of Ravensbrück" (2020), master's thesis, aquila.usm.edu/masters_theses/738.

CHAPTER 11: "I WANT TO LOOK MY DEATH IN THE FACE"

161   "Run off and hide in your barracks": Benz and Distel, *Dachau Review 1*, 231.

161   "You must be joking": Postel-Vinay, *Vivre*, Loc. 558, Kindle edition.

162   "My darling, I want to face my destiny": Ibid., Loc. 572, Kindle edition.

162   "She was very serene": Ibid.

162   "There is one thing that would really displease me": Helm, *Ravensbrück*, 469.

163   "He had hardly made this gesture": Postel-Vinay, *Vivre*, Loc. 572, Kindle edition.

163   "Afterward," she wrote: Benz and Distel, *Dachau Review 1*, 232.

164   "Anise's face appeared at the window": Helm, *Ravensbrück*, 468.

164   "That night was the worst": Benz and Distel, *Dachau Review 1*, 232.

165   "My darling *maman*": Lacouture, *Témoignage*, 196.

165   "beautiful, radiant, great spirit": Don Zimmet, "C'est à vous que je songe, Madame Émilie Tillion," *Mémoires des déportations 1939–1945*.

166   "a panoramic view where facts and arguments": Todorov, *Germaine Tillion*, 229.

166   "During this last period of the camp": Ibid., 218.

167   "*la chasse, la chasse*": Helm, *Ravensbrück*, 472.

167   "It became dangerous to be out": Ibid.

167   "Over there!": Toulouse-Lautrec, *J'ai eu vingt ans à Ravensbrück*, 331.

168   "We went to fetch it": Berriot, *Chronicles of Resistance*, 93.

169   "Constantly on the alert": Ibid., 101.

169   "My only recourse": Ibid., 102.

169   "We could see they were clearing us out": Helm, *Ravensbrück*, 474.

171   "to stay put, await the arrival": Ibid., 459.

171   "Prisoners are starving": Ibid., 462.

172   "For the rest of us, the call was over": Toulouse-Lautrec, *J'ai eu vingt ans à Ravensbrück*, 335.

173   "When I saw them crying": Helm, *Ravensbrück*, 481.

173   "I am ashamed to confess": Toulouse-Lautrec, *J'ai eu vingt ans à Ravensbrück*, 335.

CHAPTER 12: RACING DEATH

174   "My beloved little Mama": Berriot, *Chronicles of Resistance*, 51.

174   "It's over": Interview transcripts, Maia Wechsler, *Sisters in Resistance*.

176   "which most of us had lost hope": Maisie Renault, *The Great Misery* (Lincoln, Neb.: Zea Books, 2013), 98.

178   "The women whose names I am going to call": Toulouse-Lautrec, *J'ai eu vingt ans à Ravensbrück*, 336.

178   "It took me a moment to realize": L'Amicale de Ravensbrück et l'association des déportées et internées de la Résistance, *Les Françaises à Ravensbrück*, 267.

178   "They kept asking us if we were nervous": Helm, *Ravensbrück*, 504.

179   "was stupefied by our audacity": Berriot, *Chronicles of Resistance*, 94.

180   "I know these women are here!": Ibid.

180   "got nasty, threatened": Ibid., 95.

180   "You are free," he said: Renault, *Great Misery*, 102.

180   "To walk in the country": Ibid.

180   "a half-dead stick doll": Ignatius, "After Five Decades, a Spy Tells Her Tale."

181   "other terrible work": Ibid.

181   "I owe her my life": Rousseau de Clarens, "In Memoriam: Germaine de Renty."

181   "I decided I must intimidate her": Ignatius, "After Five Decades, a Spy Tells Her Tale."

182   "You won't be very comfortable": Toulouse-Lautrec, *J'ai eu vingt ans à Ravensbrück*, 339.

182   "Is it joy?": Ibid.

182   "I couldn't sleep or speak": Berriot, *Chronicles of Resistance*, 95.

183   "So we've really left Germany?": Toulouse-Lautrec, *J'ai eu vingt ans à Ravensbrück*, 341.

183   "clean beds with crisp white sheets": De Gaulle Anthonioz and Tillion, *Dialogues*, Loc. 1149, Kindle edition.

184   "the poor wretches that we were": Ibid., Loc. 1158, Kindle edition.

184   "He was helpless to do anything": Todorov, *Germaine Tillion*, 238.

184   "with so much respect and courtesy": Berriot, *Chronicles of Resistance*, 95.

185   "There was as much as they wanted": Ibid.

186   "And this is Fritz Suhren": Helm, *Ravensbrück*, 524.

CHAPTER 13: HOMECOMING

187   "Faces that were gray-green": Janet Flanner, *Paris Journal 1944–1955* (New York: Atheneum, 1965), 25.

188   "a convoy of martyrs": Helm, *Ravensbrück*, 485.

188   "There was almost no joy": Flanner, *Paris Journal*, 26.

188   "a bent, dazed, shabby old woman": Ibid.

188   "No one had thought": Interview transcripts, Maia Wechsler, *Sisters in Resistance*.

188   "has had the disagreeable courage": Flanner, *Paris Journal*, 26.

189   "The hubbub overwhelms us": Fleury-Marié, *Résistante*, 145.

190   "a veritable Ali Baba's cave": L'Amicale de Ravensbrück et l'association des déportées et internées de la Résistance, *Les Françaises à Ravensbrück, 284*.

190   "It was an absolute duty": Le Foulon, *Procès de Ravensbrück*, 76.

191   "Thanks to them": Ibid., 77.

191   "a world where we would be respected": L'Amicale de Ravensbrück et l'association des déportées et internées de la Résistance, *Les Françaises à Ravensbrück*, 297.

191   "The older women had the most difficult time": Interview transcripts, Maia Wechsler, *Sisters in Resistance*.

192   "Life is interesting": Berriot, *Chronicles of Resistance*, 43.

193   "I disappeared under an avalanche of flowers": Ibid., 52.

194   "I felt I was soaring on a cloud": Ibid.

194   "She was leaving her mother there": Le Foulon, *Procès de Ravensbrück*, 77.

195   "the most creative part": Ibid., 78.

195   "Liberation was a terrible thing": Todorov, *Germaine Tillion*, 229.

195   "For me, it was a nightmare": Le Foulon, *Procès de Ravensbrück*, 77.

195   "I remember that when I walked to the Métro station": Ibid., 78.

196   "caused me terrible pain": Ibid., 79.

198   "When we met, it was difficult": Postel-Vinay, *Vivre*, Loc. 710, Kindle edition.

198   "The only person I communicated with": Ibid., Loc. 695, Kindle edition.

198   "She needed a distraction": Chevrillon, *Code Name Christiane Clouet*, 128.

199   "to be quite old and diminished": Gildea, *Fighters in the Shadows*, 439.

200   "He was about the only person": Neau-Dufour, *Geneviève de Gaulle Anthonioz*, Loc. 2032, Kindle edition.

200   "To hear her recount the details": Ibid., Loc. 2048, Kindle edition.

200   "For Charles de Gaulle, Geneviève was like a daughter": Ibid., Loc. 1986, Kindle edition.

201   "Everyone was enthralled": Ibid., Loc. 2063, Kindle edition.

201   "We went to churches": Ibid.

202   "For days and nights": Ibid., Loc. 2077, Kindle edition.

202   "I had my own room there": Interview transcripts, Maia Wechsler, *Sisters in Resistance*.

CHAPTER 14: "THIS POWERFUL FRIENDSHIP"

204 "an entirely male affair": Helm, *Ravensbrück*, 532.

204 "Reading the wartime memoirs": Anne Sebba, *Les Parisiennes: How the Women of Paris Lived, Loved, and Died Under Nazi Occupation* (New York: St. Martin's Press, 2016), 321.

205 "had voluntarily taken the same risks": Debra Workman, "Engendering the Repatriation: The Return of Female Political Deportees to France Following the Second World War," *Journal of the Western Society for French History*, vol. 35 (2007).

206 "the principal cornerstone": Ibid.

206 "to preserve the feeling of sisterhood": Claire Davinroy, *Voix et Visages*, June 1946, ADIR archives, BDIC.

206 "voices coming through walls and fences": Ibid.

206 "A look, a squeeze of the hand": Geneviève de Gaulle, "The Return," *Voix et Visages*, June 1946, ADIR archives, BDIC.

207 "Without question": Workman, "Engendering the Repatriation."

207 "On more than one occasion, hospital administrators called": Ibid.

208 "We were beings apart": L'Amicale de Ravensbrück et l'association des déportées et internées de la Résistance, *Les Françaises à Ravensbrück*, 313.

208 "They laughed and joked": Ibid., 307.

208 "Enough of cadavers!": Sebba, *Parisiennes*, 345.

209 "If Germaine was everything to me": Rousseau de Clarens, "In Memoriam: Germaine de Renty."

210 "Don't get their hopes up": Ignatius, "After Five Decades, a Spy Tells Her Tale."

210 "I have to go back": Claude du Granrut, *Le Piano et le violoncelle* (Monaco: Rocher, 2013), Loc. 118, Kindle edition.

210 "an almost normal appearance": Ibid., Loc. 74, Kindle edition.

210 "She only spoke with her friends": Ibid.

211 "she showed no sign of sadness": Ibid., Loc. 135, Kindle edition.

211 "I can't sleep in a bed": Ibid.

211 "life in Ravensbrück was not nearly as terrible": Ibid., Loc. 150, Kindle edition.

211 "With these few words": Ibid.

211 "She had left in Ravensbrück": Ibid.

212 "even a little edge of contempt": Ibid., Loc. 167, Kindle edition.

212 "invented help by telephone": Rousseau de Clarens, "In Memoriam: Germaine de Renty."

214 a "time in her life when she really needed it": Claude du Granrut interview, *Émile*, alumni magazine of Sciences Po, Summer 2016.

214 "the extraordinary influence my mother had": Du Granrut, *Piano et le violoncelle*, Loc. 1399, Kindle edition.

CHAPTER 15: FINDING LOVE

216 "a woman whom I'm going to export": Berriot, *Chronicles of Resistance*, 32.

217 "Why not?": Interview transcripts, Maia Wechsler, *Sisters in Resistance*.

218 "I boldly set off on skis": Neau-Dufour, *Geneviève de Gaulle Anthonioz*, Loc. 2222, Kindle edition.

218 "Dad took three days to think things over": Ibid., Loc. 2252, Kindle edition.

218 "I've heard a lot about you": Ibid., Loc. 2296, Kindle edition.

218   "My wedding was like out of a novel": Interview transcripts, Maia Wechsler, *Sisters in Resistance*.

219   "Oh, but Mrs. Girard": Ibid.

219   "like a hair in the soup": Ibid.

220   "Mr. Postel-Vinay, you may be a good patriot": Ibid.

220   "When I met him, I understood": Postel-Vinay, *Vivre*, Loc. 710, Kindle edition.

221   "After what she suffered": Du Granrut, *Piano et le violoncelle*, Loc. 270, Kindle edition.

221   "had a second son": Bowers, *General's Niece*, 166.

222   THE FRUIT OF OUR LOVE: Interview transcripts, Maia Wechsler, *Sisters in Resistance*.

222   "It was crazy, considering my health": Ibid.

223   "Until then, I felt like a traveler": L'Amicale de Ravensbrück et l'association des déportées et internées de la Résistance, *Les Françaises à Ravensbrück*, 315.

223   "to bring children into the world": Neau-Dufour, *Geneviève de Gaulle Anthonioz*, Loc. 2310, Kindle edition.

223   "was life beginning again for me": Fleury-Marié, *Résistante*, 156.

223   "my second family": De Gaulle Anthonioz and Tillion, *Dialogues*, Loc. 64, Kindle edition.

223   "had a special place in our family": Ibid.

CHAPTER 16: BEARING WITNESS

224   "obsessed her from her first steps": Le Foulon, *Procès de Ravensbrück*, 84.

224   "try to understand how an educated": Ibid., 81.

226   "a desolate vision of Germany": Ibid., 135.

227   "Good! You can eat the disgusting German food": "John da Cunha," *Daily Telegraph*, July 19, 2006.

229   "for each agony, there was a collaboration": Germaine Tillion, "Le Procès de Ravensbrück," *Voix et Visages*, March 1947, ADIR archives, BDIC.

229   "First, she was cruelly bitten": Ibid.

230   "You don't straighten out men": Le Foulon, *Procès de Ravensbrück*, 130.

230   "How was such an escape possible?": "Le Procès de Ravensbrück," *Voix et Visages*, November 1947.

232   "might have stepped out of a bread line": Helm, *Ravensbrück*, 529.

232   "Elisabeth Marschall looks me in the eye": Germaine Tillion, "Le Procès de Ravensbrück," *Voix et Visages*, January 1947, ADIR archives, BDIC.

233   "almost twice as many": Germaine Tillion, "Le Procès de Ravensbrück," *Voix et Visages*, March 1947, ADIR archives, BDIC.

233   "the ogress of Ravensbrück": Le Foulon, *Procès de Ravensbrück*, 161.

233   "Irène, they are killing me!": Ibid.

234   "who actually saved your life": Germaine Tillion, "Le Procès de Ravensbrück," *Voix et Visages*, February 1947, ADIR archives, BDIC.

234   "It's times like these": Ibid.

234   "The criminals, taking advantage of the scruples": Ibid.

234   "insinuation of derogatory facts": Le Foulon, *Procès de Ravensbrück*, 178.

235   "If I'd been able to see this file": Germaine Tillion, "Le Procès de Ravensbrück," *Voix et Visages*, March 1947, ADIR archives, BDIC.

236   "carefully measured tones": Heather Stracey, " 'Enfer des Femmes': Britain and the Ravensbrück-Hamburg Trials," master's thesis, Canterbury Christ Church University, September 2017.

236   "quite unsuitable": Ibid.

236   "Because the witness cannot give": Ibid.

237   "the very complete and very serious documentation": Le Foulon, *Procès de Ravens-brück*, 178.

237   "I assume we will receive a written protest": Ibid., 179.

237   "The court procedures": Ibid., 164.

237   "It was a horrible time": Ibid., 183.

238   "What we had experienced": Ibid., 187.

238   "It's this indifference": Ibid.

239   "the infinite extension of trials": Ibid., 195.

239   "This must not be repeated": Ibid., 189.

239   "You must explain very clearly": Ibid.

240   "People like you are no longer judged": Geneviève de Gaulle Anthonioz, "Le Procés du Commandant de Ravensbrück," *Voix et Visages*, May–June 1950.

241   "due to the importance of the individuals": Ibid.

241   "Pflaum is what one would expect": Ibid.

242   "He stood out for his brutality": Le Foulon, *Procès de Ravensbrück*, 211.

242   "Suhren had defended himself": Ibid.

CHAPTER 17: "THE LAPINS ARE COMING"

243   "everything in my power": William Hitzig, report to Norman Cousins, October 20, 1958, in *Congressional Record*, April 16, 1959, Caroline Ferriday collection, U.S. Holocaust Museum archives.

244   "I will be able to swim": Undated letter from Nina Iwanska to Anise Postel-Vinay, Caroline Ferriday collection, U.S. Holocaust Museum Archives.

245   "We embodied for her": Jacqueline Péry d'Alincourt, "Caroline Ferriday," *Voix et Visages*, July–October 1990, ADIR archives, BDIC.

246   "From that moment . . . Caroline would stand": Ibid.

247   "this is a serious humanitarian problem": Caroline Ferriday, "Les Amis de l'ADIR d'Amerique Obtiennent des Indemnités Substantielles pour Cobayes," *Voix et Visages*, January–February 1962, ADIR archives, BDIC.

247   "consider the most complete reparation possible": Ibid.

248   "But Dzunia didn't get anything": Ibid.

248   "As I left the U.N. that morning": Ibid.

248   "Abandoned, sick, physically and morally diminished": Ibid.

249   "I became obsessed": Ibid.

250   "You know who he is": Ibid.

251   "If the international authorities": Ibid.

252   "atrocity stories and war": Norman Cousins, "Dialogue in Warsaw," *Saturday Review*, June 28, 1958.

252   "into the bowels of hell": Ibid.

252   "I could see a somewhat pained": Ibid.

252   "Can you provide us immediately": Ferriday, "Indemnités Substantielles pour Cobayes."

253   "a very nice young lady": Benjamin B. Ferencz, "Reimbursing Good Samaritans," benferencz.org/stories/1956-1970/reimbursing-good-samaritans/.

253   "poor Catholic girls": *Saving the Rabbits of Ravensbrück*, video, YouTube.

253   "a mission impossible on its face": Ibid.

254 "You have to put on a new trial!": Bjorn Okholm Skaarup, "The Last Prosecutor," *American Jewish Committee Global Voice*, May 5, 2020.

255 "as a hot poker": Allen Pietrobon, *Norman Cousins: Peacemaker in the Atomic Age* (Baltimore: Johns Hopkins University Press, 2022), 148.

255 "Not since I had been in Berlin": Cousins, "Dialogue in Warsaw."

255 "Don't be surprised": Ibid.

256 "I'm afraid it will be of no use": Ibid.

256 "If the Germans pay us": Ibid.

257 "had an almost magical gift": Cousins, "The Lapins Are Coming," *Saturday Review*, October 25, 1958.

257 "Dear Miss Caroline": Kristin Peterson Havill, "A Godmother to Ravensbrück Survivors," December 26, 2021, connecticuthistory.org/a-godmother-to-Ravensbruck-survivors/.

258 "Her first few days": Cousins, "Lapins Are Coming."

258 "every nook and cranny": Hitzig, report to Norman Cousins.

258 "everyday people": Ibid.

259 "their own personal harassment": Ibid.

259 "to represent not only their own cause": Ibid.

259 "Not at all," he said: Ibid.

259 "Our project," he wrote Cousins: Ibid.

260 "You would have been amazed": Ibid.

261 "You are Dr. Hitzig?": Ibid.

261 "this exciting, dynamic young woman": Ibid.

261 "courage and genius": Ibid.

262 "are still alive and are still waiting": Cousins, "Dialogue in Warsaw."

262 "electrifying generosity": Cousins, "Lapins Are Coming."

263 "He was most cordial": Norman Cousins, "The Lapins in America," *Saturday Review*, January 24, 1959.

264 "The silk glove must precede": Pietrobon, *Norman Cousins*, 149.

CHAPTER 18: "THEY ARE NO LONGER ALONE"

265 "There's nothing to worry about": Cousins, "Lapins in America."

266 "there was no longer": Ibid.

267 "An attempt is being made": Ibid.

268 "no more tinkering": "Earl Ubell's New Horizons in Science," *Anderson (Indiana) Herald*, January 28, 1959.

268 "little by little, we could see": Ferriday, "Indemnités Substantielles pour Cobayes."

269 "keep the conversational ball rolling": Lorraine Weiss Frank and Ann Battie Horvitz, "The Lapins' Visit," *Vassar Quarterly*, May 1, 1960.

270 "By the end of the week": Ibid.

270 "was almost beside herself with excitement": Ibid.

270 "Far from looking for other people": Ibid.

271 "I couldn't begin to name": Frank and Horvitz, "Lapins' Visit."

272 "As I told each goodbye": Norman Cousins, "The Ladies Depart," *Saturday Review*, June 13, 1959.

272 "I don't know how to say it right": Ibid.

272 "From the persons with whom we are living": Caroline Ferriday, "The Lapins a Year Later," *Saturday Review*, February 20, 1960.

273   "justice for the 'Lapins'": Pietrobon, *Norman Cousins*, 152.
273   "Surely there is an unbalanced scale": Editorial, *Oakland Tribune*, June 16, 1959.
273   "the Germans perpetrated these inhuman acts": Pietrobon, *Norman Cousins*, 151.
273   "It is disgusting to learn": Ibid., 152.
273   "it did not pay financially or politically": Ibid., 150.
274   "Only the highest level in the Foreign Office": Ibid.
275   "For nearly ten years": Ibid., 151.
275   "These were rested, well-groomed": Ferriday, "Indemnités Substantielles pour Cobayes."
275   "On several occasions, we went as a group": Ibid.
276   "We'll keep on marching": Pietrobon, *Norman Cousins*, 152.
276   "The gist of it": *Saving the Rabbits of Ravensbrück*, video, YouTube.
276   "nefarious Communist purposes": Pietrobon, *Norman Cousins*, 153.
276   "a short time ago, the Polish women": Ibid.
277   "In a divided world": Ferriday, "Indemnités Substantielles Pour Cobayes."
278   "courage and genius": Hitzig, report to Norman Cousins.

CHAPTER 19: "WATCHMEN IN THE NIGHT"

279   "We talked for hours": Interview with Maia Wechsler.
280   "It was so much in line": Ibid.
280   "I just could not let it go": Ibid.
281   "It was the first time I dared to leave New York": Ibid.
281   "He was the smartest person I'd ever met": Ibid.
281   "I remember Paul came to visit once": Ibid.
281   "She wanted a baby": Interview with Aline Corraze de Ziegler.
282   "I feel completely powerless": Lorraine de Meaux, *Germaine Tillion*, 194–95.
282   "Doctors told me": Interview transcripts, Maia Wechsler, *Sisters in Resistance*.
282   "terrified me": Ibid.
283   "I couldn't imagine what I could say": Berriot, *Chronicles of Resistance*, 64.
283   "People have to know this": Ibid.
283   "the duty of memory": Ibid., 2.
284   "What I came to understand": Interview with Maia Wechsler.
284   "She talked a lot about the closeness": Ibid.
284   "I said it would be the dream of my life": Ibid.
285   "It was a day of memory": Ibid.
286   "Come to L.A.": Ibid.
286   "I love what you're doing": Ibid.
286   "No one better than us": De Gaulle Anthonioz and Tillion, *Dialogues*, Loc. 1217, Kindle edition.
287   "the moral conscience of twentieth-century France": "Germaine Tillion: Resistance Fighter and Ethnologist," *Independent*, April 25, 2008.
288   "Unlike what happened in 1942": Todorov, *Germaine Tillion*, 21.
288   "hers was one of the first and loudest voices": Douglas Martin, "Germaine Tillion, French Anthropologist and Resistance Figure, Dies at 100," *New York Times*, April 25, 2008.
288   "The survivor of Ravensbrück": David S. Newhall, "Tillion, Germaine (1907–)," encyclopedia.com.
288   "I am always on the side of those": Rice and Tillion, " 'Déchiffrer le silence.' "
288   "Today, I still love my country": Todorov, *Germaine Tillion*, 11.

289 "If God wants me back in service": Liliane Charrier, "Germaine Tillion, Yacef Saadi, Deux Visages de la Résistance," TV5Monde, December 24, 2021.

289 "When I entered this large shantytown": Neau-Dufour, *Geneviève de Gaulle Anthonioz*, Loc. 2767, Kindle edition.

289 "The expression that I read on [these] faces": Ibid., Loc. 2776, Kindle edition.

290 "Our past struggles and suffering": Ibid., Loc. 2834, Kindle edition.

291 "For us," they declared: L'Amicale de Ravensbrück et l'association des déportées et internées de la Résistance, *Les Françaises à Ravensbrück*, 9.

292 "What would I have done?": Interview with Maia Wechsler.

292 "France in 1940 was unbelievable!": Interview trancripts, Maia Wechsler, *Sisters in Resistance*.

292 "Well, there were a few": Ibid.

292 "We have a very great need": Ibid.

293 "Sorry," she apologized: Ibid.

293 "has always borne the guilt": Helm, *Ravensbrück*, 469.

293 "I thought that as I got older": Postel-Vinay, *Vivre*, Loc. 834, Kindle edition.

293 "Every night for a long time": Berriot, *Chronicles of Resistance*, 44.

293 "They're always very present": Interview transcripts, Maia Wechsler, *Sisters in Resistance*.

294 "The world must pay attention": Ibid.

294 "Our time there taught me a lot": Ibid.

294 "we don't have a pessimistic, black vision": Ibid.

294 "She loved it": Interview with Maia Wechsler.

295 "I think about Jacqueline": Ibid.

295 "no matter how isolated we are": Ibid.

CHAPTER 20: "THIS BEAUTIFUL PIECE OF ART"

296 "Wait a minute": Kirk Boettcher, "Note from the Dramaturg," program, *In the Underworld*, University of Southern Maine Theater, April 18–27, 2014.

296 "I would be a wealthy man": Ibid.

297 "would be its finest jewel": Nelly Forget, "Témoignage sur l'improbable parcours d'un manuscrit,' in Despoix et al., eds., *Chanter, Rire, et Résister à Ravensbrück*, 97.

298 "an unforgettable evening": Ibid., 98.

299 "I devoured it": Ibid., 106.

300 "I dreamed that this theater": Natalie Simon, "Panthéon: Le Châtelet reprend l'opérette de Germaine Tillion," *Le Monde*, February 20, 2014.

300 "a dangerous defender": Kim Willsher, "Paris Fears for Fate of Theatre That Added Chic to Pop Culture," *Observer*, April 2, 2016.

300 a "solemn text": Simon, "Panthéon: Le Châtelet reprend l'opérette de Germaine Tillion."

301 "to be dreamed—as a way to escape": Christophe Maudot, "Note from the Arranger/Composer," program, *In the Underworld*, University of Southern Maine Theater, April 18–27, 2014.

301 "She knew the whole thing by heart": Donald Reid, "Re-mémoration et créativité," dans *Le Verfügbar aux Enfers*," 117.

301 "Could we put this on a stage?": "Une ethnologue avec le sens de l'humour," Radio France, August 13, 2021.

303 "There are surely lots of things": Catherine Simon, "Le Siècle de Germaine Tillion," *Le Monde*, May 29, 2007.

303 "avoiding trauma without minimizing the horror": Ibid.

303 "Simply put, those who have not been": Ibid.

304 "The schoolgirls, like the singers": Ibid.

304 "Would you like a glass of milk, Kouri?": Ibid.

304 "She seemed very moved": Henry Samuel, "Diary of Nazi Survivor Turned into an Opera," *Telegraph,* June 2, 2007.

304 "The operetta you are going to see": Forget, "Témoignage sur l'improbable parcours d'un manuscrit," 103.

305 "witty and imaginative": *Le Monde,* June 4, 2007.

305 "dizzyingly brilliant": *Telerama,* June 6, 2007.

305 "its strength and singularity": Agence France Presse, June 3, 2007.

305 "a masterpiece": Danielle Dumas, "A Beautiful Page of Hope," blog post, June 4, 2007.

306 "You know," she said: "*Verfügbar aux Enfers* de Germaine Tillion," France 2 television program, April 2010.

307 "Would I have gone along?": Ibid.

308 "It was such a brilliant, dark comic rendering": Interview with Meghan Brodie.

308 "My thought was that there were no men": Ibid.

309 "It was clear to me that the students' education": Ibid.

309 "We had some Jewish students": Ibid.

309 "By doing that, they had an experience": Ibid.

310 "I was crying too": Ibid.

311 "Every time I see or hear from them": Ibid.

EPILOGUE

313 "Take your place here!": Transcript, François Hollande speech, Panthéon, May 27, 2015.

313 "I was stunned": Anise Postel-Vinay interview with Léa Salamé, Radio France, May 25, 2015.

314 "It was very unsettling": Postel-Vinay, *Vivre,* Loc. 822, Kindle edition.

314 "I don't like the word 'heroism'": Bowers, *General's Niece,* xiv.

314 "Look at us, poor people": Neau-Dufour, *Geneviève de Gaulle Anthonioz,* Loc. 3961, Kindle edition.

314 "She was offered them all": Interview transcripts, Maia Wechsler, *Sisters in Resistance.*

314 "an anonymous story": Quentin Girard, "Anise Postel-Vinay," *Libèration,* May 24, 2015.

315 "the wife of an officer": Olson, *Madame Fourcade's Secret War,* 379.

315 "remembering the contributions of all": Sylvie Corbet and Jamey Keaten, "Rare Honor for 2 Women in Paris Pantheon of Greats," Associated Press, February 21, 2014.

315 "Female heroes are not limited": Frédérique Neau-Dufour, "Geneviève de Gaulle Anthonioz et Germaine Tillion: Portrait croisé," Fondation Charles de Gaulle, May 1, 2020, charles-de-gaulle.org/blog/2020/05/01/lettre-dinformation-n8-genevieve-de-gaulle-anthonioz-et-germaine-tillion-portrait-croise-par-frederique-neau-dufour/.

316 "History is not nostalgia": Transcript, François Hollande speech, Panthéon, May 27, 2015.

316   "she was obsessed with this problem of evil": Postel-Vinay, *Vivre,* Loc. 817, Kindle edition.

316   "What we stigmatized": Neau-Dufour, "Geneviève de Gaulle Anthonioz et Germaine Tillion."

316   "Now," she said: Girard, "Anise Postel-Vinay."

Bibliography

·······

ARCHIVAL MATERIAL

U.S. Holocaust Museum Archives, Bowie, Maryland
—Caroline Ferriday collection
—Violette Lecoq portfolio of Ravensbrück drawings
Bibliothèque de documentation international contemporaine (Library of International Contemporary Documentation) (BDIC), Nanterre, France
—ADIR archives

BOOKS

d'Albert-Lake, Virginia. *An American Heroine in the French Résistance: The Diary and Memoir of Virginia d'Albert-Lake*. New York: Fordham University Press, 2008.

L'Amicale de Ravensbrück et l'association des déportées et internées de la Résistance. *Les Françaises à Ravensbrück: Un grand témoignage collectif sur la déportation des femmes*. Paris: Gallimard, 1965.

Andrieu, Claire. *When Men Fell from the Sky: Civilians and Downed Airmen in Second World War Europe*. Cambridge, UK: Cambridge University Press, 2023.

Anthonioz, Geneviève de Gaulle. *The Dawn of Hope: A Memoir of Ravensbrück*. New York: Arcade, 1999.

————, and Germaine Tillion. *Dialogues*. Paris: Plon, 2015.

Bair, Deirdre. *Samuel Beckett: A Biography*. New York: Harvest/HBJ, 1978.

Benz, Wolfgang, and Barbara Distel, eds. *Dachau Review 1: History of Nazi Concentration Camps; Studies, Reports, Documents*, vol. 1. Dachau: Verlag Dachauer Hefte, 1988.

Berest, Anne. *The Postcard*. New York: Europa, 2023.

————, and Claire Berest. *Gabriële*. Paris: Stock, 2017.

Berriot, François. *Chronicles of Resistance and Deportation: Jacqueline Péry d'Alincourt and Her World*. West Kennebunk, Maine: Androscoggin Press, 2021.

Blanc, Julien. *Au commencement de la Résistance: Du côté du Musée de l'Homme 1940–1941.* Paris: Seuil, 2000.

Blumenson, Martin. *The Vildé Affair: Beginnings of the French Resistance.* Boston: Houghton Mifflin, 1977.

Bowers, Paige. *The General's Niece: The Little-Known de Gaulle Who Fought to Free Occupied France.* Chicago: Chicago Review Press, 2017.

Chevrillon, Claire. *Code Name Christiane Clouet: A Woman in the French Resistance.* College Station: Texas A&M University Press, 1995.

Cordier, Daniel. *Alias Caracalla.* Paris: Gallimard, 2009.

Despoix, Philippe, et al., eds. *Chanter, Rire, et Résister à Ravensbrück: Autour de Germaine Tillion et du* Verfügbar aux Enfers. Paris: Seuil, 2018.

du Granrut, Claude. *Dix ans en 1940.* Compiègne: Mémorial de l'internement, 2012.

———. *Le Piano et le violoncelle.* Monaco: Rocher, 2013.

Flanner, Janet. *Paris Journal: 1944–1965.* New York: Atheneum, 1965.

Fleury-Marié, Jacqueline, with Jérome Cordelier. *Résistante.* Paris: Calmann-Lévy, 2019.

Gildea, Robert. *Fighters in the Shadows: A New History of the French Resistance.* Cambridge, Mass.: Belknap Press of Harvard University Press, 2015.

Guéhenno, Jean. *Diary of the Dark Years 1940–1944.* Oxford: Oxford University Press, 2015.

Helm, Sarah. *Ravensbrück: Life and Death in Hitler's Concentration Camp for Women.* New York: Anchor, 2016.

Hofmann, Tom. *Benjamin Ferencz: Nuremberg Prosecutor and Peace Advocate.* Jefferson, N.C.: McFarland, 2014.

Humbert, Agnès. *Résistance: Memoirs of Occupied France.* London: Bloomsbury, 2008.

Jackson, Julian. *France: The Dark Years 1940–1944.* Oxford: Oxford University Press, 2001.

Knowlson, James. *Damned to Fame: The Life of Samuel Beckett.* New York: Simon & Schuster, 1996.

Lacouture, Jean. *Le Témoignage est un combat: Une biographie de Germaine Tillion.* Paris: Seuil, 2000.

Laroux, Ariane. *Déjeuners chez Germaine Tillion: Peintures et dialogues.* Lausanne: L'Age d'Homme, 2008.

Le Foulon, Marie-Laure. *Le Procès de Ravensbrück: Germaine Tillion; De la vérité à la justice.* Paris: Cherche Midi, 2016.

Loftis, Larry. *Code Name: Lise; The True Story of the Woman Who Became WWII's Most Highly Decorated Spy.* New York: Gallery Books, 2019.

Meaux, Antoine de. *Miarka.* Paris: Phebus, 2020.

Meaux, Lorraine de. *Germaine Tillion: Une certaine idée de la résistance.* Paris: Perrin, 2024.

Missika, Dominique. *Les Inséparables: Simone Veil et ses soeurs.* Paris: Seuil, 2018.

Moorehead, Caroline. *A Train in Winter: An Extraordinary Story of Women, Friendship, and Resistance in Occupied France.* New York: Harper Perennial, 2011.

Neau-Dufour, Frédérique. *Geneviève de Gaulle Anthonioz: L'Autre de Gaulle.* Paris: Cerf, 2015.

Olson, Lynne. *Last Hope Island: Britain, Occupied Europe, and the Brotherhood That Helped Turn the Tide of War.* New York: Random House, 2017.

———. *Madame Fourcade's Secret War: The Daring Young Woman Who Led France's Largest Spy Network Against Hitler.* New York: Random House, 2019.

Persson, Sune. *Escape from the Third Reich: Folke Bernadotte and the White Buses.* New York: Skyhorse Publishing, 2009.

Pietrobon, Allen. *Norman Cousins: Peacemaker in the Atomic Age.* Baltimore: Johns Hopkins University Press, 2022.

Poltawska, Wanda. *And I Am Afraid of My Dreams.* New York: Hippocrene Books, 2013.

Porch, Douglas. *The French Secret Services: From the Dreyfus Affair to the Gulf War.* New York: Farrar, Straus and Giroux, 1995.

Postel-Vinay, Anise. *Vivre.* Paris: Grasset & Fasquelle, 2015.

Renault, Maisie. *The Great Misery.* Lincoln, Neb.: Zea Books, 2013.

Riding, Alan. *And the Show Went On: Cultural Life in Nazi-Occupied Paris.* New York: Alfred A. Knopf, 2010.

Rosbottom, Ronald C. *Sudden Courage: Youth in France Confront the Germans, 1940–1945.* HarperCollins, 2019.

Rossiter, Margaret L. *Women in the Resistance.* New York: Praeger, 1985.

Russell of Liverpool, Lord. *The Scourge of the Swastika: A History of Nazi War Crimes During World War II.* New York: Skyhorse Publishing, 2008.

Schoenbrun, David. *Soldiers of the Night: The Story of the French Resistance.* New York: Dutton, 1980.

Sebba, Anne. *Les Parisiennes: How the Women of Paris Lived, Loved, and Died Under Nazi Occupation.* New York: St. Martin's Press, 2016.

Tillion, Germaine. *Ravensbrück.* Garden City, N.Y.: Anchor Books, 1975.

———. *Ravensbrück.* Paris: Seuil, 1988.

Todorov, Tzvetan, ed. *Germaine Tillion: Fragments de vie.* Paris: Seuil, 2009.

Toulouse-Lautrec, Béatrix de. *J'ai eu vingt ans à Ravensbrück: La victoire en pleurant.* Paris: Perrin, 1991.

Vomécourt, Philippe de. *An Army of Amateurs.* New York: Doubleday, 1961.

Weitz, Margaret Collins. *Sisters in the Resistance: How Women Fought to Free France, 1940–1945.* New York: John Wiley & Sons, 1996.

Wievorka, Oliver. *The French Resistance.* Cambridge, Mass.: Harvard University Press, 2016.

FILM

Germaine Tillion, in Her Own Words. Film documentary, Germaine Tillion Association, Paris, 2016.

Sisters in Resistance. Film documentary, Women Make Movies, 2000, ADIR archives, BDIC.

PERIODICAL ARTICLES

Andrieu, Claire. "Réflexions sur la Résistance à travers l'exemple des françaises à Ravensbrück," *Histoire@Politique* 2008, no. 2.

———. "Women in the French Resistance: Revisiting the Historical Record," *French Politics, Culture & Society,* 2000, vol. 18, no. 1.

Coffey, Regina. "You Must Live and Show to the World What They Have Been Doing Here: The Survival of the 'Rabbits' of Ravensbrück" (2020). Master's thesis. aquila.usm.edu/masters_theses/738.

Cousins, Norman. "Dialogue in Warsaw." *Saturday Review,* June 28, 1958.

———. "The Ladies Depart." *Saturday Review,* June 13, 1959.

———. "The Lapins Are Coming." *Saturday Review,* October 25, 1958.

———. "The Lapins in America." *Saturday Review,* January 24, 1959.

Don Zimmet, Paulette. "Bobard-Tant-Pis" et "Bobard-Tant-Mieux." *Mémoires des déportations 1939–1945.*

———. "C'est à vous que je songe, Madame Émilie Tillion." *Mémoires des déportations 1939–1945.*

———. "Un gros morceau de lard rose, translucide, fumant." *Mémoires des déportations 1939–1945.*

Hitzig, William. Report to Norman Cousins, October 20, 1958, in *Congressional Record,* April 16, 1959. Caroline Ferriday collection, U.S. Holocaust Museum.

Holden, Christine. "Joie de (Sur)Vivre: Germaine Tillion's Artistic Representation of Experiences in Ravensbrück Concentration Camp in the Operetta 'Le Verfügbar aux Enfers.'" *International Journal of Conflict & Resolution,* Spring 2017.

Ignatius, David. "After Five Decades, a Spy Tells Her Tale," *Washington Post,* December 28, 1998.

Iwanska, Janina. "Janina Iwanska." *Chronicles of Terror, 1939–45.* zapisyterroru.pl/dlibra/publication/1441/edition/1424/content.

Knowland, James, "Samuel Beckett's Biographer Reveals Secrets of the Writer's Time as a French Resistance Spy," *Independent,* July 23, 2014.

Lacoste-Dujardin, Camille. "Une ethnologue à Ravensbrück ou l'apport de la méthode dans le premier Ravensbrück de Germaine Tillion." *Histoire@Politique* 2008, vol. 2, no. 5.

Mestre, Claire, and Marie Rose Moro. "Une pensée et un engagement: Entretien avec Germaine Tillion." *L'Autre* 2004, vol. 5, no. 1.

Neau-Dufour, Frédérique. "Geneviève de Gaulle Anthonioz et Germaine Tillion: Portrait croisé." Fondation Charles de Gaulle, May 1, 2020.

Newhall, David S. "Tillion, Germaine (1907–)." encyclopedia.com.

Penson, Joanna, and Anise Postel-Vinay. "Un exemple de résistance dans le camp de Ravensbrück: Le cas des victimes polonaises d'expériences pseudo-médicales 1942–1945." *Histoire@Politique* 2008, vol. 2, no. 5.

Rice, Alison, and Germaine Tillion. "'Déchiffrer le silence': A Conversation with Germaine Tillion." *Research in African Literatures,* Spring 2004, vol. 35.

Rousseau de Clarens, Jeannie. "In Memoriam: Germaine de Renty," *Voix et Visages,* July–August 1994, ADIR archives, BDIC.

Spinney, Laura. "The Museum Director Who Defied the Nazis," *Smithsonian,* June 2020.

Stracey, Heather. "'Enfer des Femmes': Britain and the Ravensbrück-Hamburg Trials." Master's thesis, Canterbury Christ Church University, September 2017.

Veillon, Dominique, and Françoise Thébaud. "Hélène Viannay." *Clio,* January 1995.

Workman, Debra. "Engendering the Repatriation: The Return of Female Political Deportees to France Following the Second World War." *Journal of the Western Society for French History,* vol. 35 (2007).

Photo Credits

....

Page 148: Violette Lecoq portfolio, U.S. Holocaust Memorial Museum archives

Page 152: Creative Commons—Attribution: Centre des archives diplomatiques de La Courneuve

Page 160: Germaine Tillion Association

Page 167: Violette Lecoq portfolio, U.S. Holocaust Memorial Museum archives

Page 170: Violette Lecoq portfolio, U.S. Holocaust Memorial Museum archives

Page 221: Bridgeman Images

Page 222: Courtesy Aline Corraze de Ziegler

Page 232: Creative Commons—Attribution: Ława oskarżonych w procesie załogi KL Ravensbrück

Page 260: U.S. Holocaust Memorial Museum, courtesy of Anna Hassa Jarosky and Peter Hassa

Page 295: Catherine Scheinman

Page 310: Courtesy Shannon Zura

Page 313: Creative Commons—Attribution: Yann Caradec

Index

Page numbers of photos and illustrations appear in italics.

....

Picabia, Jeanine, 25–26
code name Gloria, 27
escapes to London, joins Free
French, 35
wartime activities and head of Gloria
SMH intelligence network, 25, 27,
28, 30–31
Poland
culture of, 259
government in exile in London, 55
Hitler's desire to annihilate, 51
Home Army resistance group, 51, 54,
259
military personnel fighting for the
Allies, 259
Nazis' savagery and regarding Poles
as *untermenschen* (subhuman), 51,
258
number of war deaths, 258
postwar condition of, 255–56
resistance members at
Ravensbrück, 50
Russian campaign and (1945), 148
Russian liberation of death camps in,
175
Soviet's postwar control, 244, 258, 259
Warsaw uprising, 148
Polish prisoners of Ravensbrück, 120
aid and information given to
Germaine Tillion, 49
assigned camp jobs, 75
form a committee to care for young
Poles at, 54
French inmates' acts of defiance and,
102
from Lublin, Poland, 51–52, 270
members of the Polish resistance in, 50
moroseness of, 107
Nazi's savage treatment of, 51
new arrivals at Ravensbrück in
January 1945, 148
Polish inmate as foreman of gardening
detail, 152–53
secret messages sent to outside
contacts, 54–55
survivors' organization, 246, 249, 257

Polish prisoners of Ravensbrück:
"rabbits" or *lapins*, 51–52, 248, *260*
ADIR brings victims to Paris for
medical treatment, 244
campaign to bring victims to the U.S.
for treatment, 249–64, 266–67
Dr. Hitzig visits Warsaw, 258–60
Gebhardt's medical atrocities
practiced on, 51–56, 243–45, 262
Germany pays reparations to, 277
medical treatment and cross-cultural
exchange in the U.S., 267–72
Norman Cousins visits surviving
lapins in Warsaw, 255–57
novel *Lilac Girls* based on, 277–78
Pan Am flight for *lapins* to America,
263–66, 265n
photos of the mutilations, given to
Germaine Tillion, 56, 178
postwar campaign for recognition and
reparations for, 243–78
Ravensbrück prisoners unite to save,
hide, and smuggle them out of the
camp, 154–58, 243
rebellion sparked by victims of
medical atrocities, 54–56
See also Iwanska, Nina
Postel-Vinay, André, 218–20
betrayal, arrest, and escape, 219–20
Compagnons de la Libération and, 219
in de Gaulle's administration, 220
Hamburg war crimes trial and, 237
marriage to Anise Girard, 220
wartime activities, 219–20

Ravensbrück (Tillion et al.), 225
Ravensbrück concentration camp, xiii
appearance, 43, *43*
arrival and intake of prisoners, 42–44,
45, 59, 73–74, 120
beatings and brutality at, *95*, 95–97,
128
becomes an extermination center, 147,
150–51
black transports (trucks to Auschwitz
gas chambers), 47, 48, 105

ABOUT THE AUTHOR

Lynne Olson is the *New York Times* bestselling author of *Madame Fourcade's Secret War*, *Last Hope Island*, *Those Angry Days*, and *Citizens of London*. She has been a consulting historian for the National WWII Museum in New Orleans and the United States Holocaust Memorial Museum in Washington, D.C.

lynneolson.com

Facebook.com/LynneOlsonBooks